HURON COUNTY LIBRARY

W9-CJT-071

HURON COUNTY LIB

This volume was donated by the Centennial Commission on the occasion of the Centennial of Canadian Confederation	Cet ouvrage est un don de la Commission du Centenaire à l'occasion du Centenaire de la Confédération canadienne
SPRING/1967	PRINTEMPS/1967

THE LIFE AND TIMES OF CONFEDERATION

THE LIFE AND
TIMES OF
CONFEDERATION
1864-1867

Politics, Newspapers, and the Union of

British North America

P. B. WAITE

University of Toronto Press

Copyright, Canada, 1962, by
University of Toronto Press

Second edition, with corrections
© UNIVERSITY OF TORONTO PRESS 1962

Reprinted 1967

Printed in the U.S.A.

Preface

THE LAST HISTORY OF CONFEDERATION was R. G. Trotter's *Canadian Federation*, published in 1924. Since that time much work has been done on this seminal period of Canadian history by Canadian historians, and more recently, in important peripheral studies, by American ones. Three notable contributions by Canadians have been D. G. Creighton's *British North America at Confederation* for the Rowell-Sirois Report, his *John A. Macdonald: The Young Politician* (1952), and W. M. Whitelaw's *The Maritimes and Canada before Confederation* (1934). This present book begins roughly where Professor Whitelaw's ended.

The work has developed from a suggestion by Dr. Margaret Ormsby of the University of British Columbia for an analysis of Canadian opinion of the United States at the time of Confederation. The subject slipped sideways, and the result was a study of ideas and politics in the province of Canada, 1864–1867, that was presented to the University of British Columbia in 1950. A more comprehensive thesis on British North America followed in 1953 for the University of Toronto. The debts incurred have been many and various. Dr. Ormsby and Dr. W. N. Sage of the University of British Columbia were prepared to accept a thesis on an eastern subject and even encouraged the enterprise. Professor D. G. Creighton of the University of Toronto gave prodigally of his assistance and advice when the dissertation was being prepared for the University of Toronto, and I should like to record here my appreciation of his generosity and interest. Dr. Frank MacKinnon of Prince of Wales College, Charlottetown, was kind enough to read the Prince Edward Island chapter of the thesis and to offer some useful criticism.

This book is, in several important respects, a shift in emphasis and direction, and represents an entire rewriting on the basis of other perspectives and a good deal of further research. In this connection I should like to thank Dr. J. M. S. Careless of the University of Toronto for permission to read the Brown Papers. For the acquisition of these papers every historian of the period is in his debt, and I would like to acknowledge mine. I am grateful to the Social Science Research Council of Canada and the Canada Council for a grant that allowed me to do much of the early research and also for a substantial grant toward publication of this book. The Canada Council and Dalhousie University have helped to make it possible for me to spend a year in England canvassing the British Museum newspaper collection and the Public Record Office, and in writing. From librarians and archivists throughout Canada, and in England, I have received unfailing help and courtesy. Some of the material in the book has been the result of their interest and initiative. For the remarkable facilities of the Public Archives of Canada I must express my lively appreciation. Mr. W. G. Ormsby has been particularly helpful in arranging to place research materials at my disposal, often on short notice. I should also like to thank the staff of the Archives of Nova Scotia who have willingly met repeated drafts upon their time and energy.

Colleagues at Canadian universities have also been generous. Professors W. S. MacNutt and J. K. Chapman of the University of New Brunswick have read an early draft of the chapter on New Brunswick, Professor G. O. Rothney of Memorial University of Newfoundland the chapters on Newfoundland and Canada East, Professor J. M. Beck of Royal Military College the chapter on Nova Scotia. Their knowledge and assistance have been invaluable. Finally, I should like to thank Dr. G. E. Wilson of Dalhousie University, who has not seen this book but who has contributed not a little to the education of the person that wrote it.

P.B.W.

Halifax
March, 1961

I have taken the opportunity offered by a second printing to make a few minor corrections.

P.B.W.

Halifax
September, 1962

Contents

THE LIFE AND TIMES OF CONFEDERATION

NOTE

THROUGHOUT THE BOOK the names of the colonies follow the usage of the time. British North America or British America is used for them as a group. Canada (and Canadians) applies only to what was from 1840 to 1867 the united province of Canada (now Ontario and Quebec). Canada West and Canada East were the names used at the time for the two sections of the united province. Contemporaries also continued to use Upper Canada and Lower Canada even though these names really referred to the separate provinces before their union in 1840. Other names like Newfoundland, Prince Edward Island, Nova Scotia, and New Brunswick have no complications. On the west coast there were two colonies, British Columbia and Vancouver Island, which were united in 1866 under the name British Columbia.

1. NEWSPAPERS AND POLITICAL LIFE

IN BRITISH NORTH AMERICA in the nineteenth century politics comprehended most forms of public life. Politics expressed the natural combative urges of the human species, sometimes refined into parliamentary decencies, sometimes not; it conscripted loyalties and opinions; it commanded men's public spirit and focussed their private selfishness. Opinions were held with stubbornness and expounded with conviction; political issues ran nearly as deep as religious ones. Victorians, British or British American, would probably have agreed with Aristotle's definition of man. They were ready to interpret history as politics past, view life in terms of politics present, or even perhaps to see the future, like a Fabian dream, realized by political means. In British North America the problems were material as well as political, and the materialism of the raw North American environment had plenty of force. The Grand Trunk Railway was an instructive example of the effects, good and bad, of this vital communication between material wants and their realization through politics. But politics had its own *élan vital*, expressed in the powerful, tenacious loyalties and prejudices that disposed parties and inspired men. Had the argument for British North American union been only a material one, there would probably have been no union at all. Confederation defied not a few material and geographic considerations; its creation was a political achievement. In that sense it was thoroughly characteristic of its age.

The history of the Confederation movement lies in many sources, in the despatches of governors to the Colonial Office, in the debates of colonial legislatures, in the letters of public men. It is also in the newspapers. Confederation was a great public issue and its ramifications were considerable. It fired the imagination of many men, editors not least, as newspapers from Newfoundland to Vancouver Island bear witness. Its very existence as an issue common to all provinces helped to bring their problems within a common understanding. Confederation was literally a national issue, the first and the greatest that British North Americans had to face.

This book is a history of British North America engaged upon that high adventure. The main sources have been the newspapers of the time; and although despatches and letters have been indispensable (going behind the scenes as they do), it has been the natural compass of the newspapers that has largely determined the character of the book. The newspapers reported and informed; they commented and criticized; and in the broadest sense they revealed the diversity not only of men and politics but of life itself. All the world, Thackeray once wrote, is in the paper. Society and its attitudes are the climate in which men and politics grow; it is not possible to separate men from their times, nor is it possible to separate politics from political comment. They are vital to one another. In British North America there was a practical consequence: the real interaction of politicians and newspapers. Political patronage the newspapers expected and received. They entered the cut and thrust of political life with all the verve of the politicians whose views they represented. Their remarks were vigorous, at times vindictive and downright scurrilous; they had in fact the same characteristics as politics itself. The relationship between newspapers and politics was often a matter of loyalty to friends, party, or principle: it was also, sometimes, a matter of dollars and cents. Newspapers had their principles, but newspapers, and principles, could be bought and sold. For this reason, if for no other, newspapers must be used with care. They were too often ready to trim to a fresh wind, or to alter their course, for due consideration, to a new bearing. And the aim of their editorials was persuasion. They provide the historian with much valuable, public evidence, but in a history of Confederation based upon them it is essential to use as well the more private sources of despatches, letters, diaries. The two kinds of evidence explain and illuminate each other.

The newspapers are also refreshing and useful reminders of the complexity of history. Confederation was a cause that succeeded; it was successfully imposed upon British North America by the collective power of Canada and the Colonial Office. It was a resolution of Canadian difficulties, the sovereign remedy for the ills that had beset the province for ten years. But in the Maritimes Confederation did not solve old issues, it raised new ones. Adverse economic conditions may have made Confederation acceptable: the poverty of Newfoundland was a powerful argument for union; the same was true in British Columbia; the land question in Prince Edward Island may have influenced the Islanders; the Intercolonial Railway was an essential condition for New

Brunswick. But it must also be said that New Brunswick was pushed into Union, Nova Scotia was dragooned into it, and Newfoundland and Prince Edward Island were subjected to all the pressure that could be brought to bear—short of force—and still refused. These are reasons why the newspapers may be studied with profit. It is too easy to assume that Confederation, because it established a national state, is a desideratum by which other causes are to be judged. We reason from a nationality, after the event, but men cannot be understood or history explained, without the complexity of the antecedents. British North American newspapers represent this complexity, imperfectly no doubt, but not ineffectively.

And they are fascinating in their own right. The dusty files of the *Globe*, *Le Canadien*, the *Newfoundlander*, the *Acadian Recorder*, full of Confederation, have the native vitality of life itself. Confederation was once alive and breathing; its critics and its advocates once filled the halls and marketplaces; and it is not too much to ask of history that it recover something of the liveliness of that generation. For this purpose the newspapers are wonderfully apposite; with all their limitations they remain an exciting and vital source of political life. No one can read them without discovering that newspapers since have become pallid and stodgy. The editorial writing—the heart of the paper and recognized as such—was often extreme, but it was pungent and virile, and at its best it was sharp and witty. Not the least of the delights of these newspapers was their style. They displayed a facility with the language now rare, and if the writing was ephemeral in purpose and often vitriolic in character, it rarely lacked the literary graces. Certainly its rugged vigour often carried an intensity of conviction and an integrity of purpose that was itself indicative of the spirit of political life. The following is an example from the *Perth Courier*, criticizing Macdonald and the Coalition.

He'll come home Sir John A. some time next summer, with a new Constitution for British North America in his pocket, and House and the people can go to Jericho for all he cares. . . . This is a very nice result certainly for those Reformers who brought the Coalition into existence to contemplate . . . they are the men on whom the responsibility must rest of handing the country over body and bones to Mr. McDonald and his associates. The latter gentlemen are now actually revelling in power; fairly gorging themselves in self-gratification; their slightest whims are law, and at their command Constitutions for a Continent spring into existence. Toryism in its palmiest days never enjoyed such a glut of authority.[1]

[1]*Perth Courier*, Jan. 11, 1867. (In newspaper citations the masthead will be italicized.)

The same vitality was reflected in the number of newspapers. In 1865 Halifax, with a population of 30,000, had eleven newspapers. This was the most conspicuous example, but variations could be repeated for most cities in British North America. There were in all about 380 newspapers issued weekly or oftener in 1865.[2] Many of these have now disappeared altogether. John Sandfield Macdonald's Cornwall *Freeholder* survives in only scattered copies. J. B. E. Dorion's *Le Défricheur* has apparently vanished.[3] Much recent work has gone into rescuing and microfilming files of newspapers that are still to be found in dusty little newspaper offices, particularly in Ontario. If they escape destruction by fire (and by housecleaning editors), they last remarkably well. Until the 1880's they were printed on paper made from rag (with other admixtures) and were well calculated to survive the ordinary vicissitudes of time.

Paper was sufficiently expensive to enforce an economy of space unknown at present. Newspapers were invariably one large single sheet, folded once, that is, four pages of print.[4] The front page was not unlike the London *Times* of today; it had no news, or only what overflowed from the inside pages. Page 2 was the main page and contained the editorials, newsletters, and quotations from other newspapers. Pages 3 and 4 were often largely advertising: hoopskirts and the elaborate supports thereof were displayed in detail, stoves delineated in stately engravings, wines and spirits offered in unseemly quantities, and a

[2]The following table gives approximations for 1865.

	Daily	Tri-weekly	Semi-weekly	Weekly		Total	Population (est.)
Canada West	18	20	7	176		221	1,508,000
Canada East	10	9	3	40		62*	1,150,000
Newfoundland	1	5	2	5		13	140,000
P.E.I.	0	0	1	9		10	87,000
Nova Scotia	1	9	0	26		36	354,000
New Brunswick	2	5	0	17		24	267,000
Red River	0	0	0	0	1**	1	8,000***
British Columbia	0	0	2	3		5	5,000***
Vancouver Island	3	1	0	1		5	7,000***
						377	3,526,000

*There were a larger number of monthly magazines in Canada East than in Canada West.

**A fortnightly paper.

***Not including Indians, or in the case of the Pacific colonies, Indians or Miners.

[3]The issue of 27 déc. 1866, when Wilfrid Laurier was editor, is quoted by Sir John Willison in *Sir Wilfrid Laurier and the Liberal Party* (2 vols., Toronto, 1905), I, 111–23.

[4]The weekly editions of some dailies had interleaved sheets.

remarkable plethora of panaceas with marvellous qualifications were presented. Radway's Ready Relief appeared almost universally in British North American papers:

So swift [*sic*] is the patient transformed from pain, misery, weakness, and decrepitude, to the delightful enjoyment of health and strength, that patients frequently ascribe its talismanic power to the supernatural influence of enchantment.[5]

More humble remedies were described with unbecoming grandiloquence —Ayer's Cathartic Pills, for example.

The sciences of Chemistry and Medicine have been taxed to their utmost to produce this best, most perfect purgative which is known to man.[6]

Not the least of the excitements provided were the tales of adventure by sea and land, the grisly narratives of public executions, and the occasional serial story modestly placed out of sight on the front page. The tales of adventure were often real, the sea providing many of them. The Toronto *Globe* took several issues to describe the awful details of the wreck of the *Hungarian* which drove aground one wild February night in 1860 on Cape Ledge, half a mile off Cape Sable, N.S., with the loss of 109 lives.[7] The Halifax *Morning Chronicle* gave a laconic account of how the schooner *Gypsy*, out of Maitland, N.S., was heaved over on her beam ends and all her crew lost but the captain and the mate.[8] All executions were reported, preliminaries being duly noted, and with a final emphasis on the dreadfulness of crime as well as on the grim method of its expiation. The serial stories were the worst; the mawkish mid-century taste was here served up with uninhibited abandon. ("The blood thrilled through her heart. . . .") The *Globe* did publish Wilkie Collins' *Woman in White*, but this high level of writing was the exception not the rule.[9] The front page was sometimes the woman's page, and when it was it was terrible.

The Toronto *Globe* was the conspicuous representative of what might be called a metropolitan press.[10] The railways of the 1850's had by the 1860's increased the circulation and expanded the influence of the city dailies, of which the most important were the Toronto *Globe*, the

[5]Halifax *Morning Chronicle*, July 18, 1863.
[6]Halifax *British Colonist*, Feb. 28, 1857.
[7]The wreck happened on Sunday night, Feb. 19, 1860. Toronto *Globe*, Feb. 24, 1860, *et seq.*
[8]Halifax *Morning Chronicle*, March 17, 1863.
[9]As early as 1846 the *Globe* had begun this practice, with *Dombey and Son*. The Halifax *British Colonist* also carried *Woman in White*.
[10]The *Globe*'s circulation was about 28,000. Its closest rival was probably the Saint John *Morning Telegraph*, with about 12,000.

Montreal *Gazette, Le Journal de Québec,* the Saint John *Morning Telegraph,* and the Halifax *Morning Chronicle.* The obverse of this trend was
the weakening of the small town and village papers, though the full force
of this development was only felt later. The *Globe*'s rise to power was
significant, and the political power of George Brown was inescapably
associated with the circulation of the *Globe.*

In British North America Brown was not the only person who began
as a newspaperman and ended as a politician. Howe had done it with
the *Nova Scotian* in the 1830's. As G. M. Grant remarked, "at that
time . . . it was almost impossible to be an editor without being a
politician also. . . ."[11] But it was becoming less usual in the 1860's.
Wilfrid Laurier was editor of *Le Défricheur* after J. B. E. Dorion's death
and Hector Langevin helped to begin *Le Courrier du Canada,* but
neither remained at it very long, and it was probably not the basis of
their political success. The more common practice was for a politician to
acquire influence in a newspaper in order to make it the forum for his
opinions. The difficulty lies in determining the extent of this influence
and how it was maintained.

Some newspapers were owned and edited outright and present no
problem. Edward Whelan, a member of the Prince Edward Island
Opposition, owned and edited the Charlottetown *Examiner.* In the same
category were Joseph Cauchon's *Journal de Québec,* T. W. Anglin's
Morning Freeman of Saint John, R. J. Parson's St. John's, Newfoundland *Patriot.* Dorion et Cie published *Le Pays.* In other cases there was
a family connection. Ambrose Shea's brother, E. D. Shea, M.L.A. for
Ferryland, owned and edited the *Newfoundlander,* and was sympathetic
to his brother's views on Confederation. But family connections are not
always a reliable guide. W. H. Pope, who owned the Charlottetown
Islander, opposed the views of his brother, J. C. Pope. An interesting
arrangement was that of the *Halifax Citizen,* owned by E. M. Macdonald, M.L.A. for Pictou, and William Garvie, a 27-year-old classics
tutor at Dalhousie College.[12]

More often the owner and the editor were separate and the connection
between them rather obscure. Only occasionally a disagreement produced sufficient friction to generate light. There was a dramatic quarrel
over the running of the great Liberal daily in Halifax, the *Morning
Chronicle,* when the editor became converted to Confederation and the
owner remained opposed. As a result, the owner, Charles Annand,
assumed the active direction of the paper; the editor, Jonathan McCully,

[11]G. M. Grant, *Joseph Howe* (Halifax, 1906), 28.
[12]Garvie gave up the *Citizen* in 1866, went over to London to study law in
Lincoln's Inn, and was called to the Bar there. He returned to practise in
Halifax.

resigned, bought out a moribund journal, and made it and its editor his own.[13] In the case of the *Public Ledger* of St. John's, Newfoundland, the death of the owner resulted in a reversal of the paper's Confederation policy. The widow was obliged to appoint an editor; the editor insisted that Confederation should be supported, and upon that condition took up the post.[14]

The most difficult question is that of relationships that were common knowledge to contemporaries. For example, everyone knew that *La Minerve* of Montreal expressed the views of M. Cartier, the Saint John *Morning News* the views of Mr. Tilley, and the Quebec *Morning Chronicle* those of John A. Macdonald. But documentary evidence to support such knowledge is thin. Occasionally a happy revelation turns up; Charles Tupper admitted that he wrote "almost all the political leaders in the *British Colonist* when in Halifax from 1855 to 1870."[15] But admissions of this kind are few. There is an illuminating letter to a prospective editor in whom Sandfield Macdonald was interested for the Cornwall *Freeholder*. It is clear that the establishment of the paper—the premises, plant, type—were owned by Sandfield Macdonald. These the editor leased from him and paid rent from the current profits of the newspaper. In return Sandfield Macdonald had his political views advocated in the *Freeholder*. It was essential, of course, that there be a certain correspondence in outlook between the owner and the editor; as Sandfield Macdonald put it, "There is again—before entering upon an engagement . . . a very important conference to be held—touching your views and mine."[16] Sandfield Macdonald believed that the current editor had made a good thing of his lease; but the lament sounded in the *Freeholder* hardly suggested that:

Take accounts for two hundred dollars; spend a toilsome week on the road . . . living at roadside taverns upon everlasting pork and "rot-gut" whiskey. Sum up the "tottle" at the week's end. Collections $22; expenses $18; to say nothing of lost time, heart a little heavier than before, and a few more gray hairs. . . .[17]

In addition to the *Freeholder*, John Sandfield Macdonald reputedly controlled the *Quebec Daily Mercury* (which he had leased) and got his friend Josiah Blackburn to run it; and it is known that duly upon the defeat of the Sandfield Macdonald government in March, 1864, the

13*Infra*, 208–9.
14St. John's *Public Ledger*, Dec. 21, 1866.
15E. M. Saunders, *Life and Letters of the Rt. Hon. Sir Charles Tupper* (2 vols., New York, 1916), I, 127.
16Sandfield Macdonald Papers, Sandfield Macdonald to A. McLean, March 25, 1865.
17*Stratford Beacon*, Feb. 10, 1865, quoting *Prescott Messenger*, quoting Cornwall *Freeholder*.

Mercury changed hands, and Mr. Blackburn reverted to his home which was the *London Free Press*. It is possible to speak of the Cornwall *Freeholder* as Sandfield Macdonald's paper, or of the *British Colonist* in the years 1855 to 1870 as "Tupper's paper," but to say the same thing of Tilley and the *Morning News* is more hazardous. The best that can be said of the latter is that Tilley's political views were probably represented there. Whether he wrote the leaders, as Tupper did, is another matter. John A. Macdonald reputedly "influenced" several papers, but it is highly doubtful that he ever wrote for them. Macdonald preferred to exercise his influence through private correspondence with editors and owners, a not uncommon practice. Luther Holton's correspondence with Brown of the *Globe* was considerable; more than once arguments that Holton suggested were turned and shaped into the compelling style that usually characterized the editorials of the *Globe*.[18] Holton had a similar, if not closer, connection with the Montreal *Herald*.

The key to the relation between newspapers and politicians was patronage in one form or another. Patronage helped to keep some newspapers alive, others prosperous. Each newspaper had its circle of subscribers and advertisers, but other support, in the form of private financial aid or government printing contracts, was sometimes necessary. When newspapers looked for patrons, and politicians looked for publicity, some connection between them was inevitable. The Toronto *British Colonist* rose to prominence under the patronage of John Hillyard Cameron and declined after Cameron had lost his money in the New York crash of 1857. When the right party was in power a newspaper publisher could expect government printing contracts, and governments carefully distributed these to the politically deserving. Paul Denis once taunted J. B. E. Dorion, owner and editor of *Le Défricheur*, with having a newspaper that never cleared (défriché) anything except when the honourable member's brother was the Attorney General.[19] The three Conservative newspapers in Halifax were each rewarded with contracts by a grateful administration.[20] The St. John's *Morning Chronicle*[21] was

[18]E.g. Brown Papers, Holton to Brown, Nov. 22, 1859, the argument of which is reproduced in the *Globe*, Nov. 25, 1859.

[19]Canada, Legislature, *Parliamentary Debates on the Subject of the Confederation of the British North American Provinces* (hereafter *Confederation Debates*) (Quebec, 1865), 879.

[20]The *Evening Reporter* was given the debates; the *Evening Express*, other House printing; the *British Colonist*, Government railway printing. The *Acadian Recorder*, an independent, was given Post Office printing. So alleged the *Morning Chronicle*, May 10, 1864. The *British Colonist*, May 28, 1864, replied *tu quoque*.

[21]There were three *Morning Chronicles*: St. John's, Newfoundland, Halifax, N.S., and Quebec, Canada.

proud to boast that it had survived for five years without any government support at all.[22]

The lives of editors were not always peaceful. Opinions were strongly held, prejudices deeply engrained, and editors who clashed violently enough in print, sometimes clashed in public. J. B. E. Dorion, picturesquely called "l'enfant terrible," complained to the Canadian Assembly that he had been slapped in the face by the editor of Ottawa's *Le Canada* because of an article in *Le Défricheur*.[23] One of the editors of the *Halifax Citizen* who had been criticizing Cape Breton rowdyism in the paper was himself the victim of it. William Garvie, leaving the house of some friends on Hollis Street in Halifax, was struck down and badly hurt.[24] At the height of the Confederation debate in the Nova Scotian legislature in 1866, William Miller, M.L.A., goaded by personal jibes from the Halifax *Sun*, pummelled the editor when he encountered him outside the Assembly. The assistant editor of the *Chronicle* came to the rescue and was attacked by Miller's colleague.[25] Violence was not condoned, but it was not altogether unexpected. It was only twenty-four years since Howe had fought a duel for his newspaper comments, and political life remained intense and personal. Explosions of temper in the Assemblies were not rare. Joseph Cauchon, editor of *Le Journal de Québec* and M.L.A. for Montmorency, caused a fearful row in the Canadian House in 1865 by pulling the nose of Alexandre Dufresne, M.L.A. for Iberville, when both happened to meet behind the Speaker's chair.[26] The cause was, incidentally, an unpleasant discussion that had taken place in the House on the government patronage given to *Le Journal de Québec*. A similar wrangle, on the same subject, had taken place the year before.[27]

Violence on a larger scale appeared at the polls. Elections were fought as well as contested. In the Canadian election of 1861 the Conservative supporters of John A. Macdonald fought a pitched battle in Kingston with the Reform supporters of Oliver Mowat.[28] It was reported that at a political meeting in Galt in 1867 some three hundred "roughs," primed

[22]St. John's *Morning Chronicle*, Dec. 1, 1866.
[23]Canada, Legislative Assembly, *Journals*, 1866, 257. The scene was, apparently, the new Parliamentary library. (Barrie *Northern Advance*, Aug. 8, 1866.)
[24]Halifax *Morning Chronicle*, April 11, 1866; *Halifax Citizen*, April 12,1866.
[25]*Halifax Citizen*, April 10, 1866.
[26]*Canadian Free Press*, March 10, 1865, report from Quebec from "Fag," dated March 2, 1865. (The *Canadian Free Press* was the weekly edition of the *London Free Press*.)
[27]*Sarnia Observer*, Feb. 19, 1864.
[28]D. G. Creighton, *John A. Macdonald: The Young Politician* (Toronto, 1952), 310–12.

with whisky and armed with long wooden clappers, tried to drown out the speakers.[29] In the same election, Alexander Mackenzie had to fight his way to his carriage from a rowdy school-house meeting near Sarnia, and succeeded in getting away, his two spirited horses out-distancing the howling mob who had followed in carriages behind.[30] In Newfoundland in the 1861 election virtually open war prevailed in some districts, notably Salmon Cove and Cat's Cove at Harbour Main. Salmon Cove men going to the polls found the road blocked by Cat's Cove people; shots were fired; one man was killed and several injured. The ramifications of this affray were partly responsible for even wilder scenes in St. John's when the two Harbour Main members so elected tried to take their seats in the Assembly.[31]

In Canada, Newfoundland, Prince Edward Island, and Nova Scotia the "manly practice" of open voting still prevailed.[32] In New Brunswick the ballot had been introduced in 1859, and while it may have been a vast improvement on open voting,[33] it did not prevent corruption. It was in 1862 that G. L. Hatheway, Tilley's Commissioner of Public Works, said at dinner at the Lieutenant Governor's that his supporters cost a guinea each; they were thus not so easily corrupted as those of the Solicitor General who could be got for only 3/6.[34] Nova Scotia had experimented with manhood suffrage, but the Liberal administration of Joseph Howe had abolished it just before the election of 1863.[35] There was much prejudice against universal suffrage, at least as much among Liberals as Conservatives. A Liberal newspaper in Halifax referred contemptuously to Conservatives as "these Universal Suffrage gentlemen."[36] Jonathan McCully was being characteristically Liberal when he remarked in 1867 that if *vox populi vox Dei est*, then God is pretty

[29]Reported by the *Guelph Advertiser* and quoted in the *Galt Reporter*, Aug. 16, 1867, which said the story was exaggerated.

[30]Reported however by the pro-Mackenzie *Sarnia Observer*, Aug. 23, 1867. See also Dale C. Thomson, *Alexander Mackenzie: Clear Grit* (Toronto, 1960), 100.

[31]A recent account of this affair is in E. C. Moulton, "The Political History of Newfoundland, 1861–1869," M.A. thesis, Memorial University of Newfoundland, 1960, 86–115.

[32]The expression is the Toronto *Leader*'s. It maintained that the ballot was ineffective in preventing corruption. Ballot box stuffing was an evil "from which under our manly practice of open voting, we are happily free." (Oct. 17, 1867)

[33]So said James Hannay, *History of New Brunswick* (2 vols., Saint John, 1909), II, 192.

[34]C.O. 188, Gordon to Newcastle, Dec. 31, 1862 (confidential).

[35]The new suffrage did not take effect until after 1863.

[36]Halifax *Morning Chronicle*, Dec. 18, 1865.

fickle.[37] The Reform St. Catharines *Evening Journal* provides a good example of the prejudice:

We don't desire our institutions to be the playthings of an irresponsible Executive, or the footballs of a senseless and levelling rabble, or the targets for wide-mouthed fanatics to shoot their mad ravings at. We are not money or title worshippers, but we believe that property has rights which should not be ignored and that the constitution which makes the *vox populi* the "all in all" . . . has an inherent weakness which must result in its own death.[38]

This dislike of what British North Americans thought of as American political practice was widespread. According to a Barrie paper, American legislatures were filled with "demagogues, prizefighters, and other specimens of the genus vagabond, who can handle a bowie knife much better than a pen. . . ."[39] The American practice of electing judges drew a vehement attack from the Toronto *Globe*:

That the dignified and learned wearer of the ermine, whose proudest distinction is his independence from popular clamor and prejudice . . . should become a roaring political partisan, and secure or maintain his position by force of the unwashed multitudes who boast of universal suffrage, is something so abhorrent to our traditions and convictions . . . that we cannot for a moment think of it.[40]

Such views were common in Canada and Nova Scotia. In Newfoundland some newspapers criticized the whole "cumbrous and complicated machinery of representative institutions."[41] But this reflected exceptional circumstances. Newfoundland was a colony whose parlous condition called for heroic remedies.[42] In Prince Edward Island and New Brunswick there was not so much talk of the kind that resounded in Canada and Nova Scotia. The suspicion was that in those two colonies the legislatures and the electorate were happily wallowing in their own Americanized versions of responsible government. Arthur Gordon, the Lieutenant Governor of New Brunswick, thought so and deplored it, but the Islanders, if not New Brunswickers, remained obstinately content.

There was one characteristic common to all the provinces, especially Nova Scotia, and one which is not easy to describe: it might be called restlessness. There was a pervasive feeling that colonial ambitions had reached a dead end. "The bars of these Provincial cages" were clearly

[37]Halifax *Unionist*, Feb. 6, 1867.
[38]St. Catharines *Evening Journal*, Feb. 22, 1865.
[39]Barrie *Northern Advance*, April 4, 1867.
[40]*Globe*, May 19, 1865.
[41]St. John's *Daily News*, Dec. 1, 1866. Cf. also St. John's *Public Ledger*, Feb. 22, 1867.   [42]*Infra*, 164–5.

too confining for Nova Scotia;[43] and this same feeling was reflected in the growth of territorial ambitions in Canada West. The little worlds of Halifax, Charlottetown, Fredericton, Quebec, perhaps even of St. John's, were becoming cramped for some of the politicians who had made their careers there. In this respect the politicians, and the newspapers, seem to have been ahead of the general public. The little villages of Prince Edward Island, New Brunswick, and Canada, the outports of Newfoundland and Nova Scotia, remained relatively unaffected by this restlessness, and their innate conservatism was employed to advantage by politicians who, for one reason or another, found Confederation unacceptable. This was partly responsible for the verdict against Confederation in the New Brunswick and Newfoundland elections of 1865, and in the Nova Scotian and Prince Edward Island elections of 1867. It is important therefore to distinguish between public opinion represented by the public and the electorate and public opinion in the narrower sense, as reflected in newspapers and in public speeches of legislators. It was in fact the young, energetic, ambitious journalists and politicians who expressed most vividly the frustration with colonial status. "To be a British American means nothing in the world's estimation: to be a Canadian, a New Brunswicker, or a Novascotian, is to be just next to nothing."[44] British Americans, situated between Great Britain and the United States, were incessantly tantalized by the power and renown of others.[45]

Joseph Howe was one of these. He had never forgotten a dinner he had once had with John Quincy Adams and a dozen other Americans in Washington. He envied them that "boundless field" of ambition, their nationality.

Sir, my heart rose when I compared these men with those I had left at home, their equals in mind and manners. But it sunk [sic], aye, and it sinks now, when turning to the poor rewards which British America offers. . . . Has she ever supplied a Governor . . . ? a secretary or an under-secretary of state? . . . How long is this state of pupilage to last?[46]

Howe fretted and chafed against the restrictions of being merely a provincial minister, of contending for the "petty prizes" of the colonial

[43]Halifax *Morning Chronicle*, Nov. 24, 1864.

[44]P. S. Hamilton, *Observations upon a Union of the Colonies* (Halifax, 1855), 6. Hamilton first published these observations in the Halifax *Acadian Recorder*, of which he was editor from 1853 to 1861. He was 27 years old when they were published.

[45]*Ibid.*, 4.

[46]Joseph Howe, *Speech on Union of the Colonies and Organization of the Empire* (Pictou, 1855), 30. The speech was given in the Nova Scotian Assembly, Feb. 24, 1854.

raffle.[47] He hated to fling away ambition; he felt hedged in by barriers he could not get around; he winced and smarted under slights real or imagined from British customs officers and other officials.

Tupper, after being minister for half a dozen years, was as restless as Howe. He wanted "to have a dash at somebody . . . at least to be able to shiver a lance. . . ."[48] In his speech at the Saint John Mechanics Institute, November 19, 1860, Tupper tilted at the grievances: "that colonists were tied hand and foot to the chariot wheels of Downing Street . . . that colonial statesmen were . . . nobodies unknown beyond their bailiwick, that England snubbed us at every turn. . . . *The truth of all of which,*" added the *Morning News'* report, "*no one can deny.* These facts are old stories."[49] What was there, Tupper asked, to tempt a man to go into politics? He can get nowhere when he is in. "Local politics . . ." wrote Jonathan McCully five years later, "have become a farce, nothing more or less. . . . the only politics to divide parties . . . [is] who shall be high constable of the parish, first footman in a Governor's hall, or master of ceremonies at a political pic-nic. . . . 'Small countries make small men.' "[50]

The Nova Scotians suggested three remedies. Howe's panacea was representation of the colonies in the imperial parliament. What was also necessary, in the view of Hamilton, Tupper, and Howe, was some form of imperial patronage. They complained that in the Colonial Office there was not a single colonist. A third remedy was union of the colonies. The *Quebec Daily News* summed it up. "For probably forty years the most prominent politicians and public men of Nova Scotia have been clamouring for some Colonial system which would give a larger scope to their intellectual activity. . . ."[51]

In 1859 the Toronto *Globe* had scoffed at the flights of Nova Scotian ambition: "The grandee of the backwoods settlement, the jingle of whose silver is music to his neighbours, and the nod of whose head is law to all around him, learns to his mortification that his name and fame are unknown at the Colonial Office."[52] The *Globe* in 1859 was generally opposed to schemes of this kind, union of the empire or union of the colonies. Its immediate concern was the grievances of Canada West.[53] But Brown, speaking to the 600 delegates of the Reform Convention in November, 1859, was as ambitious as any Nova Scotian.

[47][B.W.A.] Sleigh, *Pine Forests and Hacmatack Clearings* (London, 1853), 344.
[48]Saint John *Morning News*, Nov. 22, 1860; also Halifax *British Colonist*, Dec. 1, 1860. (Original italics) [49]*Ibid.* (Original italics)
[50]Halifax *Unionist*, July 10, 1865. [51]*Quebec Daily News*, Nov. 17, 1863.
[52]Toronto *Globe*, July 13, 1859. [53]*Infra*, chapter IV.

Now, Sir, I do place the question on the ground of nationality. I do hope there is not one Canadian in this assembly who does not look forward with high hope to the day when these northern countries shall stand out among the nations of the world as one great confederation. (Cheers.)[54]

By 1865 the *Globe*, and most Reformers, found the prospect of Confederation, "the assertion of our right to take a place amongst the nations of the world," a glittering one. The very thought should make the heart of every Canadian "leap with joy."[55] Bleu journals were not less expectant, though more philosophical: "un temps qui n'est peut-être pas très éloigné arrivera où nous serons laissés maîtres de nos destinées; eh! bien, nous devons nous préparer en prévision de notre passage de l'état colonial à l'état d'indépendance. . . ."[56]

Aspirations for a British American nationality were the result of ambitions frustrated by the narrow confines of colonial identities. Nova Scotia, politically mature, geographically small, felt it the most keenly. Canada, too, was confined by the thrusts of the Canadian shield against which waves of settlement beat in vain. Although union of the British North American colonies was to be a solution of Canadian political difficulties, it was not less an opportunity for Canadians to reach westward for arable land. The national ambitions of Nova Scotia and Canada were nobly stated, but the poetry concealed the motives. It should not, however, obscure them. British Americans shared the Anglo-Saxon propensity for declaring in noble language purposes that could be stated more simply. Carrying "the blessings of civilization" to the boundless west (as Brown once put it)[57] was to produce two western rebellions in the space of fifteen years. Canadian nationalism was also chauvinism: Nova Scotian restlessness, a whetted taste for office.

There was, however, not a little ignorance in the Maritimes and Canada of each other's point of view. Before 1860 it was said there was not even a Canadian map of the British North American colonies.[58] McGee remarked that when he became President of the Council the Canadian Cabinet had no Maritime newspapers on hand except an old file of the *Nova Scotian*.[59] Anthony Trollope was right when he noted that Canadians and Maritimers "seldom see each other,"[60] though that

[54]*Globe*, Nov. 16, 1859, reporting Brown's speech of Nov. 10.

[55]*Globe*, Jan. 2, 1865.

[56]Quebec *Courrier du Canada*, 25 jan. 1865. "La Constitution," XXI.

[57]*Globe*, Nov. 16, 1859, reporting Brown's speech of Nov. 10.

[58]Reported by *Stratford Beacon*, Dec. 2, 1859. In the next issue, Dec. 9, it announced that such a map would be available in 1860.

[59]McGee's speech in London, C.W., Sept. 20, 1866, reported in the Toronto *Canadian Freeman*, Sept. 27, 1866. He is referring to the year 1862.

[60]Anthony Trollope, *North America* (New York, 1862), 81.

was changing. There were conferences at Quebec in September, 1861, and September, 1862, on the Intercolonial railway,[61] and the railway itself was a "national" question, however unpleasant and even intractable the issue at times became. British North American newspapers were the principal, if not the only means of intercolonial communication, on the railway as well as on Confederation. Yet their effects were by no means unequivocal. To know a province better was not necessarily to love her more. Maritimers thought Canadian history pretty lurid, and said so. Newspapers did not soften the colours: as now they tended to make them more garish. As for Canadians, their ignorance of the Maritimes was proverbial. In Fredericton McGee amused his audience with the story of the Canadian who, asked where the river Styx was, replied it was somewhere in New Brunswick.[62] And it is altogether probable that, outside of Taché (who had been to the Maritimes in 1852 with Francis Hincks) and perhaps one or two others, McGee was the only Canadian politician who knew the Maritimes at first hand. It was entirely characteristic that in October, 1864, a Canadian who was curious about Maritimers could ask McGee, "What sort of people are they?"[63]

It was to be expected that when, in 1864, Confederation suddenly became practicable, the newspapers would have a significant role in its evolution. Not all people were agreed that Confederation was either necessary or desirable; some who believed in the principle opposed the form; others opposed both. This opposition to Confederation found in the newspapers a natural and ready means of expression. But for those who believed in Confederation the newspapers were not only useful, they were indispensable. Change had to be urged, and many who feared and distrusted change persuaded that the far-reaching change of Confederation was for political and economic advantage. In the Maritime provinces this was going to be uphill work, but it was not altogether easy amid the ancient antipathies in Canada East. But it is clear that the newspapers, whether for or against Confederation, would make a vital contribution to its history.

[61]In September, 1861, Howe, McCully, and Archibald of Nova Scotia and Tilley, Mitchell, and Smith of New Brunswick met with Cartier, Macdonald, Galt, and five other Canadians. In September, 1862, approximately the same group of Maritimers met with Sandfield Macdonald, A. A. Dorion, Sicotte, Howland, and other members of the Liberal government.

[62]Saint John *Morning Telegraph*, Aug. 10, 1864, report of McGee's speech of Aug. 8.

[63]McGee gives this story in the *Confederation Debates*, 135.

2. BRITISH NORTH AMERICA

AND

GREAT BRITAIN

AN EDITORIAL in the London *Times* put the matter briefly and to the point: "Our colonies are rather too fond of us, and embrace us, if anything, too closely."[1] By the 1860's Great Britain had worked out the political consequences of the free trade principles of the 1840's. The end of the mercantilist system had given Great Britain free trade and the British North American colonies responsible government. The bracing winds of economic freedom blew unhampered over the broad oceans; Britain sought her supplies and her markets no longer in the colonies but in the world at large. The untidy and awkward restrictions that had threatened Britain's internal prosperity and thwarted her expanding energies were swept away, and free trade rapidly acquired the status in Britain that the Trinity held in the Church. This article of faith did not lack heretics, but in England it remained essentially unshaken for many years to come. In some of the self-governing colonies, notably Canada, early attempts at protection were thought not merely unenlightened, but positively wicked.

In these circumstances the colonies themselves began to appear anomalous. What use a colony, when neither a source nor a market? The very question was significant. Colonies were not intrinsically valuable. They were certainly inconvenient to administer, and what was worse, they were often expensive. In any case their value could be calculated in economic terms. No doubt some were valuable for imperial defence; but some were of no value at all, and others were a positive danger.

After the outbreak of the American Civil War the British North American colonies were in this last unhappy position. Canada especially posed exceedingly awkward problems in Britain's relations with

[1]London *Times*, Oct. 24, 1864.

the United States. A thorough defence of the Canadian border was impossible. The ten thousand troops that were hurried to Canada early in 1862 through the winter snows of New Brunswick were no more than a useful handful if war really came. Had the Canadians evinced a powerful desire to back up British efforts, Britain might have been more willing to make the best of a difficult and disconcerting problem. But when the worst of the Trent crisis was over in May, 1862, the Canadian government was actually defeated when it attempted to appropriate half a million dollars for defence. Whatever may have been the causes of the defeat in Canada—and they were complex—the reaction in Britain was unmistakable. A colony of two and a half million inhabitants that balked at half a million dollars for its own defence could not expect Britain to make extensive efforts. The London *Spectator* put it bluntly: "it is, perhaps, our duty to defend the Empire at all hazards; it is no part of it to defend men who will not defend themselves."[2]

The Canadian action confirmed many of the current beliefs about colonies. Goldwin Smith's letters in the London *Daily News* in 1862 and 1863 were characteristic not only of his own views but also of a prevalent attitude. The possession of Canada, he said, while it might be the pride of a small class in England, gave England nothing but "endless expense, perpetual danger." Moreover, the state of colonial tutelage was not good even for Canada herself: the protection that the British government gave to Canadians quenched the spirit of self-defence they otherwise would have had. If Canadians shrank from dangers and responsibilities, that was the natural consequence of their colonial condition. "What child, if the future could be revealed to it in infancy, would not shrink from the dangers and burdens even of the most prosperous and heroic life?"[3] Canada must face her own future, and she must learn that basically she must face it alone.

The project of Confederation gave new impetus to such ideas. At long last there was some prospect that the British North American colonies would be able to take care of themselves. England seemed to heave a visible sigh of relief.[4] No sane Briton would choose Canada as a battleground in a quarrel with the United States, and if Canada

[2]*Spectator*, July 26, 1862. Quoted in C. P. Stacey's *Canada and the British Army, 1846–1871* (London, 1936), 127.

[3]Goldwin Smith, *The Empire* (London, 1863), 134–5.

[4]"Conscious as we are of our inability to protect these colonies by land in case of war, we must naturally rejoice at any event which seems to place them in a position in which they would be better able to protect themselves." London *Times*, Oct. 15, 1864.

were separated from Britain, this danger would be largely removed. That Confederation would lead to this separation was confidently (and happily) anticipated by the *Edinburgh Review* of January, 1865:

> . . . we accept, not with fear and trembling, but with unmixed joy and satisfaction, a voluntary proclamation, which, though couched in the accents of loyalty, and proferring an enduring allegiance to our Queen, falls yet more welcome on our ears as the harbinger of the future and complete independence of British North America.

Lord Lyveden in the House of Lords said much the same. "Happy and amicable separation" ought to be the natural result of a maturing relationship between the mother country and a self-governing colony.[5] And while these views were not necessarily those of the British Liberal government, members of it were influenced by them. Gladstone, the Chancellor of the Exchequer, was. Palmerston, the Prime Minister, was not.[6] Palmerston remained a staunch, even aggressive, imperialist until the day he died, October 18, 1865. Lord Russell, the Foreign Secretary and successor to Palmerston, tended to follow colonial sympathies of many years standing, and much disliked the current fashion in colonial philosophy. Edward Cardwell, the Colonial Secretary, worried, like many of the Cabinet, about North American defence, but publicly at least he was not without sentiments that suggested a more spacious sense of imperial destiny. Other countries, he said to his constituents at Oxford, had great and powerful empires, "but it has been given to England alone to be also the mother of great and free communities. . . . The time may come," he went on, "when England, as the parent of those distant communities, may be glad to have her quiver full of them."[7] This may have been merely a wafting of official amenities across the ocean, or, as the *Times* put it, "soothing with soft words his rough and querulous clients. . . ."[8] Probably Cardwell was neither an imperialist nor an anti-imperialist, but a mixture of both. As long as the colonies wished to remain connected with Britain, as long as they remained loyal, then Britain should not, would not, surrender their welfare to the flinty mercies of a coarse logic that weighed their benefits in pounds, shillings, and pence. Even the *Times* was forced to agree with that. At the same time Cardwell could look without dismay at the growth in British North America of a more independent spirit as indicative of the colonial coming of age; it would enable the colonies, while

---

[5]Great Britain, House of Lords, *Hansard*, vol. 177, 420 (Feb. 20, 1865).

[6]See also C. P. Stacey, "Britain's Withdrawal from North America, 1864–1871," *Canadian Historical Review*, XXXVI, 3 (Sept., 1955), 187–8.

[7]Cardwell's speech was reported in the *Times*, Jan. 7, 1865.

[8]Editorial in the *Times*, Jan. 7, 1865.

still, if possible, remaining British, to sustain the responsibilities that were the natural consequence of maturity. Confederation seemed to Cardwell an indication of this spirit, and it was therefore something the British government could support wholeheartedly.

Thus Britain preferred to narrow her colonial commitments, especially in those areas where they meant inconvenience, expense, and danger. She would do her duty and stand by her colonies, but she was held to her purpose by pride rather than enthusiasm, by duty rather than love. Sir Frederic Rogers, the Permanent Under-Secretary of State for Colonies, expressed this view in a letter to Henry Taylor in 1865:

I go very far with you in the desire to shake off all responsibly governed colonies. . . . But I think our present relation to Canada involves an understanding that we are not to let other people take them from us unless they like to go. And I am inclined to think that allowing them to be taken from us for fear of consequences to ourselves in the way of war or taxation would be one of those ungenerous chicken-hearted proceedings which somehow or other bring their own punishment in the long run, and indicate the declining spirit of the nation.[9]

More cynical Englishmen suspected that if the danger to Canada were less real, Canadian devotion to Britain would be less demonstrative. Certainly it was reasonable that Canada and other self-governing colonies should make their way to independent nationhood. If this meant separation from Britain it might be regrettable, but it was not unexpected. George Brown, in England in December, 1864, caught the feeling accurately and noted it in a letter to Macdonald.

I am much concerned to observe . . . a thing that must seriously be considered by all men taking a lead hereafter in Canadian public matters— that there is a manifest desire in almost every quarter that, ere long, the British American colonies should shift for themselves, and in some quarters evident regret that we did not declare at once for independence.[10]

Joseph Howe was angry at the same spirit he observed in the House of Lords in 1867: ". . . the doctrine I heard there from the mouth of a noble Marquis was this: 'These British Americans may go and set up for themselves whenever they please.' . . . Good God, said I, can that be sound English doctrine [?] The Marquis made the statement, and not a man rose to contradict him. . . ."[11]

[9]Henry Taylor, *Autobiography of Henry Taylor* (2 vols., London, 1885), II, 241, Sir F. Rogers to Henry Taylor, n.d.

[10]Joseph Pope, *Memoirs of the Right Honourable Sir John Alexander Macdonald, G.C.B.* (Toronto, [1930]), 290, George Brown to Macdonald, Dec. 22, 1864 (private and confidential).

[11]Howe's Temperance Hall speech, May 24, 1867, in Halifax *Morning Chronicle*, May 29, 1867.

The reaction in Canada and Nova Scotia to doctrines like this was often chagrin and disillusionment. A letter to Macdonald from a Hamilton Conservative shows it vividly:

It will be a bitter pill to swallow if it becomes necessary to give up our connection with the Dear Old Country to which we have clung for so long . . . and for whose dear sake we would still sacrifice our all if it would not spurn us from it—But the haughty indifference and the sneers of the men of Downing Street are becoming almost too much to bear any longer.[12]

The Conservatives were, as might be expected, staunch supporters of the British connection, Macdonald himself being an example. Macdonald was an interesting combination: his political beliefs were British, but his political techniques were Canadian and he was not without sympathy for a colonial nationality. He never believed in Britain, right or wrong, and his robust affirmations of "British" loyalty have to be read in the light of his definition of what a British subject was and what British loyalty really meant. There is no doubt that he believed in the imperial connection; but he was also a nationalist in the sense that he sought to build on the North American continent "a British nation under the British flag and under British institutions."[13] When, in 1891, he affirmed "a British subject I was born and a British subject I will die" he was referring to Canada as well as to Britain. As the Conservative *Northern Advance* of Barrie said on April 4, 1867, "We look . . . to Great Britain as our political model, and in doing so we recognize the wisdom and experience which directed the making of her laws and the modelling of her Constitution." The word "British" had two meanings, and Macdonald was a conspicuous instance of the double loyalty that it represented. At a meeting in Oshawa in January, 1865, T. N. Gibbs, a new member for South Ontario, pointed proudly to a large sign on the wall—"British principles have been triumphant"— as if it had been his adherence to these that had won him his seat.[14]

Reformers were hardly less enthusiastic. The *Globe* would have agreed that Canada wanted to remain British.[15] George Brown himself felt that British institutions were not always applicable, however, to Canada and

---

[12]Macdonald Papers, M. O'Reilly to Macdonald, March 15, 1865 (private and confidential).

[13]Macdonald's speech at a Hamilton dinner in his honour, Oct. 29, 1866, in Montreal *Gazette*, Nov. 2, 1866.

[14]Oshawa *Vindicator*, Jan. 25, 1865, reporting speech of Jan. 18.

[15]Toronto *Globe*, May 19, 1865. See F. H. Underhill, "Canada's Relations with the Empire as seen by the Toronto *Globe*, 1857–1867," *Canadian Historical Review*, X, 2 (June, 1929), 106–28.

Canadian circumstances. Perhaps the greatest difference between the Conservatives and the Reformers in their attitudes to Great Britain was the periodic interest of the latter in a British American nationality. Conservatives tended to be less articulate on this subject.

The Bleus shared many of the sympathies with British traditions, though, like the Reformers, they looked to the creation of a distinct nationality. The Bleu *Journal des Trois Rivières* echoed the *Globe*, "nous voulons rester sujets anglais jusqu'au temps où par le conseil et avec l'aide de la mère-patrie, nous serons capables de prendre place parmi les nations. . . ."[16]

There were those who, if not welcoming the approach of a new separate status, were prepared to accept it as inevitable. S. E. Dawson, in the widely circulated pamphlet, *A Northern Kingdom*, began as follows:

To all nations and peoples . . . there comes a time—a crowning period of crisis—of trial, when the landmarks which have long guided them must be left behind and the broad sea of the unknown entered. . . . Such a crisis has now arrived in the history of our country. . . . The policy which once ruled England's councils has now given place to another. To decrease responsibilities is now the policy of the nation which never before drew back its limits. . . .[17]

There was little doubt that the overwhelming majority of Canadians were staunchly loyal to the British connection. Anthony Trollope remarked upon it—"the loyalty of both the Canadas to Great Britain is beyond all question."[18] Even the outspoken and caustic Dr. Charles Mackay, the American correspondent of the London *Times*, noted, after three weeks in Canada in September, 1864, how loyal Canadians were. He admitted that the French Canadians were not as passionately devoted to Britain as were the English, but added that they exceeded the English in their dislike of the United States.[19]

The conversion of Canadian loyalties into action was another matter. Canadians tended to think of defence not as prevention but rather as a final effort to repel actual invasion, in C. P. Stacey's words, "it was time enough to begin preparing for war after war had begun."[20] From 1862 until 1864 Canadians were sceptical there would be a war,

[16]*Le Journal des Trois Rivières*, 19 mai 1865 (First day of publication). This editorial was quoted approvingly by *Le Journal de Québec*, 22 mai 1865.
[17]A Colonist [S. E. Dawson], *A Northern Kingdom* (Montreal, [1864]), 3.
[18]Anthony Trollope, *North America* (New York, 1862), 55.
[19]London *Times*, Oct. 22, 1864, report from Quebec of Oct. 2. Charles Mackay (1814–89) was the American correspondent of the London *Times* from February, 1862, to December, 1865.
[20]Stacey, *Canada and the British Army*, 136.

and they felt that large defence expenditures by them would not help matters much if there were one. After the Trent crisis passed Canadian attitudes to defence became half-hearted. In 1864 the defence that Canada made on her own behalf consisted of 25,000 half-drilled militia, scattered from Gaspé to Sarnia, and, it was said, with not enough rifles in the whole province to arm a regiment, save for those in the hands of the British army.[21] Canadian enthusiasm for defence was effectually damped by a belief that war, if it came, would not be of Canada's doing, and that if England wanted to fight the United States she should provide for most of the cost of Canadian defence herself. Canadians were ready enough to defend themselves against actual aggression, but they were not happy about being dragged into a war with the United States on the coat-tails, so to speak, of British policy. Hence the apathy about defence so disturbing to the British; hence also the resolution of the Canadian government in 1864 and 1865, which was the direct result of the St. Alban's Raid and was exemplified in the 2,000 volunteers stationed on the border and the appropriation of $1 million for defence in the 1865 session of the Canadian legislature.

In the end it was the British government who turned out to be hesitant. The best the British would do in 1865 was to appropriate £50,000, with another £150,000 promised over the next three years. The British believed that Confederation was the best defence measure. Confederation, by contrast with other forms of defence, was both cheap and simple. That was the principal reason for the unequivocal backing it received in London. Confederation cost Britain nothing but the trouble of despatches and the occasional juggling of colonial governors; ultimately it would save her the cost of administering seven, perhaps eight, colonies by making them one.

Nova Scotia was, if anything, a more loyal colony than Canada. Her connection with the North American continent was more tenuous, and her communications with England were direct, and for that time, swift. Halifax had been both a garrison town and a naval base from its inception in 1749, and it would retain for a long time to come the authoritarian stamp of its origin. It was natural, perhaps, that from Halifax should have come the schemes for reorganization of the empire which sought so earnestly to make the British parliament and the Colonial Office truly imperial. The Nova Scotians were imperial federationists

[21]From a description of the state of defence in Canada in a letter to the London *Times* from Hamilton, C.W., dated July 22, 1864 (*Times*, Aug. 13, 1864). The Montreal *Gazette* republished the letter and agreed with it. Arms for the volunteer force were usually loaned by the imperial government.

before the movement had been conceived. It need hardly be added that in Nova Scotia the question of loyalty to Great Britain hardly arose. It would have been laughed out of court.

New Brunswick was different from both Nova Scotia and Canada in her attitude to Britain, and she was perhaps unique in her relations with the United States. Her relations with Maine had been remarkably good, since the Ashburton Treaty of 1842, and it was not unnatural that the most populous and prosperous part of the province, the lower Saint John valley, was much taken up with its commercial and economic relations with the United States. Moreover, Saint John had much less direct communication with Great Britain than Halifax, and Shediac was never a transatlantic port of call, however much New Brunswickers hoped it would be. As a result, New Brunswick had a distinctly American orientation both in political thought and practice, and its relations with Great Britain resembled those of more distant colonies.

The relations of both Prince Edward Island and Newfoundland with Britain were complicated by histories of colonial grievances. In Prince Edward Island the absentee landlords were the cause of a running fight between the Island Assembly and the Colonial Office over the disallowance of provincial land legislation. In Newfoundland the French Shore controversy had strained Newfoundland's relations with Britain ever since 1857. Indeed, Newfoundland was no more ready to accept the "semi-dictation of Downing Street"[22] in 1865 on Confederation than she had been in 1857 on French fishing rights.

In respect of defence, the four Maritime colonies were as unprepared in 1859 for trouble with France as the Canadians were in 1864 for battle with the Americans. The ships and troops at the little base in St. John's, Newfoundland, were more often employed in preventing mayhem at the polls than in dealing with peremptory extensions by the French of rights on the French Shore. But then defence in the Maritimes did not seem a serious concern. The British base in Halifax was forty-eight hours from most points of danger, and with these provinces more remote from American threats and ambitions, Maritimers could breathe more easily than Canadians. The action of the British West Atlantic and West Indian squadrons at the time of the Fenian threat to New Brunswick in April, 1866, was a good example of the effectiveness of Halifax.[23] Nor were the British seriously worried about the defence of the Maritime provinces. The provinces were relatively

[22]St. John's *Patriot*, Sept. 23, 1865, quoting the Charlottetown *Patriot* with approval. Similar sentiments were expressed by the St. John's *Newfoundlander*, Dec. 5, 1864.   [23]*Infra*, 266–7.

small—an aggregate population of 850,000 compared to the 2,600,000 in Canada—and the frontier of New Brunswick with Maine, though two hundred miles long, was sufficiently remote and unpopulated to invite only local adventures like the "Aroostook War" of 1839. The Fenian threats of 1866 came in the south where sea communication with Portland was possible.

Even in the Maritimes it was becoming clear that the British government was not very enthusiastic about its North American colonies, however patent the loyalty of some might be. Of one thing British North American politicians can be sure, said the Saint John *Morning Telegraph* on September 12, 1864, "and that is that the Mother Country is becoming tired of her Colonial dependencies. This is undoubtedly the prevailing sentiment among the English statesmen. —Veterans like Lord Palmerston and Earl Derby may not *say* so, whatever they may feel; they leave the expression of such radical sentiments to the new school of politicians, to rising men of the stamp of Mr. Gladstone and Mr. Goldwin Smith. . . . We consider, then, that the time is near at hand when we shall be told to shift for ourselves; and the American difficulty, if we are not greatly mistaken, has brought the time considerably nearer . . . than it otherwise would be."

In the west, the position of Red River and the two Pacific colonies, Vancouver Island and British Columbia, became distinctly more precarious toward the end of the Civil War.[24] The Royal Canadian Rifles had left Red River in August, 1861,[25] and the Royal Engineers British Columbia in November, 1863, leaving a small detachment of the Royal Marines stationed on San Juan Island as the only British force in the whole west.[26] The Victoria *British Colonist* warned that if any overt move were started by the Americans "the whole of British territory west of the Rocky Mountains would fall like an over-ripe apple into the lap of the United States. . . ."[27] In June, 1866, when the news of the Fenian invasion of Canada arrived,[28] and when a wild rumour had it that 40,000 Fenians in California were willing and anxious to go north,[29]

[24]*Infra*, 308–17.
[25]The Red River *Nor'Wester* commented anxiously on their departure, Aug. 15, Oct. 1, 1861.
[26]See W. E. Ireland, "Pre-Confederation Defence Problems of the Pacific Colonies," Canadian Historical Association, *Report*, 1941, 41–54. By the summer of 1865 the establishment of Esquimalt as the North Pacific naval base for the British Navy had been agreed to.
[27]*Weekly British Colonist*, May 9, 1865; also Ireland, "Pre-Confederation Defence Problems," 51–2.
[28]Noted in the New Westminster *British Columbian*, June 6, 1866.
[29]Governor Kennedy of Vancouver Island scouted these rumours. C.O., 305, Kennedy to Cardwell, June 13, 1866.

the New Westminster *British Columbian* had some hard words to say about the "cold neglect" of the British government in leaving her youngest and most helpless colony "exposed to the fury of an enemy. . . ."[30] But there was nothing vicious or even unkind in the attitude of the British government; it was a kind of parental detachment, a belief, as J. S. Helmcken put it, that the colonies "might go and do as the[y] pleased; they were only children which when grown up would go their own way and be independent. . . ."[31]

A general grievance of British North Americans was that the British were not very well informed on affairs north of the American border. The *British Columbian* complained on May 23, 1865, of the ignorance prevailing in Great Britain about the west coast. The London *Times* was not free from error even about eastern affairs.[32] The Saint John *Telegraph* said the British showed "more knowledge of Kamchatka" than of their North American colonies.[33] Another irritation was the patronizing attitude that characterized the comments by British papers. Whatever else be the result of Confederation, said the Saint John *Telegraph,* Great Britain "will learn that the now fragmentary and disunited elements of the 'Colonial Empire' are not mere lumbering camps and semi-civilized homes of a rude and uneducated people, but possess the wealth and enterprise necessary for a nation. . . ."[34] When the British were informed, it was more often about Canada than the Maritime provinces. The market quotations of Canadian government bonds, the stocks and bonds of Canadian railways, that dominated the colonial sections of the *Times'* financial page, were a symbol of the British preoccupation with Canada. The Maritimers were apt to be jealous of this interest, but it was not unreasonable. It had existed even before railways and the Civil War had brought Canada into prominence. And by 1865 Canada had become not merely a question of colonial policy, but an inescapable and vital concomitant of foreign policy. Canada had become, in fact, a major problem in British relations with the United States.

[30]*British Columbian*, June 16, 1866.
[31]J. S. Helmcken, *Reminiscences*, V, 67–9, quoted in W. E. Ireland, "A Further Note on the Annexation Petition of 1869," *British Columbia Historical Quarterly*, V (1941), 68.
[32]London *Times*, Feb. 16, 1867, recalled that the Maritime delegates were in conference at "Charlotteville" when the Canadian government was defeated in June, 1864. This kind of error was unusual in the *Times*.
[33]Saint John *Weekly Telegraph*, Jan. 11, 1865.
[34]*Ibid.*

3. BRITISH NORTH AMERICA
AND THE
UNITED STATES

IF REASONS WERE NEEDED for Confederation, said McGee in 1864, they can be given in one word: *circumspice*. "Look around you in this age of earthquake . . . look around you to the valley of Virginia, look around you to the mountains of Georgia, and you will find reasons as thick as blackberries."[1] In March, 1864, Grant was given command of all the Union armies. Early in May he and General Sherman, the commander in the west, opened the summer campaign; Grant crossed the Rapidan on May 3 and, two days later with the Battle of the Wilderness, began the attacks that continued all through that summer. The casualties were frightful and by August the North was sick at heart. The war seemed to lead nowhere. Only Sherman's occupation of Atlanta, just beyond the eastern slopes of the Georgian Appalachians, early in September, gave some light in the Northern gloom. In Mexico, French troops had occupied Mexico City in 1863 and there, on April 10, 1864, Maximilian, Archduke of Austria, was named Emperor of the Mexicans. Juarez, however, continued to fight doggedly against Maximilian and the French.[2]

The British colonies watched all these events with uneasiness and trepidation. They were overwhelmed with the spectacle of the United States, "lately prosperous beyond precedent," reduced to debt, decay, and death. "The cap of peaceful liberty now adorns the heads of battle, murder and sudden death," was the brooding refrain of the Halifax *Morning Chronicle*.[3] The fall of the great republic was all but accom-

[1]Montreal *Gazette*, Oct. 31, 1864, reporting McGee's speech of Oct. 29; also E. Whelan, *Union of the British Provinces* (Charlottetown, 1865), 123.
[2]The Saint John *Morning News*, Oct. 28, 1864, considered Juarez' cause was finished.
[3]Halifax *Morning Chronicle*, Nov. 10, 1864, "Governmental Experiences in America, No. I."

plished. "Who is there, outside of the Northern States, who can doubt that it is irrevocably dissolved?"[4] But whether the South would end subjugated or separate, the state of the North American continent augured anything but permanent peace. However the war might end, the United States "will emerge . . . chafed, angry, and entertaining feelings of mortal hatred and revenge. . . . "[5] "L'ère de la colonisation pacifique est finie et l'ère militaire commence pour l'histoire des peuples du Nouveau-Monde."[6] *Le Canadien* wrote, "Tout le continent est en mouvement poussé dans la voie des transformations par un courant irrésistible. . . ."[7] Again and again the theme is reiterated. McGee, as he so often did, summed it up:

Not only at the time of the Trent affair, but at every subsequent period of the four years' civil war, American events deeply impressed themselves on every Canadian capable of observation or reflection . . . we were taught that the days of the colonial comedy of Government were over and gone, and that politics had become stern, and almost tragic for the New World.[8]

It was brutally symbolic of stern and tragic New World politics that McGee was shot dead just five months later in April, 1868.

Nor had British North Americans forgotten the history of American expansion: "They [the Americans] coveted Florida, and seized it; they coveted Louisiana, and purchased it; they coveted Texas, and stole it. . . . The acquisition of Canada was the first ambition of the American Confederacy, and never ceased to be so. . . ."[9] The Civil War had temporarily turned American energies into unprofitable channels, but the time when the war would be over was not something that British North Americans could contemplate with equanimity. It was perhaps unfortunate that the belligerent *New York Herald* was accepted as representing American opinion, but the *Herald* was not the only paper that proclaimed the ultimate American acquisition of the British colonies. Other American papers differed from the *Herald* in degree rather than in substance. Horace Greeley's *New York Tribune* joined the refrain[10] and so did the *New York Times* and the New York *World*. Anthony Trollope in his journey around the United States and Canada

[4]P. S. Hamilton, *Union of the Colonies of British North America* (Halifax, 1864), "Introduction," 6.
[5]Halifax *Morning Chronicle*, Sept. 22, 1864.
[6]*La Revue Canadienne*, mars 1865, 158.
[7]Quebec *Canadien*, 29 mars 1865.
[8]McGee's speech in the Debate on the Address, Nov. 14, 1867. Ottawa *Times*, Nov. 15, 1867; Toronto *Leader*, Nov. 18, 1867.
[9]Canada, *Confederation Debates* (Quebec, 1865), 132. (McGee)
[10]E.g., *New York Tribune*, May 10, 1867: "when the experiment of the 'dominion' shall have failed—as fail it must—a process of peaceful absorption will give Canada her proper place in the great North American Republic."

in 1861 and 1862 remarked how Canadians constantly heard that "they are to be invaded, and translated into citizens of the Union."[11]

It was natural that Canadians should react to this kind of belligerence. There was strong feeling in Canada against the North, though it was not universal.[12] The Liberal Montreal *Herald* noted on November 24, 1866, that in recent years it had "stood almost alone among our contemporaries in having even a decent word to say of American institutions or American statesmen. . . ." Nor was the feeling against the North confined to Canada. Nova Scotian newspapers, especially Halifax ones, took a sharp anti-Northern line. The principal British North American papers that expressed support for the North were the *Globe* of Toronto, the *Herald* and *Le Pays* of Montreal, the *Freeman* of Saint John, not altogether but largely on anti-slavery grounds. In New Brunswick, Prince Edward Island, Newfoundland, Vancouver Island, and British Columbia opinion generally was less pronounced, reflecting provincial preoccupations, although in those colonies, too, the sympathy tended to be with the South. Northern supporters were apt to be Liberal or Reform. Perhaps that was one reason why the *Nor'Wester*, a Reform off-shoot in Red River, supported the North so strongly.

Southern agents and exiles were plentiful in the province of Canada. They filled the private lodging and boarding houses in Toronto; the Queen's Hotel was a Southern rendezvous. Dr. Charles Mackay, of the London *Times*, visiting Canada in September, 1864, remarked the Southerners in Niagara Falls: "they sit in the cool verandas of the Clifton House . . . [l]ooking wistfully over the foaming river. . . ."[13] Even Victoria, Vancouver Island, had its meeting place of Southern sympathizers in the St. Nicholas Hotel.[14] Northern newspapers mightily resented the presence of Southerners just across the border, and their resentment was turned against the Canadians who, though nominally neutral, supported openly the Southern cause. And the war was everywhere: "The hotels have Southern tables and Northern tables. . . . Night by night Southern songs and Northern songs float discordant on the evening air; and the same piano has often to sound 'loyal' notes this evening, and 'My Maryland' or something equally 'rebel' tomorrow."[15]

During 1862 and 1863 the tension aroused by the Trent crisis

[11]Anthony Trollope, *North America* (New York, 1862), 55, 598.

[12]A useful analysis is given by R. W. Winks in his *Canada and the United States: The Civil War Years* (Baltimore, 1960), 220–8.

[13]London *Times*, Oct. 11, 1864, report of Sept. 26, from Montreal.

[14]B. F. Gilbert, "Rumours of Confederate Privateers Operating in Victoria, Vancouver Island," *British Columbia Historical Quarterly*, XVIII (July-Oct., 1954), 245. Winks, *Canada and the United States*, 162–5.

[15]Halifax *Morning Chronicle*, Sept. 29, 1864, report of Sept. 19, from Niagara Falls.

lessened, but a subterranean uneasiness remained, and late in 1863 a series of incidents began that inflamed opinion on both sides of the border. In December, 1863, the *Chesapeake* affair raised Saint John and Halifax to a pitch of excitement. Tupper was said to have been prepared to sink the U.S.S. *Dacotah* from the guns of the citadel if her commander did not release a Nova Scotian who had been captured in the fray.[16] Just before the Charlottetown Conference, in August, 1864, the C.S.S. *Tallahassee* took refuge in Halifax from her Northern pursuers, and after being recoaled, got away from their blockade by slipping out the Eastern Passage with the help of a local pilot. On the upper lakes there was the *Philo Parsons* affair of September 18–19, 1864,[17] and while the Quebec Conference was sitting came the St. Alban's Raid. On Wednesday afternoon, October 19, 1864, Confederates dressed in civilian clothes held up three banks in St. Alban's, Vermont, a town some fifteen miles south of the Canadian border. They then fled northward on stolen horses, some 25 men in all and carrying with them about $200,000. Two were caught by the Americans before they reached the border; the leader, Lt. Bennett Young, was caught by Americans on the Canadian side and forcibly released by a British major and the Canadian militia; the rest were captured by a "posse" of Canadian detectives and constables and imprisoned in Montreal. Two months later, on December 14, 1864, they were discharged by the Montreal magistrate, C. J. Coursol, for want of jurisdiction.[18]

Whatever the legal justification for this decision—and there was some—the effect on the United States was electric. The press was outraged. Dr. Mackay wrote from New York that the hubbub over the dismissal of the case against the St. Alban's raiders "almost rendered inaudible the din of war at Savannah and Nashville."[19] Charles Sumner wrote John Bright about "the Canadian storm."[20] And on December 16, 1864, the *New York Times* said in a voice heavy with menace, "We were never in better condition for a war with England." General Dix's orders for the Eastern Department were published: American army commanders were to pursue any other raiders right into Canada, and under no circumstances to surrender them to Canadian authorities, but to return them to New York for trial under martial law.[21] Some American

[16]Winks, *Canada and the United States*, 244–63.
[17]*Ibid.*, 288–95.
[18]*Ibid.*, 295–336.   [19]London *Times,* Dec. 29, 1864, report of Dec. 17.
[20]British Museum, Add. MSS, 44390, Bright Papers, Sumner to Bright, Jan. 1, 1865.
[21]Toronto *Globe*, Dec. 15, 1864; text in the Toronto *Leader*, Dec. 17, 1864. There were two orders from General J. A. Dix on this subject, one on the evening of October 19 which ordered American troops to follow raiders into Canada, and the second on December 14 which, as indicated above, went much further.

papers condemned such an extreme order, but it was generally approved, though ultimately it was disavowed by Washington. Other, more serious consequences followed.

On December 17 an executive order from the State Department required passports for all British North Americans travelling to the United States. The effects of this were felt from Vancouver Island to the east coast.[22] The new session of the American Congress at once took up the ending of the Reciprocity Treaty with renewed vigour. It should perhaps be made clear that its demise was imminent anyway. In May, 1864, Baxter of Vermont alleged that Reciprocity was a gross injustice to the United States and only "a wet-nurse to sick British colonies." Notice of abrogation had then been defeated by only three votes.[23] It was due to come before the House again on December 13, and in fact it passed the House on that day, i.e. before the news had arrived from Montreal.[24] But its passage in the Senate was made easy, and the difference between the vote in the House and in the Senate is largely explained by the fact that the former was on December 13, the latter on January 12, the one before, the other after, the objectionable events in Canada.[25]

The events of 1864 sharpened the sense of insecurity in British North America. Americans might well "cry havoc and let slip the dogs of war"; Edward Whelan quoted it forebodingly in Montreal that very October.[26] The huge Union armies and the truculence of the government that controlled them were dangers enough, but the basic indefensibility of Canada was worse. It aggravated all the difficulties for it meant that defence, to be effective, would be enormously expensive, and neither the Canadian nor the British taxpayer had much heart for it. Canada and Britain reacted adversely upon one another. If Britain had been astounded at the defeat of the Militia Bill in 1862, there was equal consternation in Canada—indeed as far west as Vancouver Island[27]— when the British government appropriated only £50,000 in 1865. Something closer to £1,000,000 was needed. When the news reached

[22]The *Vancouver Times* of Victoria, Vancouver Island, Feb. 4, 1865, carried the official notice of the American consul.

[23]United States, 38th Congress, 1st Session, *Congressional Globe*, 2503 (May 26, 1864); *ibid.*, 2509. The vote was 76–73.

[24]United States, 38th Congress, 2nd Session, *Congressional Globe*, 32 (Dec. 13, 1864). The vote was 85–57.

[25]*Ibid.*, 234 (Jan. 12, 1865). The vote was 33–8. Charles Sumner told Joseph Howe a year later that the St. Alban's Raid destroyed the treaty. Halifax *Morning Chronicle*, May 29, 1867, reporting Howe's speech of May 24, 1867.

[26]Whelan, *Union of the British Provinces*, 112.

[27]*Victoria Weekly Chronicle*, May 9, 16, 30, and June 6, 1865.

Canada Macdonald was said to have remarked in perfect seriousness that one of the zeros must have been omitted by mistake. Ministerial papers remarked that if under such circumstances Great Britain expected Canada to tax herself $5 a head for defence, she would be disappointed.[28] Subsequently, there were suggestions that annexation to the United States was better than going under in an unsuccessful war. The *Galt Reporter* and the Belleville *Hastings Chronicle* both made remarks of this kind, though their depressed state of mind was temporary.[29] The state of Canada west of Toronto was in 1865 not dissimilar to what it had been in 1812 before Brock's victories at Detroit and Queenston Heights had restored morale.

The antipathy and fear of the United States felt by many was joined to a lively appreciation of the lessons to be learnt from the collapse of its constitution. British North Americans had witnessed "the rise and fall of the Great Republic."[30] Most were agreed about that, as they were about the lessons to be learnt from it. No understanding of Confederation is possible unless it be recognized that its founders, many of its supporters, and as many of its opponents, were all animated by a powerful antipathy to the whole federal principle.[31] This antipathy was reflected, in more thoughtful journals, in opinions of the American constitution. The Halifax *Morning Chronicle* called it "a constitution of elementary mistrust."[32] James Madison in the *Federalist* had put the same sentiment in a different way: "ambition must be made to counteract ambition."[33] Madison's view of human nature justified the check and balance system in the central government. The *Morning Chronicle* extended the principle:

> The Constitution was a document of mutual suspicion, State distrusted State, individually and collectively the States distrusted the central government. . . . The Federation was a loosely bound mass of incongruity from the beginning that neither courage nor power could rebind. . . .[34]

The Toronto *Globe* was more hopeful and took a more positive view of the American achievement. The founders of the American republic were, said the *Globe*, in much the same position as British North

[28]Quebec *Morning Chronicle*, March 24, 27, 1865.
[29]Belleville *Hastings Chronicle*, quoted by Montreal *Le Pays*, 10 juin 1865. See *infra*, 157–9.
[30]Halifax *Morning Chronicle*, Sept. 28, 1864.
[31]See *infra*, Chapter V.
[32]Halifax *Morning Chronicle*, Nov. 15, 1864, "Governmental Experiences in America, No. IV."
[33]*Federalist*, No. 51.
[34]Halifax *Morning Chronicle*, Nov. 15, 1864, "Governmental Experiences in America, No. IV."

America now. American difficulties were indeed greater, and in the end it was slavery that destroyed the American constitution, not federation.[35] A Reform cohort of the *Globe*, the Oshawa *Vindicator*, went so far as to assert that federation was a sound principle and could be usefully applied to British North America.[36] But the *Vindicator*'s view was distinctly exceptional. The French newspapers, for whom it can be said that federation was a *sine qua non*, were less concerned with American analogies. Those who opposed Confederation did not need them; those who supported Confederation did not want them. In French Canada federation could stand on its intrinsic merits.

Thus, the prejudices against the United States were basically three. First, there was a deep distrust of the North with its continental ambitions and its formidable army. Second, there was a strong suspicion that federation was the cause of the Civil War; it was thought such an ambivalent principle that it was a cause of disruption rather than a basis of cohesion. Third, there was a nearly universal dislike of American political practice. The elected executive, the elected judges, the wide suffrage were associated by British Americans with bowie knives, uncut hair, ignorance, and buffoonery, and they believed that American practice had produced what they regarded as the chronic subservience of American politicians to a corrupt and depraved electorate.

Whatever positive contributions the American example provided, they were not much spoken of. Americans and their institutions were too unpopular. Nevertheless, the Americans provided one supreme example. It could not be ignored or effectively disparaged, and whether British North Americans liked it or not, it had enormous significance: the United States had created a transcontinental nation. Given time, energy, ambition, and resources it was possible for British Americans to do the same. But in the means to be used, the political machinery by which such a nation might be created from British colonial materials, British Americans turned deliberately away from the American example and looked to their own political and administrative experience. Limited though this was, it was to be the basis of their national state. For a persuasive majority, the main thing was, as Macdonald said, to "have a strong and lasting government. . . ."[37]

<hr/>

[35]Toronto *Globe*, July 15, 1864. See also *infra*, 128.

[36]Oshawa *Vindicator*, Aug. 31, 1864. See also *infra*, 128–9.

[37]J. Pope, ed., *Confederation: Being a Series of Hitherto Unpublished Documents Bearing on the British North America Act* (Toronto, 1895), 55. See *infra*, 115–16.

4. THE CANADIAN COALITION

BY 1864, after twenty-three years of existence, the legislative union of the province of Canada needed a "strong and lasting" government. The Taché-Macdonald government of 1856 had become, after the election of December, 1857, the Cartier-Macdonald one, and, except for a celebrated week at the end of July, 1858, it had remained in office and had been upheld in the election of June, 1861. Since then, however, the political stability of Canada had grown steadily more precarious. In May, 1862, the Cartier-Macdonald government was defeated on the Militia Bill; the Sandfield Macdonald-Dorion government that followed was defeated in the House a year later, in May, 1863, and called a general election. The election of 1863 showed only the increased political polarity of the province. The French Canadians tended more toward the Conservatives, the English Canadians in Canada West toward the Reformers. The Sandfield Macdonald government survived the election, reconstituted itself, and tottered on until March, 1864, when it resigned from sheer inanition.

The Conservative government that followed, the Taché-Macdonald ministry, was no better. It lasted three months. When it was defeated on June 14, 1864, few could know where the next move lay in the complex tangle of interests and parties. The two sections of the province pulled against each other more and more: the years had made the knot tighter, harder, more impossible to undo. In fact it could not be undone. It demanded an heroic remedy, not a patient unravelling.

The history of Confederation to this point in 1864 has been essayed by several, not the least of whom was George Brown in his speech to the Canadian Assembly on February 8th, 1865.[1] It was a sporadic history. Confederation appeared in Canada in fits and starts: in Lord Durham's Report of 1839, in the British-American League resolutions of 1849, and in the Canadian legislature and Canadian press from 1856

[1]Canada, *Confederation Debates* (Quebec, 1865), 84–115. His history of the Confederation movement, 110–14.

to 1859. The cause of its appearance was almost always some pressing difficulty for which Confederation could be a remedy. In 1839 it was the political crisis, in 1849 the commercial crisis, and in 1856 it was the political difficulties already discernible in the Canadian union.

These difficulties, though familiar, can be briefly stated. The *Perth Courier* described the cause in its usual trenchant manner on May 20, 1859: "the object of the Union (and there is no disguising the fact) was to swamp the French Canadians, obliterate their language, change their customs and institutions, and make them in reality, what they are in name, British subjects. . . ." The method was that each section of the province would have forty-two representatives, by which the English in the West, combining with the English in the East, would, it was presumed, overwhelm the French. The French Canadians had managed to frustrate this design. The English divided into parties, and the French, united upon vital questions of language and religion, backed whichever English party best suited their interests. This produced, for a decade or so, a nice interchange, the French-Canadian majority being almost always with the party in power. "So long as the French have twenty votes they will be a power, and must be conciliated," wrote Macdonald to the editor of the Montreal *Gazette* in 1855.[2] Howe wrote shrewdly in a similar vein a decade later in the *Morning Chronicle*.[3]

This was not unsatisfactory. But by the mid-1850's it was obvious that the population of Canada West was growing more rapidly than that of Canada East and would soon surpass it. It is significant that George Brown brought in his first representation by population—it soon became "rep. by pop."—proposals in 1853; and so powerful did the western wing become that it broke the old Reform party and allowed the Conservatives to make an alliance, and a government, with the French Canadians. The Clear Grits of Canada West remained in opposition virtually from 1854 to 1864, with the exception of a two-day administration in 1858, that was worse than nothing, and an uncertain period of supporting Sandfield Macdonald in 1862 and 1863. The demand of the Grits for political justice to Canada West became more powerful as time went on and the inexorable increase of population in Canada West continued. The census of 1861 startled even the Grits with the disparity, amounting to 285,000, between the two sections of Canada. By this time each of Canada East's members of Parliament

[2]Chamberlin Papers, Macdonald to Chamberlin, Jan. 21, 1856. Also in D. G. Creighton, *John A. Macdonald: The Young Politician* (Toronto, 1952), 226–7.
[3]Halifax *Morning Chronicle*, Jan. 13, 1865. "Botheration Letter, No. 2." See *infra*, 212.

represented an average of 17,000, while those of Canada West represented more than 21,000. This under-representation of Canada West might not have been so serious and so chronic a grievance had it not been attended by the most profound differences with Canada East in language, religion, and institutions—in fact all the ethnic differences still characteristic of Ontario and Quebec. With goodwill and common sense, and a recognition that the economy of the two sections was inseparable, the Union could be made to work. This was the view of Conservatives, east and west. But of goodwill there was little, and under the circumstances common sense was a counsel easy to urge and difficult to realize. The result was that the Conservative recognition of the economic and the political value of the Canadian union only weakened the party at the polls in Canada West.

Various solutions were offered for this state of affairs. The simplest was to give Canada West what she wanted. This not unnaturally the French Canadians refused to do, and by 1855 the English majority had neither the power nor the intention of forcing them to do so. Another solution was to give Canada West a token number—a few more members—in other words, to grant the principle but deny the substance. This was probably the basis of the abortive Brown-Dorion government of 1858.[4] A third solution was a plain dissolution of the Union, proposed by Sheppard at the Reform Convention in Toronto in 1859. Last, and perhaps most acceptable of all, was federation, either of the two sections of Canada or of all the North American colonies.

The variety of solutions proposed for Canadian difficulties prompted Joseph Rymal to lament the sad fate of the lovely youth (Canada) who was unfortunate enough to be transferred to the care of a variety of physicians.

Some of them were allopaths, some were homœopaths, some were hydropaths,—but they all bled (laughter)—they all blistered—they all sweated. (Continued laughter.) Under such treatment this lovely youth became pale and sickly. . . . [Finally] they agreed to join, and, making an admixture of their several nostrums, to administer that to the patient.[5]

But mixture or not, if remedy were necessary, it was probable that federation was not only the most feasible but the least harmful. The Conservatives included federation of all the provinces, confederation,[6]

[4]". . . nous étions prêts, en 1858, à entrer dans la voie de changements constitutionnels parce qu'il ne paraissait pas alors y avoir d'autre issue possible aux difficultés. . . ." Montreal *Le Pays*, 6 août 1864.

[5]*Confederation Debates*, 935.

[6]"Confederation" in modern political theory has the connotation of a weakly centralized federation. This was not, generally speaking, the meaning of the

in their programme in 1858; the Reformers included federation of the two Canadas in theirs in 1859.

The Conservative proposal of 1858 was the work of Alexander Galt. Galt had been a Liberal when he had first mooted the idea in the Canadian Assembly in 1856. He moved to the right and took his idea with him, and it was the basis of his entering the Cartier-Macdonald ministry in August, 1858. The alliance of Galt and Cartier was an interesting and fruitful one, and it continued through thick and thin for many years to come. Both men came from political backgrounds that can be conveniently labelled Rouge, and both drifted to the right. There is an amusing and persuasive letter of Macdonald's to Galt inviting him to become "true blue,"[7] but it may well have been Cartier's more direct contact with Galt that brought him into the Conservative fold in 1858. They were an odd combination, Galt and Cartier—Galt, expansive both in size and ideas, a financier by experience, a visionary by temper; Cartier, smaller, more compact, tough, resilient, and forceful, a bulldog who, without great ability, had reached political power by nerve and determination. Cartier was not a man of great imagination; he was a shrewd and practical corporation lawyer; but he could be persuaded, and it is more than probable that where Confederation was concerned, it was Galt that did the persuading.[8]

The proposals of Galt, and of Dorion, in the Canadian Assembly in 1856 had produced some reflective writing on the subject in 1857 and 1858, particularly among the French Canadians. J. C. Taché, co-owner with Hector Langevin of the new *Courrier du Canada*, wrote thirty-three critical and able articles on the subject in successive issues of the paper, beginning in July, 1857.[9] Joseph Cauchon, editor of *Le Journal de Québec*, published a similar series opposing Confederation.[10] *Le Canadien* supported Confederation from 1857 onward, and spoke of it as "ce grand évènement."[11] The Toronto *British Colonist*, a Conservative

---

word to Canadians. "Confederation" meant federation of all the provinces, as opposed to federation of the two sections of Canada. If anything the prefix "con" seemed to contemporaries to strengthen the centralist principle rather than to weaken it.

[7]O. D. Skelton, *The Life and Times of Sir Alexander Tilloch Galt* (Toronto, 1920), 229–30.

[8]*Ibid.*, 431.

[9]J. C. Taché, *Des Provinces de l'Amérique du Nord et d'une union fédérale* (Québec, 1858) was the republication of these articles with a brief preface added. See *infra*, 143–4.

[10]J. Cauchon, *Étude sur l'union projetée des provinces britanniques de l'Amérique du nord* (Québec, 1858). See *infra*, 144–5.

[11]Quebec *Canadien*, 23 août 1858. See also R. Toupin, "*Le Canadien* and Confederation, 1857–1867," M.A. thesis, University of Toronto, 1956.

paper, produced a long and thoughtful editorial on the subject, the gist of it being that federation was no longer the only form of government possible for British North America, railways now making feasible much more centralized forms.[12]

The Rouges and the Reformers entertained strong suspicions about such a large scheme as the confederation of all of British North America especially when brought in by Conservatives. It was another Grand Trunk manipulation, and this was confirmed by Galt's inclusion of an intercolonial railway in the scheme. It was a trick to keep the perpetrators of the "double shuffle" in power, and at the same time to reward the Grand Trunk with a few more millions, all at the expense of the public of Canada. Even in 1857 Reformers were preoccupied with their own pockets. "The politicians of Nova Scotia and New Brunswick are shrewd enough to see that Upper Canada is a fat goose," warned the *Stratford Beacon*; and, mixing its metaphor, it added, "they no doubt sincerely wish to step in to help Lower Canada fleece her. What an easy matter it would be for the corruptionists of these colonies—Lower Canada included of course—to put their heads together and vote to spend our money in their respective sections!"[13]

The Reformers, in particular, preferred the more modest federation of the Canadas. And circumstances favoured them. The Conservative proposals of 1858 for Confederation had fallen on stony ground; the author of the *Last Days of Pompeii*, who ruled at the Colonial Office, had not received the Confederation proposals with much imagination, and they elicited only a lukewarm or indifferent response from the four eastern colonies. The Duke of Newcastle, who succeeded Bulwer-Lytton as Colonial Secretary in 1859, preferred legislative union of the Maritime provinces to the more grandiose scheme, and he was abetted by the governors of Nova Scotia and New Brunswick. Consequently, the more limited project for federation of the Canadas seemed to offer hope. It was not, like Confederation "a ministerial myth"[14]; it was, the *Globe* believed, perfectly realizable. Moreover, if federation were good for British North America, it was surely good for the Canadas. "Is there anything in striking off a fourth of the population which destroys the federative principle?" Such a federation would, the *Globe* believed, "at once draw the teeth and cut the claws of Lower Canada." It would also be cheap. The local governments would be county councils on a larger

[12]Toronto *British Colonist*, Oct. 26, 1858. Also quoted in the Halifax *British Colonist*, Nov. 9, 1858.
[13]*Stratford Beacon*, Aug. 21, 1857.
[14]Toronto *Globe*, July 11, 1859.

scale, and the central government would be modest. Whatever else, things could not go on as they were.[15]

All these questions arose in concerted fashion at the Reform convention that opened with tremendous fanfare in Toronto on November 9, 1859. George Sheppard, one of the *Globe*'s best editors, spoke skilfully against federation for the Canadas alone, and at the same time showed up much loose thinking on the whole subject of federation.

Call upon them [the advocates of federation] to tell you the details of their scheme, to show its working, to define the powers which they are willing to confer upon the central government; and at once you will discover that no two agree. (Cheers.) . . . Do you think that Upper Canada will give a Federal authority over that very Treasury which has been the source of so much heartburning—so much extravagance and ruin? . . . You say that Upper Canada is to have preponderance in the federation. What does the federative principle rest upon, if not on an equality of rights, an equality of powers?[16]

Federation for the creation of a British American nationality was one thing: for that purpose its inconvenience and expense could be borne. Otherwise simple dissolution was cheaper and better. Brown's reply to Sheppard was to sum up the grievances of Canada West and show how they could be relegated to a local legislature. Brown's bill of indictment was formidable:

What is it that has most galled the people of Upper Canada in the working of the existing Union? Has it not been the injustice done to Upper Canada in local and sectional matters? Has it not been the expenditure of Provincial funds for local purposes of Lower Canada which here are defrayed from local taxation? Has it not been the control exercised by Lower Canada over matters purely pertaining to Upper Canada—the framing of our School laws, . . . the appointment of our local officials? Has it not been that the minority of Upper Canada rule here through Lower Canada votes. . . ?[17]

Brown's eloquence carried the day, and the proposal for federation of the Canadas was carried by the convention by a vote of 566–4.

It was Brown's view that from this point on no government was capable of useful life unless it dealt with the Upper Canadian problem. The fact remains that governments did carry on somehow for another four and a half years after 1859. But Brown gradually seems to have abandoned hope of real party co-operation with the French. His intemperateness made it difficult for French-Canadian Rouges, such as Dorion or Sicotte, to co-operate effectively with him or with that large

[15]*Globe*, Nov. 25, 1859 (argument suggested by Luther Holton); July 11, 1859; Oct. 1, 1859.
[16]*Globe*, Nov. 12, 1859, reporting Sheppard's speech of Nov. 10.
[17]*Globe*, Nov. 16, 1859, reporting Brown's speech of Nov. 10.

section of the Reform party that he dominated. Thus with little hope of forming a government himself, storming away in opposition, Brown, with a powerful voice and a powerful case, gradually made effective government in Canada an impossibility. The Brown Reformers provided the accumulating force that was slowly destroying the compromises and the accommodations, the whole ramshackle, quasi-federal structure of the Union. For a growing number of people in Canada West, the province of Canada was no longer viable. They disliked its restrictions, they strained its arrangements; it could neither hold their allegiance nor contain their ambition, and by 1864 they had practically brought it to a standstill. The whole burden of their grievance the Halifax *Morning Chronicle*'s correspondent summed up vividly, perhaps unfairly, with the usual bite of newspaper style: "The half civilized people of the sterile shores of the Saguenay—the shivering squatters away up by the Temiscouata Lake—had more political power vested in them than the wealthy, and substantial farmers and tradesmen on the shores of Lake Huron, or Lake Erie. The latter *paid* the taxes, the former controlled them."[18]

A few uncertain attempts were made to resolve the difficulties of the province of Canada by a coalition of parties. In the summer of 1862 there had been some ineffectual exchanges on this subject between Brown and John A. Macdonald through the offices of an interested inter-mediary, and these were renewed in the spring of 1863.[19] Then John Sandfield Macdonald, whose administration had been in imminent danger of defeat since September, 1863, began to cast desperately around for new support. On March 17, 1864 he approached Sir Etienne Taché. Taché did not refuse the overture; he undertook to consult his friends. The aim was to reconstruct the government with Taché, Cartier, and John A. Macdonald joining the "moderate Liberals," i.e. Sandfield Macdonald's Reformers. In the end the moderate Liberals were too immoderate. They wanted to keep six portfolios, four for Upper Canada and two for Lower Canada.[20] In any case, perhaps because of these negotiations, Dorion and the whole Lower Canadian wing of the Liberals resigned on March 21.[21] Sandfield Macdonald folded up the same day.

[18]Halifax *Morning Chronicle*, Sept. 29, 1864, report of Sept. 19 from Niagara.
[19]Creighton, *Macdonald: Young Politician*, 336, 339–40.
[20]Taché gives an account of these negotiations in his speech to the Legislative Council, April 1, 1864. (*Quebec Daily News*, April 2, 1864.) Other references to this episode appear in *Le Journal de Québec*, 19 mars 1864; *Le Courrier du Canada*, 21 mars 1864; Louis Taché, "Sir E. P. Taché et la confédération canadienne," *Revue de l'Université d'Ottawa* (1935), 236.
[21]Sandfield Macdonald Papers, A. A. Dorion to Sandfield Macdonald, March 21, 1864. (Photostat)

This attempt at coalition in March, 1864, had the blessing of Lord Monck who thought both before and after the March crisis that a coalition of some kind "would be much the best thing for the country."[22] But the solid and increasing polarities of Canada East and Canada West were drawing apart every administration that sought to represent both sections; in all probability a coalition would have gained only a respite. The blunt truth was stated by the *Aurora Banner*, April 1, 1864: "Here are two Provinces of different nationalities . . . and to a great extent of different customs: these two Provinces are professedly united, when in reality they are at variance, and to all appearances there is no prospect of their ever acting in unison." Coalition alone was not to be the answer. One reason why Sandfield Macdonald's reconstruction attempt failed was that he probably had no new basis upon which a coalition could be put together. No coalition was going to work for very long without something concrete to offer the 285,000 (and more) "unrepresented" inhabitants of Canada West, for whom, as the *Stratford Beacon* pointed out, there was no equivalent in Canada East but cod-fish off Gaspé.[23]

That Sandfield Macdonald's attempt failed was less significant than that it happened. It supplied a precedent, and a useful one, for the much more fruitful reconstruction that was to take place three months later. In March, 1864, before the defeat of the Sandfield Macdonald government, George Brown had moved the appointment of a select committee to enquire into and report upon federation as a solution for Canadian difficulties. The motion was not debated until the new government was in office, in May, but it was a good debate, temperate and to the point,[24] and to the astonishment of the Taché-Macdonald government Brown's motion actually carried, 59–48. Despite the opposition of Galt, Cartier, Macdonald, and Langevin to the motion—they seem to have felt it was just another excuse for the ventilation of Reform grievances—its appeal to members from Canada West could not be resisted. The vote revealed a striking and ominous division of sectional opinion. Of the 59 who voted for Brown's committee, 51 were from Canada West: of the 48 who opposed it, 44 were from Canada East.

Brown's motion passed on May 19, 1864. The first meeting of his committee was held the very next day, with sixteen of the twenty members present.[25] It reported to Parliament on June 14, suggesting, not

[22]Monck Papers, Monck to his son, Henry, March 28, 1864.
[23] *Stratford Beacon*, April 21, 1865.
[24]Brown Papers, George Brown to Anne Brown, May 18, 1864. Also Alexander Mackenzie, *Life and Speeches of George Brown* (Toronto, 1882), 221–2.
[25]Brown Papers, George Brown to Anne Brown, May 20, 1864; *Globe*, May 21, 1864.

unexpectedly, constitutional changes in the direction of federation and recommended that the matter be taken up at the next session of the legislature.[26] That same day, Tuesday, June 14, the Taché-Macdonald government was defeated by two votes. The Conservative ministers may not yet have known it, but the constitution of the united province of Canada had now come to the end of its tether.

The events that followed caused intense excitement in the Canadian parliament. Macdonald's announcement that negotiations were proceeding for a coalition was received with tremendous cheering from both sides of the House. At long last some constructive solution for the manifold problems of governing Canada was in the offing. "The time for party Governments has passed away," remarked the Hamilton *Spectator* on June 20, "and we do not think the old landmarks can ever be restored." It was, however, the failure of three previous administrations within the space of thirteen months that had educated public opinion to accept the sudden, and to some, unprincipled coalition of Brown and the Conservatives. "Nothing but a strong conviction of the necessity and patriotism of the conduct of the gentlemen who have thrown off party trammels for the good of the country, could have averted the hostile criticism which even the best men under like circumstances would have a right to expect."[27]

Brown had long distrusted coalitions as dangerous and demoralizing. He had denounced them in the past as machinations of weak men with an itch for power.[28] Besides, Brown was reluctant to enter the Government for other reasons. He was a journalist, not a politician. Certainly he liked power, but he also disliked responsibility. It could have been said of him, as Baldwin said of Lord Beaverbrook, that what he most loved was power without responsibility. Brown confessed as much writing to Luther Holton, three years later. "I want to be free to write of men and things without control. . . . To be debarred by fear of injuring the party from saying that *** is unfit to sit in parliament, and that *** is very stupid, makes journalism a very small business. Party leadership and the conducting of a great journal do not harmonize."[29] Brown could hold his tongue, but he preferred not to, and there were times when his imperious temper betrayed him. He had, as one tried

[26]Three members of Brown's committee would not sign the report: John Scoble, John A. Macdonald, and Sandfield Macdonald.

[27]Belleville *Hastings Chronicle*, July 20, 1864. (Reform)

[28]*Globe*, June 18, 1864, makes this point retrospectively.

[29]Brown to Holton, May 13, 1867, in Mackenzie, *George Brown*, 211. J. M. S. Careless elaborates this point in his *Brown of the Globe: The Voice of Upper Canada, 1818–1859* (Toronto, 1959), 249–50.

and true Grit journal confessed, "an unfortunate faculty for 'knocking the bottom out of' Administrations. . . ."[30] He was not really cut out for office, not even to be a leader of the Opposition. Even leaders of the Opposition, however wantonly they may criticize the Government have to be circumspect when dealing with their own followers. This Brown could not do. There was a Presbyterian intransigeance about the man. Sometimes he would lay about him in all directions, wild with fury against abuses, real and imagined, from whatever cause, Conservative or Reform. Brown was a great journalist and a great Reformer, but as Willison, himself a *Globe* editor, wrote many years later, "a journalist may be a powerful and effective reformer; he is seldom a sober and prudent statesman."[31] Brown recognized something of this himself. But the pressure for him to enter the Cabinet was irresistible. Lord Monck, the Governor General, wrote him urging him to do so. So did McGee. His own party were almost unanimous.[32] The announcement of the Coalition was made in the House on June 22, 1864.

Brown's speech on this occasion was one of the greatest of his life. He was excited and nervous and almost broke down during it, but he carried the whole House with him. He began realistically. "We have two races, two languages, two systems of religious belief, two sets of laws, two systems of everything. . . ." He had implored Dorion and Holton, his old Liberal allies in Canada East, to take up the matter of political justice to Upper Canada; had they done so he would never have deserted them. But, he said, "party alliances are one thing, and the interests of my country another. . . . Let us try to rise superior to the pitifulness of party politics . . . let us unite to consider and settle this question as a great national issue, in a manner worthy of us as a people." The House cheered enthusiastically. But the best was yet to come. Brown turned to the French members:

And one thing I must say. It is little sacrifice to me to accept this compromise. It is comparatively little even for the member for Sherbrooke (Mr. Galt). . . . But it is a great thing, a most bold and manly thing, for Sir Etienne Taché, and for the member for Montreal East (Mr. Cartier) to take up this question. . . . I do frankly confess, Mr. Speaker, that if I never had any other parliamentary successes than that which I achieved this day . . . I would have desired no greater honour. . . .[33]

[30]*Stratford Beacon*, March 1, 1867.
[31]J. S. Willison, "Some Political Leaders in the Canadian Federation," in Wrong, Willison, Lash, and Falconer, *The Federation of Canada, 1867–1917* (Toronto, 1917), 53.
[32]Brown Papers, Monck to Brown, June 21, 1864. McGee to Brown, June 22, 1864. On June 21 the Reform caucus carried a motion to this effect, 34–5. *Globe*, June 22, 1864.
[33]*Globe*, June 23, 1864, reporting debates for June 22.

Brown took his seat amid tumultuous and prolonged cheering from all parts of the House, and when, immediately afterward, the Speaker left the chair for the dinner recess, members from both sides crowded around him, some of the French members, it is said, reaching up— Brown was well over six feet—and kissing him on both cheeks. The next day, June 23, the Quebec *Canadien* wrote, "La séance d'hier, qu'elle ouvre une ère nouvelle dans notre existence politique . . . comptera parmi les plus mémorables de notre histoire parlementaire." It was indeed memorable.

The Rouges could scarcely believe their ears. *Le Pays* had written rather pathetically on June 16, "Nous ne sommes pas prêts à croire que M. Brown abandonne ses amis pour un aréopage d'intriguants politiques qu'il a toujours vaillamment et si efficacement combattus. . . ." Holton manfully gave a "Hear, hear" when Brown had said that he had done nothing to sever the bonds of personal friendship, but it was not going to be easy to keep them. *Le Pays* said that Cartier, Langevin, and other French-Canadian ministers were traitors;[34] and it was difficult to avoid the conclusion that Brown was too, however much *Le Pays* avoided saying so. In short, the Rouges were, as one Bleu paper put it, "beaucoup scandalisé de la coalition."[35]

The Bleus tended to be on the defensive. Their view was that Cartier and his colleagues knew what they were about and French Canadians could be confident that no essential rights would be compromised and that French-Canadian ministers would resign if there were any real danger. Sir Etienne Taché suggested the Bleu position in a letter to a fellow legislative councillor: "Pour moi c'est une grande affaire et tenant la clef de la boutique, je pourrai toujours la fermer si je m'aperçois qu'on ne peut y rien faire de bon."[36] Besides, as the Quebec *Courrier du Canada* explained, Reformers were in a minority in the Cabinet; nothing dangerous could happen with the Conservative party in control.[37]

The English in Canada East were divided over the Coalition and its proposals. In the main their reactions followed existing party divisions, for the Liberals of Canada East were not part of the Coalition. But there was also a strong undercurrent of uneasiness. Those who supported the Government hoped that by sufficiently centralizing any federation, the danger of being submerged by the French in the local government would be minimized. This was the view of the Montreal *Gazette* and the Quebec *Morning Chronicle*, both strong Conservative

[34]Montreal *Pays*, 28 juin 1864.
[35]*Le Courrier de St. Hyacinthe*, 5 août 1864.
[36]E. P. Taché to F. A. Quesnel, 9 juillet 1864 in L. Taché, "Sir E. P. Taché et la confédération canadienne," 244n.
[37]*Le Courrier du Canada*, 17 juillet 1864.

papers. The *Montreal Witness*, a militant Protestant paper with Liberal sympathies, was afraid the English Canadians of Canada East would lose their religious and political identity in a separate province.[38]

The response of Canada West to the Coalition and to Confederation was enthusiastic. The Reform press wore an air of triumph. The goal that had so long been the object of Reform agitation was now within their grasp. It was a glittering prize. Even Conservative papers were bemused with it. It was estimated that nine-tenths of the newspapers of Canada West, Conservative and Reform, supported the Coalition and its proposals.[39] But there was some surprise nevertheless. Everyone expected, said the *Berliner Journal*, that sooner or later some solution would be found for Canada's political problems, but that it would be brought in by George Brown "mit John A. Macdonald, Cartier und Galt Hand in Hand zu gehen—daran hätte gewiss Niemand in Traume gedacht."[40] And there were some recalcitrants. One of the most conspicuous was the *Perth Courier*. Like some Reformers, the *Courier* objected not only to the new company in which it found itself, but to the fact that Brown and the Reform party had abandoned a strong tactical position in order to come down onto the plain, where, like King Harold of old, they would lose their political life and identity. The *Courier* opposed Confederation for the same reason the Reformers as a whole had opposed it in 1859. It was too circuitous a method of settling the difficulties. Dubious, costly, smelling distinctly of the Grand Trunk, Confederation was to the *Perth Courier* and other Reform recalcitrants an elaborate fraud.[41]

The Conservatives of Canada West were in a difficult position. They had manfully stood by Macdonald in years past, though the assaults of the foe had left gaps in their ranks. They believed in the Union; they believed, as did the Ottawa *Citizen*, that "the evils experienced by Upper Canada have not been practically and in fact so great as is commonly supposed";[42] they believed, in short, that the Union had not outlived its usefulness; and they had resisted Reform arguments as best they could. The Coalition of June, 1864, swept the ground from beneath their feet. "Who is who?" asked the Conservative *Northern Advance* of Barrie. The whole episode was "rather embarrassing in a country where politics

[38]Montreal *Witness*, July 2, 1864. Also *infra*, 150.
[39]Oshawa *Vindicator*, July 6, 1864. Also *infra*, chapter IX.
[40]*Berliner Journal*, 23 Juni 1864. To the writer's knowledge this newspaper was the only one published in German in British North America. Berlin, C.W., is now Kitchener, Ont.
[41]*Perth Courier*, June 24, 1864; July 15, 1864.
[42]Ottawa *Citizen*, Oct. 7, 1864.

run high and where a few days since almost every man, woman and child, knew their political creed by heart, but are now, as it were, brought to a stand still, and all their preconceived ideas of the fitness of things and long settled opinions of men and measures knocked into pi."[43] They had now to accept those whom for a decade they had scorned and castigated as radicals ready to overturn a workable constitution for a mess of American pottage called federation. Macdonald's view, expressed to the editor of the Montreal *Gazette* in 1856, is suggestive of the fear of the Conservatives, especially those east of Toronto: "The Peninsula must not get command of the ship. It is occupied by Yankees and Covenanters, in fact the most yeasty and unsafe of populations."[44] The Conservatives were also jealous of the Reformers getting favours. Two days after the Coalition, a letter to Macdonald warned, "You must take care of the [Toronto] Leader That Paper will go into opposition if not managed otherwise & the cause is self-interest—"[45] The Toronto *Leader* was the principal Conservative paper in Canada West, and its attitude throughout the Coalition was one of half-suspended loyalty. This was not uncharacteristic of the Conservatives of Canada West. It was no accident that on June 27 the Conservative *Morning Chronicle* of Quebec criticized the *Leader* for not burying the hatchet. "Our contemporary may not find the new combination to his taste . . . [but] if we are never to let 'byegones be byegones' when are we to have peace? . . . let us . . . find a nobler exercise of our energies and our intelligence in a broad and common patriotism. The country needs peace and honest efforts. Why may it not have them?" Still, some Conservatives never accepted the Coalition. The St. Thomas *Weekly Dispatch* believed, as did the Rouges of Canada East, that the existing union was perfectly workable with "more patriotism and less selfishness."[46] In general, however, the Conservatives of Canada West were prepared to support Macdonald, though they did not like Reform company. Some Conservative supporters, like the Toronto *Leader*, were nervous and skittish; some, like the St. Thomas *Weekly Dispatch*, or M. C. Cameron, refused to countenance the Coalition at all. When William McDougall, one of the four Reform members of the Coalition government, went to take his by-election in North Ontario, he was actually defeated by M. C. Cameron. McDougall, rather chop-fallen, was forced to find another seat in North Lanark.

43Barrie *Northern Advance*, June 29, 1864.
44Chamberlin Papers, Macdonald to Chamberlin, Jan. 21, 1856.
45Macdonald Papers, Jacob Hespeler to Macdonald, June 24, 1864.
46St. Thomas *Weekly Dispatch*, July 28, 1864.

A powerful determinant in the attitudes of different groups to the Coalition was of course the nature of the Coalition's project—Confederation. It had now become practical politics, and much depended on its structure and its character.[47] By the end of the summer of 1864 the plan of Confederation was already well advanced. It had been in the air for years. It had been proposed and included in the Canadian government programme in 1858, and while the Nova Scotians had been the most active in promoting the idea of Confederation—even the *Globe* conceded this[48]—it was the Canadians who developed and elaborated the concrete details. As Brown noted later, "we have a great deal of talkee-talkee, but not very much practical administrative talent among our Maritime friends."[49] The Canadians had this administrative talent in abundance, though in varying qualities, in Macdonald, Galt, Cartier, and, for that matter, in Brown himself. From the moment the Coalition began the Canadian Cabinet also began work on the details of Confederation. By late August they were hard at it. Brown's letters to his wife bring this out forcibly.

We have been hard at work with our Constitutional discussions for two days & everything goes as well as we could possibly hope for. I do believe we will succeed. The discussion today lasted from 12 until 1/4 to 6 & from first to last it was highly interesting—most deeply interesting. For perhaps the first time in my political life I indulged in a regular chuckle of gratified pride. . . .[50]

There are other sources. Two years later, at a dinner given in honour of Macdonald at Kingston, Canada West, on September 6, 1866, McGee said bravely that of the seventy-two Quebec Resolutions, their honoured guest was the author of fifty. Brown, by then no longer a member of the Government, could not allow this to go by, and took it up in the *Globe*. The *Globe* denied McGee's statement, and at the same time referred to the "original preparation of the Confederate resolutions by the Canadian Cabinet. . . ."[51] The Montreal *Gazette* denied that the plan of union was cut and dried before Canadians came to Charlottetown, but the theme was taken up in Halifax and Saint John by the opposition press and made much of.[52] The whole truth

[47]See *infra*, chapter IX.

[48]Toronto *Globe*, Nov. 25, 1863.

[49]Brown Papers, George Brown to Anne Brown, Oct. 17, 1864. Also J. M. S. Careless, "George Brown and the Mother of Confederation," Canadian Historical Association, *Report*, 1960, 71.

[50]Brown Papers, George Brown to Anne Brown, Aug. 26, 1864. Also Mackenzie, *George Brown*, 226.

[51]Toronto *Globe*, Sept. 11, 1866.

[52]E.g. Halifax *Morning Chronicle*, Sept. 19, 1866.

no one knows. But there is little doubt that the Canadians came to Charlottetown with a scheme carefully worked out in detail and the members of the delegation thoroughly familiar with it. If Confederation was not cut and dried before it was brought to Charlottetown it was as close to being so as the Canadians could make it.[53]

Confederation was a Canadian solution for Canadian problems. In this respect it was thoroughly practical. It would remove at one fell swoop the principal difficulties of the Canadian political system. It was a solution proposed and accepted by three of the four major political groups in the province. It was accepted generally with satisfaction and sometimes with enthusiasm. The province was, on the whole, when the initial excitement had died down, calm and confident. Coalition and Confederation stilled the heaving waters of Canadian political life. Richard Cartwright remarked later how stormy the political life of Canada was before the Coalition and how great a strain was imposed on everyone. When the calm came Canadian politicians "enjoyed the quiet amazingly."[54] Donald McDonald, M.L.C. for Tecumseh, noted the swiftness and decisiveness of the change and added, "depend upon it, the change would not be so easy, nor would the acquiescence in it be so general, were not the great body of the community . . . weary of the old state of things. They were thoroughly dissatisfied. . . . It is good to escape from party deadlocks, and sectional squabbles and struggles. . . ."[55] A great measure had been taken in hand to relieve the tension; and although there were a variety of opinions on the kind of federation to be instituted, Canadians, particularly those in Canada West, were content. But it was to be quite otherwise in the Maritimes.

[53]Arthur Gordon, after talking to Galt at Charlottetown, wrote to Cardwell, "He developped [sic] to me at considerable length the details of the scheme which had been agreed to by the Canadian Cabinet." In Gordon's final despatch the word "agreed" is struck out and the word "discussed" substituted. New Brunswick, Lieutenant Governor, Despatches Sent, Gordon to Cardwell, Sept. 12, 1864 (confidential). The final despatch is also in C.O. 188.

[54]Richard Cartwright, *Reminiscences* (Toronto, 1912), 40.

[55]*Stratford Beacon*, Jan. 6, 1865, quoting the *Huron Signal*'s report of McDonald's speech at Goderich.

5. THE ROAD TO CHARLOTTETOWN

FOR CANADIANS CHANGE was essential. They were committed to it, and the knowledge drove them remorselessly onward. But in the four eastern colonies—Newfoundland, Prince Edward Island, Nova Scotia, New Brunswick—Confederation could not be the practical issue it had become in Canada. In the Maritimes Confederation was an abstraction, a desideratum, no doubt, but an abstract one. It was true that Confederation had appeared in years past: in Nova Scotia in 1826, 1838, 1854, and, more recently, in 1861 when a resolution in favour of it (or Maritime union) had actually passed the Nova Scotia Assembly.[1] Newfoundland in 1858 had been willing to talk about it;[2] so had New Brunswick, though more interested in its commercial concomitants, railways and trade.[3] Prince Edward Island, for tactical reasons, had in 1863 passed a resolution favouring it.[4] It had been a favourite subject with after-dinner speakers and restless (or disappointed) politicians. But it had never been a pressing issue in the Maritimes. It remained a glittering ideal that few cared to transform into the dross of everyday reality. At the Quebec Conference of September, 1862, when it might, with perfect propriety, have been considered,[5] there was no formal discussion of it at all. "It was looked upon," recalled William Annand of Nova Scotia, one of the delegates, "as a matter in the distance. . . ."[6] Confederation in the Maritimes was the remedy for no particular evils, the solution of no particular difficulties. It offered material advantages perhaps, but it offered few enough answers for

[1]Nova Scotia, Assembly, *Journals*, 1861, 128 (April 15). Discussed in W. M. Whitelaw, *The Maritimes and Canada before Confederation* (Toronto, 1934), 175–8.
[2]C.O. 194, Bannerman to Lytton, Oct. 11, 1858; Feb. 24, 1859.
[3]C.O. 188, Manners-Sutton to Lytton, Sept. 29, 1858.
[4]Prince Edward Island, Assembly, *Journals*, 1863, 142 (April 14).
[5]On the basis of Newcastle's well-known despatch, copies of which were sent to other governors and which was the formal authorization produced for the Quebec Conference of 1864: C.O. 218, Newcastle to Mulgrave, July 6, 1862.
[6]Nova Scotia, Assembly, *Debates and Proceedings*, 1865, 232 (April 12).

Maritime political problems. Confederation raised instead the prospect of vast and unsettling constitutional changes. The Toronto *Leader*'s correspondent wrote from Halifax in August, 1864, "There has not been in these Provinces a tithe of the political agitation which has distracted Canada. . . . The people here are rather content to suffer the evils they bear than fly to others they know not of. . . ."[7]

Yet, if Confederation was an abstraction, Maritime union was hardly less so. Maritime union represented the yearning of Nova Scotia for the restoration of her ancient boundaries, before Prince Edward Island, in 1769, and New Brunswick, in 1784, were taken away from her, leaving her, like modern Austria, only the stump of an originally great domain. In the 1860's Maritime union thus meant the political union of Nova Scotia, New Brunswick, and Prince Edward Island (without much reference to Newfoundland), and it was this project that had been the hope of two very earnest young men, both of them governors of New Brunswick. Maritime union, originally suggested by Sir Edmund Head when he was governor of New Brunswick, was vigorously taken up by his successors in that office, John Manners-Sutton (1854–61) and Arthur Gordon (1861–6). Like a will o' the wisp Maritime union flickered fitfully across Maritime politics from 1854 onward and was pursued with unflagging zeal by the two governors until, in 1864, when almost within Gordon's grasp, it vanished.

Manners-Sutton and Gordon seemed convinced of strong support for Maritime union, but after ten years of endeavour, public support was negligible and public enthusiasm non-existent. The whole discussion of Maritime union, concentrated as it was in the dispatches between Fredericton, Halifax, and the Colonial Office, had an air of sublime unreality. There were advantages to Maritime union: Gordon certainly thought that a larger scope for Maritime politicians was necessary. It would, if nothing else, reduce the number of them; and it might elevate the views of those politicians remaining to something higher than the sweets of office, which, Gordon grimly noted, they were wont to pursue with remarkable assiduity. But Gordon was virtually alone in his enthusiasm. The interest of Governor Mulgrave of Nova Scotia subsided. Governor Dundas of Prince Edward Island had—and continued to have—a positive genius for being non-committal. Joseph Howe was equivocal. J. W. Johnston and Charles Tupper developed periodic preferences for British North American union. Leonard Tilley preferred a Maritime customs union. In Prince Edward Island the only politician who would look at Maritime union was W. H. Pope, the

[7]Toronto *Leader*, Aug. 20, 1864, report from Halifax of Aug. 16.

Provincial Secretary and owner of the Charlottetown *Islander*. And only in Nova Scotia was there a faint public stir over the prospect of the union of the Maritime provinces. There it promised a return to the greater Nova Scotia of 1763. It would rectify, as the Halifax *Acadian Recorder* put it, April 2, 1864, "a mistake under which these colonies have been suffering for eighty years and more." The vision of one great province, as it used to be before the partitions of 1769 and 1784, periodically haunted Nova Scotians, but after almost a century of separation reunion seemed impossible. New Brunswick was not disposed to think of her existence as a "mistake" and Prince Edward Island saw Maritime union as the annihilation of Island independence and said so.

The sporadic moves for Maritime union in the 1850's and early 1860's had little concrete result. It was the Canadian deception—or what New Brunswick and Nova Scotia believed deception—over the Intercolonial Railway negotiations of 1862 that led the Maritimes into a renewed consideration of Maritime union. W. M. Whitelaw concludes that the only emotional force behind Maritime union was this dis-illusionment over the Intercolonial.[8] It developed rather suddenly in the autumn of 1863. The Intercolonial Railway had foxed the ingenuity of British North American politicians from the time railways had become practicable. Between the years 1845 and 1847 a line had been surveyed that avoided, so far as it was possible to avoid, the dangerous proximity of the American border. Howe, in 1851, came home from England thinking he had the railway "in his pocket"; but it got away from him. In the 'fifties, when railways grew apace, the Grand Trunk Railway of Canada reached Rivière du Loup, and the Nova Scotian Railway from Halifax to Truro; but five hundred miles of nearly virgin wilderness still remained for the Intercolonial Railway to traverse, defying the interest of the British, the efforts of colonials, and the hunger of the contractors. The Trent Crisis did much to stimulate active recognition of the military value of the railway, and in 1862, with the energies of Tilley of New Brunswick and Howe of Nova Scotia, with some encouragement from the Canadian Conservative government and from England, the project went forward rapidly. The defeat of the Canadian government in May, 1862, and the appearance of the Reform ministry of John Sandfield Macdonald did not arrest this progress, though it may have been that Tilley and Howe, hot for the railway, were too sanguine, and under-estimated the interest of Reformers in retrenchment and economy. Nevertheless, the Quebec Conference of September, 1862, produced substantial agreement between the three

[8]Whitelaw, *Maritimes and Canada before Confederation*, 201.

colonial governments of Canada, New Brunswick, and Nova Scotia on the sharing of costs—in the proportion 5: 3.5: 3.5. Delegates duly proceeded to England for discussions with the British government. Gladstone, Chancellor of the Exchequer, insisted upon a sinking fund as a condition for the British guarantee of the loan, the fund to be invested in solid British government bonds. New Brunswick and Nova Scotia were prepared to negotiate this question, Tilley suggesting that the fund might better be invested in colonial securities at 6 per cent instead of British securities at only 3 per cent. But the Canadian ministers, Sicotte and Howland, took exception to any sinking fund at all and made it the excuse for returning precipitately home.

Even then Tilley and Howe did not believe negotiations were broken off. "I can not suppose for a moment," Tilley wrote to Sandfield Macdonald, "that your Government will allow this great work to fall to the ground upon so trifling a point. Nova Scotia and New Bk are well satisfied with the proposals, and Howe & I will press the Measure, submitting it at an early day after the Meeting of our Legislatures."[9] So they did. Both Nova Scotia and New Brunswick in 1863 passed acts implementing the substance of the Quebec and London agreements of 1862. All the Sandfield Macdonald government passed was an irritating and deceiving Minute of Council, supporting the action of Sicotte and Howland but at the same time leaving the impression that the question was still open.[10] Thus in July, 1863, both Nova Scotia and New Brunswick responded favourably to the Canadian overtures for a comprehensive survey before construction should start, and Tupper (the new Premier of Nova Scotia) and Tilley went to Quebec in August to concert arrangements.

By this time, however, Canadian uneasiness with the whole project had become manifest. Sandfield Macdonald had survived the Canadian election of May, 1863, but had reconstituted his Ministry, adding A. A. Dorion, who, it was suspected, had resigned office in 1862 because of opposition to the Intercolonial.[11] Moreover Reformers in Canada West were distinctly uncomfortable about the railway; it seemed to them well calculated to duplicate the notorious financial adventures of the Grand Trunk. In short, opposition to the Intercolonial within the Government was strong, and in the Assembly

[9]Sandfield Macdonald Papers, Tilley to Sandfield Macdonald, Jan. 15, 1863 (private and confidential).
[10]Canada, Minutes of Council, Feb. 25, 1863. Much of the subsequent correspondence is contained in New Brunswick, Assembly, *Journals*, 1864, Appendix 8; Nova Scotia, Assembly, *Journals*, 1864, Appendix 12.
[11]*Quebec Daily News*, Dec. 5, 1863.

Sandfield Macdonald could not afford to risk a single vote. So the survey was planned, and Sandford Fleming appointed, probably to save appearances, to camouflage the fact that hopes for the Inter-colonial Railway were now going to be sacrificed to party necessity.

It was only after Tupper and Tilley returned to the Maritimes that a Canadian Minute of Council, September 18, 1863, at last made plain the unhappy truth. The negotiations of 1862 were abandoned. Any arrangement for the actual construction of the railway would have to begin from the beginning.[12] And on this issue the whole intercolonial project jarred to a stop.

Expansive and violent recriminations followed. The newspapers were articulate and uncharitable. The *Morning News* and *Morning Freeman* of Saint John, much as they disliked each other, joined in their denun-ciation of the Canadians.[13] They were supported by no less a person than Lieutenant-Governor Gordon, whose biting despatches to Lord Monck were in much the same spirit.[14] On November 5, the Halifax *Morning Chronicle* said that Canadian perfidy had set not just the Intercolonial railway but intercolonial union out of reach of the present generation. Tupper and his *British Colonist* did not join in the diatribes, but Tupper could afford to be charitable, since he had only been in power since May, 1863.[15] But few newspapers could share his magnanimity. The independent *Acadian Recorder*, which had favoured British North American union in the less unpleasant days of 1861 and 1862, was now bitter and pessimistic (November 7, 1863):

Union of the colonies is a popular fiddle to play on, and there are fools enough to dance. But what work is there for union? What Colonial man with a head on his shoulders, has done something—sacrificed something for such object? . . .

As Colonies we seem to be going in different political directions. We seem to be severing what ties there are between us. Perhaps there never

---

[12]Canada, Minutes of Council, Sept. 18, 1863. Also enclosed in New Brunswick, Lieutenant Governor, Despatches Received, Monck to Gordon, Sept. 29, 1863.

[13]*Morning Freeman*, Oct. 29, 1863; *Morning News*, Oct. 26, 1863.

[14]Notably Gordon to Monck, Oct. 7, 1863, printed in New Brunswick, Assembly, *Journals*, 1864, Appendix 12.

[15]A debate later arose in the Nova Scotian Assembly between Liberals and Conservatives on the issue of Canadian intentions. Tupper accused the Liberals of wilfully misconstruing the Canadian position. Nova Scotia, Assembly, *Debates and Proceedings*, 1864, 95–8 (March 9).

In New Brunswick A. J. Smith, in the Opposition, had defended the Canadians, including Sicotte and Howland, in 1863. (Saint John *Daily Evening Globe*, April 7, 1863, reporting debates for March 27 and 28.) Such an attitude did not however reappear after the events in the autumn of 1863.

was so much jealousy and bad feeling between these Colonies as at the present time.

It was not very helpful, either, when the *Quebec Daily Mercury*, the organ of the Sandfield Macdonald government, noting the asperity of recent Maritime newspapers, commented blandly, October 24, that "Nova Scotia and New Brunswick can hardly feel surprise when they discover how lightly their charges fall in this province." It then added pleasantly that for the delay of the Intercolonial Railway "New Brunswick, and New Brunswick alone, should be held responsible." And some in Canada West of the Grit stripe were only too pleased to see the Intercolonial Railway put by for a time.[16]

Maritime union was a natural reaction. With Maritime union, said the Saint John *Evening Globe* on November 4, "we could talk with some effect. Canada would not dare to treat us as basely as she has done." Gordon was the principal exponent, and he took full advantage of his opportunity, but he was not without help from the newspapers. In Saint John support came from the *Morning Telegraph* and *Evening Globe*; in Halifax, from three of the leading papers, the Conservative *British Colonist*, the *Acadian Recorder*, and the Liberal *Morning Chronicle*; in Charlottetown, from the *Islander* and *Ross's Weekly*. It was a generous range of political opinion that included some of the leading papers in all three provinces. In Canada some Reform papers, perhaps glad to be rid of the Intercolonial, supported the cause. The Toronto *Globe*, November 25, 1863, recognized that the failure of the Intercolonial negotiations made Maritimers angry with Canada; Maritime union was in these circumstances both reasonable and natural. The whole movement developed sufficient steam that in the spring sessions of 1864, all three Maritime legislatures proposed resolutions authorizing the appointment of delegates to a conference.

But at this point the movement flagged, probably because shattered hopes for the Intercolonial began to revive. On February 20, 1864, just after the Nova Scotian session began, Lord Monck wrote to Gordon and Doyle (Major-General Hastings Doyle was the administrator in Nova Scotia) that Canada had, on her own initiative, responsibility, *and* expense, instructed Sandford Fleming to begin the Intercolonial survey.[17] This despatch actually crossed a long and argumentative

---

[16]E.g., *Sarnia Observer*, Nov. 6, 1863. The *Sarnia Observer* often reflected Alexander Mackenzie.

[17]Nova Scotia, Assembly, *Journals*, 1864, Appendix 12, Monck to Doyle, Feb. 20, 1864; New Brunswick, Assembly, *Journals*, 1864, Appendix 8, Monck to Gordon, Feb. 20, 1864.

New Brunswick Minute of Council—seven pages of print—that Gordon had sent to Monck on February 26.[18] Sandford Fleming worked quickly; he was in Rimouski by March 10, getting ready to snowshoe the ninety miles overland to the Restigouche. He was in Fredericton[19] before the Nova Scotian and New Brunswick legislatures discussed Maritime union, and in Halifax by late April.[20] Even Fleming was not as quick as C. J. Brydges, the managing director of the Grand Trunk. He was in Fredericton by March 4, advancing the Grand Trunk cause in any Intercolonial contract that Tilley might see fit to make.[21] Tupper of Nova Scotia was also solicited.[22] Although not all of these moves were yet public knowledge, the presence of Brydges and Fleming was, and the despatches from Monck, together with the instructions to Fleming, were tabled in the New Brunswick and Nova Scotian legislatures early in March.[23] The Halifax *Morning Chronicle* of March 8 commented warmly on Canadian initiative in beginning a survey in the winter, and although there were skeptics who doubted the value of a gesture that came from so unstable a government,[24] the Canadian survey weakened Maritime union just at the time when it ought to have been at its most vigorous.

The Maritime union proposals were formally introduced first in the legislature of Nova Scotia. Gordon doubtless felt that New Brunswick would benefit from the stimulus that a brisk airing of the subject in Nova Scotia might provide. Unfortunately Nova Scotia was very little agitated. The Pictou *Colonial Standard* of March 8 said Maritime union was "a consummation most devoutly to be wished for," but the debate in the legislature was desultory and the press response negligible. Tupper introduced the resolutions on March 28, 1864. Union of British North America would, he said, be impracticable for many years; Maritime union was, on the other hand, both desirable and practicable. "What we want," said J. W. Johnston, supporting Tupper,

[18]New Brunswick, Minutes of Council, Feb. 10, 1864.

[19]Fleming created a sensation in Fredericton by going to a Government House dinner, at Gordon's express invitation, in a grey homespun suit and a red flannel shirt, L. J. Burpee, *Sandford Fleming, Empire Builder* (London, 1915), 82.

[20]Canada, Assembly, *Journals*, 1865, 2nd Session, Sessional Paper No. 8, Fleming to Provincial Secretary, April 25, 1864, from Halifax.

[21]New Brunswick, Assembly, *Journals*, 1864, Appendix 8, Brydges to Tilley, March 4, 1864.

[22]Nova Scotia, Assembly, *Journals*, 1864, Appendix 12, Brydges to Tupper, March 11, 1864.

[23]Nova Scotia, Assembly, *Debates and Proceedings*, 1864, 83 (March 4); *ibid.*, 85 (March 7). New Brunswick, Assembly, *Journals*, 1864, 86 (March 1); *ibid.*, 156 (March 24).

[24]*Halifax Citizen*, March 5, 1864; Halifax *Evening Express*, April 1, 1864.

"is to produce a real *unity*—make the parts that are now separate a homogenous whole—given them a oneness of existence and of purpose." William Miller, an independent Liberal from Cape Breton, said, however, that Maritime union was unnecessary, and that what was needed was a general colonial union. He looked forward to the day when "the inhabitants of these noble provinces, united under one government, might stand before the world in the proud national character of British Americans."[25] Tupper's resolutions for the appointment of delegates passed "without a dissentient voice"[26] the day they were introduced, March 28, 1864. It had been a feeble debate. "The indifference exhibited," said the *Halifax Citizen* the next day, "was most chilling"; the animated discussion that Gordon hoped for, which might have aroused some interest in other provinces, never developed from "the vapid generalities, listlessly uttered and indolently heard." A few days later, April 2, 1864, the *Acadian Recorder* struck off a hopeful editorial. The sectional feuds of Canada, it said, made a mockery of union; Maritime union should not resemble the unfortunate Canadian experiment.

We hope our public men will manage to annihilate all distinctions on the Colonial map and on the Colonial brain. If we are to join together, let us be one people in reality. Let the name of Acadia absorb forever the names of New Brunswick, Nova Scotia, and Prince Edward Island. Let there be no Upper and Lower, East and West, or North and South with us.

This view was a harbinger of sentiments to come with Confederation, but so far as Maritime union was concerned the *Acadian Recorder* was virtually alone, and even it lapsed quickly into silence. Tupper's paper, the *British Colonist*, had not a single editorial on Maritime union after the resolution had passed the House, not even in its summing up of the 1864 session.[27] One would scarcely have known the project existed.

In New Brunswick there was some suspicion of Maritime union. The Nova Scotian despatch containing the Speech from the Throne was sent down to the New Brunswick legislature on February 26, 1864, with a message from Gordon. The resolution for the appointment of delegates was introduced by Tilley on April 9, and passed that same day without a division.[28] Charles Fisher, like William Miller in Nova

[25]Nova Scotia, Assembly, *Debates and Proceedings*, 1864, 179; 186; 188.
[26]But not unanimously. Tupper's attempt to have the resolution made unanimous was objected to, *ibid.*, 194. The Legislative Council passed the resolution unanimously.
[27]Halifax *British Colonist*, May 10, 1864.
[28]New Brunswick, Assembly, *Journals*, 1864, 228–9 (April 9).

Scotia, wanted British American union; he thought Nova Scotian talk of Maritime union simply "grandiloquent."[29] Charles Skinner and John Hamilton Gray[30] were the only ones who supported Maritime union and both considered it incidental to the future union of British America. A. J. Smith, leader of the Opposition, said he would not oppose the resolution, but he did not think anything would come of it. This, from a representative from the Chignecto Isthmus, was significant. As for the New Brunswick newspapers, like those in Nova Scotia, they seemed hardly aware of the project.

In Prince Edward Island the debates reveal clearly how reluctant the Islanders were to abandon their cherished legislature in Charlotte-town. Edward Palmer in the Legislative Council admitted that the Island would have a natural disposition to keep its own legislature, but he thought it discourteous to refuse to reply to mainland solicitations for a conference. A. A. Macdonald remarked that there was no point in having delegates at all if they were just going to say no. The Government intimated that although Prince Edward Island had no wish to join any union, questions might arise at the Conference that might be of importance.[31] Upon this the resolution passed, 6–4. In the Assembly the resolution met a similar reaction. George Coles, leader of the Opposition, said he would consider the "higher ground" of federal union of British North America, but nothing else.[32] J. H. Gray, the Premier, spoke out and said, "I would not allow myself or my country to be swamped by any body of men on earth. We, Sir, are here to maintain our rights, and we shall never enter a Union which will deprive us of this birthright."[33] Edward Whelan said the whole thing was a farce while the colonies remained tied to the "apron strings" of Great Britain.[34] Only the Provincial Secretary, W. H. Pope, spoke at all warmly for Maritime union. The Island could not, he felt, be left to her own devices much longer. She was composed of an irreconcilable

[29]Saint John *Morning Telegraph*, April 12, 1864, reporting debates for April 9.
[30]There were two John Hamilton Grays. One (1814–89) was a Bermudian, a lawyer, and member for Saint John County in the New Brunswick Assembly; the other (1812–87) was a native Prince Edward Islander and Premier of the Island from 1863–4.
[31]Prince Edward Island, Legislative Council, *Debates*, 1864, 111 (April 30, 1864).
[32]There are three different reports of the debates in the Island legislature in 1864: (1) the official report; (2) the *Islander*'s ordinary reports and those of other newspapers; (3) an extended version of the "debates on union" that the *Islander* published in June. For example Coles' remark is found in the Assembly, *Debates*, 35; the *Islander*, April 22, 1864; the *Islander*, June 10, 1864. All three sources have been used in the following analysis.
[33]*Islander*, June 3, 1864, debates of April 18.
[34]*Ibid.*, April 22, 1864, debates of April 18.

mixture of 35,000 Irish Catholics and 45,000 Scottish Protestants. "I fear that if left to ourselves, we shall share the fate of the Kilkenny Cats."[35] Coles replied sweetly that this argument for Maritime union was "a piece of political clap-trap."[36] In the end, a watered down resolution passed the Assembly 18–9, which authorized the appointment of five delegates to confer, not on Maritime union, but on the "expediency" of it.[37] It gave no authority for any real negotiations.

In the mainland provinces and in the Island the newspapers preserved an almost incredible silence on the subject of Maritime union. When one considers how greatly Confederation dominated the public print for the next three years, it is remarkable that Maritime union, upon which so much stress has been laid, created so little stir. The fact was that Maritime union was never a serious possibility. Even many who did support it did so as a step toward general British American union. It never touched the imagination of the public. Once the exacerbation with Canada over the Intercolonial had been soothed by the resumption of Canadian initiative, the press fell silent and public interest in Maritime union seemed non-existent. The faithful *Islander* said ruefully on June 24, 1864, that it "appears to be attracting but little attention among our neighbours. Their Press scarcely ever alludes to it. In this Island . . . the newspapers have generally declared against it. . . ." The Charlottetown *Examiner* opined on July 4 that delegates to a conference might be appointed in a forthcoming Council meeting on July 5. But they were not. "Local politics," said the *Examiner* wearily some days later, on July 11, "are at a dead stand at present." Maritime union was over before it started. Jonathan McCully of Nova Scotia, in his usual forceful manner, remarked later that it was not merely unfinished, but "unbegun."[38] In short, by the early summer of 1864, Maritime union was all but forgotten. There was no conference arranged; neither date nor place had been set. At this point it was at best a hope, nothing more.

It was almost as if the Maritimes expected Confederation instead. The debates in all three legislatures in the spring of 1864 had revealed a surprising amount of support for general union. When the news of the defeat of the Canadian government reached the Maritimes the *Islander*, June 24, shrewdly observed that Canada could not continue as she was. Government in Canada, it said, "has already become *all but* an impossibility, and we should think that the statesmen of that great

[35]*Ibid.*, June 3, 1864, debates of April 18.
[36]*Ibid.*, June 10, 1864, debates of April 18.
[37]Prince Edward Island, Assembly, *Journals*, 1864, 64–5 (April 19).
[38]Edward Whelan, *Union of the British Provinces* (Charlottetown, 1865), 166. McCully was speaking in Toronto, Nov. 3, 1864.

Province must . . . seek in a *repeal* of the Union . . . or in a further *Union* the remedy for those causes which now prevent the formation of a Government possessing any elements of stability." Under such circumstances Confederation was simply "a question of time." But not even the *Islander* knew how soon that time was to be.

By sheer accident, by fortuitous circumstances, on a question that had nothing to do with the Maritimes, a Maritime union conference suddenly became imperatively necessary. The Canadians had asked to come to it. Of course the cause of the Canadian request was the defeat of June 14, and the Coalition that followed. If this revolutionized politics in Canada, it had equally drastic effects in the Maritimes. If the Canadians were going to come to a Maritime union conference, then there had to be a conference for them to come to. That seemed logical. But where or when? Or for that matter, whom to send? None of these things had been arranged. Such were the questions raised by Governor MacDonnell of Nova Scotia in his despatch to the Colonial Secretary, written from the schooner *Daring* on July 18, 1864.[39] Governor General Monck had written MacDonnell and the other Maritime governors on June 30, asking permission for the Canadians to attend the Maritime Union conference. MacDonnell thought the whole proceeding rather irregular and said so, but he was prepared to help.

It was another week before anything was done. About July 24, the *Daring* put into Charlottetown, and it was there, in discussion with Governor Dundas and some of his Council, that Charlottetown was fixed as the place for the conference and the 1st of September as the date. MacDonnell's despatches leave the impression that the initiative was largely his, and this was probably true. At any rate, the Prince Edward Island and New Brunswick governments appointed delegates, and Nova Scotia, somewhat later, followed suit.[40] It had all been done in haste, but it had been done.

Thus it was only after the Canadian request of June 30 that the question of Maritime union was taken up again in the Maritimes. This time it was with the Canadian proposal looming over the horizon, with the prospect of two unions not just one. The two governors, Gordon of New Brunswick and MacDonnell of Nova Scotia, were in no doubt about which to choose. Both men were convinced that Maritime union was both sensible and logical.[41] Furthermore, it had the additional advantage of not precluding the larger union should that be desired.

[39]C.O. 217, MacDonnell to Cardwell, July 18, 1864.
[40]MacDonnell felt obliged to write to the Colonial Office for authorization.
[41]Gordon said later that if Canada had not interfered, Maritime union would have been effected. C.O. 188. Gordon to Cardwell, Sept. 21, 1864 (confidential).

What they did not want—and were forced ultimately to accept—was a British North American federal union with each of the Maritime provinces left intact. Gordon's despatches bear exhaustively on this point. He thoroughly disliked having provincial legislatures at all. They were corrupt; men willing to stand for them wanted only the sweets of office, and they would subserve any prejudice of their constituents, or any conspiracy of their friends, to stay in power. In short, provincial politicians were, in Gordon's pungent phrase, "needy, rapacious and ignorant."[42] He believed that there were not enough men of sufficient talent, education, or public spirit to run a federal system, even if— Heaven forbid—such a system were created. This was not his only objection to the federal system, but it was the one he felt most strongly about.

The best evidence of the stir the Canadian proposal created was the rapid appearance in Maritime newspapers of editorials and comment on the subject. These began in mid-July when the Canadian request to attend the Maritime union conference became known. In Nova Scotia opposition newspapers were reluctant to see the Maritime union swallowed up by the Canadian proposal for a British American one. In this respect they agreed with MacDonnell and Gordon. It was not simply that the Maritimes distrusted Canada; they objected to the principle of federation. The *Morning Chronicle* warned Canada that its proposition for federal union was both presumptuous and dangerous. It was obvious to Maritimers that Canadian difficulties were the occasion for Canadian overtures, and, the *Chronicle* said bluntly, the Maritimes had no desire to be "make weights for balancing the machinery, of a new, untried, and more than doubtful expediency adapted to the exigencies of Canadian necessities. . . ."[43]

The *Halifax Citizen*, a Liberal journal with an independent manner, had more to say. It had a lively interest in Canadian affairs and had followed the Canadian crisis in June with an abundance of informed editorials. Like the *Morning Chronicle*, the *Citizen* was not at all sure it wanted to see the Maritimes and Canada mixing in each other's political affairs. The federal experiment would be better tried out in Canada before any broader application of it was attempted. Legislative union of the Maritime provinces was "convenient, practical, and safe; a federal union with Canada, at present, would be almost impossible and of doubtful utility at best."[44] But the Canadian newspapers kept arriving, all through July, heavy with editorials on Confederation,

[42]C.O. 188, Gordon to Cardwell, Nov. 21, 1864 (confidential).
[43]Halifax *Morning Chronicle*, Aug. 4, 1864.
[44]*Halifax Citizen*, July 12, 1864.

and the *Citizen* took a much sharper look at the whole business. The objection to federal union on the ground that it was American, or un-British, was nothing but a "sentimental quibble." The real objection to a federal union was that it solved nothing. "It is a new theory of peacemaking, this attempt to settle a quarrel by giving the parties to it the weapons with which to fight it out more effectually." Such a federal plan would be fatal to the "national hopes of British Americans." It would unite only for costly non-essentials and leave British Americans disunited on all that really mattered.[45]

The government papers of Nova Scotia were no different from the opposition ones in quietly burying Maritime union after it had passed the Assembly. But when the Charlottetown Conference became a reality, the *British Colonist* felt obliged to defend the Government against any suggestion that the Conference would be turned aside by Canadian blandishments. The Charlottetown Conference was being held to discuss a legislative union of the Maritime provinces. If Canada had any proposition to make about British American union she would be heard, but the *Colonist* was not very hopeful. The idea was no doubt interesting, but "it will not prove of easy accomplishment."[46] The *Evening Reporter* and *Evening Express*, also government papers, were more hopeful, but they were inclined, like the *Colonist*, to be cautious.

The Halifax *Acadian Recorder*, like the Liberal opposition, thought the whole idea of a federal union thoroughly disreputable. That Canada should be contemplating giving up her own legislative union was bad enough; extending the federal principle to the Maritime provinces was worse. The *Acadian Recorder* shook an admonishing finger:

The federal principle, let us remember, is at the root of the American war. . . . Some day, no doubt, a grand national structure will rise here in northern North America, but if the Federal principle is introduced, it may lurk like a Guy Fawkes under the building. . . . If Canada is to come to our conference we beg that she may not come with her mouth full of "Federal" preaching, that she may come with a determination to pave the way to cement British America into one indivisible whole.[47]

In New Brunswick there was less philosophizing about political principles and a sterner concentration on economic and political realities. The *Morning Telegraph* of Saint John, an independent paper,

[45]*Ibid.*, July 28, Sept. 1, Sept. 8, 1864.
[46]Halifax *British Colonist*, Aug. 6, 1864; Aug. 13, 1864.
[47]Halifax *Acadian Recorder*, July 30, 1864. Quoted approvingly by the Saint John *Daily Evening Globe*, Aug. 4, 1864.

currently opposed to the Tilley government,[48] said British American union was altogether premature. It had never been discussed outside of a select circle, and "the mass of the people have never given it a thought."[49] No government would dare put through such a measure. Besides, what reason had New Brunswick to pull Canadian chestnuts out of the fire? The *Evening Globe,* an opposition paper, thought the whole business rather precipitate. The *Evening Globe* admitted that "we have all at different times had our dreams of a future when the British possessions in America should become one great nation. For the first time we are being brought face to face with the reality." But New Brunswickers had not had time to consider this reality. Further, it was important that Maritime union should not be lost sight of.[50] The *Morning Freeman,* a Roman Catholic opposition paper, largely ignored the question.

The government newspapers in New Brunswick, unlike those in Nova Scotia, were more cordial toward the general union and less so to Maritime union. The Saint John *Morning News,* reflecting the views of Leonard Tilley, was ready to abandon Maritime union and concentrate on the Canadian proposals. Said the *Morning News* on July 18, "if these provinces are ever to attain that greatness which is their manifest destiny, this Union will have to be consummated." And federation was, after all, sensible. The *Morning News* agreed with the Charlottetown *Examiner*: local interests in the Maritimes were too substantial to expect provincial legislatures to vote themselves out of existence.[51]

As for the Islanders, the new orientation in affairs hardly affected them at first. The Island summer sailed serenely into August. Canadian newspapers came and went. It was not until after MacDonnell had proposed Charlottetown as the place and September 1 as the date, for the Conference that the Island newspapers woke up. Out of a summer's lazy silence came, on August 4, an editorial in the *Monitor* entitled "Confederation." The Canadian papers and MacDonnell had finally had their effect. Throughout August the *Monitor* developed the theme of Confederation with increasing enthusiasm. By August 25 it was looking forward to next week's meeting as "the most important event —as far at least as the future destiny of these Colonies is concerned— that has occurred during the present century." It hoped that the Conference would result in the creation of "a great nation in this western hemisphere."

[48]Though not opposed to Tilley personally. The *Telegraph* later supported Confederation.   [49]Saint John *Morning Telegraph,* July 7, 1864.
[50]Saint John *Daily Evening Globe,* Aug. 4, 1864; Aug. 29, 1864.
[51]Saint John *Morning News,* Aug. 29, 1864. For the *Examiner* see below.

Then George Coles, leader of the Opposition, commented in a long letter to Edward Whelan's paper, the *Examiner*. Coles, like most Islanders, could not contemplate the extinction of the local legislature. Consequently, the Canadian proposal of federal union appealed to him much more than Maritime union.[52] He even suggested a plan of union.[53] The grand touch was the last sentence:

> Besides, in case of Union, Charlottetown, no doubt, would become the place for the meeting of the United Legislature; for no part of North America enjoys such a healthy and invigorating climate as that of P.E. Island in the summer months; and our Canadian friends will be glad, I am sure, to spend a month or two in public business here, if only to escape the fever and ague of their own Province.[54]

The *Examiner* commented in long editorials on August 22 and September 5. Whelan was sceptical. It was all very well to produce schemes of union; no one would disagree with Mr. Coles on the necessity of retaining the Island legislature. The trouble was that Islanders were not prepared to part with even a vestige of their local independence.

> They think . . . perhaps justly enough, that under one large Parliament, legislating hundreds of miles away, their wants would not be as well cared for as they would be by a Parliament sitting within a day's drive of all of them, and directly under the control of all. When a man pays taxes he does it grudgingly, but it is nevertheless a consolation to his troubled spirit to see the money laid out in improvements all around him.[55]

Even so, the *Examiner* thought Confederation should be considered. It was a measure that would make the North American colonies more independent of Great Britain; it would "lay on the shelf with other rubbish those antiquated notions of loyalty for which she [Great Britain] herself has not now that sentimental regard. . . ."[56] Most important of all, Confederation would "relieve us from that provoking intermeddling of the Colonial Office in our local legislation."[57] But no one need have any doubt that the kind of union the Islanders had in mind was a federal one. "Our little Parliament is a poor concern, the

[52]Charlottetown *Examiner*, Aug. 22, 1864, letter from George Coles.
[53]In which the lieutenant governors of each province would be elected. There would be bicameral provincial legislatures, with each house elected, together with an elected central assembly that would approve all laws passed by the provincial legislatures. The comment of the Saint John *Daily Evening Globe* (Aug. 26, 1864): Mr. Coles "favors, however, a Federation—and such a Federation!"
[54]Charlottetown *Examiner*, Aug. 29, 1864, letter from George Coles.
[55]*Ibid.*, Aug. 22, 1864, "Union question, No. 1."
[56]*Ibid.*
[57]*Ibid.*, Sept. 5, 1864, "Union question, No. 2."

Lord knows . . . but bad as it is, we are disposed to keep it. . . ."[58] If any delegates still believed Maritime union was possible the Charlottetown *Monitor*, on September 1, was at pains to enlighten them. "If . . . the Conference which is to assemble here today is to be productive of any very beneficial results, 'a wider range' will have to be given to its deliberations. . . . This, we are inclined to think, will inevitably be the case. . . ."

About this time Newfoundland appeared briefly and almost surreptitiously on the scene. Newfoundland was the Cinderella of the Maritimes. No one had ever thought of *her* coming to the Ball! On August 18, the St. John's *Newfoundlander* asked if Newfoundland was sending delegates. The same day the Premier of Newfoundland, Hugh Hoyles, was in Halifax asking Tupper about the Conference and about Newfoundland's participation in it.[59] It was however too short notice for Newfoundland, and it came at an inconvenient time, just upon a change of governors.[60] All the same, the Newfoundland government was criticized for not sending delegates.[61]

Something more concrete than editorials in the Saint John *Morning News* or the Charlottetown *Monitor* was applied to help popularize Confederation in the Maritimes. This was the visit of a hundred Canadians to New Brunswick and Nova Scotia in mid-August. For the purposes of Confederation the timing of this visit could not have been better, but the time chosen was the result of chance, not design. The visit had nothing to do with the Canadian project: it had been planned even before the June crisis in Canada. The visit was one of the many strokes of luck with which Confederation was favoured, and its effects can hardly be underestimated. The Canadians had little need of conversion, for they were convinced of the merits of Confederation whether they had seen the Maritime provinces or not, but the Maritimers had developed a considerable suspicion of the Canadians. Canada had a lurid history: rebellions in 1837, the Governor General pelted with rotten eggs in 1849, the Grand Trunk scandals punctuating the 1850's, and the crowning touch, the Canadian treachery after the Intercolonial Railway negotiations of 1862. The history of the past thirty years had shown how untrustworthy, how irresponsible, how impossible, Canadians were. Incapable of running their own Union, bogged

[58]*Ibid.*

[59]Newfoundland, Minute of Council, Sept. 12, 1864, in Newfoundland, Assembly, *Journals*, 1865, Appendix, 845. Also St. John's *Courier*, Feb. 4, 1865.

[60]Anthony Musgrave reached Halifax just before the delegates arrived there from Charlottetown. At Halifax Musgrave transshipped for Newfoundland.

[61]St. John's *Patriot*, Sept. 6, 1864.

down in a welter of debt and bad finance, they were, all too often in the Maritime eyes, bent on relieving themselves of their embarrassments at the expense of others. They were suspect; their good faith was not something that Maritimers were prepared to take for granted. The removal of this miasma of hostility and suspicion was not to be the work of three halcyon weeks in August, 1864. No one reading the Maritime newspapers for the three years after 1864 can escape the conclusion that it continued to exist. But there is no doubt that the manifest goodwill of the Canadians, combined with the warmth of their reception in Saint John and Halifax, produced an atmosphere of geniality that radiated sunlight through the fog and gloom of Canadian-Maritime relations. And, coming as it did two short weeks before the Charlottetown Conference, it achieved its maximum effect at the time when it was most needed.

The visit had developed from a casual conversation between two inveterate British North Americans, Sandford Fleming and Thomas D'Arcy McGee. McGee had been in Halifax and Saint John before and was well known. He was last in Halifax in July, 1863, when the *Morning Chronicle* had noted with regret (July 21) that McGee had chosen to lecture on the Intercolonial and the future of British America; not all people were hardy enough to believe at that time that either had a future. But with an august assembly on the platform, including Tupper, Howe, Johnston, and Tilley (who was in town at the time), McGee filled Temperance Hall anyway and in an eloquent speech said that what was most needed was an Intercolonial Railway to tunnel through the ignorance that kept Canadians and Maritimers apart.[62] It was in consequence of views of this kind that Fleming and McGee's conversation developed in the following winter.[63] The upshot was that when Fleming reached Halifax in April, 1864, he approached Tupper with the suggestion that Nova Scotia might sponsor a Canadian visit. Tupper, be it said, demurred. But the Saint John Chamber of Commerce welcomed the proposal, and Halifax, not to be outdone by the upstart across the Bay of Fundy, followed suit. Invitations to the Canadians appeared in May and June.

[62]Halifax *Morning Chronicle*, July 23, 1863, reporting McGee's speech of July 21. Joseph Howe, who could often be touched by eloquence, his own or others', at the end of McGee's two-hour address called out, "Go on, I am with you." This is recalled by Hiram Blanchard, in Nova Scotia, Assembly, *Debates and Proceedings*, 1868, 142 (Feb. 19). A fine description of McGee's style is in G. W. Ross, *Getting into Parliament and After* (Toronto, 1913), 3–4.

McGee made a similar speech at Saint John, a week later, July 28, 1863, which was apparently well received. Saint John *Daily Evening Globe*, July 29, 1863.

[63]Sandford Fleming's role is discussed in Burpee, *Sandford Fleming*, 90–2.

At first not much was expected; before the Canadian Coalition it was thought that Canadians would be too busy solving their own problems to take full advantage of an opportunity to see the Maritimes. (This turned out to be true of the Canadian cabinet—McGee was the only member that came; the others were getting ready for Charlottetown.) But the proposals for Confederation that were in the air by the end of June made the Maritime invitation all the more interesting to Canadians and they availed themselves of it with a will. All the important newspapers were sent invitations and most accepted, twenty-three in all. Conservative newspapers represented included Montreal's *La Minerve*, the Montreal *Gazette*, *Le Journal de Québec*, the Toronto *Leader*, and the Hamilton *Spectator*; but there were important Liberal, Reform, and independent newspapers also, such as the *Quebec Daily Mercury*, the Toronto *Globe*, and Quebec's *Le Canadien*. In addition to the newspaper correspondents, there were eighteen members of the Canadian Legislative Council, thirty-two from the Assembly. Together with about forty other gentlemen, the Canadians made a substantial party of about one hundred.

In Saint John, according to a preview printed by the *Morning News* on August 3, the forthcoming visit was "the chief topic of conversation at street corners . . . and at every other place of public resort." The tour began inauspiciously enough, at Portland, Maine. At four in the afternoon of Thursday, August 4, the Canadians were on the wharf at Portland, wet and morose in the pouring rain, sitting on barrels or whatever was to hand, waiting for the boat which, when it arrived, could only provide cabins for three-quarters of the party.[64] Many had to sleep in open spaces below decks. "Sleep is a great leveller," wrote the Saint John *Morning Telegraph*. "There lay the Toronto *Globe* with the *Leader* stretched lovingly beside him. The Montreal *Witness* and *Telegraph* snoozed peaceably together, while the *Gazette* clung affectionately to the neck of the *Herald*."[65] The next day spirits rose with the appearance of fine weather off the New Brunswick coast, and the ship made its way past the rocky and wooded islands toward Saint John, where they arrived about eight in the evening, to be greeted at Reed's

[64]Toronto *Leader*, Aug. 12, 1864, report of Aug. 6, from Saint John; *Quebec Daily Mercury*, Aug. 8, 1864, report of Aug. 8, telegraphed from Saint John. There were as many accounts of this trip as there were newspapers. The best was probably that of the Toronto *Leader*'s able editor, Charles Belford. The *Quebec Daily Mercury*, the Montreal *Gazette*, the Kingston *Daily British American*, have useful accounts. The Toronto *Globe*'s (C. J. Harcourt was the correspondent) was disappointing.

[65]*Morning Telegraph*, Aug. 9, 1864.

Point Wharf by a vast concourse of people, variously estimated by the astonished Canadians at from 6,000 to 15,000. "Not only were the wharves in the neighbourhood of the landing place crowded to excess; but every foothold had been eagerly secured hours before," wrote Charles Belford of the Toronto *Leader*.[66] The greeting of the Saint John *Telegraph*:

> You come, proud sons of a noble state
> Too long estrang'd and too long unknown. . . .[67]

The next day was bright and warm; handbills posted over the city invited citizens to meet the Canadians at a levee in the Court House, after which the visitors were driven around the local sights. That night the Saint John Chamber of Commerce produced an enormous dinner the menu of which daunts the imagination and which must have staggered even copious Victorian digestions. Despite all this, the speeches were undistinguished. The great speeches were to come after the Charlottetown Conference rather than before.

Sunday was, as usual, given over to private concerns, but on Monday, August 8, the delegates embarked once more, this time on the European and North American railway,[68] which took them to Rothesay, all of ten miles, where they boarded a special steamer, the *Anna Augusta*, for the journey to Fredericton. It was an impressive voyage. The Kennebecasis and the lower Saint John river valleys offered the best the province could show, and on that day the river was delightful: ". . . the heat [was] gently softened by the summer breeze, and the fleecy clouds which hung in the sky above us seemed but the shadows of the glorious earth."[69] The band of the 15th Regiment[70] played, and the French Canadians, who comprised a good quarter of the party, interspersed the band music by singing "A la claire fontaine" and other old paddling songs, swinging imaginary paddles from side to side of invisible canoes as they sang. Their most graphic song for Maritimers was "Mademoiselle Marianne," during which they "hugged each other so affectionately, and laughed over so many bars in succession that the admiring audience caught

[66]Toronto *Leader*, Aug. 12, 1864, report of Aug. 6 from Saint John.

[67]Saint John *Morning Telegraph*, Aug. 6, 1864. Also quoted by the Montreal *Gazette*, Aug. 11, 1864.

[68]The name of the Saint John-Shediac railway that was owned and operated by the New Brunswick government.

[69]Saint John *Morning Telegraph*, Aug. 10, 1864, report of Aug. 8 from Fredericton.

[70]A battalion of 15th Regiment, part of the contingent of 1861, had been stationed in Fredericton since that time.

their enthusiasm." "Jolly Good Fellow, Johnny Canuck!" was the response in Halifax.[71] So successful was French-Canadian good humour and courtesy that Maritimers "will labor under the impression . . . that French is the universal language in Canada and that French songs are as familiar to all Canadians as 'John Brown's soul'. . . ."[72]

Fredericton produced a less elaborate reception than Saint John, but both Tilley and McGee were in good form and both spoke hopefully of the prospects of union, McGee of political union, Tilley cautiously confining himself to a customs one. At the end of his speech Tilley took the hand of Benjamin Weir of Nova Scotia on his right, and that of T. R. Ferguson of Canada on his left, and thus joined the three were warmly applauded by a charmed audience.[73] Still, it was not wise to be optimistic. The Saint John *Morning Telegraph* was still inclined to be sharp, especially with George Brown. "Mr. Brown . . . will be glad to turn any spasmodic and unsuccessful conference at Prince Edward's Island to the best account, to suit his own purposes. It will be well if the hon. gentleman does not mistake the wishes of these Lower Colonies. . . ."[74] The editor of a Saint John paper told Charles Belford that "if a proposition were made in Parliament to join with Canada and Nova Scotia in a political union, it would be hooted down."[75] New Brunswickers were cautious about union, though the Canadians made ample use of the opportunity to sound out, and perhaps to influence, opinion on the subject.

By August 10 the Canadians were in Nova Scotia, arriving at Windsor by the *Emperor*, the ancient and perilous steamer that ran regularly from Saint John, and were met by Tupper, Annand, Howe, and others who accompanied them to Halifax.[76] The days were filled with sunshine and Nova Scotia displayed herself to advantage. Having spent part of Thursday, August 11, at a "bonnet hop" on board H.M.S. *Duncan*,[77] the Canadians were next invited to join the Royal Halifax Yacht Club's annual picnic, called by the unsettling name of "Hodge-Podge and

[71]*Halifax Citizen*, Aug. 13, 1864; also *Quebec Daily Mercury*, Aug. 20, 1864, "Letter XII."

[72]Toronto *Leader*, Aug. 22, 1864, report of Aug. 19 from Portland.

[73]Saint John *Daily Evening Globe*, Aug. 10, 1864.

[74]Saint John *Morning Telegraph*, Aug. 13, 1864.

[75]Toronto *Leader*, Aug. 16, 1864, report of Aug. 9, from Saint John.

[76]Some Canadians stayed with leading Nova Scotians. Howe said later that he had entertained two Canadians for a week. Halifax *Morning Chronicle*, June 7, 1867, reporting Howe's Truro speech of June 4.

[77]Ottawa *Citizen*, Aug. 23, 1864, report of Aug. 12. *Duncan* was the 81-gun flagship of the Admiral, Sir James Hope, K.C.B. It carried a complement of about 900 men.

Chowder Party."[78] It began at eleven in the morning, on a glorious day with a stiff breeze to swell the sails of the yachts and stream out the bunting with which they were decorated.[79] The rendezvous was Prince's Lodge on Bedford Basin, where the Canadians disembarked and walked up to the grounds of the Duke of Kent's old house, whose foundation stones—and a pretty circular music room down by the water—were the only recollection of Queen Victoria's father and his mistress, Julie St. Laurent. Here long tables laden with a sumptuous feast were arrayed on the grass and on the long terrace "manly and exhilarating games were vigorously carried on."[80] The resulting spectacle rather belies the conventional picture of Victorian gentlemen. The august legislators of Canada never looked less so than on this occasion. Charles Belford's account, honest in most respects, might perhaps be trusted:

. . . leap-frog at once became the order of the day and a lively scene ensued. Members of the Upper House backed members of the Lower House with an agility that was wonderful. Blue-noses sprang over Canadians with a shriek of delight. Canadians bounded over New Brunswickers and tripped over Nova Scotians. Editors and correspondents mingled in the fray and perilled their valuable persons by seeking the bubble reputation. . . .[81]

Then all were summoned to the "substantials." Of course there were speeches. McGee made a merry speech—one of his best—and Howe was given the appropriate task of toasting sweethearts and wives. Howe and McGee often set off each other, the one with the familiar half-yankee style of Nova Scotia, a racy idiom of homely allusions informed by history, the other with a poetic, elegant, rather studied manner, full of Irish wit and vivacity. Howe, who knew McGee by this time—they had met on several occasions before—always retained a great affection for him. "Of D'Arcy I would speak tenderly," said Howe later, "because, whatever be his errors, he is a man of genius—an elegant writer, and eloquent speaker, and a pleasant fellow over a bottle of wine."[82] After the speeches came the sound of the bagpipes, and several adept Scotsmen danced the Highland fling, including the nimble old Mayor of Fredericton, who, it was said, danced "the friskiest carle" of them all.[83] And

[78]Hodge-podge was mutton boiled up with vègetables. Canadian reaction varied. The *Leader* thought it quite palatable. The *Quebec Mercury* thought it was flavoured with ashes! Chowder was "haddock sliced and boiled until a rather suspicious mixture is produced" (Toronto *Leader*). This description suggests the Canadian reaction to chowder.

[79]Toronto *Leader*, Aug. 20, 1864, report of Aug. 13 from Halifax.

[80]*Halifax Citizen*, Aug. 13, 1864.

[81]Toronto *Leader*, Aug. 20, 1864, report of Aug. 13.

[82]*Morning Chronicle*, May 15, 1867, reporting Howe's speech at Mason Hall, Halifax, May 9, 1867.　　　　[83]*Halifax Citizen*, Aug. 13, 1864.

when the evening began to gather, and as the revellers set off for town, a full moon rose like an exhalation above the spires of spruce and shone over Bedford Basin.[84] "One o'clock and all's well!": one Canadian editor turning into bed the night before had heard the cry of the Halifax watch and expressed the hope that all *was* well.[85] So far, it could hardly have been better.

On Saturday night, August 13, the dinner was given at which Howe, under the mellowing influence of wine and the occasion, gave the speech that he was later to have flung back at him so often.

He was not one of those who thanked God that he was a Nova Scotian merely, for he was a Canadian as well. He had never thought he was a Nova Scotian, but he looked across the broad continent . . . and studied the mode by which it could be consolidated. . . . And why should union not be brought about? Was it because we wished to live and die in our insignificance?[86]

On Monday, August 15, H.M.S. *Lily*, the little 700-ton corvette to which Howe was attached, was pressed into service and took the visitors out to sea. Of the return to harbour, Charles Belford wrote, "Nature smiled upon us . . . on one side the city of Halifax looking resplendent in the fullness of the noon-day sun, and on the Dartmouth side . . . the fields still green and lively with pretty cottages peeping out from charming clusters of trees."[87]

So the Canadians departed home, full of the splendours of the Maritimes, delighted with the warmth of their reception, and dreaming national dreams. "Everywhere," wrote the Ottawa *Citizen*'s correspondent, "the Canadians were welcomed like newly found members of the great Confederation of the British North American Colonies."[88] How faithfully they reported their trip was revealed in the Canadian papers which came down to the Maritimes "groaning under the weight of their correspondents' letters. . . . It is evident," said the Halifax *Morning Chronicle* of September 1, "that they diligently inquired into the views of Nova Scotians and New Brunswickers with reference to the plan of Federation that has been mooted by Mr. McGee, and so ably and

[84]Montreal *Gazette*, Aug. 23, 1864, report of Aug. 13.
[85]*Ibid.*, Aug. 22, 1864, report of Aug. 12. The watch in Halifax was begun about 1818 and lasted until the seventies.
[86]Halifax *Morning Chronicle*, Aug. 16, 1864. Of this speech Howe commented three years later: "Some people may be inclined to doubt that even I was sober then,—however I really think I was; but who ever heard of a public man being bound on an occasion like that?" Halifax *Morning Chronicle*, June 7, 1867, reporting Howe's Truro speech of June 4.
[87]Toronto *Leader*, Aug. 22, 1864, report of Aug. 17 from Saint John.
[88]Ottawa *Citizen*, Aug. 23, 1864, report of Aug. 18 en route to Portland.

strenuously advocated by himself and other leading politicians in all the Provinces." Canadian speeches had been well primed with union sentiment. Here the Toronto *Leader*'s correspondent cautioned his readers. "I think I may say with the fullest confidence that there is no earnest desire among the people of Nova Scotia and New Brunswick to change their state at present. . . ."[89] The Halifax *Morning Chronicle* agreed. "There is no tangible evidence to prove that either Nova Scotia or New Brunswick entertain a strong desire to be united with Canada. It is true that in certain circles the project is popular, but the idea of Confederation, after all, is little more than a sentiment."[90] But sentiment was something, and perhaps even more than the *Chronicle* would have conceded a month before. Sentiment was an indispensable quantity. It may have been nothing; on the other hand, it was everything. Without it Canadian overtures at Charlottetown might have fallen on merely polite ears. Even the Saint John *Morning Telegraph* had to admit on August 19 that after all "the Canadians are good fellows and a jolly set, and . . . we are sorry to part with them. . . ." In Nova Scotia, Sir Richard MacDonnell remarked on the vivacity and friendliness that had animated the Canadians' six-day visit to Halifax. He concluded that the visit "must be regarded as having had, and as being intended to have had, an influence on the deliberations at Charlottetown"; that Her Majesty's Government must expect to find Confederation of the British North American provinces "more extensively supported, than was at all probable six months ago."[91] The Halifax *British Colonist*, which had been cool to Confederation was quite won over.

They [the Canadians] were strangers, they are now acquaintances, friends . . . and let us hope, will aid materially in forwarding that grand scheme which all the more intelligent politicians of our common country seem to have at heart—a complete political consolidation of these British North American colonies.[92]

Confederation was not yet popular, but it had already taken hold of a powerful and persuasive group of politicians and journalists. Whether for good or ill, there was a national spirit stirring in the Maritime provinces.

[89]Toronto *Leader*, Aug. 20, 1864, report of Aug. 16 from Halifax.
[90]Halifax *Morning Chronicle*, Sept. 1, 1864.
[91]C.O. 217, MacDonnell to Cardwell, Aug. 18, 1864.
[92]*British Colonist*, Sept. 8, 1864, being reflections on the Canadian visit.

6. THE CHARLOTTETOWN
CONFERENCE

IT IS CLEAR that it was only by Canadian initiative—interference perhaps
—that the Charlottetown Conference was held at all. It is understandable
also why the Conference was to be turned aside so easily from its
ostensible purpose. To some contemporaries the impression was left
that the Canadians swooped down upon Charlottetown, corrupted the
delegates with champagne and promises, and steamed them up to
Quebec, where, with further inducements, they were persuaded to sign
the Quebec Resolutions. A contemporary Sackville newspaper attributed
it to wizardry:

> Reader you know as well as I,
> How there 'mid scenes of revelry,
> At festive boards, at midnight balls,
> With dance and song, in lordly halls . . .
> Where'er they turned, on every hand,
> They met the Wizard with his wand,
> He sparkl'd in the ruby wine,
> He glitter'd in the dresses fine . . .
> Yet there amid these scenes they laid
> The cornerstone of what they said,
> Would make of us a mighty nation,
> And christen'd it, "Confederation."[1]

There was just enough in the Canadian argosy to lend colour, even
substance, to this view.

The Canadians embarked at Quebec on the evening of Monday,
August 29, 1864. Eight of the twelve members of the Cabinet came,
well briefed with proposals and the arguments to sustain them, and
probably already allotted their respective tasks. The trip down the St.
Lawrence in the *Queen Victoria* was a delight for everyone. The

[1]Sackville (N.B.) *Borderer*, March 17, 1865.

beautiful weather of that sunlit summer still held;[2] the Canadians enjoyed themselves, sprawled in deck chairs, and watched the steep north shore of the great river recede below the horizon.[3] The steamer followed the south shore; James Ferrier recalled how he stood at Rivière du Loup and watched the *Queen Victoria* go by and wished them all God speed.[4] By early Thursday morning, September 1, the *Queen Victoria* had sighted the western tip of Prince Edward Island and thence followed the low, red ochre shoreline, with its green fields and white cottages. Brown, who was up for the sunrise and a salt water bath, described it, "as pretty a country as you ever put your eye upon." After coming into Hillsborough Bay, about noon they came quite suddenly upon Charlottetown.[5]

Charlottetown was then a modest little place of about 7,000 inhabitants. Its principal boasts were the fine Georgian structure that housed the legislature, and a pretty Government House beside the bay, set, like many of the handsomer houses, in a grove of fir. The town itself lay on a slight elevation from the harbour; the houses were "chiefly of a Quakerish brown and drab hue, clustered together methodically . . . and the straight parallel streets run down to the water's edge like the red lines of a ledger."[6] The quiet of Charlottetown was deceptive; indeed, Prince Edward Island politics generally were belied by the Island's bucolic charm. Besides, Slaymaker and Nichols' Olympic Circus was in town, from August 30 to September 2; the Charlottetown *Examiner* had carried advertisements of excursions to Charlottetown on August 22 and 29, and by the end of the month Charlottetown's twenty modest hotels were well taken up with visitors.

The Nova Scotian delegates had arrived in the late afternoon of Wednesday, August 31. The boat was late, and the Nova Scotians, so the *Examiner* said, "were suffered to find out by rule of thumb, where they could find something to eat and a bed to lie upon."[7] As for the New Brunswickers, who arrived at 11 P.M. the same night, "neglect and indifference was measured out to them . . . with beautiful impartiality." It was not quite true. The members of the Prince Edward Island government could not be deprived, apparently, of their opportunity to see the

[2]Weather reports from Father Point, Aug. 29, 30, 31: "Weather clear and beautiful." Montreal *Gazette*, Aug. 30-Sept. 1, 1864.
[3]Brown Papers, George Brown to Anne Brown, Sept. 13, 1864.
[4]Canada, *Confederation Debates*, 195.
[5]Brown Papers, George Brown, to Anne Brown, Sept. 13, 1864. Also in J. M. S. Careless, "George Brown and the Mother of Confederation," Canadian Historical Association, *Report*, 1960, 68.
[6]Saint John *Morning Telegraph*, Aug. 31, 1864, report from Charlottetown by "Shadow." Cf. descriptions of Halifax and Saint John, *infra*, 194–5 and 229–30.
[7]Charlottetown *Examiner*, Sept. 5, 1864.

circus and the duty of meeting the delegates was given to W. H. Pope, the Provincial Secretary, who escorted the New Brunswickers safely to their lodging in the *Mansion House*; and the *Islander* said he had done his best for the Nova Scotians as well.[8]

And he was still going strong the next day, when the Canadians arrived. The *Queen Victoria* had anchored with not a little *éclat*: the Islanders' style was more modest. The Island government was now busy with the Conference about to open, and Pope was deputed once more. He hurried down to the harbour and was rowed out to meet the Canadians, in an unprepossessing little oyster boat, "with a barrel of flour in the bow, and two jars of molasses in the stern, and with a lusty fisherman as his only companion. . . ." The story is probably authentic,[9] though *Ross's Weekly* may have embellished it:

He . . . made a respectful official visit alongside the Canadian steamer "Queen Victoira" [sic] seated on an unclean barrel, and in full command of an imbibing oyster boat propelled by a paddle and an oar. The Stewart [sic] of the steamer, taking the Secretary for a *Bumboater*, said, "I say, skipper, what's the price of shell-fish?" But William the Secretary opened not his shell.[10]

The Canadians then went ashore amid the stares of the populace. Brown's description of this occasion is lively and revealing:

Having dressed ourselves in correct style, our two boats were lowered man-of-war fashion, and being each duly manned with four oarsmen and a boatswain, dressed in blue uniforms, hats belts, etc. in regular style, we pulled away for shore and landed like Mr. Christopher Columbus who had the precedence of us in taking possession of portions of the American continent.

The Charlottetown Conference met about 2 P.M. that same afternoon, without the Canadians. Col. J. H. Gray, Premier of the Island, was made Chairman. The Conference took only a short time to decide that the question of Maritime union could be deferred, whereupon the Canadians were at once introduced, hands were shaken all around, and the Conference stood adjourned until 10 o'clock the next morning. Canada was to have four days in which to make her case for Confederation.[11]

[8]Saint John *Morning Telegraph*, Sept. 5, 1864, report of Sept. 2 from Charlottetown; Charlottetown *Islander*, Sept. 9, 1864.
[9]Charlottetown *Vindicator*, Sept. 7, 1864. The Halifax *British Colonist*, Tupper's paper, said that Pope came out personally and conducted the delegates ashore (Sept. 13, 1864). This report was copied by the *Islander*, Sept. 16, 1864.
[10]Charlottetown *Ross's Weekly*, Sept. 8, 1864.
[11]Brown Papers, George Brown to Anne Brown, Sept. 13, 1864. Also in Careless, "George Brown and the Mother of Confederation," 69.

There were few accounts of the actual meetings of the Conference. The Saint John *Telegraph* of September 5 reported that some members had been in favour of making its proceedings "an open court," but that this was overruled. Instead business was to be conducted in a conversational manner; thus "buncombe speeches will be out of place, and politicians will for once deal with naked facts. This will facilitate matters greatly. . . ." No doubt it did. The Charlottetown papers complained about the lack of information. The *Examiner* of September 5, after giving some of the gossip, said nothing else was known about the Conference. Why "the awful and pompous air of mystery?" it asked, a fortnight later. There were however some sources. The Saint John *Telegraph* sent a correspondent to Charlottetown, and the Charlottetown *Vindicator* published a timetable that was much copied.[12] These accounts were however second-hand; the only important first-hand source is George Brown.[13]

On Friday and Saturday, September 2 and 3, Canada opened up with her powerful guns. Cartier, Macdonald, and probably Galt spoke,[14] Cartier and Macdonald developing the general arguments for Confederation, and Galt laying out the basis of the financial settlement. It was known, even at that time, what the basis was: the general government would assume all debts, and would in turn provide revenue for the provinces, apportioned on the basis of population. The principle of the debt allowance may have been set forth.[15] The Saint John *Telegraph* described vividly the telling effect of all this on the Maritime delegates:

New Brunswick, Nova Scotia and Prince Edward Island have all been within the range of her [Canada's] big guns since Friday morning last, and

[12]Saint John *Morning Telegraph*, Sept. 2–Sept. 13, 1864; Charlottetown *Vindicator*, Sept. 7, 1864, which the Charlottetown *Monitor*, Sept. 8, 1864, copied. The Halifax *Morning Chronicle*, Sept. 10, 1864, has a useful report, perhaps from Jonathan McCully. The Toronto *Globe*, Sept. 21, 1864, gives excerpts from all three of the above. There are three reports, dated Sept. 3, 5, and 8, in the Kingston *Daily British American*, Sept. 16, 17, 1864. See also W. M. Whitelaw, *The Maritimes and Canada before Confederation* (Toronto, 1934), 220–4; D. G. Creighton, *John A. Macdonald: The Young Politician* (Toronto, 1952), 365–7. The differences here reflect in part the disparities in the newspaper accounts.

[13]Brown Papers, George Brown to Anne Brown, Sept. 13, 1864. J. H. Gray of New Brunswick published an account of Confederation in 1872, but his references to the Charlottetown Conference are very brief. (J. H. Gray, *Confederation: or the Political and Parliamentary History of Canada from . . . October 1864 to . . . July 1871* (Toronto, 1872).)

[14]The *Telegraph*, *Vindicator*, and *Daily British American* all say Galt spoke on Monday, Sept. 5; Brown says he spoke Saturday.

[15]From a semi-official release, presumably arranged by the Canadian Cabinet, dated Sept. 23, and which appeared in the Quebec *Courrier du Canada* and the Montreal *Gazette*, Sept. 26, 1864. Other papers followed.

great it is said has been the effect. Indeed her ordnance is of a superior kind, and embraces such well known pieces of artillery as the Cartier, the Brown, the Macdonald and the Galt. . . . I am told that the speeches have been able and powerful and the arguments almost irresistible. Furthermore . . . our own delegates are still more favourable to [BNA] Union than they were, and as they consult and converse with the Canadians, the difficulties in the matter of detail vanish.[16]

And the entertainment proceeded apace. At three on Friday, September 2, the Conference adjourned to meet at Pope's house for a fine buffet luncheon, replete with Island delicacies. That night was clear, with a full moon, and the Canadians appear to have spent it as they pleased. Brown, for example, who was staying with W. H. Pope in Pope's fine house by the bay, sat quietly on the balcony looking out over the moonlit sea in all its glory.[17] At three o'clock the next day, Saturday, September 3, the Conference adjourned to the *Queen Victoria* for lunch, with the Canadians as hosts.

The Canadians had had, by that time, two good days of it. Though still rather ill at ease, they had begun to warm to their theme, and the Maritimers, though not without suspicion of the motives that brought these eight imposing Canadians steaming into Charlottetown, were disposed to be hospitable and interested. If Mr. Pope had been generous the previous day, the Canadians were princely. Nothing was spared then, or later, to do whatever could be done with good food and good wine to make Islanders like Canadians, or Nova Scotians appreciate New Brunswickers. Lord Elgin, ten years before, had negotiated a difficult treaty in Washington by luck, charm, and champagne, and who was to say that the Canadians could not emulate him. In those opulent days, before prohibition and taxes, no one was disposed to stint either in the provision or the consumption of wine and spirits, except perhaps Leonard Tilley, the druggist from Saint John, who already believed in temperance. The Canadian Cabinet never hesitated when it came to a few thousand dollars for entertainment; enough members of it were convinced that splendid intoxication was splendour sufficient for ordinary mortals, newly acquainted, and engaged in portentous public business. At four o'clock lunch began on the *Queen Victoria*. The work was over until Monday; everyone was in good spirits; champagne corks punctuated the talk which soon waxed merrily. Cartier got up and in his forceful accents[18] extolled a new continental nation; Brown expanded

16Saint John *Morning Telegraph*, Sept. 8, 1864, report of Sept. 5 from Charlottetown.

17Brown Papers, George Brown to Anne Brown, Sept. 13, 1864.

18Cartier "never mastered the English idiom, pronunciation or accent. . . ." A. W. Savary of Nova Scotia, quoted by J. Boyd in *Sir George Etienne Cartier* (Toronto, 1917), 370.

the theme to transcontinental dimensions, and in the warmth of eloquence and champagne, the ice melted completely. The occasion took hold of everyone; so much so that the banns of union were read, and when no one demurred the British North American provinces were declared affianced and so it was proclaimed.[19]

This luncheon on the *Queen Victoria* in Charlottetown harbour was, in a significant sense, the beginning of Confederation. There were no resolutions and no signatures, only toasts and talk, but perhaps for the first time, some of the twenty-three delegates at Charlottetown began to drink the deeper draught of nationalism. Was Confederation within reach? It actually began to seem possible. Some began to think so, to believe so, and with thought and belief came a radiant confidence that filled speeches with conviction and purpose. Perhaps the greatest single achievement of the Conference was the messianic fervour that the converts to Confederation were endowed with, and the luncheon aboard the *Queen Victoria* visibly marked a stage in that conversion.

On Monday Brown addressed the Conference on the constitutional aspects of Confederation, particularly the manner in which the local and general governments might be established. About this question there was much speculation in the newspapers. On September 5 Whelan gave in the *Examiner* a list of federal powers that included control of public lands and power to enforce uniformity of education. A much more accurate list appeared in the Halifax *Morning Chronicle* of September 10, in a letter from Charlottetown, signed "Index." Index's list was substantially that which finally appeared in the Quebec Resolutions. Index's list of local powers was equally accurate and was essentially the same as that given by *Le Courrier du Canada* from official sources.[20] Some newspapers had access to reliable information.

Tuesday, September 6, the Conference discussed details, and that day the Canadians closed their case, leaving to the Maritime delegates the decision about what was to be done. It did not take long on Wednesday morning to decide that Maritime union was hopeless. The Canadians were told that the Maritime delegates were unanimous in believing Confederation to be highly desirable, if satisfactory terms could be agreed on, and that the question of Maritime union would be waived. At this point the Conference adjourned to Halifax.

The rest was holiday. That same afternoon, Wednesday, September 7, the Canadians were hosts to the Dundases and a large number of ladies.

[19]Fredericton *Head Quarters*, Sept. 14, 1864; Brown Papers, George Brown to Anne Brown, Sept. 13, 1864.
[20]Quebec *Courrier du Canada*, 26 sept. 1864. This list included also the suggestion of protection for minority rights by the central government.

Thursday was excursion day, with trips to the north side of the Island, presumably to the sand and the warm sea-bathing. That night, as the final touch, a grand ball was given at Province House. It began at ten in the evening, supper was at one o'clock, and after supper there were speeches that lasted for nearly three hours.[21] Something of the extravagance of the occasion struck John Ross, the editor of *Ross's Weekly*, who combined what seems to have been a Puritan morality with a remarkably flamboyant vocabulary. The ball in Charlottetown, by this description, was perilously akin to the worst excesses of the Roman empire:

A few days after the close of the circus, a great public "Ball and Supper" is announced; the evening of the day arrives; the proud and the gay, arrayed in fashion's gauds, flock to the scene where revelry presides. . . . Pleasure panoplied in lustful smiles meets and embraces exuberant Joy. . . . the fascinating dance goes merrily, and the libidi[n]ous waltz with its lascivious entwinements whiles in growing excitement; the swelling bosom and the voluptuous eye tell the story of intemperate revel. . . . In this scene, where intrigue schemes sin . . . our moralist mingles; here he rocks his piety to sleep, and cradles his morality in forgiveness; and the saint who could not tolerate satan in the circus, embraces the Prince of Darkness in the gilded scene of fashion's vices, and the reeking slough of debauchery.[22]

The comment of the sober Saint John *Telegraph* on September 19: "There are some desperate fellows in the Island Press. . . ." It added that Ross must have lost his way going to the ball and found himself in quite a different establishment!

It was nearly five o'clock in the morning, on Friday, September 9, when the Canadians, Nova Scotians, New Brunswickers, and Islanders, went down to the foggy harbour and crowded aboard the *Queen Victoria* for the journey to Nova Scotia. From Pictou to Halifax most of the delegates went by land; Macdonald, Langevin, and McGee voyaged leisurely through the Gut of Canso in the *Queen Victoria*, and she was in Halifax harbour blowing off steam when the other delegates arrived by train.[23] That day, Saturday, September 10, the Conference met again, in the Legislature in Halifax, and again on Monday, when

[21]See Creighton, *Macdonald: Young Politician*, 366–7.
[22]*Ross's Weekly*, Sept. 15, 1864. The reason for the animus of John Ross was the criticism of the circus by the Charlottetown *Protestant* (Sept. 10, 1864) for the way the circus had been fleecing the public. Ross not only supported the cause of the circus but especially disliked the patronizing and contemptuous tone of the Conservative paper. The *Protestant* in its turn was outraged that "a social gathering of some of the most virtuous and respectable persons in the community [should be] . . . characterized as a 'slough of debauchery' . . . ." (Sept. 24, 1864).
[23]Charlottetown *Islander*, Sept. 23, 1864.

it was adjourned, *pro forma*, to Saint John.[24] By this time the decision had been reached to hold a further Conference at Quebec on October 10.

Monday, September 12 it rained heavily in Halifax. At long last the dry summer seemed to be over, and that evening, while the rain fell in torrents and thunder rumbled overhead, a "sumptuous" dinner took place at the Halifax Hotel—the one decent hotel that Halifax could boast of.[25] The speeches were remarkable, said the once-sceptical *Morning Chronicle* on September 13, "for good sense, sound reasoning, and fervid eloquence." The *Acadian Recorder*, September 14, called this plain long-windedness and censured Brown for taking an hour and a quarter.[26] Brown shared the floor with nine others; yet he gave a long, rather arid speech freighted heavily with statistics.[27] Still, J. H. Gray remembered it, eight years later, as a speech of great power.[28]

And it was a great occasion. It was the first public dinner where the delegates gave something of the spirit of their deliberations. Most of them felt this sense of occasion.[29] Macdonald rose to it handsomely. "Everyone admits," Macdonald said, "that Union must take place sometime. I say now is the time." "For twenty long years I have been dragging myself through the dreary waste of Colonial politics. I thought that there was no end, nothing worthy of ambition, but now I see something which is well worthy of all I have suffered. . . ."[30] The Halifax *Evening Express* caught the same idea, "three or four millions of us, under one paternal government. . . . Was there anything more grand and noble."[31] But the *Citizen*, sarcastic and trenchant, fired a parting shot as the delegates left for Saint John. There was nothing wrong with union except the method proposed to effect it.

[Nova Scotians] have learned to distrust that combination of union and disunion—that expensive double machinery of government, that attempts to

---

[24]The Charlottetown Conference was officially adjourned, *sine die*, in Toronto, Nov. 3, 1864. C.O. 217, MacDonnell to Cardwell, Feb. 5, 1865.

[25]Halifax papers complained of the lack and they were joined by the Saint John *Morning News*, Sept. 16, 1864: "There is really not one conveniently arranged and commodious Hotel in the place. The 'Halifax Hotel' is large and well kept . . . but . . . badly arranged."

[26]Brown wrote to his wife six months earlier, "They used to charge me with being long-winded, but Cartier outdoes all the world, past present and to come." A. Mackenzie, *Life and Speeches of George Brown* (Toronto, 1882), 220.

[27]E. Whelan, *Union of the British Provinces* (Charlottetown, 1865), 27–37.

[28]Gray, *Confederation*, 33.

[29]Noted by Sir Richard MacDonnell. C.O. 217, MacDonnell to Cardwell, Sept. 15, 1864.

[30]Whelan, *Union of the British Provinces*, 46, 42.

[31]Halifax *Evening Express*, Sept. 26, 1864.

neutralize sectional feelings and interests through a general government while perpetuating these feelings by means of local legislatures. . . .[32]

There were many more shots to come from this armoury.

The Charlottetown Conference arrived in Saint John on September 14, and already opposition newspapers were eyeing its proceedings a little suspiciously. The Fredericton *Head Quarters* of that day wrote,

Rumour or report has it that the New Brunswick delegates . . . were much struck, and they say converted by the arguments of the Canadian ministers. From all accounts it looks as if these gentlemen had it all their own way . . . and that, what with their arguments and what with their blandishments, (they gave a champagne lunch on board the *Victoria*, where Mr. McGee's wit sparkled brightly as the wine), they carried the Lower Province delegates a little off their feet.[33]

It was perhaps fitting that at the banquet given that night in Stubbs' Hotel in Saint John the toast of the evening was given by the New Brunswickers to their fellow delegates, and was quaffed to the raucous singing of "For they are jolly good fellows."[34] Cartier wound up the evening's proceedings, standing up and singing, in his unlovely voice, "God Save the Queen" in English and in French. The enthusiastic reporter for the Saint John *Morning News* described it as one of the happiest occasions he had ever attended.[35]

The next morning they all set off for Fredericton by steamer,[36] up the broad river between rain-swept fields with misted hills beyond.[37] In Fredericton Cartier, Brown, and Galt stayed with the Governor, Arthur Gordon, who seemed to have kept the Canadians up half the night asking them questions and doubtless offering much gratuitous advice. This curious young man—the son of Lord Aberdeen—had a good opinion of his political *savoir-faire*, and he made large demands on the patience of everyone. His despatches and private letters were, however, full of information, and it is from these that the work of the Charlottetown Conference begins to appear in perspective.

It was of course a preliminary to Quebec. Nothing seems to have been set down systematically; there were no resolutions embodying the thought of the Conference. But this does not alter the fact that the Charlottetown Conference had discussed, if not decided, many of the

[32]*Halifax Citizen*, Sept. 13, 1864.
[33]Also quoted by the *Morning Telegraph*, Sept. 16, 1864.
[34]Saint John *Daily Evening Globe*, Sept. 15, 1864.
[35]Saint John *Morning News*, Sept. 16, 1864.
[36]Saint John *Morning Telegraph*, Sept. 16, 1864 reported that McGee and Cartier had left at once for Portland; but Cartier went to Fredericton.
[37]The return trip down river was made in happier weather. (*Morning News*, Sept. 19, 1864)

points. The Legislative Council had been the subject of lengthy discussion,[38] but its method of selection and the basis of its composition had been, for the time being, decided.[39] It was Newfoundland's appearance on the scene at Quebec that upset the *modus vivendi* already agreed upon, and McDougall and Mowat proved to be intractable about giving up the elective principle.[40] The appointment of judges had also been discussed at length. Gordon described discussion on this point as "very animated"; two of the New Brunswickers, E. B. Chandler and Leonard Tilley, had argued forcibly for federal appointment of all judges.[41] Index's view had been that the judges would be appointed by the federal government.[42] As to the division of powers, Gordon remarked that the French Canadians were ready for as much local power as the circumstances would permit. Other delegates, however, wanted to reduce the local legislatures "to the smallest possible dimensions."[43] Gordon said nothing about the financial settlement, but the Montreal *Gazette* and *Le Courrier du Canada* did in their issues of September 26, and so did George Coles of Prince Edward Island, who stated specifically that the Charlottetown Conference agreed that £200,000 sterling—or possibly the annual interest thereof—would be given to the Island to buy out the land proprietors. This was the "talk of the town" when it was published in Charlottetown.[44] It was never denied by his colleagues, though the proposition

[38]*Le Courrier du Canada*, 30 sept. 1864, and Gordon agreed on this point. C.O. 188, Gordon to Cardwell, Sept. 22, 1864 (confidential).

[39]C.O. 188, Gordon to Cardwell, Sept. 22, 1864 (confidential): "With regard to the [Legislative Council] . . . less difference of opinion was found to exist than I should have anticipated—It was agreed that the Federal Legislative Council should consist of 60 members, 20 from Upper Canada, 20 from Lower Canada, and 20 from the Maritime Provinces."

[40]McDougall writes, "I moved and Mr. Mowat seconded a motion for the elective principle. About 1/3rd of the delegates voted for the proposition—Brown arguing and voting against it." McDougall's copy of the *Confederation Debates*, 35, in the University of Toronto Library.

[41]The reasons Chandler gave were interesting: "Those who wished to enter public life at all would naturally look to the Federal Legislature as the scene of their labours, and if the local Governments were allowed to appoint Judges to be selected from their own supporters in the local assemblies the Bench would be speedily filled with obscure and incompetent men. He therefore strongly urged that the appointment of all the Judges should be vested in the Central Government and he was warmly supported by Mr. Tilley. . . . On the other hand considerable reluctance was exhibited by several of the legal members of the Conference to forego prizes now apparently within their grasp." C.O. 188, Gordon to Cardwell, Sept. 22, 1864 (confidential).

[42]Halifax *Morning Chronicle*, Sept. 10, 1864.

[43]C.O. 188, Gordon to Cardwell, Sept. 22, 1864 (confidential).

[44]Charlottetown *Examiner*, Sept. 19, 1864.

was omitted from the Quebec Resolutions much to Coles' astonishment and disgust.[45]

There were also some significant omissions from the Charlottetown "constitution," notably the power of disallowance, and the manner of appointing the lieutenant governors.[46] A combination of circumstances was probably responsible for these significant additions at Quebec. Pressure from the Governor General and from lieutenant governors like Gordon may have had some effect; more likely it was the apparent acceptance of the Charlottetown proposals with only little demur that persuaded the centralists at Quebec to press further. Not the least important factor in the final analysis was the mood of the Quebec Conference itself. With the American government growing visibly more threatening as the autumn drew on, a strong central government seemed a necessary buttress against the truculence below the border.

Of course what was missing from the Charlottetown "constitution" was something much more obvious: Maritime union. Enough has been said already to show how weak the movement was. It reached the Conference by a power not its own, and there it simply fell to pieces. It had never caught the popular imagination. Maritime union was an historical conception; it looked to a condition before 1784, before 1769, and it was one that only Nova Scotians could thoroughly appreciate. And even the Nova Scotians were neither persuaded nor persuasive on the subject. Maritime union seemed to look backwards, and in the new world of young and growing provinces, a century past was an age beyond recapture. P. S. Hamilton put it very well: "To the British American, as such, the past is a blank."[47]

By contrast, British American union, whatever may be said of the Canadian manipulation of it, gave to Canadians and Maritimers alike some hope of national glory. This hope may have been illusory; it may have been chauvinism, another variation of the active North American appetite for space; it was unrealistic, perhaps, given the limited colonial resources of men, money, and talent. But then all dreams are apt to be unrealistic, transcontinental ones not less than others.

[45]Charlottetown *Islander*, March 17, 1865, reporting Assembly debates for March 2. Other sources: Kingston *Daily British American*, Sept. 17, 1864, report of Sept. 8, from Charlottetown; Charlottetown *Protestant*, Sept. 10, Oct. 1, 1864; Charlottetown *Vindicator*, Sept. 21, 1864.

[46]Gordon maintained that the federal appointment of lieutenant governors was absolutely essential.

[47]P. S. Hamilton, *Observations upon a Union of the Colonies* (Halifax, 1855), 9.

At the same time, the Canadian success had been deceptively easy. The Canadian expedition to Charlottetown had been all and more than they could have dared hope. The Canadians had swept the board. Their speeches in Halifax, Saint John, and later in Canada, rang with confidence. Their proposals had been accepted with unbelievable alacrity. Public opinion, though uncertain, cautious, even sometimes hostile in the Island, was, in the mainland cities of Halifax and Saint John, lively and encouraging. Indeed, the Canadians acquired quite a misleading impression of Maritime opinion. Viewed from Charlottetown, Halifax, and Saint John, the Maritimes seemed far readier for Confederation than they actually were.[48] The Canadians also forgot that they appeared volcanically, as it were, thrust upon the British North American scene by the upheavals of Canadian politics. And after all, as the Saint John *Morning Telegraph* had said—on September 16, 1864, the Canadians *"invited themselves* to the Conference!" Canadians were not helped greatly either by the lack of realism among the Maritime delegates who were also caught up in nation-building. The Canadians had had a long, hard schooling in political realities, but the Maritime leaders were more sanguine.[49] And although some of the delegates felt they were on uncertain ground,[50] many were caught and won by the sheer virtuosity of the whole conception. To build a nation! The Halifax *Witness* remarked upon the change on September 24:

. . . since the recent visit of the Canadians who were entertained in St. John and Halifax, and especially since the meetings of the Intercolonial Convention in Charlottetown, Halifax and St. John, a very manifest change has been creeping over the spirit of our leading politicians, and we believe, of the people generally. There is less aversion to Canada. Indeed, there seems to be a positive desire for union. . . . The distinguished men whom Canada has sent . . . have succeeded in removing some prejudices, and

[48]William Annand a few months later offered a caution on the same subject. "The city of Halifax is not the Province of Nova Scotia. . . ." Nova Scotia, Assembly, *Debates and Proceedings*, 1865, 232.

[49]Francis Shanly, in Nova Scotia and New Brunswick on a Grand Trunk survey in December, 1864, remarked on the sanguineness evident in the leaders. Shanly Papers, Shanly to Brydges, Dec. 21, 1864.

[50]One New Brunswick delegate remarked that some of his colleagues felt that they were "upon delicate, if not uncertain ground; that individually they were in some doubt as to how far their views and opinions would meet the approbation of people in their respective Provinces." Halifax *Morning Chronicle*, Sept. 15, 1864. The Saint John *Morning Telegraph*, the next day, Sept. 16: "We cannot but express our indignation at the pusillanimous conduct of the Lower Province delegates. They were sent to Charlottetown . . . to discuss the question of a Union of their own Provinces. Under the blandishments of Canadian politicians, (who *invited themselves* to the Conference!) they placed the Union of the Lower Provinces entirely in the background. . . ."

greatly modifying some real obstacles to union. As things look at present we must have a Colonial Union of some kind with the least possible delay.

The Charlottetown Conference was preliminary to Quebec, but Quebec was also the natural conclusion to Charlottetown. The Quebec Resolutions refined and systematized conclusions already suggested, points already agreed upon. What is surprising is not how much was concluded at Quebec, but how much had been arranged at Charlottetown. J. H. Gray's remark at the Quebec Conference, in the discussion of the House of Commons, is suggestive: "I fancied we were fully agreed on these points at Charlottetown, and that our discussion was to be about details."[51] The records of the Quebec Conference are replete with references of this kind. Of course the Charlottetown Conference did not complete its work in six days, any more than the Quebec Conference did its work in sixteen. Much of the work had been done beforehand. The Canadians presented the delegates at Charlottetown if not with a *fait accompli*, at least with a matured plan of action. The Conference enthusiastically accepted it. What is more important, the Charlottetown Conference established Confederation as a political reality. It gave Confederation the initial *élan*, the sense of common destiny, that for a time seemed to sweep all before it. It even submerged the instinctive independence of some Islanders. J. H. Gray was one. It also established the relationships, personal as well as political, which made acceptance of the Canadian proposals possible and which was going to help to sustain them in the future. McGee once said in Halifax that all that was needed to carve out a glorious future for British North America was "union, authority, and moral courage."[52] The Canadians had a good deal of all three at their disposal. They went ashore at Charlottetown feeling like conquerors. The Maritimers would have resented this. They had resented Canadians and Canadian methods before and they would do so again, but, for the moment at least, the glitter of a future that would end their insignificance, the audacious realism of the means, and the surging vitality of the men who proposed both ends and means, swept obstacles aside. Charlottetown was more than just a Canadian triumph: it was the first appearance of an authentic national spirit.[53]

[51]J. Pope, ed., *Confederation: Being a Series of Hitherto Unpublished Documents Bearing on the British North America Act* (Toronto, 1895), 70.
[52]Halifax *Morning Chronicle*, July 23, 1863, reporting McGee's speech of July 21.
[53]"The Conference at Charlottetown will be looked upon by many as being, as the phrase is, historical; the beginning of a great change in the fortunes of the British North American Provinces." Fredericton *Head Quarters*, Sept. 14, 1864.

7. QUEBEC, 1864

QUEBEC, THE CAPITAL of Canada in 1864, was at once imposing and tawdry. The old walls stood; the city retained, from a distance at least, the rock-like grandeur it had possessed from its very inception two and a half centuries before. To a correspondent of the Saint John *Morning News*, returning early one September evening from Montmorency Falls, it looked ravishing. "The sun was throwing its last declining rays upon the glittering domes and lofty battlements of the grand city, bathing it in a flood of light. The shadow of the Citadel was thrown far out upon the tranquil waters of the St. Lawrence."[1] Unfortunately some of the city, upon closer inspection, was less grand. The roads of Quebec beggared description. Anthony Trollope had had some choice words to describe them when he was there in 1861.[2] They were no better in 1864. For aches and pains a rueful correspondent from the Halifax *Morning Chronicle* recommended taking a *calèche*, "drawn by a lively French pony, driven by a chattering French Canadian, and traverse these wood-paved streets for an hour. Bump—thump —jump you go from one stick to another—out of one deep hole into another, till you are well nigh shaken to pieces." There seemed to be hardly a yard of stone pavement in the city. Sidewalks were wooden, and the ones in Quebec were positively dangerous. In short, "wood in some form or other answers for all things."[3] In the Upper Town were the Parliament buildings, a temporary, plain and "paltry" structure of brick, three stories high.[4] The shadow of Ottawa and the Queen's decision had been on the building from the beginning, wrote the Montreal *Gazette*, dwarfing and diminishing all its proportions. But if the Parliament buildings had nothing to recommend them "either to the eye or to the understanding" the site they stood on was magnificent. They stood

[1]Saint John *Morning News*, Sept. 30, 1864, "Impressions of Canada," Sept. 8, 1864, from Quebec.
[2]Anthony Trollope, *North America* (New York, 1862), 50.
[3]Halifax *Morning Chronicle*, Sept. 24, 1864, report of Sept. 12 from Quebec.
[4]*Ibid.*; cf. also Montreal *Gazette*, Oct. 28, 1864.

on the grounds of the old Chateau St. Louis, between Laval University and the steep hill that plunged down to the Lower Town. Below them, "Mountain-hill street dips down to the broad river, as steep as a stair or a timber-slide"; above, the Citadel towered, its grand battery buttressing the very walls.[5] The Parliament buildings commanded the splendid view down the St. Lawrence, toward Montmorency and Ile d'Orléans. It was here, in the spacious reading room of the Legislative Council, on the second floor, that the Quebec Conference met, on Monday, October 10, 1864.

The Quebec Conference was the focus of many lines of British North American history. Political union, defence, railways, the Northwest, relations with Great Britain and the United States, all converged upon Quebec. Most of the familiar issues of British North American history came together around the crimson, book-littered table in that large room. And with the windows streaked with rain, the grey distant view of the Lower Town and the St. Lawrence beyond, surely the problems that faced the Conference seemed the more urgent. It was a stern world, and the future seemed to grow visibly more stormy and uncertain. The asperity of differences may have been softened by the thought that failure to solve them meant a return to the bleak world that each province would have to face alone. Alexander Campbell's sombre analysis was not without truth:

We cannot remain as we were. . . . he [the hon. member] overlooked the changed character of the times, the dangers with which we were menaced, and the feeling growing up in Great Britain that it would be better to leave us to our own resources. The hon. member wanted no change whatever, when in fact everything was changing around us. . . .[6]

Robert Harris' sketches of the Quebec Conference are in the Charlottetown Library, and although Harris did his sketches years afterward, one is made to feel the earnestness of the men assembled at Quebec. Was it the prevailing tone in all Victorian portraiture? William Notman's careful photographs never seemed to betray a smile, though one reason for solemnity was the fact that the exposure took a minute and a half.[7] And the high Victorian fashion is misleading. The long, narrow trousers, the high boots, the funereal aplomb of mutton-chop

[5]The Montreal *Gazette*, Oct. 28, 1864, gives an excellent description of the Quebec Conference, its personalities and setting, which had to be reprinted, Oct. 31, 1864.

[6]His speech in the Debate on the Reply, *Quebec Daily News*, Jan. 25, 1865, reporting Legislative Council debates for Jan. 23.

[7]W. Notman and F. Taylor, *Portraits of British Americans* (3 vols., Montreal, 1865-8).

whiskers, all conspire against the observer; they belie humour and humanity. Still there was no doubt that the delegates were in earnest. The Quebec Conference was an occasion that could be fittingly portrayed in attitudes of resolute dignity and august composure. In this sense Harris' sober and austere sketches were true.

A powerful nationalism pervaded the Conference. The ambitions called into existence by the Charlottetown Conference were now aroused; provincial horizons began to melt away, and there appeared the breathtaking possibility that a transcontinental nation might be created by the colonists themselves, upon their own initiative, by their own energy, and with their own resources. S. E. Dawson wrote just at this time, "Never was there such an opportunity as now for the birth of a nation."[8] This kind of nationalism gave to the Conference a remarkable spirit. That there were differences at Quebec goes without saying, but a powerful majority believed in union, and with that belief differences could probably be overcome.

At the same time the Canadians and Maritimers had different purposes, and it is useful to distinguish them. The Canadians were conscious of the necessity that lurked behind them like a shadow. Action was essential: they could not turn back. Among those who were most conscious of this was George Brown. In a broad sense Brown was a British American nationalist, but he was first and foremost a powerful advocate of justice for Canada West. He was out to extinguish the interference of the French Canadians (as he regarded it) for ever: ". . . we can't wait," Brown told Gordon in Fredericton, "we are *not going to be tied to Lower Canada* for twelve months more."[9] Reformers generally were in a hurry.[10] Macdonald, clear-headed and unabashed, had made a virtue of necessity and put his shoulder resolutely to the wheel. Cartier, who loved office and power, had taken a quick, shrewd look at Confederation and gambled. Of all the Canadians, Galt, romantic, unstable, and over-sensitive as he was, seemed to offer, with McGee, the most genuine dedication to the national principle.

On the other hand, the Maritimers had not so much to gain by

[8]A Colonist [S. E. Dawson], A Northern Kingdom (Montreal, 1864), 13. The words quoted were published by the leading English ministerial journal in Quebec while the Conference was sitting (Quebec *Morning Chronicle*, Oct. 17, 1864).

[9]Gordon's recollection, a postscript in a personal letter to Cardwell, Dec. 19, 1864, in P.R.O., 30/48–6/39, Cardwell Papers. (Gordon's italics)

[10]Note the following from the *Sarnia Observer*, three years later: "Had it been known, in June, 1864, that it would take three years to make Confederation the law of the land, the Reform party could not possibly have been brought to accept it." (June 28, 1867)

Confederation and they took great political risks to achieve it. Tupper, Tilley, Gray, McCully, Pope, and Whelan, all put their political careers at stake. Most of them suffered for their opinions. They were neither more nor less altruistic than the Canadians, but their purposes were different. They saw in Confederation broader fields of enterprise, more spacious meadows of reward, an end to the littleness of provincial pastures. Whelan was characteristic—a loyal Islander before the Quebec Conference, and afterward speaking of dull old Charlottetown, or of the Island as a "patch of sandbank in the Gulf."[11] Feeling more acutely the limits of their provincial identities, the Maritime delegates were caught up more readily than the Canadians by the appeal of a broader nationalism. The customs examination at the provincial frontiers made a visit by a Nova Scotian to New Brunswick, or to Canada, seem like a visit to a foreign country. "Each little Province," wrote Tupper in the *Colonist*, "is a little nation by itself. . . ."[12] But, as the Halifax *Morning Chronicle* had said on September 22:

Let these Provinces . . . be organized into one vast Confederation . . . and we should soon possess all the prestige and command all the respect to which our numbers and our position would entitle us. . . . Our ships would be British American, our character, our position and our influence, would be known the world over. . . .

Nothing was accomplished at the Conference, McGee said later, without full deliberation and hard work.[13] By the time a week had passed the Conference was sitting from ten in the morning until two in the afternoon, meeting again at half-past seven and sitting late into the night.[14] Delegates seem to have consistently underestimated how long it would take.[15] The unanimity at Charlottetown had been deceptive, and the formal registration at Quebec of the more informal conversations at Charlottetown was necessarily difficult.

Trouble was first encountered over the Senate. On Thursday, October 13, John A. Macdonald moved, seconded by Oliver Mowat, that the three sections of British North America, Canada West, Canada East, and the four Maritime provinces, should be represented equally in the upper house with twenty-four members each. The riposte from

[11]Charlottetown *Examiner*, April 10, 1865; Dec. 26, 1864.
[12]Halifax *British Colonist*, Nov. 17, 1864. Brown made the same point in Canada, *Confederation Debates* (Quebec, 1865), 99.
[13]Toronto *Globe*, Dec. 29, 1864, reporting McGee's speech at Cookshire, C.E., Dec. 22.
[14]Halifax *Morning Chronicle* Oct. 25, 1864, report of Oct. 18 from Quebec.
[15]Brown estimated a week, at least. W. H. Pope, on Oct. 15, thought it would take until Oct. 20 (Charlottetown *Islander*, Oct. 17, 1864).

the Maritimes came at once, moved by Leonard Tilley of New Brunswick and seconded by R. B. Dickey of Nova Scotia: Canada West and Canada East should each have twenty-four members and the four Maritime provinces thirty-two.[16] Over this seemingly minor problem was a major battle joined. The Senate was vital; it was considered the *fons et origo* of the whole federal principle.[17] And even those who, like Tupper, were unsympathetic to the principle were ready to press claims for seats in the upper house. The entry of Newfoundland into the proceedings had disrupted the neat Charlottetown arrangement,[18] and the process of accommodating Newfoundland in a way satisfactory to the two sections of Canada and the Maritime provinces was arduous, and rapidly became critical. All groups were sensitive to any change from Charlottetown. Canada East, for example, seemed to suspect a disposition on the part of Canada West to tinker with the basic equality of the two sections in the Senate.[19] All day Friday, October 14, the question was debated "with considerable warmth."[20] At 4 P.M. that day Whelan wrote pessimistically, "with so much diversity of opinion, it is very difficult to say whether the Convention will not be compelled to break up prematurely. Matters do not certainly look very promising. . . . I do hope there may be concession and reconciliation, but I have very grave doubts respecting a satisfactory result."[21]

By this time everyone was feeling tired and a little dismayed. Progress was so slow, and the weather was so wretched. "The weather here has been fiendish since the Conference opened. It has rained every day more or less, and rains as I write." Thus the correspondent of the Halifax *Morning Chronicle*.[22] He seemed unperturbed, but the *Globe*'s correspondent wrote on Friday, October 14, that "everyone here has had a fit of the blues."[23] The ball given that night by the Canadian govern-

---

[16]J. Pope, ed., *Confederation: Being a Series of Hitherto Unpublished Documents Bearing on the British North America Act* (Toronto, 1895), 11; [A. A. Macdonald], "Notes on the Quebec Conference, 1864" (ed. A. G. Doughty) *Canadian Historical Review*, I, 1 (March, 1920), 34.

[17]*Infra*, 110–11.

[18]Charlottetown *Examiner*, Oct. 24, 1864, report of Oct. 15. All of Whelan's reports to the *Examiner* during the Quebec Conference will be cited from the printed version: P. B. Waite, "Edward Whelan reports from the Quebec Conference," *Canadian Historical Review*, XLII, 1 (March, 1961), 23–45. Cited as "Whelan reports," and in the above instance, "Whelan reports," 36.

[19][A. A. Macdonald] "Notes on Quebec Conference," 34; "Whelan reports," 43–4.

[20]"Whelan reports," 34.

[21]*Ibid.*, 35.

[22]*Morning Chronicle*, Oct. 25, 1864, report of Oct. 18 from Quebec.

[23]Toronto *Globe*, Oct. 15, 1864, report of Oct. 14.

ment came as a welcome relief. Among the eight hundred guests, dancing quadrilles, polkas, and waltzes, the Canadian ministers then, as later, performed prodigies of terpsichorean endeavour. "The Cabinet Ministers—the leading ones especially—are the most inveterate dancers I have ever seen," wrote the ubiquitous Edward Whelan of a later ball, "they do not seem to miss a dance during the live-long night. They are cunning fellows; and there's no doubt that it is all done for a political purpose; they know if they can dance themselves into the affections of the wives and daughters of the country, the men will certainly become an easy conquest."[24]

The ladies were no inconsiderable group at Quebec. There were of course the local belles. Whelan, who began by preferring the beauties of the Maritimes, rapidly succumbed to the charm of the *Québecoises*. The Maritime delegates seem to have taken the Quebec Conference as a heaven-sent opportunity to launch their daughters into British American society. George Sala, the famous correspondent of the London *Telegraph*, who was at Quebec, described them at New York afterward, a group of "Nova Scotians, Newfoundlanders, New Brunswickers and Prince Edward Islanders, stalwart Saxon-looking yeomen, with comely wives and pretty daughters. . . ."[25] Tupper brought his wife and daughter; so did A. G. Archibald, and George Coles. R. J. Dickey of Nova Scotia, Charles Fisher, W. H. Steeves, and J. H. Gray of New Brunswick brought their daughters. The Bachelors' Ball, given a week later by the "bachelors of Quebec" was therefore entirely appropriate.

Saturday night, October 15, the Quebec Board of Trade gave a dinner in the best Quebec style at Russell's Hotel in Palace Street. One hundred and fifty guests sat down to a lavish feast and a lengthy roster of toasts and speeches. The Maritime delegates were the principal speakers, but it appeared that Sir Etienne Taché carried off the honours. In Whelan's view at least he spoke with more good humour and "more common sense" than anyone else.[26] The decorations of the "concert hall" in Russell's on this occasion give the setting of many similar occasions afterward. Flags—mostly Union Jacks—were suspended from the balcony, and the walls were covered with alternating strips of bunting and evergreen boughs. Below these, around the walls, were hung the names of the five provinces, Nova Scotia and Prince

[24]"Whelan reports," 41.
[25]London (England) *Daily Telegraph*, Nov. 23, 1864, report of Nov. 7 from New York.
[26]"Whelan reports," 37. The speeches are given in E. Whelan, *Union of the British Provinces* (Charlottetown, 1865), 62–79.

Edward Island on one side, Canada, Newfoundland, and New Brunswick on the other, each painted in large letters and wreathed elaborately in evergreen. On the two end walls were blazoned "Ships, Colonies and Commerce" and "Union is strength," while over the gallery was suspended an imposing "Intercolonial Railroad."[27]

Well might the Intercolonial Railroad be imposing. Gentlemen representing a variety of interests were lobbying at Quebec for contracts. C. J. Brydges was solicitous but remained for the moment in the background; but R. J. Reekie, of Brassey, Betts, Peto and Jackson, was in full cry.[28] The International Contract Company was represented by Mr. Levesy, who had been an assiduous advocate at both conferences. This was probably the "grey-headed cockney fop" that Whelan spoke of, who had been "dogging the steps of the Delegation through the Provinces," and who, "without influence or position," had the nerve to escort Mrs. Tupper into the Government Ball.[29]

Newspapers sent a considerable company of correspondents. At the Board of Trade dinner they had even been distinguished by a special table, and the toast in their honour was replied to by George Sala, of the London *Telegraph*. The London *Times*, London *Morning Herald*, and the *New York Herald* had correspondents at Quebec, to say nothing of those from British American papers. Despite this massive coverage, many of the newspapers are not very detailed or explicit. There is nothing comparable to the reports of Hewitt Bernard or A. A. Macdonald[30] except in Whelan's *Examiner*. The Conference met behind closed doors, which, however indispensable, gave it the air of a conspiracy. "Shut the door after ye, that's the fashin here," ran the satire in *Barney Rooney's Letters*.[31] The correspondents petitioned for admission, or for at least a daily official report, but neither was forthcoming.[32] The crumbs available were not very filling, though the Montreal *Gazette* and the Toronto *Leader* managed well enough. The *Globe* reported gossip by telegraph, but Brown, like most of the delegates was scrupulous about giving anything away. *La Minerve* was quiescent, as was

---

[27]*Quebec Daily Mercury*, Oct. 18, 1864.

[28]The Reekie-Tupper railway correspondence is published in Nova Scotia, Assembly, *Journals*, 1865, Appendix 7.

[29]"Whelan reports," 36. The Halifax *Morning Chronicle*, Nov. 17, 1864, spoke of Levesy's "tracking the delegates." A similar report appeared in the *Islander*, Nov. 11, 1864.

[30]Bernard's report is in Pope, ed., *Confederation Documents*.

[31][William Garvie], *Barney Rooney's Letters on Confederation, Botheration and Political Transmogrification* (Halifax, 1865), 12. First published in the *Halifax Citizen*, Nov.-Dec., 1864.

[32]Pope, ed., *Confederation Documents*, 7–8, 10–11.

Le Courrier du Canada. Tupper's *British Colonist* seemed to languish in his absence. The *Newfoundlander's* connection with Ambrose Shea availed it little. W. H. Pope's *Islander* used mainly the reports of other newspapers. But Jonathan McCully sent telegraphic reports to the Halifax *Morning Chronicle* of which he was the editor, and Edward Whelan sent a complete series of reports to the *Examiner* in Charlotte-town. The *Examiner* from October 17 to November 7 provided a running digest of Conference affairs. Whelan was even accused by Edward Palmer of spending his time at the Conference board writing things for the *Examiner*.[33]

This accusation came during the post-Conference *imbroglio* in the Island.[34] In the rough and tumble many things were said which help fill in the details in the Conference portrait.[35] The three main difficulties that the Conference encountered all involved the Island to a considerable degree, and the Island's exacerbation, highly inconvenient for the Conference, is very useful for historians. The three problems were the Senate, the House of Commons, and the financial settlement.

Of the first, the Senate, the points at issue hardly need further emphasis. The battle over the apportionment of representatives went on despite the great ball given by the Canadian government, and it was not until Monday, October 17, a week after the Conference opened, that Macdonald broke the deadlock by accepting a motion of Tupper's of the previous Friday that simply adhered to the original Charlottetown arrangement, and offered Newfoundland four Senators in her own right.[36] But other issues connected with the Senate dragged on alarmingly: qualifications of members, and, notoriously, the method of their selection, whether by existing provincial executives or by the central government, and how the choice was to be made.[37] It was not until

[33]Charlottetown *Examiner*, Dec. 12, 1864, letter from Palmer of Dec. 5: "You were, in fact, nearly the whole time occupied in writing something, which I suspect more immediately concerned yourself, or your Paper."

[34]*Infra*, 179–80.

[35]D. G. Creighton has given a fine account of the Conference, with Macdonald as the central figure (*John A. Macdonald: The Young Politician* (Toronto, 1952), 372–81); W. M. Whitelaw gives a useful study under the title of "The Maritime Interests at Quebec," in *The Maritimes and Canada before Confederation* (Toronto, 1934), 238–59, and also provides an excellent paper on the general setting of the Conference in "Reconstructing the Quebec Conference," *Canadian Historical Review*, XIX, 2 (June, 1938), 123–36, much of which is based on the account in the Montreal *Gazette*, Oct. 28, 1864.

[36]Pope, ed., *Confederation Documents*, 13–14; [A. A. Macdonald], "Notes on the Quebec Conference," 35–6; "Whelan reports," 37–8.

[37]Pope, ed., *Confederation Documents*, 61–6; [A. A. Macdonald], "Notes on the Quebec Conference," 37–8; "Whelan reports," 38.

Wednesday afternoon, October 19, that the Senate was finally disposed of, and it was to reappear in ingenious and diabolical forms in subsequent despatches and at London in 1866.

From this point on, however, things began to go rather better. As Edward Palmer put it, "The current seemed to set with the Canadians." His general summation is of interest.

> For the first few days the leading delegates of the Lower Provinces exhibited caution and vigilance upon every question affecting the interests of these Provinces. . . . As the business proceeded, and the details of the federal union were from day to day laid down, parties evinced a visible elasticity of judgement, and were observed gradually to harmonize with those whose opinions they had previously met in a style more polemical in character. The current seemed to set with the Canadians. The maritime delegates one after the other, were observed to drop into the stream; and, with few exceptions, the members appeared to float along with it, scarcely producing a ripple on its now gentle surface.[38]

But before smooth water was reached a further difficulty had to be settled. This was the question of the representation in the House of Commons. Edward Palmer said at the Conference that as far as he was concerned the Island's support of union depended entirely upon how many representatives she was given in the lower house.[39] Ambrose Shea of Newfoundland interjected and said that it had been agreed at Charlottetown that Prince Edward Island should have only the five members her population entitled her to. Palmer turned on Shea and said it had *not* been so decided at Charlottetown. Besides, what did he, Shea, know about it anyway? He had not even been at Charlottetown. To Palmer's chagrin both J. H. Gray and W. H. Pope rose to support Shea's interpretation.[40] At this point—it happened on Wednesday night, October 19—the Island delegation apparently retired to iron out its differences, as well it might. They agreed to ask for six representatives to the House of Commons, but the Conference, the next day, would not accept the suggestion. J. H. Gray and Edward Whelan did not seem to have much heart for pressing the point. J. H. Gray

[38]Charlottetown *Monitor*, Dec. 1, 1864, letter from Palmer of Nov. 30. Also *Islander*, Dec. 9, 1864.

[39]*Monitor*, Dec. 22, 1864, letter from Palmer of Dec. 19: "I well recollect turning to Dr. Tupper . . . and repeated my opinion . . . that as regarded Prince Edward Island, the question of Union, I thought, would almost entirely depend on *what number of representatives* would be allowed [her]. . . ." (Original italics) Also *Islander*, Dec. 30, 1864.

[40]*Monitor*, Dec. 22, 1864, letter from Palmer of Dec. 19. Bernard records a speech by Shea not unlike Palmer's recollection of it, but not Palmer's reply. Gray's speech in this connection is given, but not W. H. Pope's. (Pope, ed., *Confederation Documents*, 69–70.)

said later that several members of the Conference had been surprised at Palmer's position and that George Brown remarked out loud that Palmer's objections were "perfectly absurd."[41] Whelan wrote to the *Examiner* the common sense of the matter: he could not see what difference five *or* six representatives would make in a house of 194 members.[42] Palmer, two days later, wrote to David Laird, the editor of the Charlottetown *Protestant*, "I am thoroughly disgusted at the course things have taken here and would be disposed to 'sit by the waters of Babylon and weep' for years, if I thought our Island people would be taken in by the scheme. . . ."

Nevertheless Palmer said that "the great principles . . . are pretty nearly decided upon, and secondary principles and details are now under discussion. These are as you may imagine, the most difficult to adjust: but still I think a scheme will be agreed to. . . ."[43] This was on Friday, October 21. By this time the powers of the central legislature had been put forward by Macdonald and were being debated *seriatim*, with much discussion on the question of the concurrent jurisdiction in agriculture. Criminal law called forth strong opinions, of which the most striking was Oliver Mowat's: "I quite concur in the advantages of one uniform system. It would weld us into a nation."[44] But oddly enough it was on Monday, October 24 that the most interesting discussion ensued, in connection with the powers of the local legislatures, and it brought out sharply the centralist philosophy that animated many of the Conference members. E. B. Chandler of New Brunswick struck at once at Mowat's resolutions on the local powers. "I object," said Chandler forthrightly, "to the proposed system. You are adopting a Legislative Union instead of a Federal." He maintained that local legislatures should not have their powers specified; if they do they will become "merely large municipal corporations." But Tupper replied: "I have heard Mr. Chandler's argument with surprise. Powers— undefined—must rest somewhere. Those who were at Charlottetown will remember that it was fully specified there that all the powers not given to Local should be reserved to the Federal Government. . . . It was a fundamental principle laid down by Canada and the basis of our deliberations." George Coles of Prince Edward Island and R. B. Dickey of Nova Scotia agreed with Chandler, but J. M. Johnson, Col. J. H. Gray of New Brunswick, and John A. Macdonald supported

[41]Charlottetown *Monitor*, Dec. 29, 1864, letter from J. H. Gray of Dec. 24. This is not in Bernard's reports.
[42]"Whelan reports," 39.
[43]*Monitor*, Dec. 15, 1864, quoting Palmer to Laird, Oct. 21, 1864.
[44]Pope, ed., *Confederation Documents*, 82.

Tupper. Jonathan McCully went so far as to cite the New Zealand Act of 1852 in support of his views, and though Macdonald could not accept this he was clearly sympathetic. J. M. Johnson, and W. A. Henry, the Attorney General of Nova Scotia, both warned against defining the powers of the general legislature in anything but the broadest possible terms.[45]

Two days later, on Wednesday, October 26, the last full session of the Conference (it lasted until midnight), the final stage of the Island's difficulties at Quebec was reached, and it revealed, once again, the importance of what was said and done at Charlottetown. It had been agreed at Charlottetown, apparently, that £200,000 (or possibly the interest on it yearly[46]) would be given to the Island to buy out the land proprietors. When the Finance Committee of the Conference reported, Coles was "struck with amazement" when this provision was omitted.[47] Coles expressed himself freely on the subject; it was resolved that the Finance Committee should reconsider. But Newfoundland and New Brunswick rose to the defence of their interests. The result, according to Coles, was that Newfoundland received an extra $150,000 yearly,[48] New Brunswick $63,000, and Prince Edward Island nothing at all. Coles protested. George Brown retorted that the Island would have more income than she would know what to do with. As if to pile treachery upon insult, W. H. Pope agreed with Brown. "I stated at the Conference when they refused my proposition . . . that they might as well strike Prince Edward Island out of the constitution altogether."[49] And Coles' opinion was shared by the Charlottetown *Vindicator* which declared the £200,000 was "a sine qua non of our acceptance of a Confederation."[50]

The Canadians, Palmer said, were clever and ingenious. They knew that "their government must stand or fall in the accomplishment or failure of the Union."[51] Whelan was more kind. "Canada has, I think, shown a very honest and generous disposition so far. . . ."[52]

[45]*Ibid.*, 84–7.

[46]Whelan's view, *Examiner*, Nov. 23, 1864.

[47]Prince Edward Island, Assembly, *Debates*, 1865, 68.

[48]This was to be in return for Newfoundland's surrender of her Crown lands to the central government.

[49]Charlottetown *Islander*, March 17, 1865, reporting debates for March 2. Also, Prince Edward Island, Assembly, *Debates*, 1865, 5–9. None of this discussion is recorded in Bernard's notes; A. A. Macdonald refers to it (45–6), but reports mostly his own speech.

[50]Charlottetown *Vindicator*, Sept. 28, 1864.

[51]*Monitor*, Dec. 15, 1864, quoting Palmer to Laird, Oct. 21, 1864.

[52]"Whelan reports," 43.

There was in fact little doubt of Canadian sincerity. Canada was not going to desert the Maritime delegates the way she had done after the previous Quebec Conference two years before. As for generosity she had already committed herself to the Intercolonial Railway and several other responsibilities.

Canada was also generous in other respects. The Canadian Minutes of Council showed that nothing was stinted for entertainment. Hotel claims after the Conference was over came to $15,000.[53] "The Canadians—who must, after all, be generous hearted fellows—appear to have great faith in the power of good feed, champagne, and torch light, as much more potent than dry argument. They seem to think that turning the head is a synonymous phrase with convincing the mind. . . ."[54] The delegates were all billeted in the St. Louis Hotel, where, according to McCully of Nova Scotia, they constituted "a very merry party."[55] They were having such a rousing good time, said the *Berliner Journal*, that whatever they did in their forthcoming visit to Canada West they could hardly expect any worse hangovers ("lauter Katzenjammer") than they had acquired already.[56] George Brown wrote feelingly at 2 A.M. Saturday, October 15, "We have had such a week of it!"[57] He talked of the hard work, but the *Quebec Daily News* wondered what the homespun farmers of Canada West would think of their hero who, "instead of thundering forth his complaints of their grievances, in the very same building, on the very same floor, he is now as lithe and gay as the merriest courtier of the old tory compact?" And what of Oliver Mowat —"pious little Oliver—when they hear that he, too, has thrown away his bible, and has gone in among the Philistines?" The sad truth was, concluded the *News*, that just six short months of office have sufficed to convert both Brown and Mowat away from "their gloomy, plodding notions of government," and to make good courtiers of them.[58] And much was made later of this festive side of the Conference. The *Perth Courier*, March 17, 1865, jibed at the Quebec scheme as "the measure of the Quebec ball-room and the oyster supper statesmen. . . ." A. J. Smith evoked roars of laughter from his Sackville audience with similar

[53]The Canadian Minutes of Council record claims, as of January 5, 1865, of $14,983.55. But it was not until June 29, 1867 that all the claims were finally adjudicated and settled.
[54]Fredericton *Head Quarters*, Oct. 4, 1865.
[55]Halifax *Morning Chronicle*, Oct. 25, 1864, report of Oct. 18.
[56]*Berliner Journal*, 27 Okt. 1864.
[57]Brown Papers, George Brown to Anne Brown, Oct. 15, 1864. Also in J. M. S. Careless, "George Brown and the Mother of Confederation," Canadian Historical Association, *Report*, 1960, 71.
[58]*Quebec Daily News*, Oct. 24, 1864.

sallies. "They had nice times going up [to Quebec] and nicer after they got there. . . . dinners, balls, champaign [*sic*], suppers, and only when surrounded with such influences were they fit to form a new empire."[59] *Barney Rooney's Letters* were the most blatant of all; when the delegates got back "afther a hard day's conspirocy," the party started.

John A. ". . . but hand us the tipple iv ye iver stop suppin' to see iv it's strong enough; and toss a lemon to Tilley, the sowl, iv he must do penance like a patriarch."

"I'll hae whuskey," sez Jarge [Brown]. . . . "My certie, ye're richt though, Darcie lad, aboot the danger o' gangin' ower early tae the polls. . . . Dinna ye think sae, Mister Crupper?"

"Sir," sez Tupper, as he dried the bottom iv his tumbler, and held it handy to D'Arcy's ladle, "the well understood wishes iv the people are so notoriously in favor iv this scheme that it would be a reckless and infamous policy to put them to the trouble of expressing themselves. . . ."

. . . the whole set staggered on to the Confrince omnibus, in the top of good humour, Brown droning out "Soggarth Aroon" to plaze D'Arcy, and Darcy blarneying the Scotch to plase Brown, and McCully and Tupper swearin' etarnal friendship on Confederashun. . . .[60]

Like all satires, *Barney Rooney's Letters* had a germ of truth. And the Conference omnibus *was* in the top of good humour. "Picture it ye enthusiasts! What a Canadian prospect and Acadian delight . . . a national Paradise. . . . Mr. Brown loving Mr. Galt, Mr. Galt loving Mr. Brown, and Mr. Macdonald loving everybody continually. What could be more lovely?"[61] The celebrations at the end of the Conference lifted the spirits of nearly everyone; even George Coles (at Ottawa), and Edward Palmer (at Toronto), seemed, in their speeches at least, to partake of it. The verse on the programme of toasts at Montreal seemed to be true even for the delegates:

> Then let us be firm and united—
> One country, one flag for us all;
> United, our strength will be freedom—
> Divided, we each of us fall.[62]

The reception at Montreal was quite imposing—but for the weather. The Conference met on Friday, October 28, to revise the Resolutions[63]

---

[59]Sackville *Borderer*, Jan. 27, 1865, reporting Smith's speech at Sackville of Jan. 20. Cf. Saint John *Daily Evening Globe*, Nov. 8, 1864: "It is not holiday work to make an empire. . . ."

[60][Garvie], *Barney Rooney's Letters*, 6–18, *passim*.

[61]Hamilton *City Enterprise*, Oct. 22, 1864.

[62]Whelan, *Union of the British Provinces*, 92, 114.

[63]Several minor but significant alterations were made. (Whitelaw, *Maritimes and Canada*, 260–2.)

and the Minutes. That evening another huge ball—attended by 1000 guests—was held, which Whelan called an "exceedingly gay and brilliant party."[64] The following morning the Conference concluded the revision and adjourned after two o'clock for luncheon in the St. Lawrence Hotel. This *déjeuner*, as it was called, produced wonderful speeches. Whelan, smiling, seemed to suggest the spirit when he hoped that political absolution would be given the delegates for their long silence and then touched the champagne glass in front of him to show "how earnestly we are all doing penance."[65] Cartier, not being much given to silence (or penance) and feeling the time was now ripe for a few disclosures, lifted the curtain with a few not very oblique rhetorical questions, but he said less than the newspapers had already revealed, despite Whelan's later remark that he told as many secrets "as he could think of."[66] The Montreal *Gazette* said quite truthfully on October 31 that it had "already published much more in these columns than any delegate felt fit to announce." J. H. Gray of New Brunswick and McGee were in marvellous form, and even Carter and Shea, the two rather silent delegates from Newfoundland, were moved to eloquence. But what was most remarkable of all, as the Montreal *Gazette* said, "was that these men, all bred in small communities, and raised to positions of influence amid the contests of jarring petty factions, showed complete forgetfulness of all personal difference, all local distinctions, and spoke as they acted (we have reason to believe) at Quebec, with a large hearted patriotism which it warmed one's heart to witness."[67] Finally, amid calls of "McGee! McGee!," the curly-haired Irishman got to his feet and gave a stirring speech of which the paragraph summing up the Quebec Conference deserves to be remembered.

. . . they had not gone into the Chamber to invent any new system of Government, but had entered it in a reverent spirit to consult the oracles of the history of their race. They had gone there to build, if they had to build, upon the old foundation—(Cheers)—not a showy edifice for themselves, with a stucco front, and a lath and plaster continuation—(Laughter)—but a piece of solid British masonry, as solid as the foundations of Eddystone, which would bear the whole force of democratic winds and waves, and resist the effect of our corroding political atmosphere, consolidate our interests, and prove the legitimacy of our origin. (Loud cheering)[68]

---

[64]Whelan, *Union of the British Provinces*, 85.
[65]*Ibid.*, 111–12.
[66]"Whelan reports," 45.   [67]Montreal *Gazette*, Oct. 31, 1864.
[68]There are at least four different versions of this speech: the *Gazette*'s (Oct. 31, 1864), the *Globe*'s (Oct. 31, 1864), McGee's (*Speeches and Addresses* (London, 1865), 110), Whelan's (*Union of the British Provinces*, 123). The *Gazette*'s is the most complete; it used four shorthand writers for the purpose.

The tour of Canada West was a triumph. It began by steamer, up the Ottawa river. Whelan described the soft, rich landscape of late October and what a delight it was, with "the emerald glories of summer" struggling in vain against the onset of autumn. Nor were voices wanting to sing the lines from the Canadian Boat Song, now half a century old, "Blow, breezes blow, the stream runs fast, The Rapids are near, and the daylight's past."[69] In Ottawa the streets were filled with dense crowds, and a torchlight procession escorted the delegates to Russell's Hotel.[70] W. A. Henry, the Attorney General of Nova Scotia, remarked the next day at the luncheon in the half-finished Parliament Buildings, "We were, indeed received like conquerors, like warriors returning from a great victory. . . ."[71] The next day, Wednesday, November 2, the special train taking the delegates to Toronto was stopped at Kingston by arrangement[72] and at Belleville by public enthusiasm. Cheers and the waving of handkerchiefs greeted the delegates at Belleville, and bumpers of champagne were drunk in the failing light of late afternoon on the Grand Trunk station platform. Supper was in Cobourg, at the Solicitor General's, after which Cobourg firemen and a band escorted the delegates back to the waiting train. It was half past ten before the train arrived in Toronto. There the reception was overwhelming. The delegates were taken by a huge procession to the Queen's Hotel, amid a blaze of torchlight, the firing of rockets, and three or four brass bands. Brown, Tilley, Tupper, and Whelan, all spoke from the balcony of the Queen's to the crowds below. As McCully said the next day, "we have been received with a continued ovation; it has been one carnival, from the beginning until now."[73] This triumphal progress showed clearly the blazing elation of Canada West. "The end is as good as accomplished," wrote the Kingston *Daily News* enthusiastically.[74] Brown could scarcely believe this, but he was exuberant at the success so far. His note to Anne Brown on October 27: "All right ! ! ! Conference through at six o'clock this evening—constitution adopted—a most creditable document —a complete reform of all the abuses and injustices we have complained of!"[75]

Whatever the future might be, there was little doubt that the Quebec

[69]Whelan, *Union of the British Provinces*, 126.
[70]Owned by Russell's Hotel of Quebec.
[71]Whelan, *Union of the British Provinces*, 132.
[72]C. J. Brydges, who had provided the train, also produced lunch at the Kingston station, *ibid.*, 147–8.
[73]*Ibid.*, 165.
[74]Kingston *Daily News*, Oct. 29, 1864.
[75]Brown Papers, George Brown to Anne Brown, Oct. 27, 1864. Also in Careless, "George Brown and the Mother of Confederation," 72.

Conference inspired the great majority of its members with a messianic
zeal for the cause. The dinners and speeches were the outer display of
inner dedication. The achievement of the seventy-two resolutions was
itself remarkable, but the greatest of the achievements of the Conference
was the spirit it engendered. Again and again, the letters that go back
and forth between Brown, Galt, Macdonald on the one hand, and Shea,
Whelan, Tupper, Tilley on the other, reveal this spirit. How refreshing
it is, wrote Shea to Galt from Newfoundland a month afterward, "to
have a question like this in the place of those wretched broils which so
much disfigure & disgrace a great part of our Colonial life. . . ."[76] Tupper
wrote that his colleagues, Liberals though they were, "behave like
trumps and deserve every consideration. . . ."[77] Whelan in Charlottetown wrote that he and Pope were not dismayed by the odds against
them; nor were they in doubt that "ultimately, even here, the Cause will
be triumphant."[78] "We must fight it through," wrote Tilley to Brown,
"and 'no surrender' be our Motto."[79] J. H. Gray appealed to the Island
public: "Shall we form part of a nation extending from Halifax to
Vancouver. . . ?"[80]

The irreverent Islanders labelled this sort of talk "the *glory* argument
. . . as frothy as the sparkling champagne whose effervescence may
almost be termed its inspiration."[81] Certainly this dedication was
caricatured by the opponents of Confederation as job hunting on a grand
scale. "Ye may be sure our big dellygates weren't forgotten by no manner
iv manes. Ministerial portfolios and judges' ermines, and court suits, and
bouncing salaries . . . were settled all round. . . ."[82] Charles Tupper's
new title was to be "Charles, Duke of Parrsboro Snag."[83] And in return
for these benefits, it was said, the delegates sang the praises of Confederation. "They dream dreams, they see visions. . . . Bubble blowing is their
all. They delight in grand and magnificent schemes—they delight to
build castles in the air, and cities by the seaside, to extend railways on
paper, and construct fleets in an hour. . . ."[84] Listening to two of the

[76]Canada, Minister of Finance, Letters Received, Shea to Galt, Dec. 15, 1864.
Also in W. G. Ormsby, "Letters to Galt concerning the Maritime Provinces and
Confederation," *Canadian Historical Review,* XXXIV, 2 (June, 1953), 167–8.
[77]Ormsby, "Letters to Galt," Tupper to Galt, Dec. 13, 1864.
[78]*Ibid.,* Whelan to Galt, Dec. 17, 1864.
[79]Brown Papers, Tilley to Brown, Nov. 21, 1864 (private and confidential).
[80]Charlottetown *Islander,* Nov. 18, 1864, letter from Gray, of Nov. 16.
[81]Charlottetown *Protestant,* Dec. 10, 1864.
[82][Garvie], *Barney Rooney's Letters,* 17–18.
[83]*Ibid.,* 16.
[84]Halifax *Morning Chronicle,* July 3, 1865. The *Chronicle* became anti-
Confederate in January, 1865. See *infra,* 209.

delegates—in the train between Halifax and Truro—"you would think that the Shubenacadie [river] would be turned into molasses, tea would grow in the barrens, and tobacco would be exported from Chezzetcook, as soon as Union was consummated. . . ."[85]

It is a disservice to history to assume the altruism of the delegates. They were politicians and cannot be freed from a nice judgement of their own interests. Not a few of the delegates could look forward to being ministers, senators, lieutenant governors, judges. Gordon noted that the political ideas of some of the delegates went hand in hand with their personal interests.[86] Nor, in the *élan* of national union, will it do to lose sight of the struggle for power that went on still between Canada East and Canada West. The French Canadians feared Canada West, especially its Reform party, and according to Taché they were looking to the Maritime provinces for help in "curbing the grasping ambition of Upper or Western Canada, which now threatens to overshadow the Lower Province."[87] To George Brown the triumph of Confederation was also the triumph of Canada West over the French Canadians.[88]

Yet, when nationalism is discounted by chauvinism, dedication by self-interest, and present sacrifice by future expectations, there remained in not a few delegates a glimpse of something more spacious, and perhaps more elevated, than the cramped little corners of Charlottetown and Fredericton, St. John's and Halifax, or even Quebec. It was a hope that a more transcendent spirit might prevail in a land with a larger compass and a more purposive national existence. That these hopes were not entirely fulfilled after 1867 helps explain the Canada First movement of the 1870's, and perhaps it was not until the twentieth century that there appeared once more the same spirit of national destiny. The Confederation movement was characterized by this spirit; it was more than a mere exercise in political survival. Something of the character of the movement is given by the correspondent of the Halifax *Morning Chronicle*, writing from Niagara Falls, Canada West, two weeks before the Conference:

All the newspapers discuss the proposed changes in every issue. . . . It is felt that the task to which these Provinces are called is no light or unimportant one;—they are now laying the foundations of Empire, of an Empire that may last as long as the human race and whose bounds shall extend from the cold and sterile coasts of Newfoundland to the noble hills

[85]*Morning Chronicle*, Feb. 20, 1865.
[86]C.O. 188, Gordon to Cardwell, Sept. 22, 1864 (confidential).
[87]Whelan's account of a conversation with Sir E. P. Taché, "Whelan reports," 43.
[88]Brown Papers, George Brown to Anne Brown, Oct. 27, 1864.

and peaceful havens of Vancouver's Island. . . . This is our destiny, and the Provinces from the least to the greatest should prove themselves worthy of it.[89]

The real question was, as the Montreal *Gazette* said when the Conference was over, "Will the people follow the example, and rise to the level of the occasion—to settle now the destiny of this northern country and the people that dwell here. . . ?"[90]

[89]Halifax *Morning Chronicle*, Sept. 29, 1864, report of Sept. 19.
[90]Montreal *Gazette*, Oct. 31, 1864.

8. CONFEDERATION
AND THE
FEDERAL PRINCIPLE

CONFEDERATION WAS TO BE a reality in 1865. Before all else was the determination of the leaders of the movement—Brown, Cartier, Macdonald, Tupper, Tilley, Gray—to strike while the iron was hot. Every delegation to the Conference had represented the two major parties in each colony, and while no one was very sure of Prince Edward Island, Carter and Shea from Newfoundland seemed optimistic and Tupper of Nova Scotia and Tilley of New Brunswick had some cause to be. In Nova Scotia and New Brunswick there seemed no reason why the combined power of the two parties should not be effective. The expiry of the life of the New Brunswick legislature in June, 1865, and that of the Newfoundland legislature in October, 1865, was inconvenient; elections would come too soon to be sure of public opinion. But Tilley and Shea were sanguine of success, and Tupper was, if anything, more so. All was to be in readiness by the spring. Then, Tilley assumed, Confederation would be "a fixed fact."[1] The timetable was breathtaking: Brown was to go at once to England; Galt (and perhaps Brydges) were to go to the Maritimes to discuss the Intercolonial in relation to the existing railway assets of Nova Scotia and New Brunswick.[2] Moreover, the imperial government's enthusiastic approval of the scheme, soon to be forthcoming, was warrant that the full power of the Colonial Office

[1]Shanly Papers, Tilley to Shanly, Dec. 20, 1864. Cf. Lord Monck, who opened the Canadian parliament in January, 1865 with the hope that it would be the last Canadian provincial parliament ever to assemble. (Monck Papers, Monck to his son, Henry, Jan. 20, 1865.) Cf. also *Sarnia Observer*, June 28, 1867: "in 1864 the universal expectation of the country was that the Federation, either of all the Provinces together, or of the two Canadas together . . . would be carried in about a year from 1864. . . ."

[2]P. B. Waite, "A Chapter in the History of the Intercolonial Railway, 1864," *Canadian Historical Review*, XXXII, 4 (Dec., 1951), 356–69.

would be placed at the disposal of Confederation. The imperial government would, if requested, legislate the provinces into union in the summer of 1865.[3] "The time is short," wrote Cardwell to MacDonnell, on December 8, 1864. His despatch was the reflection of lengthy and recent conversations with George Brown. "The time is short, since those who have undertaken this great measure desire to bring it forward during the ensuing session for the decision of the Imperial Parliament:—and it is impossible to say what evil consequences might not follow the unnecessary interposition of a year's delay. . . ."[4] There was to be no delay. It "only wants the Lower Provinces to say aye, and it is done."[5] "Rarely, if ever," wrote MacDonnell, "has there occurred in history so remarkable and fortunate a concurrence of circumstances to enable distinct Provinces to frame equitable conditions of a Union."[6] There were to be none of the hesitations and fumbling that had characterized so many intercolonial arrangements in the past; the process of joining the colonies together was to be short, swift, and sure.

The Quebec Resolutions were first published on November 8, 1864, little more than a week after the end of the Conference, in *Le Journal de Québec*. Two days later, from another source, they appeared in the Charlottetown *Monitor*.[7] From these two sources they soon spread over all five eastern provinces.[8] Almost every paper published them, in full more often than in part; even a paper as remote from the scene of events as the *Standard*, of Harbour Grace, Newfoundland, took space to print them.[9] They excited much comment. Information had been made public during both Conferences, but except for the brief semi-official report on

[3]Note the following from the independent *London* [C.W.] *Evening Advertiser*, Jan. 28, 1865: "It is thought desirable, too, that the subject should pass the several Provincial legislatures in time to lay it before the Imperial Parliament during the ensuing summer, and that all may be prepared for a general election by the end of the year. . . ."

[4]Nova Scotia, Lieutenant Governor, Despatches Received, Cardwell to MacDonnell, Dec. 8, 1864. This despatch had a curious fate. MacDonnell had part of the despatch (including the quotation above) withdrawn from the regular series and made a Separate. The reason seems to have been that Cardwell's answers to MacDonnell's allegations of personal motives on the part of Tupper and others could hardly fail to be embarrassing if published.

[5]Halifax *Morning Chronicle*, Feb. 4, 1865.

[6]MacDonnell to Monck, Jan. 9, 1865 (confidential), enclosure in C.O. 42, Monck to Cardwell, Jan. 20, 1865 (confidential).

[7]The source of the *Monitor*'s information was almost certainly Edward Palmer. W. M. Whitelaw, *The Maritimes and Canada before Confederation* (Toronto, 1934), 265 analyses the differences in the documents printed in Canada and the Maritimes.

[8]*Halifax Citizen*, Nov. 17, 1864; Chatham *Gleaner*, Nov. 19, 1864; *Newfoundland Express, Newfoundlander, St. John's Daily News*, Dec. 1, 1864.

[9]Harbour Grace *Standard*, Dec. 14, 1864.

the Charlottetown Conference, there had been nothing official until Cartier's speech in Montreal on October 29, and Brown's more revealing one in Toronto on November 3. Even these were no more than informative outlines. The battle for Confederation was thus begun long before the legislatures of the several provinces met, and its course was determined, at this critical stage, not by resolutions of legislatures, but by public opinion. In the Maritimes the newspapers, issue after issue, were filled with editorials, letters to the editor, and reports of meetings. Prince Edward Island was the most lively of all. The Saint John *Telegraph* said that the Island papers "come to us completely filled with Confederation. The little Island is determined to assert the truism that small people sometimes make the greatest fuss in the world."[10] But New Brunswick papers were little different. Even in the small towns along the north shore of New Brunswick, Confederation became "the subject matter at the corner of the streets, and at 'a thousand and one firesides.' "[11] When the Newcastle Debating Club invited Peter Mitchell and the Attorney General, J. M. Johnson, to publicly discuss Confederation, Newcastle Temperance Hall was filled to overflowing. The crowds at the meetings in Charlottetown, Moncton, Saint John, Truro, and Halifax, testify how powerful—even explosive—an issue Confederation had become. This public discussion continued for many months to come, and crowded every other issue into insignificance.

The Quebec Resolutions, once published, had to be expounded and explained, to be clothed with institutional and political meaning. Tilley and Gray began this process in New Brunswick, a bare week after they had returned from Quebec, and shortly after the Quebec Resolutions had appeared in the Saint John papers. The first meeting, held in Saint John on November 17, was by all accounts not a success since neither Gray nor Tilley seemed to have the broad grasp of the subject necessary to give it coherence. Tilley in particular failed to give any general financial structure for Confederation or to indicate by what means the proposed central government could sustain its admittedly large commitments.[12] One of Tilley's characteristics—his capacity for understatement —showed here to his disadvantage. Tilley lacked the "extraordinary facility of statement which on such subjects distinguishes Mr. Galt. . . ."[13]

It was Galt, in fact, who gave the best exposition of any of the delegates. He was the first Canadian minister to give a thoroughly comprehensive analysis of the financial and legal basis for Confederation.

[10]Saint John *Weekly Telegraph*, Dec. 14, 1864.
[11]*Ibid.*, Jan. 11, 1865, letter from "Veni, Vidi," Dec. 31, 1864, from Miramichi.
[12]Saint John *Morning Telegraph*, Nov. 19, 1864. See also *infra*, 236.
[13]Montreal *Gazette*, Oct. 28, 1864.

His speech at Sherbrooke on November 23 was given before 300 people and took over three hours. It was, despite its length, well received and became at once a textbook for the supporters of Confederation. Widely circulated in all of British North America, it became, as the Saint John *Telegraph* predicted it would, December 19, 1864, "a storehouse from which arms and ammunition may be drawn without limit to defend the holy cause of Confederation. . . ." Galt, never one to hide his light under a bushel, mailed off numerous copies of his speech to cohorts in the Maritimes. Tupper wrote, "many thanks for your speech—by far the ablest exposition of the Confederation scheme altho' a little too much from the Canadian point of view to suit this meridian." Whelan thanked Galt for several copies and for "the immense service you have done to the cause of Confederation. . . ."[14]

The financial aspect of Galt's analysis is well known and it would be redundant to give it again.[15] But his legal and constitutional analysis was also sound and serves to introduce the British North American reaction to this interesting and complex subject. The proposal is, Galt said, "to go back to the fountainhead, from which all our Legislative powers were derived—the Imperial Parliament—and seek at their hands a measure. . . ."[16] The sovereign authority of Westminster simplified wonderfully the task of uniting British North America. All that was necessary was an address to the Queen from each of the colonial legislatures, praying that an act be passed to unite them. There were no ratifying conventions, no elections to decide who should compose them, both of which had made the passing of the American constitution an uncertain, tortuous, even unscrupulous business. The British Parliament had merely to pass an act. Some were, indeed, disturbed by this sovereignty, "one and indivisible," from which all power flowed.[17] A considerable issue was to arise in 1866 in French Canada under this

[14]Tupper to Galt, Dec. 13, 1864; Whelan to Galt, Dec. 17, 1864, in W. G. Ormsby, "Letters to Galt Concerning the Maritime Provinces and Confederation," *Canadian Historical Review*, XXXIV, 2 (June, 1953), 167–8.

[15]R. G. Trotter quotes Galt's tables fully in his *Canadian Federation* (Toronto, 1924), 120–2. D. G. Creighton's "British North America at Confederation," an Appendix to the Rowell-Sirois Report uses Galt's work with discernment.

[16]Galt's Sherbrooke speech was widely printed. The Toronto *Globe* published it in 12 columns of fine print, Nov. 28, 1864. Extensive extracts appeared in the Saint John *Morning Telegraph*, Dec. 5; Halifax *Morning Chronicle*, Dec. 1; Charlottetown *Examiner*, Dec. 12; St. John's *Courier*, Dec. 21, 1864, to give a few examples. Galt published it himself as *Speech on the Proposed Union of the British American Provinces* (Montreal, 1864). The above quotation is from page 8 of this edition.

[17]Montreal *Herald*, Jan. 18, 1867. E. G. Penny, the editor, published his views in a pamphlet, *The Proposed British North American Confederation: Why It Should Not Be Imposed upon the Colonies by Imperial Legislation* (Montreal, 1867).

head; it was feared that changes would be silently introduced into an imperial act by delegates in London, against which there could be no recourse.[18]

Some Bleu newspapers recognized that imperial sovereignty could usefully define the powers of the central and local governments and be the guarantor of the constitutional boundaries so established. Such was the clear-headed and sensible view of *Le Courrier de St. Hyacinthe*, October 28, 1864:

Le fait est que les pouvoirs du gouvernement fédéral, comme ceux des corps locaux émaneront également du parlement impérial, qui seul a le droit de les déléguer. Chacun de ces gouvernements sera investi de pouvoirs absolus pour les questions de son ressort et sera également souverain dans sa sphère d'action. . . .

Le Courrier du Canada of Quebec expressed similar, though less well-defined, views.

Imperial sovereignty certainly simplified constitutional changes, but even for those with a clear-cut theory of federation, the role of the new central government was rather novel. An intermediate government, between Great Britain and British colonies, so to speak, had never been created before. The London *Times* said that the proposed changes "violate the Constitution of the whole empire."[19] When responsible government had been established in 1848, Britain and the self-governing colonies divided the sphere of government between them. No systematic division was then attempted and Canada had found the omission convenient for pre-empting more for her share as time went on. Nevertheless, the division was not less real for being unsystematic. However, a third government might have seemed rather anomalous. The Montreal *True Witness*, a shrewd judge, said (July 8, 1864) that a central government in British North America would inevitably "encroach upon the legitimate functions either of the Imperial or of the Provincial Government."

Remarks such as this were rare. There were, perhaps, few critics acute enough to recognize the problem. A more convincing explanation is that British North Americans never thought of their central government in quite these terms. The new central government for the Dominion of Canada was simply an expansion of the government of the old Province of Canada. The central government would not be "interposed" between the imperial government and the provincial governments: it would be the provincial governments of old, rolled into one. The really

[18]*Infra*, 276–7.
[19]London *Times*, July 21, 1864. Despite these remarks the *Times*, by the end of 1864, was a strong supporter of Confederation.

new governments would be the "local" governments, called local and meant to be what they were called, half-municipal bodies, the remnants of the old provincial governments. Galt said as much in Sherbrooke.[20] No great difficulty was therefore anticipated with the new constitutional arrangements. The central government at Ottawa would take over most of the existing functions of the old provincial governments, leaving them with such limited powers and responsibilities that they could be appropriately called "local" rather than "provincial." "The theory will be," said the Montreal *Herald*, June 22, 1864, "that the Federal Government is the fountain of power. . . ." The Montreal *True Witness* was afraid this would happen:

We oppose the proposed plan of *Colonial* Federation, since no matter in what terms it may be conceived, it proposes to saddle us with a sovereign central government which in our actual position must derive its authority, not from within, or from the States over which it is to bear rule, but *ab extra*, and from an Imperial Government with which our connection must cease ere many years be past; and to which, and to the plenitude of whose authority, the said central government would then inevitably succeed. Our position would then be that of a subject Province, not that of a State or independent member of a Confederation. (September 23, 1864.)

The French-Canadian Liberals (Rouges) unquestionably sympathized with such a view, but it is safe to say that the prospect intimidated only a few others.

There was thus a general division of opinion in British North America about the kind of government the new colonial union ought to be. Some wanted a federal system in the present-day meaning of the word "federal": that is, a clear recognition of what would now be called "co-ordinate sovereignty,"[21] with the provinces and the central government each having clearly defined powers and protected against encroachment by the other. But this was not a widely held view, nor was it characteristic of those men who created the Quebec Resolutions. The word "federal" was used to describe the Quebec plan, not because it defined the proposed relation between the central and the provincial governments, but because it was the word the public was most familiar with. "It is astonishing," noted the Kingston *British American*, "the looseness with which the term 'federal' is used in these discussions, indicating but an indifferent acquaintance with the actual meaning of the word. . . ."[22] The French Canadians and the Prince Edward Islanders insisted that the constitution be federal, and the constitution was certainly

[20]Galt, *Speech on the Proposed Union*, 15.
[21]K. C. Wheare, *Federal Government* (London, 1953), 11.
[22]Kingston *Daily British American*, Dec. 19, 1864.

called federal; what it was really intended to be was another matter. The Montreal *Gazette* was not far off the mark when it suggested that the constitution would be a "legislative union with a constitutional recognition of a federal principle."[23] In Britain, Goldwin Smith amplified the point, early in 1865.

They intend to create not a federation, but a kingdom, and practically to extinguish the independent existence of the several provinces. . . . They hope, no doubt, that the course of events will practically decide the ambiguity in favor of the incorporating union.[24]

The *Westminster Review* said much the same.[25] This was undoubtedly true of Macdonald, who wanted elbow room for the central power. Tupper of Nova Scotia frankly preferred legislative union. So did Galt. Brown, for the moment at least, was largely satisfied with "rep. by pop." Cartier, like Sir Etienne Taché, was confident, perhaps too confident, that French-Canadian privileges could be defended better by French-Canadian ministers in a central government than by a local legislature.

The members of the Canadian Coalition had originally agreed to address themselves to negotiations "for a confederation of all the British North American provinces."[26] Should this fail to be realized, then the federal principle would be applied to Canada alone. This seemed, on the face of it, simple enough. The question was, what was the federal principle? Macdonald said that under Confederation local matters would be committed to local bodies, and matters common to all to a general legislature. He then went on to say that the general legislature would be constituted on "the well understood principles of federal government." A revealing debate took place on this very point and it was for the government, particularly the French-Canadian members of it, rather embarrassing.[27] What it revealed was that most of the members of the

[23]Montreal *Gazette*, Sept. 9, 1864. Cf. Monck's remark: "So far from the word 'Federal' being an apt designation . . . its general meaning conveys an idea the direct contrary of . . . the intent of the Quebec plan." Monck to Cardwell, Sept. 7, 1866 (confidential), in W. M. Whitelaw, "Lord Monck and the Canadian Constitution," *Canadian Historical Review*, XXI, 3 (Sept., 1940), 301.

[24]Goldwin Smith, "The Proposed Constitution for British North America," *MacMillan's Magazine*, March, 1865, 408.

[25]"The Canadian Confederacy," *Westminster Review*, April, 1865, 259: "It is impossible to mistake the direction in which these [centralizing] provisions point, and they are calculated to raise the question whether there exists the most perfect conformity and good faith between the semblance and the essence of the yielding to local interests in the name of federation."

[26]Toronto *Globe*, June 23, 1864. Also J. Pope, *Memoirs of the Right Honourable Sir John Alexander Macdonald* (Toronto, [1930]), Appendix V.

[27]This debate is discussed briefly in P. B. Waite, "The Quebec Resolutions and *Le Courrier du Canada*, 1864–1865," *Canadian Historical Review*, XL, 4 (Dec., 1959), 296.

Canadian Coalition government thought of federation largely in terms of the composition of the central legislature. In the lower house there would be "rep. by pop."; in the upper house there would be representation by territory, "equal" representation as the Canadians described it. What could be simpler? Of course local powers would be given to local bodies, but that was taken as a matter presenting little difficulty. The basis of the federal principle lay in the central legislature and in the balance between the House of Commons on the one hand and the Senate on the other. Of the constitution of the House of Commons there could be no doubt, and the constitution of the Senate became of critical importance.

The Charlottetown, Quebec, and London Conferences laboured hard on this very point. It was considered the heart of the system. At the same time, the local governments were apt to be regarded merely as conveniences for dissipating sectional prejudices or absorbing sectional difficulties. Consequently, the division of powers between the central and the local governments which bulks so large in any modern analysis of federation was not a particular difficulty. It never really became so, even when the Maritime delegates appeared on the scene. The general effect was unmistakable. It gave the central legislature and its institutions a preponderant role; it is also the answer to the puzzle of everyone's preoccupation with the Senate. The same problem had existed at Philadelphia seventy-seven years before, and the result was not dissimilar. The Senates of both Canada and the United States caused enormous difficulties, and the division of powers seemed relatively easy. One explanation is that government was neither so pervasive nor so complex in the nineteenth century as in the twentieth. Jurisdictional problems were anticipated by Dunkin and others, but the "difficulties of divided jurisdiction," to use the title of Professor Corry's work,[28] were not very apparent. That the division of powers is the heart of the federal system is a modern proposition, not a nineteenth-century one.

On this point the Quebec Resolutions themselves were enigmatic. No definition of federal was given; perhaps one was not intended. The formal symmetry of the American constitution was probably not even considered desirable. There is much in the argument that Confederation was a practical answer to a political difficulty. "Rarely indeed," said the London *Times*, November 24, 1864, "has constitutional legislation been conducted in so practical and unpretending a style." Macdonald himself has been described as a "natural empiricist in action."[29] Empiricism can

[28]J. Corry, "Difficulties of Divided Jurisdiction," Appendix to Rowell-Sirois Report, 1940.
[29]T. W. L. Macdermot, "The Political Ideas of John A. Macdonald," *Canadian Historical Review*, XIV, 3 (Sept., 1933), 264.

be emotional as well as practical and the reference of British Americans to their British political inheritance was both. The Quebec Resolutions remained a working outline; their purpose was practical, their ideas empirical, and their solutions sometimes circumstantial. The Conference had not believed in putting its assumptions into ordered prose; these assumptions remained to be discovered, some implied within the seventy-two resolutions that were the blueprint of the system, others not.

Not without reason did the *Times* of London remark on December 13, 1864, that it was "exceedingly difficult" to construe the clauses on the division of powers. The *Edinburgh Review* said that "the distinction attempted to be drawn between general and local matters is in some respects scarcely traceable. . . ."[30] The Halifax *Morning Chronicle* referred to this question as the "binomial theorem of government."[31] The Montreal *True Witness*, January 13, 1865, cunningly observed that the unintelligibility of the resolutions on the division of powers was inevitable; the Quebec Conference was "attempting to 'define the powers' of a government intentionally armed with indefinite power." That was the matter in a nutshell.

Most British American newspapers fought shy of these thorny problems of political theory, and when analysis of the federal principle was attempted, many newspapers, and not a few politicians, simply bogged down. Ambrose Shea's explanations to the Newfoundland Assembly in February, 1865, were barely comprehensible.[32] The debate in the Canadian Assembly on the "well-understood principles of federal government" largely indicated that they were not well understood at all. Christopher Dunkin's brilliant and devastating analysis in the Canadian Confederation debates was one of the few successful attempts of its kind.[33] Numerous other examples can be given of the difficulty that Canadians and others had in interpreting the division of powers, and, in a more general sense, in understanding the federal principle at all. It was so often referred to in a manner thick with prejudice. The following is from the *Canadian Quarterly Review and Family Magazine* of April, 1865.

The federation and confederation system is the adoption of the principle that *each* member of the "*body politic*" shall, while apparently under the control of a supreme head[,] at the same time possess a separate and independent mind or controlling power, each capable of working, like a *false* rule in arithmetic to the injury of all the other rules or members of the

---

[30]"The British American Federation," *Edinburgh Review*, Jan., 1865, 191.
[31]Halifax *Morning Chronicle*, Oct. 16, 1865. Discussed *infra*, 218.
[32]St. John's *Newfoundlander*, March 16, 1865. See *infra*, chapter XI.
[33]*Infra*, 153–4.

"body politic." . . . A sound system of government requires no *checks* and *guarantees*, for its head is supreme; so all true principles possess internal evidence to prove that they are sound, *immutable* and *ultimate*.

To many sovereignty must reside somewhere and it ought to be at the centre where it belonged. It could be said of the Maritime provinces that their traditions of responsible government made their prejudice against the federal system understandable, but this explanation is less satisfactory for Canada. Canadians had been familiar with forms of double legislation, with "the Federal principle recognized in the Union Act [of 1840]," as Galt put it.[34] The extension of these devices had grown with the years; by 1864 it had gone so far that the province of Canada was ready to separate into its two halves. Certainly federation had been thought of before as a solution for Canadian difficulties. But after four years of civil war in the United States, fought, it would appear, because of the federal principle, the principle itself was suspect. Indeed the most conspicuous single feature of British North American discussion of Confederation was the prevalent fear of what might now be considered its basic principle. There were exceptions and important ones, particularly the French Canadians, but many Canadians, including a preponderant majority of the English, found the federal principle a wind which, once sown, would reap the whirlwind of civil strife. As the Mount Forest *Examiner* put it,

. . . will the application of the federal principle heal the sectional difficulties under which we labor? On this point we may refer to the experience of our neighbours across the lines, where under the fostering care of this same "Federal principle," the sectional difficulty has grown, in one generation, to proportions so gigantic as to astonish the world by the "irrepressible conflict" waged in its interest.[35]

Or the Ottawa *Union*, September 8, 1864,

It is not a little singular . . . how the federation idea should be taken up in British America at the very time that war, ruin, and demoralization are its effects in the American republic. . . . A war of secession in the future . . . must flow from copying the errors in statesmanship of our republican neighbours.

The Hamilton *City Enterprise*, October 22, 1864, though more optimistic, was entirely characteristic:

We do not say nor do we wish to believe the popular cry of today that the federation of the Provinces will bring trouble upon us if consummated.

---

[34]Galt, *Speech on the Proposed Union*, 4.
[35]Mount Forest *Examiner* (Conservative) quoted in the Toronto *Leader*, July 2, 1864.

We would rather trust that our case will prove an exception to the many instances. . . .

The general proposition was, appropriately, stated by the *Halifax Citizen*, November 19, 1864, "a sectional legislature under a general congress is only a nursery of sectional feeling, a fruitful factory for local jealousies, grievances and deadlocks to progress." Federation was like a drug: efficacious it might be, in small quantities for relieving the pain of the patient, but it was dangerous when used indiscriminately. This quantitative view of federation was a significant feature of Canadian discussion of the subject. "Canadians and Acadians alike will infuse as little of the federal principle into their union . . . as will suffice to meet the absolute necessities of the case." Thus the Montreal *Gazette* on August 24. The *Globe*, October 15, was not dissimilar: "Federation is, in a large degree, but an extension of our political system, and is sustained by precisely the same reasoning as are municipal institutions." This last was too much for the Montreal *True Witness*, and on October 28 it read both papers a lesson in political theory. Federation was not a quantity. It was not analogous to municipal institutions. It differed from a legislative union "not in degree but in kind." There was a "formal and essential difference" between legislative and federal union.

This was a lesson that few British North American newspapers and politicians learned, and their ignorance was indisputably part of their conception of Confederation. With some significant exceptions, they did not believe that federation meant the fundamental recognition of the sovereignty of both central and local governments. They would have regarded with suspicion a principle that would establish such governments in a way that would make each "co-ordinate and independent."[36] If that was the federal principle, they did not want it. Most, however, never fully understood the principle that they were opposing.

It is worth noting a popular and perhaps influential pamphlet published between the Charlottetown and Quebec Conferences, called *A Northern Kingdom*.[37] It was one of many published in 1864, and afterward, on Confederation, part of a considerable body of literature whose uneven merits still remain to be assessed. *A Northern Kingdom*

[36]Wheare, *Federal Government*, 11.
[37]It was written by S. E. Dawson of Dawson & Co., Montreal, publishers. Published anonymously by "A Colonist" (Montreal, Dawson, 1864). S. E. Dawson (1833–1916) was the son of the Rev. Benjamin Dawson, born in Halifax and who came to Montreal with his father in 1847. S. E. Dawson later became owner of the firm.

summed up in eighteen pages much of the current wisdom of British North Americans. Its views on federation were repeated again and again.

Federation! Have we not seen enough of federations with their cumbrous machinery of government, well enough in fair weather, but breaking up with the least strain—with treble taxation—with staffs of state functionaries, and of supreme functionaries, and with harassing disputes of various jurisdictions? Shall we not draw wisdom from the errors of others? Must we steer our bark on that rock on which the neighbouring magnificent union has split? . . . The main problems of government have been solved for us. The problem of a federal union has been worked out—a failure. The problem of a Legislative union has been worked out—a success.[38]

The ministerial paper in Quebec, the *Morning Chronicle*, published this extract as the leading editorial, on October 17, while the Quebec Conference was sitting. The Saint John *Evening Globe*, which was to become the foremost advocate of legislative union in New Brunswick, cited it as well on September 26. The pamphlet was quoted and commented upon by many newspapers, and probably achieved a wider currency than any other published at the time.[39] That it did so was as much a tribute to its views as to the succinctness with which they were expressed.

Canadian Confederation was a native creation. There was no intention of imitating the United States. On the contrary, in legislative union, many believed, lay the unequivocal, sovereign design of political excellence. A compromise with the realities of British American political circumstances was necessary, but it was not to be allowed to weaken the structure of the whole. Federation was essential, but it was federation in a unique, and to some at the present time a strange and twisted, form embodied not so much in the relation between the general and the local governments as in that between the House of Commons and the Senate. The great compromise between representation by areas and by population that lay at the heart of the American Congress was understood to be the basis of the federal principle and so accepted; but even here the Senate of Canada was not intended to be similar to its American counterpart. The Canadian Senate was peculiar in its use of regional, as opposed to state, representation. It is conspicuous that no attempts were made in the Quebec Conference, and few outside to develop the American view. Thus, while it is fair to say that the federal principle in its application to the central legislature reflected the

[38]*Ibid.*, 13.
[39]E.g., Charlottetown *Examiner*, Oct. 3, 1864; Halifax *Acadian Recorder* Sept. 28, 1864; Saint John *New Brunswick Courier*, Oct. 1, 1864.

American example, it is also probable that American ideas did not, in any sense more specific than this, determine the character of Confederation. The immediate character of Confederation was determined by British North American political experience and political traditions. And it may well be asked if Macdonald did not suspect that the principle of cabinet government might weaken fatally the Senate in its federal capacity, and thus its principal *raison d'être*. Christopher Dunkin was to suggest that the federalization of the Cabinet was inevitable. It is impossible to believe that Macdonald, and perhaps others, were not shrewd enough to see the gist of this point: that a responsible Cabinet would suck in, with silent, inexorable, vertiginous force, the whole regional character of the Senate and with it all the strength that lay in the Senate's regional identities. In circumstances such as these, the question of whether Confederation really was a federation or not was perhaps irrelevant. The French Bleus thought it was, but for a powerful majority of others Confederation was an attempt to put aside the insidious federal contrivances that had grown up within the Union of Canada, to relegate the questions that had caused them to the care of subordinate, local legislatures, and to establish at Ottawa a strong, cohesive, sovereign, central government.

9. CANADA WEST

CANADA WEST, from the Ottawa River to the Detroit, was in 1864 the home of a million and a half British North Americans. Protestant in religion,[1] empiricist in temper, expansionist in design, they provided the driving energy which was gradually destroying the twenty-three-year-old union of the province of Canada. Its commercial strength growing as rapidly as its population, its land hunger unappeased, it was buoyant, aggressive, and powerful. The backbone of Canada West was then, as it still is, the line of the Grand Trunk, the upper St. Lawrence, the north side of Lake Ontario, through Toronto westward toward the American border. Toronto was the centre of other railway enterprises: the Northern Railway ran north through Barrie to Georgian Bay; the Great Western went southwest through London to the Detroit River. This railway network and the fertile hinterland that it served gave Toronto her commercial power. Wheat was then Toronto's stock in trade, as lumber was Ottawa's.

Wheat, wheat, wheat, is the exhaustless staple of this region. . . . Now that the harvest has been gathered in, the tack is to forward the results of a year's toil to the seaboard. Canal boats by the hundred—by the thousand—railway cars in countless multitudes, are groaning day and night with the precious burden from the overflowing granaries of the fertile west.[2]

Toronto was also the centre of a considerable lake traffic. The *Morning Chronicle* correspondent described the scene below the Esplanade on a calm September evening—"when the great full harvest moon is rising over the calm lake, and when steamers and pleasure boats are passing to and fro, well freighted with the sons and daughters of song, it is as lovely a harbour as Upper Canada can show."[3]

Northward and westward from Toronto lay the force that thwarted

[1]According to the 1861 census, 82 per cent of the population were Protestant.
[2]Halifax *Morning Chronicle*, Oct. 8, 1864, report of Sept. 20, from Toronto.
[3]*Ibid.*

even the energies of the Canadians of Canada West. It appeared first in brief outcrops in the fields, then in the straggling clumps of birch pitched inexplicably on rock, and then, with awful finality, the Precambrian Shield claimed the land. Arable land lay a thousand miles distant across a region few Canadians now remembered. Sault Ste Marie was an outpost reached occasionally in summer by steamer; beyond lay Lake Superior, unknown, oceanic, fearful, with the Shield commanding the brooding, massive hills of its north shore even more imperiously than it dominated the little lakes at Muskoka. Fort William, fifty years ago, had been as well known as Sarnia was in 1864, but the Canadian fur trade was no more. A generation had gone since the North West Company closed its books in 1821, and the carousing *voyageurs*, whose merriment had split the summer nights, had long ago either abandoned canoes or gone to join the Hudson's Bay Company. Canadians had advanced into other lucrative but less heroic enterprises. But those in Canada West had not forgotten the Northwest; it slumbered on in their memories, and it had, these ten years past, been revived by the *Globe* and George Brown.

A hundred miles west of Fort William lay the border between Canada and the chartered territory of the Hudson's Bay Company. It was no more than a dotted line on the maps, but here began an empire which surpassed even Canada in size. Canadians of the Grit stripe had long believed that the rule of the Hudson's Bay Company was an anomaly, that the Company's charter was worthless, and that the sooner Canada acquired the territory the better. These ambitions were distrusted by more responsible politicians in Canada. No doubt in time the Hudson's Bay Company would have to surrender its charter, but the Conservative government of Canada had no wish to force the issue. Acquisition of the territory was only the easiest task. "The great point is," said Edward Ellice, the old Nor'Wester, "how to govern the territory."[4] In the eight years since that letter had been written none of the problems had become easier and their urgency had grown mightily. The Civil War would end sometime, and when it did the whole western half of British North America, from Lake of the Woods to Vancouver Island, would be in imminent danger of being absorbed by the United States, in the same inexorable way that Oregon had been swallowed up only eighteen years before. The acquisition of the Northwest was Brown's theme and he urged it with great persuasiveness in parliament and in the *Globe*. Brown's voice was stentorian enough

[4]Edward Ellice to John Rose, Oct. 6, 1856, in D. G. Creighton, *John A. Macdonald: The Young Politician* (Toronto, 1952), 244.

in the House, but it was marvellously compounded and amplified in the *Globe*. The *Globe* had indeed the most magisterial and imposing voice of any newspaper in British North America. Its circulation was 28,000; it was in every hotel, book stall, and railway station in Canada West, and its friends and foes alike were eager to see what it had to say.[5] Its adherents ranged from Ottawa to Sarnia, and in Red River and little New Westminster and Victoria, on the West Coast, it was the authority on Canadian affairs.

In the twenty years since the *Globe* had become established, George Brown had become loved and hated as no man in Canada. He had great ability and sterling integrity. He had courage and determination. He appealed to the youth of Canada West, as well as to a long heritage of Free Kirk instincts, and he and his brother, Gordon Brown, made the *Globe* a political force in its own right.[6] No political party in Canada ever had a more potent champion than the Reformers had in George Brown. Brown had however some conservative characteristics. It is tempting to describe him as a conservative by instinct and a Grit by profession, for if the leading causes of his agitation are removed he tends to become conservative.[7] George Sheppard, one of the editors of the *Globe*, had an instructive opinion of him. "Take him onto the ground of abuses . . . and he is the strongest public man in Canada. . . . But off this ground he is an ordinary man. He has never studied political principles. . . . He is a vigorous *colonial politician*—no less and certainly no more."[8] Brown was not an easy man to work with, nor did he himself find coalition harness very pleasant. He was suspicious of Macdonald, uncertain of Galt; with Cartier, oddly enough, French and Catholic though Cartier was, Brown felt more at ease. At least with Cartier one knew where one stood. A *rapprochement* between Brown and Cartier posed a danger to Macdonald and the Conservatives of Canada West, and Macdonald was at some pains to avoid it. That he did so was as much due to Brown's impetuousness as to his own astuteness. Brown's trouble was that he had been a newspaper editor too long—he was perpetually up in arms about something.

[5]Halifax *Morning Chronicle*, Oct. 8, 1864, report of Sept. 20 from Toronto. The *Globe* of July 19, 1861, gave its circulation as 27,996.

[6]It was said that Gordon Brown did most of the real literary work of the paper, that George Brown's articles could be picked out by "their big type and prodigality of italic, exclamation points, and capitals." R. Sellers, "Reminiscences of 1856," in *History of Canadian Journalism* (Toronto, 1908), 177.

[7]The *London Free Press* (Liberal-Reform) said of Brown, "his instincts and feelings have always been Conservative. . . ." (Aug. 25, 1864)

[8]Sheppard to Clarke, July 5, 1859, quoted in J. M. S. Careless, *Brown of The Globe: The Voice of Upper Canada, 1818–1859* (Toronto, 1959), 302–3.

Macdonald had a long experience in administration, Brown, in agitation.

It is no discredit to Brown, or to Cartier, to say that Macdonald emerged as the man who decisively influenced the form and character of Confederation. Brown and Cartier supplied the political capital for the enterprise; Macdonald was its architect. Confederation was only possible through the support of Brown and Cartier; Macdonald would have been the last person to deny it. But when it came to the design of institutions for the future Confederation that would take up smoothly the empirical realities of the present, Macdonald exercised a formidable influence. Macdonald's preference for a legislative union of British North America is well known. He consented, with some reluctance, to the scheme for federal union. Having taken the project in hand, however, Macdonald rapidly became aware of the political value of the word "federal." Under its protection he could proceed with a measure that in many respects was to bear the impress of his ideas about legislative union. Macdonald made oratorical gestures to the excellence of the American constitution, but where British North America was concerned, the fewer concessions made to the federal principle, the better.

Nor did Macdonald expect the Quebec Resolutions to cover the whole field of government. He wished nothing stated unless it had to be, nothing specific unless there was a plain necessity to specify. As Macdonald wanted as little concession to local governments as possible, so also did he want as little of a written constitution as possible. The constitution, he said at Quebec, "should be a mere skeleton and framework that would not bind us down. We have now all the elasticity which has kept England together."[9] "Mere framework," "elasticity": these are the ideas of Macdonald on Confederation. In this respect the Quebec *Morning Chronicle* was faithfully reflecting its chief's ideas when it said that a written constitution "checks progress, and keeps a nation in the swaddling clothes of its birth."[10]

Canada West saw in Confederation the opportunity to achieve an end long sought: representation by population. And this was the real source of the solid block of opinion that united behind the Coalition and its proposals. The Coalition had united Macdonald and Brown in political harness; it followed that Canada West was politically one. This view is borne out by the vote on Confederation in the Canadian

[9]J. Pope, ed., *Confederation: Being a Series of Hitherto Unpublished Documents Bearing on the British North America Act* (Toronto, 1895), 59.
[10]Quebec *Morning Chronicle*, Oct. 17, 1864. A similar opinion is expressed in the Kingston *Daily News*, Oct. 26, 1864.

legislature. Of the 65 members from Canada West, only 8 voted against Confederation on March 10, 1865.[11] This vote is, however, misleading. Most, but not all, Reformers supported Confederation; most, but not all, Conservatives did.

Conservatives did not like the Coalition. Some were not even sure they liked Confederation. Even those who did accept it were not above criticizing it. The editor of the Conservative *Canadian Freeman* wrote Macdonald, "I presume it is already known to you that the most active oppositionists to Confederation are to be found among the Conservatives. They cannot tolerate the scheme at all. They fancy it involves the surrender of U. Canada to the Grits."[12] Some Conservatives who stood loyally by Macdonald were apprehensive. As one follower wrote, "we are willing to follow you in the experiment and help to row the Boat ashore or sink—"[13] This explains a certain coolness to and criticism of Confederation by Conservatives. Being less enthusiastic than Reformers, they were often more judicious and not without shrewd criticisms of points that appeared to them peculiar or even retrogressive.

One of these points was the question of a general election. The Toronto *Leader* and the Hamilton *Spectator*, both Conservative, thought that the drastic change heralded by the results of the Quebec Conference warranted an appeal to the people. The Government took the view that an election was unnecessary, that public approval had been given by the newspapers, and that therefore delay served no useful purpose. But the real reason behind the government attitude was a sound instinct to let sleeping dogs lie. An appeal to the country might awaken the French electorate from the comfortable soporific of their Bleu allegiance. Nothing could be gained from the turmoil of a general election; the Government had good reason to think an election could hardly strengthen its position and might conceivably weaken it. The public position of the Government was stated by two powerful government papers, the Conservative Montreal *Gazette*, a paper "held in high esteem throughout Canada and . . . to be met with everywhere,"[14] and the Toronto *Globe*. As might have been expected, the *Gazette* said that in British practice the Canadian parliament would be perfectly justified in asking the Queen for constitutional changes without the prior consent of the Canadian electorate. "If there be a settled doctrine of the British Constitution it is that the people's representatives in Parliament are

[11]Canada, *Confederation Debates* (Quebec, 1865), 962.
[12]Macdonald Papers, J. G. Moylan to Macdonald, Dec. 19, 1864 (private).
[13]*Ibid.*, E. Cook to Macdonald, Feb. 5, 1865.
[14]Saint John *Morning Telegraph*, Dec. 19, 1864, report of Dec. 9 from Quebec.

not mere delegates charged with certain specific duties, but are, in fact, the people in their political capacity. . . ." The *Gazette* deprecated proposals for an election; it would be a plebiscite after the French mode, or "after the style of our democratic neighbours." The *Globe* agreed. The idea was "one of those dreadful American heresies against which we are so often warned now-a-days."[15]

Notwithstanding, the Hamilton *Spectator*, on November 10, 1864, still thought an election desirable and expressed surprise and regret at the *Globe*'s attitude. The Toronto *Leader*, November 22, said no one was asking for a constitutional convention, and it was nonsense for the *Globe* and the *Gazette* to talk as if they were. Parliamentary methods were perfectly acceptable; "all that is asked is that Parliament should not make sweeping constitutional changes" without a popular mandate. The Reform *London Free Press* of November 17, said much the same. The Reform Hamilton *Times* chimed in with characteristic verve:

If their [the people's] *direct* decision on the confederation question is unnecessary, we know of no question that has arisen in the past, we can imagine none in the future of sufficient importance to justify an appeal to them. The polling booths thereafter may as well be turned into pig-pens, and the voters lists cut up into pipe-lighters.[16]

This homespun sentiment was characteristic of a number of Reform newspapers who had reason to dislike the Coalition.[17] The same view appeared in New Brunswick, and it was partly responsible for forcing Tilley into the election of February, 1865.[18]

On the issue of Confederation itself, the Conservative papers of Canada West were divided into three groups: first, the ultras, who opposed Confederation from the beginning, largely because it was a federation; second, the critics, like the *Spectator* and the *Leader*, who, though critical of Confederation, supported it in the end; third, the stalwarts, who supported Macdonald, the Coalition, and Confederation through thick and thin.

There were several ultras among the Conservative newspapers, but none were very powerful or significant, for example, the Simcoe *British Canadian*, the Woodstock *Times*, the St. Thomas *Dispatch*. In the Assembly their spokesman was M. C. Cameron, the member for North Ontario who defeated William McDougall when McDougall tried to

[15]Montreal *Gazette*, Nov. 2, 1864 (note the characteristic pejorative use of the word "democratic"). Toronto *Globe*, Nov. 5, 1864.
[16]Hamilton *Times*, quoted by the Ottawa *Union*, Nov. 24, 1864.
[17]E.g., Goderich *Signal, Berliner Journal, Perth Courier.*
[18]The Saint John *Morning Telegraph*, Nov. 25, 1864, quoted the Toronto *Leader* with satisfaction and approval. See also *infra*, 241.

win the seat in July, 1864. M. C. Cameron reveals the perplexity of staunch Conservatives with the sudden turn of events. He wrote pathetically to Macdonald, "I scarcely know where I am or what I am."[19] The proposal to end the old Union, the federal system, the sweeping changes, altogether gave him no confidence in the future. He saw only a sea of troubles. W. F. Powell, Conservative member for Carleton, wrote disagreeably to Macdonald from Ottawa about the "constitutional revolution or federation or whatever you call it. . . ."[20] The St. Thomas *Weekly Dispatch* had elaborated this point on July 14. Federation would be ruinously expensive and was in any case "thoroughly republican." It was this seam of republicanism running through federation that made almost any other alternative preferable, even dissolution of the Union.

Macdonald's reply to this argument is full of interest, and is contained in a letter to M. C. Cameron. Macdonald liked Cameron for his integrity and thorough-going Conservatism. He had rather enjoyed Cameron's defeat of McDougall in July. Macdonald wrote suavely and reassuringly:

My dear Cameron—
    . . . As to things political I must try to discuss the Federation Scheme with you. . . . I am satisfied we have hit upon the only practicable plan— I do not mean to say the best plan. . . . we have avoided exciting local prejudice against the scheme by protecting local interests, and, at the same time, have raised a strong Central Government. . . . If the Confederation goes on you, if spared the ordinary age of man, will see both Local Parliaments and Governments absorbed in the General Power. This is as plain to me as if I saw it accomplished now[—]of course it does not do to adopt that point of view in discussing the subject in Lower Canada.[21]

Indeed it would not do. Such assurances could hardly appear in print, and in any case they did not prevent M. C. Cameron from voting against Confederation in March, 1865.

The critics shared the same views as the ultras, but did not carry them *à outrance*. The Hamilton *Spectator*, for example, thought federation a dangerous and unworkable arrangement. The sectional troubles of Canada had developed because of the federal elements which existed in the Union constitution, notably equal representation for each section of the province. The *Spectator* urged the Quebec Conference to have

[19]Macdonald Papers, M. C. Cameron to Macdonald, Dec. 3, 1864.
[20]*Ibid.*, W. F. Powell to Macdonald, Dec. 18, 1864. See the acid interchange between Powell and Macdonald in the *Confederation Debates*, 716. Powell voted for Confederation, however.
[21]Macdonald Papers, Macdonald to M. C. Cameron, Dec. 19, 1864.

nothing to do with federation, but to adopt a legislative union.[22] By the end of October enough information was available from Quebec to make the *Spectator* feel much relieved. The Montreal *True Witness*, October 28, remarked that to call Confederation "federal" was sheer hypocrisy; the *Spectator*, October 31, 1864, was pleased to be able to agree.

The first principle of the new Constitution is that the Central Government shall be, under the Crown, absolute and supreme in the country. Give us the details to work out fairly that idea, and we care not whether the Union is called federal or legislative. . . . A strong supreme central government, delegating to the local legislatures certain powers for the management and control of local interests and objects, even controlling their action so as to protect the rights of minorities in each section, and reserving to itself absolute and unchecked control over all subjects not so especially delegated, is certainly the simplest and most innocent form in which the "federal" principle could be presented to us.

Thus the *Spectator*, though it believed an election desirable, found consolation in the form of the proposed constitution. It was a mild and gentle critic.

The Toronto *Leader* was a more stern and thoughtful one. The *Leader* competed energetically with the *Globe* for power in Canada West, but it was "distanced greatly in the race."[23] It was "never a paper of the people" the way the *Globe* was, despite its being the first to introduce, 1860, the cent daily.[24] It was, however, the major Conservative paper; it had an elevated sense of public liberty, and was disposed to bridle at the Canadian government's determination to push Confederation through at all hazards. Observing the defeat of Tilley and other Confederation supporters in the New Brunswick election, the *Leader* remarked, March 4, 1865, "If the people [of New Brunswick] are not opposed to Confederation, they are thoroughly opposed to the high handed way in which it is attempted to be carried; and if they will believe us, we assure the Canadian Ministers that they are not a whit more popular than the three gentlemen who have lost their elections in New Brunswick." Like the St. Thomas *Dispatch*, the Toronto *Leader* thought the Union of the Canadas should still continue. It was not necessarily worn out; all that was needed to make it work was a little mutual forbearance.[25] The *Leader* was perhaps encouraged by an apparent willingness on the part of the Rouges to make concessions as an alternative to Confederation. French Canada might accept, *l'Ordre* had suggested on December 12, 1864, "la modification de

[22]Hamilton *Spectator*, Oct. 13, 1864. Also Oct. 14, 15, and 21.
[23]Halifax *Morning Chronicle*, Oct. 8, 1864, report of Sept. 20 from Toronto.
[24]Sellers, "Reminiscences of 1856," 177.
[25]Toronto *Leader*, Feb. 27, 1865.

nos rapports avec cette province [Canada West] tout en conservant l'union." It is noteworthy that on this question three very different elements in Canada agreed, that is, the Rouges, the extreme wing of the Reform party, and the *Leader*'s group of Conservatives.

On the issue of federation the *Leader* shifted its ground. It began like the Hamilton *Spectator* believing that the local governments must be closely checked and controlled. But after September, 1864, the *Leader* changed. Fearing the Coalition and its power, it took up a premise reminiscent of the *Federalist* or of Lord Acton: "it is the nature of all unchecked power to run riot or to become despotic." By the time of the Quebec Conference the *Leader* was applying the premise to the proposals emanating from Quebec. "Where is the necessity for such an extreme degree of strength in the federal government?"[26] By early 1865 the *Leader* was convinced that the design of Confederation was inimical to local independence, and local independence had now become an important bulwark against a despotic central government. It warned, March 2, 1865,

There is an evident tendency to belittle the local governments as much as possible, to make them, even in their own spheres, subordinate to the federal authority. . . . It only remains to make the local machinery as feeble as possible; and we shall be surprised if this does not turn out to be the meaning of the "simple and inexpensive local governments" of which we hear so much.

This was directed at the local constitutions favoured by George Brown and the *Globe*.

By April 3, 1865, when New Brunswick had arrested what the *Leader* regarded as the headlong rush of events, "the monstrous haste . . . to carry the scheme at all hazards," the *Leader* became sweetly philosophical. There was no cause for regret that the Quebec Resolutions, matured in a few weeks, were not hurriedly adopted; indeed, "much good may result from the check which has been given. . . ." Brown's withdrawal from the Government in December, 1865, prevented it from pursuing its opposition much further. There is some evidence that the *Leader*'s course was dictated partly by pique, and once Brown was out of the Government the *Leader* did tend to be less restive. By September, 1867, its editor, James Beaty, was running as a Conservative in Toronto East.

The third group of Conservative papers, the stalwarts, were the smaller journals whose opinions fluctuated as they were subjected to the cross-currents from the larger city dailies, but who, in case of doubt,

26*Ibid.*, Oct. 20, 1864.

followed a reliable ministerial paper like the Montreal *Gazette* or the Quebec *Morning Chronicle*. The Kingston *Daily News*, a good supporter of Macdonald, found occasion to disagree with the Toronto *Leader*. (The principal difficulty with assessing these smaller papers is that complete files of them rarely exist. They seem to have varied considerably in the degree of independence they displayed. In this respect they are a contrast to the small Reform papers, such as the *Newmarket Era*, Oshawa *Vindicator* or *Perth Courier*, which showed a sturdier self-reliance.)

The Reform party after the Coalition was filled with triumph. Its main aim, that for which it had bent most of its energies for more than a decade, was at one fell swoop conceded. The Reformers were animated by a powerful antipathy to anything that would interfere with the realization of this goal. They opposed delay, they opposed changes, they opposed an election. Brown carried the great majority of his supporters with him. There were some who would not shift their ancient dislike of Conservatives; of these the *Perth Courier* was the most notable example among the newspapers, and in the House that group of Reformers sometimes called "Liberals," who followed John Sandfield Macdonald, were also conspicuous by their opposition to the Coalition and Confederation. But by and large the Reform party of Canada West offered Confederation its dedication and determination against which the few recalcitrants in their ranks, and the opposition of the John Sandfield Macdonald "tail," were ineffective. Like the Christian soldiers in the old hymn, Reformers were marching to victory, over popery, French Canadianism, and political injustice, and nothing was going to be allowed to stand in the way. The Free Kirk of Scotland, though its adherents numbered only 8 per cent of the population, was the strongest of all the Protestant sects in political energy and almost wholly Reform in politics, and it carried with it the support of a large army of Methodists.[27]

If the *Leader*'s attitude to Confederation can be described as liberal Conservatism, the *Globe*'s was conservative Reformism. The *Leader* wanted an election: the *Globe* said an election would be a waste of time and money. The *Leader* wanted stronger local governments: the *Globe* said they would be absurd. The reason for the *Globe*'s attitude lay largely in the determination of Reformers to get "rep. by pop."

[27]Toronto *Leader*, Nov. 3, 1864. It noted that Auld Kirk Presbyterians (like Macdonald) were almost exclusively Conservative. The Church of England also leaned toward Conservatism, though in the *Leader*'s opinion, its clergy exercised very little political influence.

George Brown made this determination abundantly clear in his great speech before the Assembly on February 8, 1865. The events of the past seven months, he said, can never be obliterated. The solemn admission of men of all parties cannot be erased. Anyone who opposed Confederation must not forget that there could never be a return to the *status quo ante*. No one should oppose Confederation who cannot produce something better, something acceptable to French as well as English Canada. "This scheme," Brown went on, "can be carried, and no scheme can be that has not the support of both sections of the province." Cartier interjected: "Hear hear! there is the question!" "Yes," said Brown, "that is the question and the whole question."[28] Everyone who raised his voice in hostility to the measure must bear in mind all the perilous consequences of its rejection. Brown did not mince his words. His whole speech was irradiated with a prodigious sense of power. The Rouge paper, *L'Union Nationale*, said it was the best of all the ministerial speeches. "Si nous étions haut-canadien, nous élèverions une statue de bronze à ce redoutable politicien."[29] *Le Canadien*, an independent paper halfway between Rouge and Bleu, spoke glowingly of Brown's speech. "Il a parlé en homme d'Etat, qui relègue dans l'ombre tous les souvenirs irritants du passé, pour ne songer qu'à l'avenir de la confédération canadienne. . . . En l'écoutant, il était impossible de ne pas se laisser entraîner à croire avec lui ces perspectives grandioses."[30]

Confederation, Brown had said at Quebec, must be a federal one. Brown meant it; he knew well enough that Cartier and the French Canadians would accept nothing else. He himself had long been an advocate of federal union having proposed it to the Reform Convention of 1859. But Brown had no clear-cut doctrine, and this lack was manifest despite his obvious earnestness. Brown's insistence on federal union in the debates of 1865 was because he knew he had to carry through an honest bargain with the French Canadians. British North American union had to be federal because federation was the only basis upon which Lower Canada would concede "rep. by pop." For this concession Lower Canada had been given equality in the Upper House. "On no other condition could we have advanced a step."[31] But this was the main problem of federation as far as Brown was concerned. The fact that the local governments would be municipal in character did not affect the issue. He was quite prepared to insist on federal union and at the same time demand that local governments be subordinate to the central government.

28*Confederation Debates*, 87. 29Montreal *Union Nationale*, 13 fév. 1865.
30Quebec *Canadien*, 10 fév. 1865. 31*Confederation Debates*, 88.

The *Globe* reveals these same characteristics. It never noticed the formal distinction between legislative and federal union. The distinction between them was something few British Americans bothered about. Macdonald preferred to ignore it in the hope that time would settle the ambiguity, as Goldwin Smith put it, in favour of legislative union. In a moment of reflection the *Globe* said, August 1, 1864, that it was "unphilosophical that the part should be deemed greater than the whole." Hence the reverse was true, the whole must be greater than the part. But the middle ground, where the whole and the part were sovereign equals, i.e. federation, the *Globe* did not conceive of. Federations, it believed, had failed in the past because the central power was too weak.[32] British North America would not repeat this error. Nevertheless, the *Globe* did not cite the United States as the *locus classicus* of the danger of federation. Federation had been a positive, not a negative contribution to the American polity. "The wonder is, not that federation should have allowed this war to occur, but that its marvellous adaptation to . . . circumstances . . . should have so long delayed an outbreak." The worst enemy of Confederation could not pretend that the sectional difficulties of Canada were anything like those of the United States.[33] Hence nothing was to be feared from federation. If the right emphasis were put on the central power Confederation would be sturdy and secure. As for legislative union, said the *Sarnia Observer*, Canada had had more than enough already of the cat-and-dog life of the Canadian union.[34]

The Reform Oshawa *Vindicator* went a little further. It declared federation positively good. It produced the argument that might have been expected everywhere in British North America, one that might now be conceived as the common sense of the matter.

No system of government could be fairer, or could be better calculated to give satisfaction . . . than the federal system. . . . Legislative union works very well in England. . . . But with such diverse interests as would be brought together in a British American union extending eventually over the whole of British North America, a system of government more like that under which the United States have grown to such vast proportions, is what is plainly required. . . .[35]

What is astonishing about this view is its rarity. It is not to be met with anywhere else in Canada West, New Brunswick, Nova Scotia, or New-

[32]Toronto *Globe*, Aug. 8, 1864.
[33]*Ibid.*, Oct. 15, July 9, 1864.   [34]*Sarnia Observer*, Oct. 14, 1864.
[35]Oshawa *Vindicator*, Aug. 31, 1864. But even the *Vindicator* added that it was not urging the adoption of the American system, for "time has shown wherein it may be improved upon."

foundland. It appears in a different form in Canada East and Prince Edward Island, basically as justification for the preservation of local institutions. Few indeed there were who were ready, as the Oshawa *Vindicator* was, to accept the federal principle at its face value, and to apply it to the whole of British North America as a suitable and sensible means of uniting diverse societies into one nation.

The *Globe* also seemed conservative in its attitude to the appointed Senate proposed in the Quebec Resolutions. The existing Canadian Legislative Council had been made elective in 1856; the life members were to be replaced, as they died, with elected members. By 1864 the Canadian Upper House was already two-thirds elective. At the Quebec Conference the elective principle was abandoned without much opposition. Brown agreed with the abandonment for he had never much liked the elective upper house; he felt it was inconsistent with responsible government. McDougall and Mowat, who urged the elective principle, believed that an active body springing directly from the people would have a salutary influence on the whole system of government. But as far as the Canadian Legislative Council was concerned, neither the hopes of its advocates nor the fears of the opposition were realized. As the *Globe* put it, "the change in the constitution of the Upper House did not change its character." This also applied, the *Globe* believed, to the future Senate of British North America. Appointed or elected—it probably made little difference. In any event, "its influence in the government and legislature of the country will be of a negative and not of an affirmative character." The *Globe* could not applaud the decision of the Conference—so it said—but it was not frightened by the prospect of an appointed upper house.[36] While most of the Reform party would have preferred an elected upper house, the lack of opposition to the appointed one suggests that, despite MacDougall and Mowat's anguish on the subject, most Reformers did not lose much sleep over it. A few Conservative papers, notably the Toronto *Leader*, thought Crown nomination was a retrograde step, but most Conservatives were pleased. Reformers had their eye on the House of Commons where the goal of "rep. by pop." would be realized. And with the prospect of 82 members in the future House of Commons, Canada West as a whole could probably afford to be philosophical about the Senate.

The Oshawa *Vindicator* noted that about 90 per cent of the Reform papers were behind the Coalition, and it may be inferred that a similar majority were in favour of Confederation. Their instinctive independence subordinated by a great remedial measure, the Reform legions of

[36]Toronto *Globe*, Oct. 20, 1864; Oct. 26, 1864.

Canada West trooped behind the *Globe*: the Carleton Place *Herald*, Cobourg Star, *Barrie Examiner*, Owen Sound *Comet, Stratford Beacon*, St. Catharines *Journal*, and others.[37] But not all. As the Conservative party had its ultras, so did the Reform party. There was some resemblance between an ultra-Conservative view of Confederation, represented by the St. Thomas *Dispatch*, and an ultra-reform one, such as that of the *Perth Courier*. Both opposed the federal principle; both agreed it was expensive in operation and divisive in its effects. Both believed in union of the colonies, but said that the Quebec constitution was nothing but a disconnected jumble. The *Perth Courier* emphasized this point, November 25, 1864. The constitution was called federal, but "in the very principles of its foundation, it is not federal. . . ." It was a "mongrel system without a specific character. . . . It is neither federal nor legislative, but is what many will consider a bad mixture of both." It was bad because it pretended to be something it was not. It was called federal but it was federal in nothing but name, and, the *Courier* added emphatically, expense. The local governments proposed by the Quebec Resolutions could have been made county councils for all the work they did. "These proposed local governments amount to just nothing at all but a means of patronage in the hands of the Ministry of the General Legislature." Sir John Willison, fifty years later, remarked that none of the opponents of Confederation seemed to have fully realized the immense patronage the federal government of Canada would exercise.[38] But the *Perth Courier* anticipated it. Reform papers had been fighting Conservative patronage long enough to recognize the opportunities for patronage when they saw them. A correspondent in the Reform Goderich *Signal* complained on December 2, 1864, that with Confederation "every twentieth man in Upper Canada will be an office holder." It was possible to pay "too dear for our whistle." The Reform Ottawa *Union* wrote, "The country is to be loaded with debt and taxes —burthened with the support of poorer colonies—it must expend millions in constructing a railway—staffs of costly officials are to be imposed on the country, and finally we are to be driven towards separation from the mother country. . . . Such is the end the country may expect."[39] This theme was introduced in Canada, but variations on it, with more powerful orchestration, were soon to appear in Nova Scotia.

[37]Some of these files still exist, but where missing, as for example the *Barrie Examiner*, their views must be taken from other journals.

[38]Sir J. Willison, "Some Political Leaders in Canadian Federation," in Wrong, Willison, Lash, and Falconer, *The Federation of Canada, 1867–1917* (Toronto, 1917), 50.

[39]Ottawa *Union*, March 4, 1865. Cf. J. B. E. Dorion's remarks, *Confederation Debates*, 859.

A third group in Canada West opposed to Confederation were the Sandfield Macdonald Reformers. Sandfield Macdonald and his career illustrate the peculiar difficulty of moderate Liberals in Canada West. They were Liberals rather than Reformers. They were Roman Catholic, rather than Protestant. They aimed at tolerance, at more equitable school laws; they tried to co-operate with French Liberals like Dorion or Sicotte. They believed the present Union adequate for present needs and that more generosity on the part of everyone would prevent further difficulties. The trouble was that Sandfield's *modus vivendi*, the principle of the double majority, a moderate solution of a difficult problem, never really became a *modus vivendi*. The double majority principle may never have been capable of sustaining the pressure that it was called upon to bear. Indeed it failed on its first serious test.[40] But Sandfield Macdonald did not resign when it did fail. He stood condemned on his own ground. In effect, the double majority system was an admission in practice of what the Liberals of Canada West could not concede in principle. It was in effect federalization of Canada, but without any discrimination of what was a local question and what was not. It was difficult enough to apply: Sandfield Macdonald found it more than difficult to adhere to. Unfortunately few Liberal journals exist to present Sandfield Macdonald's views. The Cornwall *Freeholder*, which did express his ideas, has gone. The *London Free Press*, which usually supported him, went over to Confederation.

Sandfield Macdonald, though a Roman Catholic, was not the leading spokesman for the Roman Catholics of Canada West. The greater part of them—about 75 per cent—were Irish. Sandfield Macdonald was a Scot, and his support from the Irish Catholics was not considerable. Joseph Lynch, the Catholic Bishop of Toronto said in 1867 that the great majority of his flock were "Conservatives and have always supported the Conservative government."[41] In other words the Irish Catholics of Canada West looked to D'Arcy McGee rather than to Sandfield Macdonald. The policy of the Irish Catholics of Canada West on Confederation was simple. They preferred not to have it at all. Canada West being 82 per cent Protestant, Roman Catholic privileges might well disappear once a local legislature, dominated by Protestants, gained control of education. If there is Confederation, said the Toronto *Canadian Freeman*, the organ of the Irish Catholics, on December 15, 1864, then it must "approach as nearly as possible to the character of a legis-

40R. W. Scott's "improvement" of the Upper Canada Separate School legislation, passed in the teeth of opposition from Upper Canada members.
41Joseph Lynch to R. P. Jamot, July 8, 1867, quoted by *Le Journal de Québec*, 15 juillet 1867.

lative union." Like the Protestants of Canada East, the Catholics of Canada West naturally regarded federation as dangerous. All the provincial minorities in Canada favoured legislative union. And as the Manitoba School question of 1890, and the Ontario School Regulations of 1912 were to show later, the suspicion of local provincial legislatures was justified. With the Catholics of Canada West their belief in legislative union was pure self-defence. They had no commercial axe to grind as did the English Protestants of Canada East. It was a simple alternative: legislative union and protection for their privileges, or federal union and sectional intolerance. Not unnaturally, Confederation was placed before them by the *Canadian Freeman*, and by McGee, as a legislative union in all but name. The *Canadian Freeman* also remained extremely suspicious of the *Globe*. It was hardly to be expected that the Free Kirk and the *Freeman* would be happy in coalition. The *Freeman* growled away at the *Globe*; it sniffed at its editorials and worried at its doctrines, until finally the editor drew a reproving letter from Macdonald, asking for an amelioration of its tone. J. G. Moylan, the editor, replied:

What has been said in the "Freeman" in reference to the Confederation scheme, was elicited by the *Globe* and purely intended as a check on that paper. The saving clause "we have every confidence in the liberality, statesmanship, and honesty of purpose of Messrs. J. A. Macdonald Galt and Cartier, to apprehend bad results", or language to that effect was always inserted.[42]

Such were the difficulties of coalition.

Thus, there were cavils against Confederation by several groups in Canada West. Conservatives, Reformers, Liberals, all found reasons to criticize it. The themes reiterated were basically three: a demand for a general election, a dislike of the divisive character of the federal principle, an objection to the expense of a multiplicity of governments. But opposition to Confederation was found among only a small part of the Conservative and Reform parties. On the other side Conservatives and Reformers produced a powerful majority for Confederation. Of all the parts of British North America, Canada West was the most powerful and devoted advocate of Confederation. The support of the Reform party in particular was indispensable, and had the Reformers wished, they could probably have forced further concessions to local government. But the Reform party and the *Globe* were far from preaching such a doctrine. Representation by population blinded them. If federation were necessary to achieve "rep. by pop." that was perfectly satis-

[42]Macdonald Papers, J. G. Moylan to Macdonald, Dec. 19, 1864 (private).

factory. The French Canadians wanted local autonomy: the Reformers were glad to give it to them. The Reformers did not in fact concern themselves much about local government; the end they sought was equally a concomitant of legislative or federal union. The Reformers would give Macdonald his way on centralization, partly because they believed in it, but also because they were not particularly interested in local government. The development of the Reform and Liberal doctrines of provincial rights were to come after 1867, not before.

Confederation may have been a necessity, a convenience, or both. But most in Canada West understood it, not as a question of principles or of co-ordinate powers, but as one of practical utility, a system of local governments to be added to existing institutions in order to lighten the heavy load of sectional differences they had hitherto been obliged to carry. To Reformers Confederation was a reward for years of strenuous endeavour. To Conservatives it was the dangerous nettle out of which they might yet be able to pluck the flower, safety.

10. CANADA EAST

MONTREAL IN 1864 WAS THE METROPOLIS of British North America. Its population of 100,000 was almost double that of its nearest rival, Quebec, which had 53,000. (Toronto was third with 49,000.) The Victoria Bridge, built by the Grand Trunk Railway at a cost that not even the opening by the Prince of Wales could assuage, was the gateway to a "city increasing in wealth, in extent, in population, and in splendour of external appearance at a rate unparalleled in British American history."[1] Palatial hotels, horse railways, regular lines of omnibuses, clean, well-watered streets, all proclaimed to the visitor the power and opulence of Montreal. The Grand Trunk had its headquarters here; so did the steamship companies. The terminus of the canal system and the focus of the Ottawa timber trade, Montreal stretched along the St. Lawrence, its mile of wharves a prickly tangle of masts and yards, with occasional black funnels looming incongruous amid the welter of sails and halyards. "Scarcely an hour of the day or night," wrote the impressionable Maritimer in 1864, "but trains and steamers and ships come and go well freighted with men and merchandise. The mighty St. Lawrence rolls laden with tribute from the distant west."[2] It was a city of merchant princes as it had been for decades past beginning with the McGills, the MacTavishes, and the MacGillivrays, who came there after 1760 to take over the fur trade from the French. A petition to the Governor General in December, 1864,[3] shows some of them: Peter Redpath, president of the Board of Trade; William Molson, president of Molson's Bank; Hugh Allan, president of the Merchant's Bank and of the Allan Line; T. B. Anderson, president of the Bank of Montreal; Thomas Paton, general manager of the Bank of British North America. Here was assembled the powei and wealth of

[1]Halifax *Morning Chronicle*, Oct. 1, 1864, report of Sept. 15 from Montreal.
[2]*Ibid*. Cf. also [B. W. A.] Sleigh, *Pine Forests and Hacmatack Clearings* (London, 1853), 234–41.
[3]A petition for investigation into the discharge of the St. Alban's Raid prisoners. (Toronto *Leader*, Dec. 27, 1864.)

Canada. Montreal was no longer the political capital of Canada, but it was still the commercial and financial one, and it was to retain this position for many years to come.

Of the total population of Canada East—some 1,100,000—the English-speaking Protestants were only 15 per cent; but it is a truism that they exercised an influence out of all proportion to their numbers.[4] Joseph Cauchon, the editor of *Le Journal de Québec*, once said that a French-Canadian editor spent the best part of his time translating, "péniblement et longuement," English into French. That was, he said, the reason why most French newspapers appeared only twice or three times a week.[5] It was a comment on the English dominance of the province of Canada as a whole, and none cherished this dominance more than did the English of Canada East. They had been the commercial leaders of the province since 1760. They controlled Montreal and Quebec. They were at the geographical and financial centre of the province. The disruption of this arrangement by a federal union was the last thing they wanted. The plain fact was that in a federated British America the English would be a minority in a French province. They had much to lose and little to gain by the division of Canada in Confederation. It could compromise their commercial dominance; it could threaten their religious and educational privileges; it could leave them politically helpless. J. W. Dawson, the Nova Scotian who was Principal of McGill University, wrote to Howe:

I suppose scarcely any one among the English of Lower Canada desires Confederation, except perhaps as an alternative to simple dissolution of the Union, but many would like to have a legislative union were that possible. Among the French nearly one half are against the Scheme; and in Upper Canada it is supported principally as a means of dissolving the existing Union. . . . The English in Lower Canada in general take a very despondent view of the position of affairs feeling themselves politically powerless; and believing that . . . if the Imperial Parliament pass an act in accordance with the Quebec Scheme, the old English dominion will be destroyed beyond redemption. . . .[6]

Upon Galt and the English Conservatives supporting the Government fell the full responsibility of allaying this anxiety of the English Protestants of Lower Canada. Galt was their minister in the Cabinet, and their most persuasive spokesman. His financial skill was a characteristic

[4]About 25 per cent of the population of Montreal were English-speaking Protestants.
[5]*Le Journal de Québec*, 30 avril 1864, announcing its change from tri-weekly paper to a daily.
[6]Howe Papers, J. W. Dawson to Howe, Nov. 15, 1866.

product of their society. Galt did his best in working out the financial terms of Confederation to ensure the dominance of the central government. In his massive Sherbrooke speech he assured his audience that the Protestant fear of the local power was unjustified. The local legislatures would be, he said, simply "municipalities of larger growth," and in the event of their colliding with the central government the whole matter would be reported by the lieutenant governor to "superior authority."[7] The Protestants liked the sound of this. "Superior authority" had a comforting and reassuring ring about it. Yeoman work was also done by the principal Conservative papers, the Quebec *Morning Chronicle* and the Montreal *Gazette*. The *Morning Chronicle* reflected Macdonald rather than Galt, but the result was much the same. The best summing up of its position was its own fervent underlining of an editorial in the Saint John *Globe*: "One of the worst features of the Union plan proposed by Canada is, that it will leave our local legislature still in existence."[8] The Montreal *Gazette* was of a similar mind; if anything, it urged its views with more resourcefulness and defended them more skilfully. Galt, Macdonald, and Brown and the newspapers that represented their views, the Montreal *Gazette*, the Quebec *Morning Chronicle*, and the Toronto *Globe*, all were warrant that the Protestants of Lower Canada would not be abandoned to a provincial legislature against whose power they would have little or no recourse. As far as the Protestants were concerned, a powerful provincial government was tantamount to absolute dissolution of the Union, and that they would not have. When dissolution was suggested by the Rouge *Union Nationale*, it was repudiated by the Quebec *Morning Chronicle*.[9] As the *Quebec Gazette*—a commercial and shipping journal—said later, December 7, 1864, the Rouge papers and anyone else "very much mistake the sentiment of the Lower Canada English if they think such an alternative feasible."

It was hardly to be expected that the French ministerial journals would say the same thing. The Bleus had no such assurances for the realization of their views as the Protestants had for theirs. The Bleus had good reason to believe that legislative union of British North America was acceptable to many Canadians; by October the Nova

[7]A. T. Galt, *Speech on the Proposed Union of the British North American Provinces* (Montreal, 1864), 14–15.

[8]Saint John *Daily Evening Globe*, Oct. 17, 1864; Quebec *Morning Chronicle*, Oct. 29, 1864. Also quoted by the Fredericton *New Brunswick Reporter*, Oct. 28, 1864.

[9]Montreal *Union Nationale*, 3 sept. 1864; Quebec *Morning Chronicle*, Sept. 10, 1864.

Scotian and New Brunswick papers were giving evidence of similar desires in two of the Maritime provinces. The Bleus also knew well the minds of Macdonald and Galt; and George Brown, though his intentions were honourable enough, was hardly a person to give Conservative French Canadians much confidence. The tone of the whole English press, Conservative and Reform, was generally inimical to federation. The collective power of the English of Canada West, Canada East, Nova Scotia, and New Brunswick would be used to effect the kind of union the English found acceptable. The Rouges in fact spoke darkly of the Durham Report—only a generation old—being revived in the form of Confederation.[10] "On le sait," warned *L'Union Nationale* on September 3, 1864, "l'Union [des Canadas] ne devait être que le premier pas dans la voie de notre anéantissement. . . ." The second step would be Confederation. The Bleu leaders did not believe this, but if many of their followers did the Bleus were finished. Taché, Cartier, Langevin, and others took the gravest risks. The Halifax *Morning Chronicle*'s assiduous correspondent wrote on September 19, "A storm is brewing in Lower Canada before which Cartier and D'Arcy McGee are likely to quail." No pains were being spared to rouse "an overwhelming tempest of opposition. Mr. Cartier's only chance is to win the clergy. If he does so, if the clergy actively support him, or even stand aloof from the contest, he may succeed; but if they join the popular current, the case seems to me hopeless. . . ."[11] The Rouges were out for blood; the Bleus could not rest. They had to justify Confederation or perish. Series of articles supporting Confederation appeared as early as July in the Quebec *Courrier du Canada* and later in *Le Journal de Québec*.

It is hardly necessary to reiterate the Halifax paper's point about the Church. The close connection between the Bleus and the Church was essential to carry Confederation. Hector Langevin's brother was Bishop of Rimouski, and it was fortunate for Confederation that the Bleus were in good odour with the church while the Rouges were not. The Church sensibly refused to be drawn into the question at this stage, but its benevolent neutrality had probably been secured by the spring. The Vicar General of Canada, E. A. Taschereau, wrote from Rome on March 9, 1865, permitting Catholics to support Confederation.[12]

---

[10]Montreal *Pays*, 21 juillet 1864. At the Quebec Board of Trade dinner, October 15, Taché seized the nettle and praised Lord Durham. E. Whelan, *Union of the British Provinces* '(Charlottetown, 1865), 76. However Maurice LaFramboise made the same point as *Le Pays*, with long quotations from the Durham Report, in Canada, *Confederation Debates* (Quebec, 1865), 850–6.

[11]Halifax *Morning Chronicle*, Sept. 29, 1864, report of Sept. 19.

[12]Quoted by Montreal *Minerve*, 10 avril, 1865.

When the chips were down, in the spring of 1867, the Church was called upon to publicly support Confederation, and this it did with the full power of all five bishops.[13] *Le Courrier du Canada* was generally considered the special spokesman of the clerical viewpoint,[14] and it never hesitated. Five days after the announcement of the Coalition, it announced the republication of J. C. Taché's pro-Confederation articles of 1857, and a few days afterward it began a series in which it tried to show that Canada East "n'a été ni sacrifié, ni trahi, et encore moins livré—que M. Cartier ne s'est pas jeté au genoux de M. Brown . . . nous rassurerons les lecteurs effrayés du *Pays*, de la *Tribune*, de *l'Ordre*, du *Journal de St. Hyacinthe*."[15] The readers of *Le Courrier* and other Bleu journals were not, presumably, "effrayés." The Bleus were, in short, on the defensive. The initiative for Confederation lay with Canada West. The French, like the English of Canada East, had much to lose and only Confederation to gain. Everything depended upon what kind of constitution it was. There was no point in giving up the present equality with Canada West to secure only the status of a half-municipal local government in an essentially English Confederation. The Bleus were committing the French Canadians to leaving a comfortable home furnished to their taste for a dubious and uncertain structure set upon foundations of "rep. by pop." The Bleus had to show not only that conditions warranted the change but necessitated it. *La Revue Canadienne* put it thus to its readers, January, 1865: "Il ne faut pas nous aveugler: des changements constitutionnels sont nécessaires aujourd'hui. . . . Il est inutile de songer à revenir au fonctionnement pur et simple de l'Union. . . ." *La Gazette de Sorel* (14 jan. 1865) also: "Les évènemens [*sic*] de ces dernières années qui sont encore frais dans la mémoire d'un chacun, démontrent cependant clairement que la continuation de l'ordre de choses actuel est impossible."

It was understandable however that the Bleu ministers might say one thing in Cabinet and another in the press. There are instructive differences between what Taché and Cartier might have conceded in Cabinet and what the Bleu papers said. Statements by the Bleu papers could also be useful preliminaries to Cabinet negotiation. Thus *Le Courrier du Canada* wrote on July 11, 1864, that the proposed central

---

[13]*Infra*, 300–1.

[14]*Le Courrier du Canada* was considered "to echo the sentiments of the Catholic clergy. . . ." (Saint John *Morning Telegraph*, Dec. 19, 1864, report of Dec. 9 from Quebec.) *Le Défricheur* (21 juillet 1864) wrote that *Le Courrier du Canada* was "organe du chef du cabinet, M. Taché, et organe du clergé." *Le Courrier* replied that it was the organ of neither but it did support their principles (25 juillet 1864).   [15]Quebec *Courrier du Canada*, 4 juillet 1864.

government "n'aurait pas le droit de venir mettre la main dans nos affaires locales qui resteraient sous le contrôle de notre législature locale; puisque la législature fédérale n'aurait pas le droit de toucher à l'éducation, à l'administration de la justice, enfin à l'économie interne de chaque province." *La Minerve* of Montreal went further, July 16, 1864: "Il [le Bas-Canada] aura son gouvernement particulier dont l'autorité s'étendra à tous les objets qui suivent le cours ordinaire des affaires, intéressant de la vie, la liberté et la prosperité des citoyens . . . il sera maître chez lui en tout ce qui regarde son économie sociale, civile et réligieuse."

As for the Rouges, their position looked stronger than it really was. On the face of it they had only to say Confederation was bad, that it was a threat to the French Canadians, and turn the Bleus out of office if they appealed to the people. But the Bleus had no intention of having an election. The Government continued to resist the demand in the face of some pressure from Canada West. And in actual fact the alliance of Brown with the Bleus put the Rouges in a most difficult position. The Rouges had been willing in the past to consider some remedy for Upper Canada's grievances; the Bleus had not. The suggestion that Dorion made in May, 1864, of giving one more representative to Canada West was at least a concession in principle to what the Rouges probably could not fully concede in fact.[16] It could be said that the Rouges were the authors of their own defeat by failing to take up their proposed remedies with sufficient energy. But whatever the cause, the Rouges, after the Coalition, were in the peculiar position of opposing concessions to Canada West when they had been the first to suggest them. And it must be said that by destroying the alliance between Lower and Upper Canadian radicalism George Brown did much to destroy Dorion's power as a French politician.[17]

It was unlikely therefore that the Rouge attitude to the Coalition would be that of sweet reasonableness. It was not. *Le Pays* said on July 14, "la nationalité canadienne française est sacrificiée à l'égoisme, à la fièvre de domination qui ronge quelques hommes dont la carrière politique ne laisse après elle que des hontes et des ruines. . . ." As for Confederation,

[16]During the debate on the appointment of Brown's Committee, May 19, 1864, Dorion moved an amendment that had the effect of increasing the representation of Canada West by one member—provided that the committee were dropped. Dorion's amendment was defeated, 74–32. (Canada, Assembly, *Journals*, 1864, 223–6.) Cf. also *Le Pays* on Dorion in 1858, *supra*, 37n. Note the following from the Toronto *Globe*, Nov. 2, 1866, "Mr. Dorion has surely not forgotten that in 1858 he entered a Government pledged to seek a solution of these difficulties."

[17]J. L. Morison, "Parties and Politics, 1840–1867," in *Canada and Its Provinces.* V. *United Canada* (Toronto, 1914), 83.

said *L'Ordre*, August 24, 1864, "nous n'avons absolument rien à y gagner et nous y avons tout à perdre!" The exclamation mark was significant. So was the appearance of *L'Union Nationale*, early in September in place of the feeble *La Presse*.[18] The Bleu journals— "feuilles vendues," *Le Pays* called them—could only tell the poor, deceived French Canadian, "ATTENDRE ET ESPERER!"[19]

This is what the Bleu papers were doing. Even *Le Canadien*, inclined to be independent, agreed that this was the best course.

La seule conduite patriotique à suivre, c'est de ne point diviser la population bas-canadienne et de ne point épuiser nos forces en d'inutiles alertes, c'est de conserver aux chefs que nous avons accepté la confiance dont ils ont besoin pour mener à bonne fin l'œuvre politique dont ils ont assumé la responsabilité. . . . Le Bas-Canada n'aurait rien à gagner à s'isoler sur de simples soupçons des hommes qui sont tenus par honneur comme par intérêt de le protéger.[20]

Thus engaged, Bleu journals also found themselves with an enemy in the rear, the English papers who were undermining the Bleu defence. By August, 1864, both the Montreal *Gazette* and the Toronto *Globe* were criticizing the views of the Bleu papers and were assuring their readers that Confederation would be strongly centralized and that the powers of the local governments would be weak and delegated. The *Gazette* in particular was making disconcerting statements that Confederation should be a legislative union.[21] That the Rouges should object to this was understandable, but the Bleus joined the Rouges in attacking the views of the *Globe* and the *Gazette*. *Le Canadien* said firmly (August 24) that Confederation was and should be "un certain nombre d'Etats souverains, déléguant une partie définie de leurs droits et leurs pouvoirs à un gouvernement central." Otherwise the local governments

[18]The first issue of *L'Union Nationale* was 3 sept. 1864. The opening editorial was signed by L. A. Jetté, L. O. David, Médéric Lanctot, and others.

The report of a committee, "nommé à l'assemblée des citoyens de Montréal," was printed in this issue and recommended dissolution of the Union. Among the signers of this report were G. E. Clerk, editor of the Montreal *True Witness*, and Wilfrid Laurier, then a law student in Montreal.

The formation of *L'Union Nationale* was discussed in an editorial on French Canada in the Halifax *Acadian Recorder*, Sept. 21, 1864.

[19]Montreal *Pays*, 14 juillet 1864.

[20]Quebec *Canadien*, 22 juillet 1864. Cf. also the view of *La Gazette de Sorel*, during the Quebec Conference, 22 oct. 1864: "D'ailleurs, l'intélligence, le savoir, l'honnêteté l'habilité que tous s'accordent à reconnaître chez nos représentants à la conférence, sont des garanties positives que nos justes droits seront scrupuleusement sauvegardés. . . ."

[21]*Gazette*, Aug. 24, 1864. The *Globe* was conspicuously more gentle with the Bleu papers than was the *Gazette*.

would be nothing but mere municipalities, without any real independence, completely at the mercy of the central power. *La Minerve* agreed. The result was an unseemly row between the two leading ministerial papers in Montreal. The *Gazette* spoke for the English Conservatives, *La Minerve* for the French Conservatives. Their positions were poles apart. *La Minerve* warned sternly, August 30,

La Gazette est certainement dans l'erreur si elle croit que dans le Bas-Canada l'opinion publique est favorable à une union législative. Au contraire, les Canadiens-Français feront toujours à cette mésure l'opposition la plus décidée. . . .
Nous voulons une confédération dans laquelle le principe fédéral serait appliqué dans toute son étendue. . . . Nous voulons que chaque état, pour les questions qui se rapportent à son existence particulière, soit complètement indépendant. . . .

But the *Gazette* was not to be deterred. It even reiterated its position. "We said then [August 24], and we repeat it now, that any union between these colonies must be as nearly as possible, a legislative union. . . . We re-assert these as the fundamental principles on which the union must be based."[22] This quarrel went on for over a fortnight.[23] Neither side could afford to back down. *La Minerve* could not safely allow the *Gazette*'s talk of legislative union to go unchallenged; neither could the *Gazette* allow consideration of a confederation where the federal principle would be applied "toute son étendue." Behind each paper was a quick, sensitive, and powerful public.

The whole incident illustrates how fearful were both the French and English of Lower Canada of Confederation, and how difficult would be the readjustment of the delicate balances already achieved within the old Union. The incident illustrates indeed the very achievement of the old Union. Problems of a similar kind had been obscured, blurred, perhaps half-forgotten in Canada East by the functioning, however imperfectly, of the old Union constitution. Now Confederation threatened to resurrect all the old troubles. In all probability neither paper would have gone as far as it did if nearly all the ministers had not been away at the Charlottetown Conference. Finally on September 16 *Le Courrier du Canada* stepped in and told both papers to cool off until the project had been elaborated, revealing perhaps the hand of the Premier in Quebec, Sir Etienne Taché. But a mending of fences was clearly required; French and English Conservatives would have to

[22]Montreal *Gazette*, Sept. 2, 1864.
[23]The Saint John *Telegraph* remarked, "The French of Lower Canada are working themselves into a fever. . . ." (Sept. 19, 1864)

agree somehow. This was perhaps the reason, on September 26, for the semi-official statement on the result of the Charlottetown Conference.[24]

The statements by the Bleu papers between July and September were significant. They took a position more extreme than that of the Bleu ministers, but in all probability they were intended to do so. They were part of the manœuvring of the Bleus for a safe position, not only in Cabinet discussions, but also in face of the great unknown: the reaction of French Canadians to Confederation. The Bleu papers could afford to be generous in giving powers to the local governments, and they had not stinted. By the time of the Quebec Conference the general French-Canadian reaction had begun to appear, and the French-Canadian ministers could breathe more easily. But in the Conference and out of it, they were watchful.

They needed to be. Dorion and the Rouges continued to do the utmost "to inflame the French population against the Scheme."[25] Dorion's address to the electors of Hochelaga, on November 7, condemned the Quebec scheme out of hand. What kind of independence would the provinces have, he asked, if deprived of control over criminal law, over commercial law? Or deprived of the right to constitute their own courts, name their own judges? "Ce n'est donc pas une confédération qui nous est proposée, mais tout simplement une Union Législative déguisée sous le nom de confédération. . . ."[26] That the Rouge efforts failed was in part a measure of the political power enjoyed by the Bleus, but Dorion's past connections both with Brown and with Sandfield Macdonald were much to his disadvantage.[27] The Bleus made strenuous efforts on their own behalf, particularly after the Quebec Resolutions had been published on November 8. By this time they were obliged to recognize the facts, though they put the best gloss on them they could. The interpretation of the Quebec Resolutions given by the Bleu papers even after the Quebec Conference differed noticeably from that of the *Globe* or the *Gazette*.

Le Courrier du Canada and some other Bleu papers, notably *Le Courrier de St. Hyacinthe*, frankly accepted the word "federal" in

[24]*Ibid.*, 26 sept. 1864; Montreal *Gazette*, Sept. 26, 1864; *Globe*, Sept. 27, 1864; Ottawa *Citizen*, Sept. 27, 1864; *Halifax Citizen*, Oct. 11, 1864.

[25]Saint John *Morning Telegraph*, Dec. 19, 1864, report of Dec. 9, from Quebec.

[26]*Le Pays*, 8 nov. 1864. Dorion's address was widely reprinted, even in government journals, e.g. Toronto *Globe*, Nov. 9, 1864; *La Minerve*, 10 nov. 1864. It was even published in Newfoundland (*Newfoundland Express*, Dec. 20, 1864).

[27]E.g., "Quand M. Brown combattait le Bas-Canada . . . les rouges étaient ses amis. . . . Maintenant qu'il met bas les armes . . . ces *grands amis* du Bas-Canada nous avertissent qu'il est à craindre!" *La Minerve*, 7 juillet 1864.

the Quebec Resolutions at its face value. They believed that the Quebec plan framed an essentially federal constitution and they explained and justified it on this ground. *Le Courrier de St. Hyacinthe* said that each government, central and local, must be entirely distinct.[28] *Le Courrier du Canada* noted that the Conference had difficulty in dealing with the question of the division of powers, but that the problem had been resolved by leaving "aux gouvernements locaux des garanties suffisantes pour les protéger contre toute tentative d'impiète-ment de la part du gouvernement central, et elle donne au gouverne-ment central une somme de pouvoirs suffisante pour lui permettre de travailler, sans être gêné, au bien-être matériel et à l'agrandissement des différents états de la confédération. . . ."[29]

This last was part of a series of twenty-one articles on Confederation that *Le Courrier du Canada* published in December and January.[30] They were a careful and comprehensive attempt to justify the Quebec Resolutions to the better educated public—notably the clergy. They were the second series that *Le Courrier* had published on Confederation, the first being in 1857. A comparison between the two series suggests the changes in thinking occasioned by the events of the seven years. *Le Courrier*'s articles of 1857 envisaged a rather more decentralized constitution. Power devolved upward—as the *True Witness* wanted it to in 1864[31]—and the residual power was held by the provinces. Although large powers were then given to the central government, these did not include the sweeping powers of taxation given by the Quebec Resolu-tions or power over agriculture and immigration.[32] The central parlia-ment would have a Senate and an Assembly, the former with equal representation from each province. In both series *Le Courrier* looked confidently forward to British North American independence.[33]

This summary does little justice to what was a considerable and thoughtful work. Influences from the United States were apparent even in 1857, and Taché warned about "ce germe de dissolution enfoui mais non détruit lors de l'adoption du pacte fédéral. . . ."[34] J. C. Taché's work seems to have influenced Galt's plan of 1858, and it remains

[28]*Supra*, 108.
[29]*Le Courrier du Canada*, 26 déc. 1864, "La Confédération," X.
[30]This series is discussed in more detail in P. B. Waite, *"Le Courrier du Canada* and the Quebec Resolutions, 1864–1865," *Canadian Historical Review*, XL, 4 (Dec., 1959), 294–303.
[31]*Supra*, 109.
[32]J. C. Taché, *Des Provinces de l'Amérique du Nord et d'une union fédérale* (Québec, 1858), 148.
[33]*Ibid.*, 155–6; *Le Courrier du Canada*, 25 jan. 1865, "La Confédération," XXI.
[34]J. C. Taché, *Des Provinces de l'Amérique du Nord*, 105.

one of the most comprehensive studies of a question that lent itself all too easily to pretty imaginings and glorious phrases, empty of solid political and constitutional content. In the 1864 series a note of urgency is clearly discernible. Canada in 1864 was faced with as dangerous a situation as in 1775. There was no third choice between Confederation and annexation.[35] Factions, animosity, jealousy had been the conspicuous features of recent political life in Canada; Brown, the principal author of these troubles, had also offered a major solution for them. In a courageous gesture, he had offered his support in solving, "d'une manière définitive, les graves difficultés qui entravaient depuis plusieurs années la marche des affaires."[36] For this condition Confederation was "le seul remède." It was necessary, therefore, to place "dans la balance les graves intérêts qui demandent cette union. . . ."[37]

Joseph Cauchon's work in *Le Journal de Québec* was rather different. Cauchon was a less thoughtful writer, for he had the swashbuckling manner of the journalist; he can be compared, not unfairly, with Jonathan McCully, the editor of the Halifax *Morning Chronicle*. Both Cauchon and McCully had the quick pen, the ready simile, the slashing style of the newspaperman. Both were politicians, but they were better editors. Both commanded powerful engines: the Halifax *Morning Chronicle* and *Le Journal de Québec* can be aptly compared in both circulation and influence. *Le Journal* was one of the most widely read of all the French papers,[38] and the only daily among them. Cauchon himself was thought by one correspondent to be "the ablest political writer in Lower Canada . . . [and] represents the feelings and aspirations of the great majority of the French people of Lower Canada."[39]

In 1858 Cauchon had praised the Canadian legislative union as logical, practical, and inexpensive. At that time he thought a federal union of the colonies was useless, for Canada had no need to change her political *métier*. If a change was necessary, even "rep. by pop." would be better than a federal union for the federal principle was no protection for a state or a province, as the centralizing tendencies of American history proved. "La constitution des Etats-Unis [est] impuissante à

[35]*Le Courrier du Canada*, 5 déc. 1864, "La Confédération," I.
[36]*Ibid.*, 9 déc. 1864, "La Confédération," III.
[37]*Ibid.*, 25 jan. 1865, "La Confédération," XXI.
[38]According to the Liberal Montreal *Herald* (July 28, 1864), the three most influential French papers were *Le Journal de Québec*, *La Minerve*, and *Le Canadien*.
[39]Saint John *Morning Telegraph*, Dec. 19, 1864, report of Dec. 9 from Quebec.

protéger l'état chez eux. . . . ."[40] In other words, in 1858, Cauchon felt
no cause to support the constitutional revolution that the Galt proposals envisaged. The imperial power was still prepared to defend
Canada, and the dangers of provincial isolation in an unfriendly world
were not yet obvious.

By 1864, however, Cauchon believed these conditions no longer
obtained. The powerful external forces that were brought to bear on
Canada seemed to act upon Cauchon, as upon so many others, as
hydraulic pressure, overcoming inertia, forcing changes, bending principles. In 1864 Confederation seemed to Cauchon the only choice, save
annexation to the United States. It was too early for British North
American union, really—the colonies were not ready for it—but there
was nothing else to be done. It was a case of union or annihilation.[41]
Cauchon accepted and explained the Quebec Resolutions in the light of
this necessity. His interpretation of them was more like Macdonald's
than that of such other Bleu papers as *Le Courrier du Canada*. Legislative union was the most logical form union could take; that being
impossible, it was still desirable, nevertheless, that Confederation should
be highly centralized. "Oui! le projet de constitution de la convention
de Québec, dans son ensemble, a été sagement conçu! Oui, la pré-
pondérance de l'unité dans la constitution, avec les conditions qui
l'accompagnent, est préférable, à tous les points de vue, à la souve-
raineté des Etats. . . !"[42] Fortunately British North America had the
means of avoiding the dangers that were latent in the American constitution. French Canadians must have the will to establish "notre
nationalité future [British North American] sur des bases plus fermes,
des éléments plus homogènes et des principes plus indissolubles."[43]

Cauchon did not envisage conflicts between the central and the local
governments. The veto, which alarmed some French Canadians, was
not for Cauchon a serious danger. Its abuse could be averted, he felt,
by the action of French-Canadian members in the federal parliament.
Many Bleus took a similar view. It was characteristic to look to the
central legislature, or to the central cabinet, for redress of constitutional abuses. *Le Courrier du Canada* said blithely, January 13, 1865,
that there would be no arbitrary exercise of the veto power by the central

---

[40]J. Cauchon, *Étude sur l'union projetée des provinces britanniques du nord*
(Québec, 1858), 11, 16.
[41]J. Cauchon, *L'Union des provinces de l'Amérique britannique du nord*
(Québec, 1865), 30. Reprinted from *Le Journal de Québec*; this particular
reference, 20 déc. 1864, "Le Projet de constitution de la convention de Québec," 7.
[42]Cauchon, *Union des provinces*, 51.
[43]*Ibid.*, 54.

government; "dans le gouvernement fédéral nous aurons des ministres pour défendre nos droits, si jamais il arrivait que le droit de réserve fut exercé d'une manière arbitraire." Cartier in the Confederation debates crossed swords with the redoubtable Christopher Dunkin on this point.

Mr. DUNKIN— . . . there is the grand power of disallowance by the Federal Government, which we are told, in one and the same breath, is to be possessed by it, but never exercised.

Hon. Atty. Gen. CARTIER—The presumption is, it will be exercised in case of unjust or unwise legislation.

MR. DUNKIN—The hon. gentleman's presumption reminds me of one, perhaps as conclusive, but which DICKENS tells us failed to satisfy his Mr. BUMBLE . . . that a man's wife acts under his control:—"If the law presumes anything of the sort, the law's a fool—a natural fool! (Laughter)[44]

That effectively silenced Cartier. As J. B. E. Dorion shrewdly observed, "from the moment that you bring the exercise of the right of *veto* more nearly within the reach of interested parties, you increase the number of opportunities for the exercise of the right—you open the door to intrigues."[45]

Le Canadien of Quebec tended to be philosophical, and it may perhaps be the best index to the temper of the French. While compared to the Maritime provinces there was not much opposition in French Canada, there was not much enthusiasm either.[46] *Le Canadien* (February 3, 1865) reveals very well this faintly melancholy state of mind. "Nous avons donc accepté la confédération sans inutile regrets pour le passé, sans vaines craintes pour l'avenir, mais aussi sans enthousiasme, résolus seulement à nous en tirer le mieux que nous pourrions. . . ."

The French Bleus were, generally speaking, distinguished by a genuine sympathy with the principle of co-ordinate authority. *Le Journal de Québec* leaned toward centralization and *Le Canadien* away from it, but both, together with *Le Courrier du Canada*, *Le Courrier de St. Hyacinthe*, and later, in 1865, the new *Journal des Trois Rivières*, can be considered useful sources for a coherent and not unintelligible theory of federal government. *La Minerve*'s views tended to be rather derivative and did not seem especially distinguished by anything, save what the *True Witness* called, in a moment of exasperation, "mutton-like

[44]*Confederation Debates*, 502. Dunkin was only slightly misquoting *Oliver Twist*.

[45]*Ibid.*, 860. (Original italics)

[46]Cf. also R. Rumilly, *Histoire de la province de Québec*. I. *George-Etienne Cartier* (Montreal, n.d.), 36.

innocence."[47] While the early views of the Bleu papers, those in July, August, and September of 1864, were unquestionably in favour of a more decentralized constitution than that projected in the Quebec Resolutions, their later readings of the Resolutions themselves were fair enough. The Quebec Resolutions were perfectly susceptible of the "federalist" interpretation given them by the Bleu papers. Different interpretations were possible, and the different views of the English-Canadian and French-Canadian papers reflected the penumbra of uncertainty that surrounded a document that assumed so much, left so much inexplicit, as the Quebec Resolutions did. It must also be said that Taché, Cartier, Langevin, all cabinet ministers in the existing Canadian government, felt that the presence of French-Canadian ministers in the future central cabinet was guarantee sufficient to resolve any difficulty that might involve the rights of the French. That the future was often to prove them right does not alter the fact that constitutionally it was a precarious doctrine, impossible to define precisely.

Doubts on this and other points assailed the Rouges. They were alarmed about the danger to French-Canadian privileges, and they opposed Confederation as an attempt to swallow up the sectional—and perhaps temporary—difficulties of Canada in a grandiose and haphazard union of British North America. Such a proceeding was replete with dangers for French Canada, and Dorion was not convinced that Cartier was fully aware of them. The Rouge view of federation was based upon the concept of the sovereign province, and a devolutionary central government. Some Rouge statements, particularly those of J. B. E. Dorion, reflected the American ideas that had been a tradition in the party. *L'Avenir*, an early paper of J. B. E. Dorion, had looked frankly to union with the United States as the natural destiny of British America.[48] In the opposition to Confederation Rouge sympathy with American ideas flared up again. The moderate *L'Ordre* said, June 7, 1865, "nous n'hésitons pas à le dire . . . qu'à tous les points de vue, nos institutions, notre langue, et nos lois seront mieux protégées avec la confédération américaine qu'avec le projet de confédération de l'Amérique Britannique du Nord." In the United States, Canada East would be a sovereign state: in British North America, only a municipality.[49] But the Rouges did not urge such arguments very

[47]Montreal *True Witness*, Dec. 16, 1864.

[48]*L'Avenir* stopped publication in 1853, and Dorion apparently did not return to newspaper work again until he founded *Le Défricheur* in 1862.

[49]Montreal *Ordre*, 12 juin 1865. Cf. also the annexation movement in Canada West, *infra*, 158–9.

strongly. The United States was too unpopular. A. A. Dorion's paper, *Le Pays*, was not convinced that suggestions of annexation were practicable. J. B. E. Dorion, though he said Canada East would be better off as a state similar to Louisiana than as the province of Quebec, insisted none the less that he was not advocating annexation. Nor, he added, did the French people desire it.[50]

The Rouges frankly preferred the old Union of the Canadas. Nearly all the public meetings they stirred up on Confederation included in their proceedings a resolution stressing the great advantages of keeping the Union. There was no need for a change: sectional difficulties were only minor and were "susceptibles d'une solution équitable,"[51] not one as dangerous and extreme as Confederation. Some of the resolutions of a public meeting in St. Jean-sur-Richelieu, on December 20, 1864, will suggest the state of mind of the Rouges:

Que la confédération . . . n'est ni nécessaire ni désirable . . .
Que nous devons être, au reste, prêts à accorder au Haut-Canada toutes les reclamations légitimes qu'il espère obtenir au moyen de la représentation basée sur la population . . .
Que le système proposé aurait l'avantage de ne pas augmenter les dépenses . . . de remédier aux griefs actuels et de ne faire à la constitution que les changements nécessités par les circonstances au lieu de nous livrer aux hasards d'un avenir inconnu.[52]

Several Rouge public meetings advocated similar concessions to Upper Canada. Probably many French Canadians, when brought face to face with Confederation, wished heartily that they had conceded something to the demands of Canada West before the movement had gone to such lengths. The attempt to keep the Union intact was now failing, and the Rouges could only see in the vast changes unrolled before their eyes by Confederation, evils of the direst consequences: "la langue française noyée, la réligion persécutée, la nationalité submergée, la race franco-canadienne bafoulée et maltraitée, ses droits ravis, ses libertés foulées aux pieds. . . ."[53] It may be, as Skelton suggested, that the Rouges professed an anxiety they did not entirely feel.[54] It

[50]*Confederation Debates*, 870–1.
[51]Montreal *Union Nationale*, 6 fév. 1865, report of a meeting of L'Institut Canadien-Français, 30 jan. 1865. This institute was formed in 1858 by the withdrawal of 150 members of L'Institut Canadien, over the question of immoral books.
[52] *Le Pays*, 27 déc. 1864. In December and January *Le Pays* reported a large number of public meetings, especially in the eastern townships. Note, however, the complaints against the way the meetings were held, by J. H. Bellerose (Laval), *Confederation Debates*, 477–8.
[53]*Le Pays*, 5 août, 1865.
[54]O. D. Skelton, *The Life and Times of Sir Alexander Tilloch Galt* (Toronto, 1920), 364.

would, however, be fairer to say that the anxiety they felt was not entirely due to Confederation. The Saint John *Telegraph* put it succinctly: "Their present violence is an indication of the desperate condition of their cause."[55] They were cut off from their natural alliances in Canada West by Brown's coalition with the Bleus. How often must Dorion have looked across the floor at the serried ranks of the Coalition, Conservatives, Bleus, Reformers, and speculated on the strange turn of affairs!

Fortunately for Dorion, there were ranged beside him some formidable English critics, mostly Liberals like Luther Holton, though Christopher Dunkin was a Conservative. The English critics were by no means powerless for they commanded about half the English newspapers of Montreal. The paper closest to the Rouges in sympathy was the weekly Catholic journal, the Montreal *True Witness*, edited by G. E. Clerk, who had been educated at Eton and had come to Montreal in 1848. In many ways, it was superior to the Rouge papers. The Rouges were preoccupied with the defence of French nationality; the *True Witness* took a larger, Catholic view,[56] and its analysis of Confederation was quite the ablest in Canada.[57] Like the Rouges, the *True Witness* would have preferred the old Union to continue, but if there was to be a change outright repeal of the Union was the only sensible course. Not even a federation would suit Canadian conditions. The two Canadas stood to each other as South to North; their differences lay deep in their aspirations and their point of view.[58] Canada East wanted her institutions and her religion, Canada West a Protestant ascendancy. Between these views there could be no compatibility; no system made could provide for such divergences.[59] In any case the Quebec Resolutions were full of anomalies and crotchets. Why not a Senate on some systematic basis?[60] "Wherein lies the utility, what is the meaning, of an Upper House named virtually . . . by a majority for the time being of the Lower House?" The answer unfortunately was all too obvious: "the delegates had not, never seem to have had, any clear or definite idea of what constitutes Federation."[61]

It was ironic that Confederation should have thrust the *True Witness*,

[55]Saint John *Morning Telegraph*, Dec. 19, 1864, report of Dec. 9 from Quebec.
[56]The *True Witness* was founded in 1850. See Agnes Coffey, "The *True Witness and Catholic Chronicle*," Canadian Catholic Historical Association, *Report*, 1937–8, 33–46. R. Rumilly says that the *True Witness* was founded at the suggestion of Bishop Bourget. (Rumilly, *Cartier*, 38.)
[57]*Supra*, 109, 112.
[58]Montreal *True Witness*, June 24, 1864.
[59]*Ibid.*, July 1, 1864.
[60]The London *Times* also made this point, Feb. 21, 1867.
[61]Montreal *True Witness*, Nov. 4, 1864.

Irish Catholic in sympathy, into the company of the Montreal *Witness*, which was Scottish Protestant. Cartier amused the House with the irony. "The *True Witness* . . ." he observed, "said that if it [Confederation] were adopted the French Canadians were doomed; while his brother in violence, the *Witness*, said that the Protestants were doomed. (Hear, hear, and laughter.)"[62] The *Witness* was basically a religious paper, but it had a large circulation and it was one of the two Montreal dailies opposed to Confederation. Its principal *bêtes noires* were "Popery, Slavery, and Rum," to which might be added the Grand Trunk Railway. Its political comment was limited by its preoccupations, and it never ceased to preach the wickedness of Brown's coalition with the Bleus, which would leave the Protestants of Lower Canada at the mercy of the Catholics when Confederation should establish a provincial legislature in Canada East.[63] Like some other English Protestants, it preferred the Union left as it was.

The Montreal *Herald*, the favourite daily of many of the commercial interests of Montreal, followed a similar line. It tended to reflect the views of Luther Holton and the English Liberals generally. Thus the Montreal *True Witness*, *Witness*, and *Herald* were joined to the French journals in Montreal opposed to Confederation, and together they constituted the "very considerable influence [that] is being brought against the project in Montreal."[64]

Indeed, the forces against Confederation by December, 1864, were not inconsiderable. To the refractory members of the Conservative and Reform parties of Canada West were added the Rouges, some uneasy Bleus, and the forceful English Liberals of Canada East. Rumours of opposition began to spread.[65]

Thus the crisis in American relations came at an opportune time. The dismissal of the St. Alban's raiders by C. J. Coursol, the Montreal magistrate, on December 14, was an affront to the United States.[66] It did not help matters when it was learned that Coursol was married to the Premier's daughter. Actually, for the release of the St. Alban's prisoners the Canadian government was not primarily responsible, and it rapidly did what it could to make amends. The raiders were re-arrested. The next most obvious step was to secure the border: first against further attempts by Confederate soldiers to take refuge in Canada from acts of violence against Northern civilians; second, to

[62]*Confederation Debates*, 61.
[63]Montreal *Witness*, July 2, 1864.
[64]Saint John *Morning Telegraph*, Dec. 19, 1864, report of Dec. 9 from Quebec.
[65]*Quebec Daily News*, Nov. 30, 1864.
[66]*Supra*, 31–2.

prevent Northern soldiers from pursuit upon Canadian soil; and third, against possible raids by the Fenians, who were reported readying an attack for January 15.[67] "There is great excitement in Canada," wrote the Saint John *Telegraph*'s correspondent on December 19. "Rumours of war abound. The people are aroused. . . . Between the Raiders, the Fenians, General Dix, intercepted telegrams,[68] the order for thirty Companies of Canadian Militia . . . the good people of Canada are having a lively time."[69] Two thousand volunteers were called out. Troops left Quebec on Monday, December 26 amid the greatest concourse of people seen since the visit of the Prince of Wales in 1860.[70] The volunteers were not very sure of whom they might be fighting; if anyone, they thought it would be the belligerent Yankees. At Toronto Major-General G. T. C. Napier felt obliged to remind his troops that they were being called upon to aid the civil power in controlling the border rather than to defend Canada against a Yankee invasion. It would also appear that the dispositions of the militia were designed to create as much sensation as possible, perhaps with the purpose of extracting the maximum political advantage abroad, and be it added, at home. The volunteers from Quebec, with additions from Montreal and Brockville, were sent westward through Toronto to Windsor. A large crowd turned out in Toronto to see them —400 men and officers, dressed in dark grey overcoats and fur caps. Companies from Woodstock, Canada West, were sent eastward to Vermont. Volunteers from Barrie and Collingwood went down to Niagara.[71] By January, 1865, some 2,000 Canadian militia were stationed along the American border. In the meantime, orders for the re-arrest of the prisoners had brought them into custody once more; Coursol was suspended pending an inquiry; and when Parliament opened, on January 19, the Canadian Government proposed, in the Speech from the Throne, to reimburse the St. Alban's banks, and to pass an act to close the loophole in the extradition provisions.

For this purpose, and for Confederation, the Government marshalled its forces. It would tolerate no refractoriness. During the last week in January it had been stiffening its supporters, and when the Alien Bill

[67]Macdonald Papers, memorandum of Dec. 17, 1864. Also in R. W. Winks, *Canada and the United States: The Civil War Years* (Baltimore, 1960), 324–5.

[68]From the Confederate Commissioner, C. C. Clay, to confrères in Halifax and elsewhere. See Winks, *Canada and the United States*, 277.

[69]Saint John *Morning Telegraph*, Dec. 29, 1864, report of Dec. 19 from Quebec.

[70]Quebec *Morning Chronicle*, Dec. 27, 29, 1864.

[71]*Globe*, Dec. 27, 1864; *Leader*, Dec. 27, 1864.

was brought in on February 1, it passed in short order by the thumping majority of 107–7.[72] It was a display of power that Canadians had not seen for many a year. The day after it passed, the Premier, Sir Etienne Taché, rose in the Legislative Council to introduce the Quebec Resolutions to the Canadian Parliament.

Sir Etienne Taché is a shadowy figure whose views, while screened by his native urbanity, have been suggested in *Le Courrier du Canada*. "Under a refinement of manners only too unusual in this age," wrote the Montreal *Gazette*, "he concealed a latent fire and determination of character. . . ."[73] In 1864 Taché had sought neither place nor power. He had loved his retreat from the buffetings of public life, but had yielded to the solicitations of his friends and had become Premier.[74] He was now almost seventy; his hair was white; and on this occasion his startling feebleness of voice suggested he was not far removed from the grave. He spoke with candour and earnestness, in a singularly impressive style.[75] It was a wise and tolerant speech, and its brief five pages at the beginning of the *Confederation Debates* recall a kindly and dignified old man, who moved lightly and gracefully through the portentous passions of the time. Macdonald, who knew him well, gave him a glowing tribute at the time of Taché's death, July 30, 1865. He was, said Macdonald, "as pure and open-hearted as the day; and as sincere and truly honorable a gentleman as ever moved in public or private life."[76]

The Confederation debates were remarkable in many ways. That they were recorded at all was an indication of the Canadian government's determination to give them all the weight the occasion demanded. No other Canadian debates were so reported.[77] They also gave an opportunity for every member, if he wanted, to speak for the record, and over a thousand stout, double-columned pages show the advantage

[72]The division on 3rd reading. Canada, Assembly, *Journals*, 1865, 62 (Feb. 2). The division on second reading was 104–4.

[73]Montreal *Gazette*, Oct. 28, 1864.

[74]Montreal *Evening Telegraph*, quoted by Belleville *Intelligencer*, April 1, 1864.

[75]Saint John *Weekly Telegraph*, Feb. 15, 1865, report of Feb. 4 from Quebec.

[76]Belleville *Intelligencer*, Aug. 4, 1865, reporting a speech of Macdonald's in Kingston.

[77]Nova Scotia and Prince Edward Island regularly, and New Brunswick intermittently, reported their debates. Note the following from the Saint John *Daily Evening Globe*, Feb. 19, 1864: "The House of Assembly has resolved not to have any authorized debates published this year. This is quite right. The official debates were always a great humbug. Nobody read them but the reporters who wrote them; the members for whom they were written . . . and the unfortunate proof readers who put the finishing stroke upon them."

that they took of it.[78] The debates were held at a critical time; many of the speakers felt powerfully the circumstances that made vital, perhaps imperative, some change in the isolated helplessness of the North American British colonies. Cartier's remarks were suggestive of many others. "Confederation was . . . at this moment almost forced upon us. We could not shut our eyes to what was going on beyond the lines. . . . We could not deny that the struggle now in progress must necessarily influence our political existence."[79] After the ministerial speeches many an aspiring member followed, and ultimately it was the opposition speeches that aroused the most interest. The newspapers liked both Dunkin and J. B. E. Dorion, the former for his comprehensiveness and mastery, the latter for his incisiveness.

Christopher Dunkin was an independent Conservative, the member for Brome County, on the American border in Canada East. On Monday night, February 27, 1865, and the next night, Dunkin delivered a criticism of the Quebec Resolutions that towers over every other. A thin, sick, tired little man, a "bag of bones" as one correspondent described him,[80] he stood there, for four hours each night. His speech was comprehensive, it was exhaustive, and it showed Confederation as a shambling, illogical mixture of compromises and rule-of-thumb methods. Dunkin could not, did not, believe that in seventeen days thirty-three gentlemen could contrive a constitution that was a judicious blend of the best in the British and American systems. Far from the Quebec Resolutions having taken the best in each, Dunkin maintained they had taken the worst, and this, together with concessions to Lower Canada and compromises for the benefit of the Maritimes, had produced an indescribable jumble. Dunkin's speech was largely devoted to showing what these weaknesses were and what would be their effect in the future. He could not believe either that the haste with which Confederation had been suggested, put together, and brought before the House was justified by the nature of the project or by the circumstances of the time. Nothing good would come from such haste, and much that was anything but good. This provoked McGee to remark, "If 'twere done, 'twere well 'twere done quickly." McGee must have realized as soon as he spoke that the allusion was unfortunate. Dunkin retorted that McGee was a good

[78]The cost of printing them came nearly to the total of the bills for entertaining the Quebec Conference, $14,490.65. (Canada, Assembly, *Journals*, 1865, Appendix 2, 15.)

[79]*Confederation Debates*, 55; for Taché on the same thing, *ibid.*, 7; Macdonald, 32; Brown, 114; McGee, 131.

[80]London (C.W.) *Canadian Free Press*, March 10, 1865, report of Feb. 28 and March 1 from Quebec, signed "Fag." Dunkin lived however until 1881.

enough scholar to know that it was to something very bad. "The hon. gentleman is welcome to all he can make of his quotation. . . ."[81]

Even the Montreal *Gazette*, March 6, 1865, although a little pained at Dunkin's desertion of the Conservatives, admitted that Dunkin's speech was a perfect chart of all the shoals and reefs ahead of Confederation. The Oshawa *Vindicator*, March 8, thought it the ablest of all the speeches. So did the St. Thomas *Dispatch* (May 18). "What a pity," said the *London Free Press* correspondent, "Mr. Dunkin was not made a Minister . . . and what a vast improvement the scheme of union would have shown upon its present bungling and crude condition if he had been called to aid Her Majesty's Councils. . . ."[82]

By this time almost a month had elapsed, and gradually after Dunkin's speech an air of weariness crept over the debate. It was said that the Opposition were talking against time in order to circulate petitions against Confederation. The Quebec *Chronicle* lamented:

The Confederation discussion is growing wofully [*sic*] stale; not a new idea is to be coined and honorable gentlemen are doomed to talk to the clock and empty benches of the Legislative Chambers. . . . In truth the question of the Union of the Provinces . . . is worn threadbare, and no one cares to listen to vain repetitions, worse and worse, presented as each fresh speaker brings the dead carcase of a worn-out argument to fill up the leaden periods he is endeavoring to make acceptable to an unwilling and wearied audience.[83]

This was Monday, March 6. The debate, it is true, was becoming insufferable, dragging its slow length along at about three hours a day. On February 24 there were only 20 members present—a bare quorum;[84] and although Dunkin had enlivened things, the debate soon resumed its heavy plodding while the Belleroses and the Fergusons addressed their constituents "at Buncome town." On March 7, John A. Macdonald moved the previous question. He did so on grounds of defence; it was desirable that Canadian ministers be in England as soon as possible to discuss defence and Confederation. But there was another reason. The defeat of Tilley in New Brunswick had been revealed over that weekend —gleefully announced to the House at 3 A.M. Saturday, March 4, by Sandfield Macdonald.

The full extent of Tilley's defeat was not yet known, but defeat it was. At one stroke the headlong progress of Confederation was suddenly

[81]For Dunkin's speech see *Confederation Debates*, 482–544.

[82]*Canadian Free Press*, March 10, 1865, report of March 1 from Quebec, by "Fag."

[83]Quebec *Morning Chronicle*, March 6, 1865. Cf. also Montreal *Gazette*, March 9, 1865; Barrie *Northern Advance*, March 15, 1865.

[84]*Stratford Beacon*, March 3, 1865, report of Feb. 25 from Quebec.

stopped. Confederation could survive the troubles that were besetting it in Prince Edward Island, the uncertainties that were appearing in Newfoundland—the immediate adhesion of those two colonies was not vital—but in Nova Scotia Tupper could only get Confederation through the House provided New Brunswick passed it.[85] New Brunswick had in fact torpedoed Confederation. The ship was still afloat, but she could have little steerage way until the damage was rectified.

In Canada, where New Brunswick had been counted for a dead certainty,[86] the Government was staggered and the Opposition much heartened. The defeat of Tilley gave them new hope, and the monotonous tenor of the debate was now enlivened with strong bucking from the Opposition. Sandfield Macdonald, Holton, Dorion, and others sprang into life; Macdonald's moving of the previous question and the New Brunswick defeat gave them a pair of weapons with which to attack the Government. It was in these circumstances that J. B. E. Dorion made his speech, one which even the government press admitted was remarkable.[87] Dorion was trenchant and ironic by turns. Paul Denis, who followed him, had to admit his cleverness at agitation and the skilful distortion of the Government's position.[88] "Could you inform me, Mr. SPEAKER," Dorion asked, "what has become of the $100,000 question?"[89] Swallowed up in the scandalous Coalition, was Dorion's own answer. The Canadian constitution had hampered the "curvetings and prancings of our leading chiefs too much,"[90] and it was therefore abandoned and by a piece of legerdemain that denied every political principle.

None of the Opposition, Dunkin and Dorion included, had much to suggest as a substitute for Confederation. Yet a return to the old state of affairs was probably impossible. The Reform party had come too far. "He must be a sanguine man," said the Montreal *Gazette*, March 3, 1865, "who thinks that, after an acknowledgement that Upper Canada is entitled . . . to seventeen more members than Lower Canada, the agitation can ever again be quelled." The Opposition that Dunkin and the Dorions offered was criticism, able certainly; but they had little to substitute for the measure they so effectively ridiculed. Their real work

[85]So Tupper told Gordon when in Fredericton, in June, 1865. P.R.O., Cardwell Papers, Gordon to Cardwell, June 5, 1865 (private).
[86]*Stratford Beacon*, March 10, 1865, report of March 6 from Quebec.
[87]Hamilton *Spectator*, March 10, 1865.
[88]*Confederation Debates*, 872.
[89]This was a reference to the reputedly unauthorized advance of this amount to the City of Montreal by the Conservative government, which had caused the defeat of the Government on June 14, 1864.
[90]*Confederation Debates*, 857–8.

was in pointing out the problems that faced Confederation, and to render the supporters of it if possible less complacent. The Confederation debate ended early on Saturday morning, March 11, with recalcitrant desk-rattling, whispering and bird singing from some members when the speaker was not to their taste.[91] A lively account of the last hours of the debate was given by the Parliamentary correspondent of the *Stratford Beacon*:

. . . the House was in an unmistakeably seedy condition, having, as it was positively declared, eaten the saloon keeper clean out, drunk him entirely dry, and got all the fitful naps of sleep that the benches along the passages could be made to yield. For who cared at one, two, three, and four in the morning, to sit in the House, to hear the stale talk of Mr. Ferguson, of South Simcoe, or to listen even to the polished and pointed sentences of Mr. Huntingdon? Men with the strongest constitutions for Parliamentary twaddle were sick of the debate, and the great bulk of the members were scattered about the building, with an up-all-night, get-tight-in-the morning air, impatient for the sound of the division bell. It rang at last, at quarter past four, and the jaded representatives of the people swarmed in to the discharge of the most important duty of all their lives.[92]

At 4:30 A.M. the main motion was agreed to, 91–33.[93] At this the House broke into ringing cheers, and as the Speaker was leaving the Chair the French Canadian members burst out with some old paddling song, the English Canadians following with "The Queen," and the whole bawled forth with the same sorry energy characteristic of the fag end of a public dinner. And over by the St. Charles River the convent bell was ringing five as the members trooped wearily home to their lodgings.[94]

With the end of the session and the departure of Macdonald, Brown, Cartier, and Galt for England in April,[95] came also the end of the American Civil War. There was a sudden stir caused by Lincoln's assassination—the *Globe* came out in black[96]—but gradually, imperceptibly perhaps, a calm descended on Canadian politics. Confederation had been passed; Canada West had accepted it even before the session had ended.[97] As the *Newmarket Era* said on March 17, "With us here

[91]Joseph Cauchon had an irritating habit of imitating bird calls in late sittings of the House. (Oshawa *Vindicator*, March 15, 1865). In later years he seems to have taken up the Jew's harp. (G. W. Ross, *Getting into Parliament and After* (Toronto, 1913), 82.)

[92]*Stratford Beacon*, March 17, 1865, report of March 11 from Quebec.

[93]*Confederation Debates*, 962; Canada, Assembly, *Journals*, 1865, 191.

[94]*Stratford Beacon*, March 17, 1865, report of March 11 from Quebec.

[95]Cartier and Galt went with C. J. Brydges, via Halifax. See *infra*, 214–15.

[96]Several papers did, as far west as Vancouver Island.

[97]Goderich *Signal*, March 7, 1865.

in Upper Canada the plan of Confederation was received by the greater part of the people from its very inauguration at the Conference. . . ." By June, 1865, Canadians found themselves upon as calm a sea as they had known for years. If in politics a calm precedes a storm, wrote *Le Canadien*, June 16, 1865, then there is going to be a hurricane, "car d'un bout à l'autre de la province l'opinion publique est plongée dans un répos profond." But there was no storm. Not even the Rouges could stir one up. News seemed almost to die out: "peu de nouvelles; les journaux sont réduits à la famine. . . ." This was the theme of the monthly events column in *La Revue Canadienne*.[98]

What remained was to convince the Maritimes to accept Confederation. That was not going to be easy, but there seemed little Canadians could do at the moment except to encourage and to hope. They were helpless to effect changes in the Maritimers, who were, as one paper said with a fine disregard of geography, "a perverse people, stubborn and stern as their snow-capped mountains and inhospitable valleys. . . .[99]

The perversities of the Maritimers reacted upon Canada. It was at this point—the summer of 1865—that a transitory but significant annexation movement developed briefly in Canada West.[100] It was born out of the apparent hopelessness of the political impasse in which Canada West found itself. Confederation seemed to be nowhere, and a few journals began to wonder what future Canada West could have in an empire where Britain was so willing to let her North American colonies go, or in a Canada where effective government now appeared an impossibility. The St. Catharines *Post* came out flatly for annexation;[101] the *Galt Reporter* temporarily cast eyes in the same direction.[102] There was also the fear that Canada might become a battleground between Great Britain and the United States, with Canada losing no matter who won. This was the attitude of the Belleville *Hastings Chronicle*.[103] The Hamilton *Times* reflected gloomily that in a country that was all frontier defence was impossible. "We cannot afford to have the spectacle of Denmark played over again. . . . in no case will Canadians consent to take part in a war of which the issue would be,

[98]*La Revue Canadienne*, juin 1865, 380.
[99]*Perth Courier*, March 17, 1865.
[100]For Canada East, *supra*, 147–8.
[101]The relevant issues of the *Post* no longer exist, but there are numerous references to its point of view in the Niagara *Mail*, notably Oct. 4, Oct. 18, 1865.
[102]*Galt Reporter* quoted in Toronto *Globe*, May 16, 1865; also in Toronto *Irish Canadian*, May 17, 1865; *Berliner Journal*, 18 Mai, 1865.
[103]Belleville *Hastings Chronicle*, in *Le Pays*, 10 juin 1865. But the *Hastings Chronicle* opposed annexation in 1866 when it appeared in the form of the Banks Bill. (*Hastings Chronicle*, Aug. 1, 1866.)

to them, hopeless defeat."[104] At the Detroit Convention, in July, 1865,[105] Hon. Malcolm Cameron underlined this point. "I would not spend one shilling for defence. (Applause.) I dare say this will be reported to our government, and I have a nice fat office under it[106] . . . but I say we want no defence except 12½ or 14 feet of tide water in the sill[s of our canals]."[107]

And the end of the Reciprocity Treaty that loomed ahead was already worrying Canadians. The efforts made by them, and the Maritimers, in the next nine months to forestall the abrogation of the treaty were a good indication of the concern of all British North Americans for their commercial future; and concern for their political future was an inescapable concomitant. Alexander Campbell wrote pessimistically to Macdonald from Kingston: "I trust that you may succeed [with Confederation and defence]—the country is depressed beyond example —and men talk of annexation who a few months ago would have resented as an insult any imputation of the sentiments they now openly profess. Our Quebec Conference has certainly had a marked influence in directing men's thoughts to the alternatives before the country."[108] The alternatives were Confederation or annexation, and there seemed little enough hope for the former. "How light and worthless . . . are all the fruits of the British connection," wrote a Canadian correspondent in the *New York Tribune*; Canada is the "coon up the tree": Uncle Sam had only to wait at the bottom, for down Canada must come.[109] Perhaps the over-all influence and extent of the annexation movement in 1865 has been made too much of; Campbell's letter, for example, represented in part the pessimism of an often gloomy state of mind; but though the movement was small and ephemeral, it was real enough. With Canadian national consciousness still weak, annexation

[104]Hamilton *Times*, quoted in *London Evening Advertiser*, March 18, 1865 and March 15, 1865. The reference to Denmark is of course the Schleswig-Holstein war.

[105]See *infra*, 215–16.

[106]Malcolm Cameron (1808–76), former Clear Grit Politician, was Queen's Printer, 1863–9.

[107]*London Evening Advertiser*, July 14, 1865, reporting speech of July 12.

[108]J. Pope, ed., *Correspondence of Sir John Macdonald* (Toronto, 1921), 26, Campbell to Macdonald, May 18, 1865.

Note the following comment on the Canadian annexation movement, by the Victoria (Vancouver Island) *Weekly Chronicle*: "Let the people of the Colonies only understand that by annexation they must . . . abandon that happy mean they now enjoy betwen the arbitrariness of English institutions on the one hand, and the tyranny of the many in democratic America on the other. . . ." (July 18, 1865)

[109]*New York Tribune*, Aug. 4, 1865, letter from Montreal July 30.

movements, however ephemeral, could not be taken lightly. Annexationism was in fact a chronic condition, outbreaks of which could be expected "when ever the country is afflicted with bad harvests, and financial depressions"; in this case it was aggravated by "the temporary failure of the Confederation scheme. . . ."[110] Love of country, said the *London Evening Advertiser*, "grows naturally from attachment to home, and the home feeling is so weak among us, partly because the country is so new, and partly because of the migratory habits of the population. . . . where is the Canadian who will not sell out if only he gets his price?"[111]

However, Consul-General J. F. Potter's senseless and provocative speech at Detroit in favour of annexation had given Canadians a fine opportunity of getting up a little loyal indignation,[112] and Macdonald's appeal, in his Ottawa speech of September 28, 1865, was designed to encourage Canadians to a more positive view. Macdonald was possessed of an unpretentious but genuine nationalism. He was not given to oratory. He distrusted it, as he distrusted all splendid pomposity. But he was quite prepared to use it, and he was not without his own brand of it.

You may read in the papers about obstructions in one colony or another, but I do not speak incautiously . . . when I say that the union of all the Provinces is a fixed fact. . . . The mere struggle for office and fight for position—the difference between the "outs" and the "ins" have no charms for me; but now I have something worth fighting for—and that is the junction of Her Majesty's subjects in all British North America as one great nation. . . .[113]

When hopes for Confederation could be renewed, when the Fenian menace began to develop, and when the good harvest of 1865 was gathered in, the annexation movement would gradually slow and disappear, to set in and disappear again in years to come.

But the Canadian doldrums did not go unnoticed. On September 14, 1865, there was a stinging editorial from the London *Times* on the apathy of the Canadian people on the question of Confederation. Canadian replies to this jibe were part acknowledgment, part angry

[110]Belleville *Intelligencer*, May 26, 1865.

[111]*London Evening Advertiser*, Sept. 6, 1865. Cf. J. S. Helmcken's remarks in British Columbia, *infra*, 321.

[112]Goderich *Signal*, July 28, 1865; also *London Evening Advertiser*, Aug. 1, 1865. J. F. Potter was appointed American Consul-General in Montreal in July, 1864.

[113]Ottawa *Citizen*, Sept. 29, 1865. Cf. also Macdonald's speech in Halifax, Sept. 12, 1864, *supra*, 80.

denials. The St. Thomas *Dispatch*, October 15, agreed there was a great deal of apathy on the subject of Confederation, as did *Le Journal de Québec*, October 9: ". . . la politique est en ce moment au calm plat le plus absolu. . . ." The *Globe* (October 2) growled that the *Times* correspondent was only a crotchety old man. Dr. Charles Mackay, the gentleman referred to, was only 51, but he had, it was true, a considerable knack for getting into trouble. The Victoria *Weekly Chronicle* of Vancouver Island suggested that Dr. Mackay had an unhappy affinity for the opinions of unsympathetic minorities.[114] The Montreal *Gazette*, judicious as it often was, remarked on October 6 that Canadians were not apathetic, but it was true that Confederation had been accepted and passed, and there were some natural consequences.

There is no agitation of this subject; there are no public meetings; there is even comparatively little discussion in the press. All that is true enough. But there is a better reason than apathy. Canadians feel they have done all that can be done for the cause. The battle has been fought and won. One very short but brilliant campaign settled it. Why agitate, therefore?

Why indeed? But in the Maritime provinces, where the whole country was "one vast debating school,"[115] it was another story.

---

[114]Victoria *Weekly Chronicle*, Nov. 20, 1865, editorial entitled, "The London Times on Canada."

[115]Belleville *Intelligencer*, Feb. 24, 1865.

11. NEWFOUNDLAND

TO THE EAST WAS Newfoundland, remote and unknown. It was imposing enough in area; even excluding the Labrador it was nearly the size of the other three Maritime colonies put together. Most of it was quite uninhabited. Its coasts were charted, but its interior was an unmapped and forested wilderness of the same haunting brutality as the vastnesses north of Lake Superior, which it rather resembled in character if not in geology. Unfortunately it had less than a vital minimum of arable land. J. B. E. Dorion of Canada was exaggerating when he said that Newfoundland was "utterly useless for cultivation," but he was uncomfortably close to the truth. "The whole island does not produce enough hay for the town of St. John's. . . ."[1] Exaggerated, no doubt, also, but the cargoes of hay and flour that went from Canada and Shea's advertisement for the sale of Canadian butter in the *Newfoundlander*,[2] were indicative. Newfoundland's 65 square miles of cultivated land was not enough even for her small population of 140,000.[3]

This population was settled in the extreme southeastern corner of the province, with three hundred miles of rugged terrain separating it from the Gulf of St. Lawrence. This eastern orientation was partly due to the French Shore which had prevented the active settlement of the west coast.[4] The French Shore stretched from Cape Ray in the extreme southwest along the whole west coast to Cape Norman in the north, and around to Cape St. John in the northeast; it thus included virtually half the huge coastline of the island of Newfoundland. The origin of the French Shore question—as with the Nova Scotian inshore fisheries—was the Treaty of 1783, and the whole issue was a fertile source of exasperations, less between Great Britain and France than between Newfoundland and Great Britain.

[1]Canada, *Confederation Debates* (Quebec, 1865), 861.
[2]St. John's *Newfoundlander*, Nov. 22, 1866.
[3]Newfoundland, Blue Book, 1867, C.O. 199; also Newfoundland censuses, for 1857 and 1869.
[4]By 1869 there were, however, some 5,400 settlers on the west coast.

Newfoundland faced eastward also because of her position as a European fishing station. There were settlements on the Burin and Bonavista peninsulas; however, most of them were concentrated on the Avalon peninsula. In St. John's the west coast of Newfoundland seemed more remote than the Labrador, and Ottawa further away than London.[5] St. John's is at the easternmost point of North America, on a forbidding and mighty coast, where the great cliffs rise out of thirty fathoms of sea upwards for five hundred feet; like implacable sentinels they watch, lonely and austere, over the great ocean. St. John's looked out from its bottle harbour, half hidden behind the rock walls, east along the great circle route's 1,640 miles to Ireland. The town was pitched mainly on the north hillside of the harbour, and seemed to pile up along the harbour edge in a welter of jetties and jobbers; along the cliffs at the harbour entrance the fish sheds and drying racks perched like spiders, half on the grass and rock, half on stilts over the sea. They symbolized the economy of the country, bound up as it was with fishing, fishing largely controlled by the "merchant princes" of St. John's, whose wharves on the harbour were only the back door to their commercial enterprises that faced along Water Street. St. John's had a population of about 30,000, declining rather than growing.[6]

Newfoundland in 1864 was almost destitute. Her fisheries were stricken; her population was demoralized by a grim combination of bad fishing and sheer famine.[7] Newfoundland depended almost altogether on fishing and the seal hunt; a bad spring, a few summer gales, any fortuitous bad luck tipped the scales toward beggary and destitution. The fishing both inshore and on the Grand Banks had been bad all through the early 1860's, and it was to continue so, with slight variations, until 1869. But it was the inshore fishing that was the worst, and this affected the small independent fisherman who clung as precariously to his livelihood as did his home to the rock of the outports. The sealing had been poor. Potatoes were a staple and were picturesquely cultivated on patches of arable land, with cod-heads marking the rows and cod viscera used for fertilizer, but the potatoes were hit with blight. By 1865, one-third of the revenue of Newfoundland was being expended on direct relief. Governor Musgrave proclaimed Friday, January 13, 1865, a day of fasting and humiliation.[8]

[5]Henry Renouf, member for St. John's West, in the Assembly. *Newfoundlander*, Feb. 16, 1865, report debates for Feb. 3.

[6]The population of St. John's dropped from 30,476 in 1857 to 28,850 in 1869. In 1874 it was 31,576.

[7]St. John's *Patriot*, Jan. 6, 1866, reported someone dying of starvation.

[8]St. John's *Day-Book*, Jan. 12, 1865.

Two or three years of difficulties of this kind had already tempered (or numbed) the sharp religious and political asperities of Newfoundland politics. The change may have been attributable also to the fairness of the Hoyles *régime* since it took office in 1861. Hugh Hoyles himself, an able lawyer and a gentleman after Governor Bannerman's own heart, had conned the lessons of the riots of 1861, and his administration, Conservative and Protestant though it certainly was, had tried to mitigate the conspicuous partiality that had hitherto characterized Newfoundland governments. Nevertheless, it is fair to say that the coalition of 1865, which developed after Hoyles' retirement, was evidence as much of the desperate condition of Newfoundland as of the uneasy peace that had settled down in these grim years between Catholic and Protestant.

In these circumstances it was natural that Confederation should appear to some as an unmixed blessing. The attitude of the majority of St. John's newspapers toward Newfoundland's independent future was profoundly pessimistic.

If any one of the Provinces more than another should seek a change, it is this. We do not mean to assert that we should adopt a change blindly, but unlike our Sister Colonies, our circumstances—the condition of our Trade— the depressed state of our people, demand a change, even if Confederation had never been proposed. . . . A state of things so injurious, so anomalous, and so baneful to the well-being of an integral part of a powerful state would command decisive measures, and the power and authority of the General Government would not be fruitless, though our local means have failed.[9]

If Confederation would only sweep away "this serfdom," said the *Day-Book* on November 30, 1864, "if it shall be the broom which will thoroughly purge this Augean stable—piled up with pauperism, nurtured, fostered, cherished pauperism,[10]—piled up too with dirty exclusiveness . . . then we say by all means let us have Confederation, or anything else that will promise relief." The bitterness reflected the disgust of a widely read and popular journal at conditions in Newfoundland.[11] The "dirty exclusiveness" was a comment on the monopoly of the merchant princes who dominated the south side of Water Street. "If Confederation were only to break down this grinding monopoly," wrote one Newfoundlander in Nova Scotia, "it would in itself

[9]*Newfoundlander*, Jan. 5, 1865.
[10]For explanation of this remark see *infra*, 164–5.
[11]The *Day-Book* claimed the largest circulation in Newfoundland. In 1865 it changed its name to the *Morning Chronicle*.

be a blessing."[12] The *Public Ledger* spoke in the same vein on November 30. The fisherman no longer thought of the merchant as a kind Providence "who will exercise a paternal care over him, and feed and cloth[e] himself and his family, in return for the produce of his toils." No; a new generation has come who look upon the merchant as an enemy or as fair game. "Let confederation come then, and should it slightly increase our taxation, it will make amends by cheapening for us the necessaries of life. . . . A central Government, with larger views than any local legislature could entertain, will initiate improvements and open up our resources. . . ." The *Newfoundland Express* talked on November 26 of the glory of British North America "united in one nation, from the Atlantic to the Pacific," but it was clear that the principal force for Confederation in Newfoundland was not so much a feeling of national glory as one of domestic degradation.

Doubts existed about the usefulness of responsible, even representative government. Some remarks suggest that responsible government could as well have ended in 1866 as 1934. Newfoundland cannot stand responsible government much longer, wrote the *Public Ledger*, early in 1867. The *St. John's Daily News* remarked that the "cumbrous and complicated machinery of representative institutions" was hardly suitable for little, poor colonies like Newfoundland.

Small and isolated communities with sparsely scattered populations,—infantile in wealth, influence and position—have suddenly encased themselves in political habiliments out of all proportions to the capacity of the body politic. And, like so many infants, with their parents' boots, hats, caps and coats on, they stagger about the world scarcely able to put one foot before the other . . . much to the amusement of the grown-up people who see themselves mimicked in the unfortunate struttings and strivings of the young folk.[13]

In the decade since responsible government had been inaugurated, in 1855, the problems of Newfoundland had become worse, not better. The franchise had been given to every householder, and this meant that about 60 per cent of the adult males were electors. This broad franchise together with the widespread pauperism produced most unfortunate results. Members of the Assembly could buy popularity by voting larger appropriations for relief and by promoting easier methods of obtaining it. Governor Musgrave stated the problem in an aphorism: Newfoundland was the victim not of taxation without

[12]St. John's *Courier*, July 14, 1866, quoting a letter signed "Vindex," which had been published in the Halifax *Evening Express*, July 4, 1866.
[13]*St. John's Daily News*, Dec. 1, 1866.

representation, but of representation without taxation.[14] Most newspapers felt that Newfoundland would be better off if the political
system were considerably simplified, an opinion that Musgrave shared.[15]
Thus the loss or the atrophy of the Newfoundland legislature under
Confederation was thought by many to be a blessing in disguise. The
"monarchical spirit" of the Quebec Resolutions would obviously be
opposed to any strong local power; thus the machinery of government
in Newfoundland will be "much diminished," said the *Newfoundlander*
on December 5, 1864. To those who opposed Confederation because
it would rob Newfoundlanders of the privilege of their own legislature
the *Daily News* replied, December 9, that having their own legislature
was not privilege at all. "Is it one of our glorious privileges to be taxed
to the extent of one-third of our revenues annually for pauper relief to
our starving people? . . . What a *bonne-bouche* we shall be for her
[Canada]! How greedily will she roll the sweet morsel under her
tongue!"

It was understandable therefore why Ambrose Shea should be
optimistic about the adoption of Confederation by Newfoundland.
He wrote to Galt, "We do not apprehend any serious difficulty in the
passage of the Scheme in our Legislature, but it is not wise to be over
confident."[16] Like Tilley and Tupper at this same moment—December,
1864—Shea was hopeful. He admitted that some of "our Mercantile
men" feared an increase in the tariff and that their fear could alarm
"the masses," but Shea proposed to allay this fear with concrete facts,
and asked Galt for returns from Canada on customs, excise, debt, and
taxation.[17] Musgrave, too, was optimistic. He wrote Monck that
"from all I have been able to gather in various quarters I am of opinion
that the proposal of the Conference will meet with little or no important
opposition."[18]

But despite these hopes, the reaction to Confederation in New-

[14]C.O. 194, Musgrave to Cardwell, July 19, 1865. Musgrave wrote this
despatch to accompany the Newfoundland Blue Book for 1864, and it is probably the best summary available of Newfoundland's problems at the time. Arthur
Blackwood minuted on Sept. 11, "Mr. Musgrave's first report and a most
creditable one to the author. . . ." Note however D. W. Prowse's comment, *infra*,
175n.
[15]C.O. 194, Musgrave to Cardwell, Dec. 27, 1864.
[16]W. G. Ormsby, "Letters to Galt concerning the Maritime provinces and
Confederation," *Canadian Historical Review*, XXXIV. 2 (June, 1953), 167–8,
Shea to Galt, Dec. 15, 1864.
[17]*Ibid.*
[18]Musgrave to Monck, Dec. 27, 1864, enclosure in C.O. 42, Monck to Cardwell, Jan. 11, 1865. Musgrave said much the same in a despatch to Cardwell,
C.O. 194, Musgrave to Cardwell, Dec. 27, 1864.

foundland was ambivalent and cautious. Confederation had come rather unexpectedly to all the Maritime provinces: in Newfoundland it had hardly been thought of.[19] The Premier, Hugh Hoyles, had on his own initiative broached the question of Newfoundland's participation in the Charlottetown Conference to Tupper in August, 1864.[20] The appointment of two delegates to the Quebec Conference aroused no particular public interest: the *Newfoundlander* pointed out they were only there as observers.[21] "The subject of a Union of the Provinces, Federal or Legislative, has never been before our Legislature," wrote Hoyles to Macdonald, "we have, therefore, no authority to commit them."[22] Nevertheless some of the St. John's papers began printing reports of the Conference and of the speeches of the Newfoundland delegates, on which the St. John's *Times* of November 9, 1864, coldly commented: "Very little seems to be known of the object of those who are just now agitating the question of Federal Union of the Provinces." But even those cool to Confederation felt a mild glow of pride that Newfoundlanders should have acquitted themselves so well at Quebec.[23] By November newspaper columns thickened with information about the Conference. Such details of Conference business as were available in the Toronto *Globe* appeared in the Harbour Grace *Standard*, though desultorily, with comments on the Newfoundland delegates from the Montreal papers.[24] On December 1 the Quebec Resolutions came out in four of the leading St. John's papers, and were soon copied by the others. By December 7 it was possible for the Harbour Grace *Standard* to say that "Confederation of the British North American Colonies seems to be the all-absorbing question just at present. . . ." But it also added characteristically, "This is certainly a matter of vital importance to this country, and should be approached with the greatest caution by the people of Newfoundland." This sudden rush of talk about Confederation made Newfoundlanders wary. They had not been prepared for it. The general feeling on all sides seemed to be that it was a vital question that required much consideration.

[19]It was true that Newfoundland had been willing to discuss Confederation in 1858, but the reply to Canada was half-hearted and the issue itself seems to have aroused little interest. C.O. 194, Bannerman to Lytton, Oct. 11, 1858; Feb. 24, 1859.
[20]*Supra*, 65.
[21]*Newfoundlander*, Sept. 22, 1864. They did not, however, function as observers, but voted and discussed as if they were delegates.
[22]Newfoundland, Assembly, *Journals*, 1865, Appendix, 847, Hoyles to Macdonald, Sept. 13, 1864.
[23]St. John's *Patriot*, Nov. 22, 1864.
[24]Harbour Grace *Standard*, Nov. 16,1864; Nov. 23, 1864.

Those opposed to Confederation had little faith in a political union with distant Canada.[25] Newfoundland could only be "the contemptible fag-end of such a compact." It was no doubt "a brilliant thing on paper —this Confederation—this Great United British America . . . but its brilliancy does not dazzle us. . . ."[26] Nor did it dazzle Charles Fox Bennett. Bennett was a merchant and mining magnate, who owned about one million acres of land and a successful copper mine. Bennett was subsequently to play a prominent part in rallying Newfoundland against Confederation in 1869, and in many respects his performance in 1864 is comparable. His letters to the *Newfoundlander* early in December were, with the editorials in the *Patriot*, the first guns fired against the scheme. Bennett's main point was that Confederation would deprive Newfoundland of her right of "independent legislation." It would "transfer the right of taxation from the people of this Colony to the people of Canada." The Newfoundland legislature would then become "little better than a second or third rate corporation."[27] The central government would not only control the main sources of revenue, but would in Newfoundland's case also control Crown lands, mines, and minerals.[28] Worse, the young men of Newfoundland would be required to man the ships of a Canadian navy, or defend the Canadian boundary against the United States, "leaving their bones to bleach in a foreign land."[29]

In reply to Bennett the *Newfoundlander* admitted that Confederation would deprive Newfoundland of her right of independent legislation. It simply denied that having a legislature was the privilege Mr. Bennett thought it was. "The colony has been going down hill for years past and what has our independent legislation been able to effect?"[30] If Newfoundland would transfer her power to a strong, central government, her interests would be better cared for. Here the *Newfoundlander* cited the example of Scotland's union with England in 1707, when Scotland had relinquished her right of independent legislation to her own great benefit.

This open skirmish greeted the Newfoundland legislature when it met on January 27, 1865. The Speech from the Throne asked for a

[25]St. John's *Patriot*, Nov. 29, 1864.
[26]*Ibid.*, Dec. 6, 1864.
[27]*Newfoundlander*, Dec. 5, 1864, letter from C. F. Bennett of Dec. 3; Dec. 12, 1864, letter from Bennett of Dec. 10.
[28]By Resolution 66 Newfoundland was given $150,000 a year for this surrender.
[29]*Newfoundlander*, Jan. 12, 1865, letter from Bennett of Jan. 9. Cf. Bennett's well-known reference to "the desert sands of Canada" in the 1869 election.
[30]*Ibid.*, Jan. 12, 1865.

"calm examination" of the Quebec scheme.[31] The Premier gave notice that he would move the House into committee to discuss the Quebec Resolutions. A report from Carter and Shea on the Quebec Conference was at once tabled.[32] The report recited familiar themes: for example, the belief that collision between the central and local legislatures would be avoided by "all powers of a general nature being vested in the General Government, and local questions being reserved for subordinate bodies." It also noted that the reason for Newfoundland's surrender of her Crown lands was that she needed the $150,000 per annum in order to avoid local direct taxation. Carter and Shea then praised the Conference itself: "no inquiry was ever conducted under a higher sense of the responsibility of the occasion."[33] Hoyles' motion for a Committee of the Whole did not prevent a debate on Confederation arising in the discussion of the Reply to the Speech from the Throne.[34] From this debate it was clear that the non-committal attitude that the Government had taken in September, 1864, was going to be continued.[35] Confederation was to be an open question. Certainly the words in the Reply were innocuous enough. They agreed with the Speech; Confederation was of great importance and should be approached in "a spirit of calm enquiry."[36]

The discussion of Confederation in Committee, delayed by the illness of the Premier, began on February 20, 1865. The Premier gave a long speech in which he followed the spirit of the *Newfoundlander*. Hoyles agreed that under Confederation Newfoundland would give up most of the control of her own affairs. He justified this by the hoary doctrine of the social contract: Newfoundland going into Confederation was like the savage giving up rights upon going into society! Newfoundland was well rid of her right of independent legislation. The history of Newfoundland since the introduction of representative government in 1832 was "not one on which we could look with satisfaction." Strong powers had been given to the central government; Hoyles admitted that. But he appealed to the large view. "But how

[31]Newfoundland, Assembly, *Journals*, 1865, 2 (Jan. 27).

[32]Carter and Shea's report, dated Jan. 21, 1865, was published in the St. John's *Courier*, Feb. 1, 1865; *Newfoundlander*, Feb. 2, 1865.

[33]*Ibid.*

[34]The Reply in Newfoundland was not simply an echo of the Speech from the Throne. A committee composed of different groups in the House drafted a reply, which was then submitted to the House. Debate often arose at this point. See C.O. 194, Musgrave to Cardwell, Feb. 20, 1866.

[35]A Minute of Council, Sept. 12, 1864, said that Confederation "should not be treated as a party question."

[36]Newfoundland, Assembly, *Journals*, 1865, 13 (Feb. 6).

could a confederation be formed without such powers? How could we form a confederation which we expected to be permanent, and to become, in the course of time, large and powerful, without such powers of taxation? Large powers were necessary to sustain national existence."[37]

Two weeks of animated debate followed. Ambrose Shea, at this time leader of the Opposition, gave a major speech supporting Hoyles on February 21. Shea asked that the Committee should endorse the Quebec plan in principle. The syllogism he urged was this: all unions are beneficial; Confederation is a union; therefore Confederation is beneficial. Shea's examples were revealing. France was "confederated" under Henry IV and under Richelieu "confederated" even more.[38] The union of Scotland with England, cited in Newfoundland to argue the advantages of union,[39] seemed to be the kind of union that Shea had in mind for British America. An interesting example of Shea's application of this meaning was his analysis of the taxing powers of the central and local governments. First, Shea assumed that the general power to tax given in Section 29 to the central government was the power to levy only indirect taxes.[40] Direct taxes were, he said, "reserved for the Local Legislatures."[41] Second, the central government had an ultimate control over both methods of taxation in the form of an emergency power. It must be borne in mind that in Newfoundland there was no local revenue for municipal purposes. The whole revenue of the colony came from indirect taxes, largely customs duties. Every expenditure, for whatever purpose, was charged upon the general revenue of the colony. Thus was engendered what Musgrave called a "morbid apprehension" of direct taxation.[42] Perhaps it was natural that Shea should have limited his definition of direct taxation to taxation upon property. Hence the power of the central government of Confederation to tax virtually had to be construed by Shea as the power to levy only indirect taxes. But his emergency doctrine is interesting, and his attempt to explain it on the question of taxation

[37]*Newfoundlander*, March 16, 1865, reporting debates of Feb. 20. (Erroneously stated in the paper to be for Feb. 14. The debate had, however, been postponed.)

[38]Cf. McGee's remark, "all governments have been more or less confederations in their character." *Confederation Debates*, 145.

[39]The anti-Confederates often cited, with equal relevance and more effect, the experience of Ireland.

[40]Section 29, sub-section 5: "the raising of money by all or any modes or systems of Taxation."

[41]*Newfoundlander*, March 2, 1865, reporting Shea's speech of Feb. 21.

[42]C.O. 194, Musgrave to Cardwell, July 19, 1865.

170   THE LIFE AND TIMES OF CONFEDERATION

especially so. Certainly it is altogether probable that Shea understood the powers of the local legislature to be essentially municipal in their nature and purpose.

Those in the Assembly who opposed Confederation agreed that the principle of union had much to recommend it, but they questioned the applicability of the principle to Newfoundland. Henry Renouf, member for St. John's West, said Mr. Shea's arguments ignored the fact that Newfoundland was separated from the rest of British North America by six hundred miles of sea.[43] In the Legislative Council R. J. Pinsent said much the same, "there is little community of interest between Newfoundland and the Canadas. This is not a Continental Colony. . . ."[44] This attitude, and petitions from St. John's merchants,[45] multiplied the reasons for caution on the part of the Government. The *Newfoundlander* claimed that there was a majority of 16–13 for Confederation in the Assembly,[46] but if so, many of the members did not have the courage of their convictions. As early as February 23 the Government had realized that postponement of Confederation was inevitable; they recognized that a hostile vote on the question should not be risked.[47] And the news of Tilley's defeat arrested whatever slight momentum Confederation might still have had. On March 6 the Premier introduced a resolution in the House postponing Confederation until after the next election, "particularly as the action of other Provinces does not appear to require that it should be hastily disposed of."[48] The St. John's *Times* of March 29 seemed to be reflecting public feeling when it said, "Every sensible person we think must rejoice that so momentous a question as the Union of this Colony with the projected Confederation has been postponed through the timely and exceedingly prudent resolution of the Premier. . . ."

The fact was that a large proportion of the voters were wholly ignorant of the subject, and the Government had to proceed with the greatest caution lest prejudices and opinions be inflamed by needy politicians using the opportunity to get into power. So Musgrave interpreted matters to the Colonial Office: "it would not be difficult by

[43]It depends upon where one takes one's distance. From Cape St. George, on the west coast, to Gaspé is about 250 miles.

[44]*Newfoundlander*, March 6, 1865, reporting debates in the Legislative Council for Feb. 14.

[45]Petitions urging postponement of any decision were presented on Feb. 13 and Feb. 20. St. John's *Patriot*, Feb. 14, 1865; St. John's *Public Ledger*, March 10, 1865.

[46]*Newfoundlander*, March 9, 1865.

[47]C.O. 194, Musgrave to Cardwell, Feb. 23, 1865; April 19, 1865.

[48]Newfoundland, Assembly, *Journals*, 1865, 37.

incaution to produce a state of public feeling which would not only postpone indefinitely any federal arrangement, but very seriously embarrass the judicious conduct of local affairs for some time to come."[49] Musgrave said in his speech closing the session that he might have regretted the lukewarm attitude of the legislature but for the fact that the other colonies would not make any definite move in 1865. "But," he warned, "the nation has a right to expect the Colonies to accept . . . their legitimate portion of the charges and responsibilities . . . of self-government and free political institutions. . . ."[50] It was a threat that other governors were soon to be called upon to use.

That same month, April, 1865, significant changes took place in the Ministry. The Premier retired and became Chief Justice. His place was taken by F. B. T. Carter, who promptly enlisted Ambrose Shea the leader of the Opposition and his colleague on the Quebec delegation. This was, of course, a coalition. What Shea had predicted in December was realized.

With us in this Colony the question [of Confederation] will break up our local parties and if even for no other reason I should hail its introduction on this account—In these small Provinces we have no really different interests to form legitimate causes of separation & grounds of party action and the disputes necessarily become sectarian & personal, and engender a very low state of public feeling.[51]

Confederation had helped to bring Government and Opposition together, and the resulting coalition contained the ablest and most experienced men in the colony. It was a union not only of Conservatives and Liberals, but also of Protestants and Catholics, Carter being Protestant, Shea Catholic.[52] The real question was, whether the Government felt strong enough to make Confederation a government measure.

On the face of it there was reason why they might. A majority of the St. John's newspapers supported Confederation: two Conservative papers, the *Daily News*, and the *Newfoundland Express*; the Liberal *Newfoundlander*; the independent *Courier*. The *Public Ledger*, a Conservative paper, was mildly critical, but was to come over to Confederation definitely in 1866. The *Times* opposed Confederation, but it was primarily a commercial paper. The only two important opposition papers were the Conservative *Day-Book* (changed in 1865 to the *Morning Chronicle*) and the Liberal *Patriot*.

[49]C.O. 194, Musgrave to Cardwell, April 19, 1865.
[50]Newfoundland, Assembly, *Journals*, 1865, 134 (April 7).
[51]Ormsby, "Letters to Galt," Shea to Galt, Dec. 15, 1864.
[52]About 40 per cent of Newfoundland's population was Roman Catholic.

But the press of St. John's, like that of Halifax, was not an accurate guide to the feeling in the province as a whole. This was not simply because of the differences between town and country attitudes, which were probably not very significant in Newfoundland. Rather it was the difference between the press and the public, between the articulate newspaper and the much less articulate voter. The newspapers often reflected the views of the more educated, and it was these who, like Ambrose Shea, were usually the most dissatisfied with the existing state of affairs. Some of the newspapers were also instruments of government policy. The St. John's *Morning Chronicle*, which boasted of surviving without government help, accused other newspapers of scrutinizing every public question through government spectacles.[53] The newspapers were also misleading in respect of the attitudes of the St. John's merchants. Probably a majority of the merchants feared the Canadian tariff and its effects. The merchants began by sponsoring a public meeting on February 11, 1865, which passed a resolution to the effect that Confederation should be submitted to the people.[54] This was followed six months later by an outright condemnation of Confederation by the St. John's Chamber of Commerce, which said it was simply a scheme to bail Canada out of her difficulties at the expense of the other provinces.[55] Thus, though a majority of the St. John's newspapers supported Confederation, all of the members in the Assembly representing St. John's felt and responded to public pressure to oppose it.

There was also resentment against the pressure applied by the British government to persuade Newfoundland and other Maritime provinces to join Confederation. This was particularly the case with the despatch of June 24, 1865, which went to all the Maritime provinces. It set forth unequivocally that "the Colonies must recognize a right and even acknowledge an obligation incumbent on the Home Government to urge with earnestness and just authority the measures which they consider to be most expedient. . . . it is an object much to be desired that all the British North American Colonies should agree to unite in one Government."[56] The harsh reply to this despatch by the anti-Confederate government of New Brunswick[57] was praised by the St. John's *Patriot* as

. . . a State Paper calculated to immortalize its authors, as containing the whole text of Responsible Government. . . . A Charlotte-town contemporary

[53]*Morning Chronicle*, Dec. 1, 1866; Dec. 22, 1866.
[54]*Day-Book*, Feb. 9, 13, 1865.
[55]*Patriot*, Aug. 12, 1865. Commented on in C.O. 194, Musgrave to Cardwell, Aug. 19, 1865.
[56]C.O. 195, Cardwell to Musgrave, June 24, 1865.   [57]See *infra*, 249.

remarks—and we unhesitatingly endorse the observation—"if Nova Scotia, Newfoundland and P. E. Island were only to follow the noble example of their sister colony . . . the Home authorities would at once abandon the delusion that the semi-dictation of Downing Street, though backed by Canadian diplomacy and the intriguing of a few scheming politicians among ourselves, can ever force upon nearly one million British colonists a measure . . . prejudicial to their prosperity and happiness." Would that Newfoundland possessed an Executive Council of the same spirit. . . ![58]

Newfoundland's Executive Council may have had spirit and ability, but they showed a decided reluctance to commit themselves on Confederation. Premier Carter said later, by way of justification, that not all the members of the Government were in favour of Confederation.[59] But most were. Despite the fact, each member of the Government and of the Assembly went to the polls on his own record, not on Confederation. To all intents and purposes Confederation was not an issue in the 1865 election. The Confederate press made no attempt to make it an issue. Their policy was, said the *Patriot*, September 2, 1865, "to preserve a death-like silence upon the subject. . . ." The election was quiet. The *Newfoundlander* commented on the absence of issues and considered the general serenity of opinion unusual. It was unusual. In the previous election in 1861 people were killed in Harbour Grace and Harbour Main and a hundred troops had to be sent from Halifax to quiet things down. There was nothing remotely resembling that in the election that took place in November, 1865. The entry of Roman Catholics into the Conservative, Protestant government had clearly had some effect in tempering the fierce religious passions that had so often made a Donnybrook of the hustings.

Although nearly all the members of the House who had favoured Confederation were returned at the polls, the *Newfoundlander* of November 20 frankly admitted that the "convinced confederationists" would be in a minority in the new House. The *Newfoundlander* had cause to be frank. One of the convinced Confederationists who would be missing altogether was the editor of the *Newfoundlander* himself. E. D. Shea, who had been the Finance Secretary, was replaced in Ferryland by an anti-Confederate, Thomas Glen.[60] On November 28, the *Morning Chronicle*'s figures were: for Confederation, 10; against, 16; doubtful, 4. And though the Government was "confessedly the strongest Govern-

[58]St. John's *Patriot*, Sept. 23, 1865. The Charlottetown paper was probably the *Herald* or the *Patriot*, neither of which is available for 1865.
[59]*Newfoundlander*, March 1, 1866, reporting Assembly debates of Feb. 12.
[60]It was reported in the *Public Ledger*, Nov. 21, 1865, that E. D. Shea did not contest the election. He was appointed to the Legislative Council in 1866.

ment" that Newfoundland had ever had,[61] it was clear its support of Confederation would be exceedingly gentle. Shea said later that the feeling in Newfoundland was, "Don't be in a hurry; let us have time to think over it, and understand it, before any action is taken that will definitely settle it."[62]

Musgrave wrote the Colonial Office that if Confederation was to make any progress in the 1866 session some despatch would have to be sent to Newfoundland to "neutralize the impression . . . that there is now no present intention of urging further dealing with the subject." The Colonial Office rallied to the cause. Musgrave got his despatch. "I wish you clearly to understand," wrote Cardwell obligingly, "not only that there is no change in the views of Her Majesty's Government but that we hope that mature consideration will have satisfied the Lower Provinces of the advantages to be derived from such an Union. I rely upon your discretion in giving effect to the known wishes of Her Majesty's Government in the way most likely to be successful."[63] It was to a similar despatch that the *Morning Chronicle* replied irreverently, "another terrible shot in our Anti-Confederate locker—a shot, too, direct from the Imperial foundry."[64]

With such a despatch Musgrave might well urge Confederation upon his Council. But they were hesitant, and the Speech from the Throne on January 30, 1866, was a compromise. It admitted the abstract advantages of union: the only question was that of terms.[65] To this the Assembly replied with mixed feelings. The new member for Ferryland, Thomas Glen, proposed a stiff rejoinder, that Newfoundland "could not think for a moment" of giving up her status as a separate colony. This was defeated, 18–7.[66] Thomas Talbot, member for St. John's West, proposed a resolution that well illustrated the equivocal attitude of many Newfoundlanders: that while the abstract advantages of Union were obvious, the feeling in Newfoundland was against entering Confederation. This, too, was defeated by the Government.[67] But the Reply that finally passed

[61]*St. John's Daily News*, Nov. 18, 1865.

[62]*Newfoundlander*, April 5, 1866, reporting Assembly debates for March 7.

[63]C.O. 194, Musgrave to Cardwell, Nov. 14, 1865; C.O. 195, Cardwell to Musgrave, Dec. 20, 1865.

[64]St. John's *Morning Chronicle*, Dec. 20, 1865, commenting on a similar despatch (C.O. 195, Cardwell to Musgrave, Nov. 24, 1865), in which Cardwell urged that Confederation would facilitate re-negotiation of the Reciprocity Treaty.

[65]Newfoundland, Assembly, *Journals*, 1866, 10 (Jan. 30).

[66]The *Morning Chronicle*, Feb. 8, 1866, published Glen's resolutions in large type on the editorial page.

[67]Newfoundland, Assembly, *Journals*, 1866, 27–30 (Feb. 16).

was hardly more enthusiastic. It simply said that although the advantages of union were obvious, great diversity of opinion prevailed as to terms. And the Assembly would not even consider what terms it would accept.[68]

Musgrave acknowledged this Reply by again pressing the question of terms on the Assembly. "Minor objections on the part of detached Colonies," he said firmly, "must of necessity give way before the pressure of the more weighty motives of national interest."[69] Her Majesty's Government was ready to adjust details, and Newfoundland should not be placed in a position unfavourable to continuation of negotiations. Musgrave called this maintaining "gentle pressure" without "exciting factious opposition";[70] but his gentle pressure was too strong. The House gave more resistance this second time. The next day, G. J. Hodgsett, a well-known opponent of the Government,[71] gave notice of motion to reconsider Confederation on February 27; that day it was postponed. The *Patriot* (March 3, 1866) considered this the end of the scheme. "Well!" it exclaimed cheerfully, "after a great deal of talk the House of Assembly have left the question of Confederation just where they found it." But the *Patriot* was a little premature; the opposition were not to be robbed of an opportunity to embarrass a divided government. The Assembly went into Committee on March 5, 1866, and three days later the debate was over. Resolutions condemning union outright were once more defeated by the Government majority, but the Assembly declared, on motion of the Premier himself, that despite the momentous character of Confederation, it was not expedient "to enter upon its discussion with a view to any decision thereon."[72] The House would not be pushed. Like Newfoundland herself, the Assembly, while not unsympathetic to Confederation, was not prepared to act decisively. All that Musgrave could say at prorogation on May 1, 1866, was that the matter would remain for the next session to decide.[73]

At this moment came Nova Scotian intervention. It became obvious, after the New Brunswick elections of May and June, that New Brunswick

[68]*Ibid.*

[69]*Ibid.*, 35 (Feb. 20).

[70]C.O. 194, Musgrave to Cardwell, Feb. 20, 1866.

[71]Member for Harbour Main, and whose election in 1861 had caused so much trouble for the Hoyles government. He was re-elected in 1865.

[72]Newfoundland, Assembly, *Journals*, 1866, 52 (March 8).

[73]*Ibid.*, 197. D. W. Prowse, member for Burgeo and LaPoile at this time, and a supporter of Confederation, wrote many years later of Musgrave: "Sir Anthony was an amiable man and painstaking administrator; he was thought a great deal of at the Colonial Office as an able writer of despatches, and no doubt he made the Home Government believe that he was able to carry confederation in the Colony; he never, however, had any real power or influence in Newfoundland." *A History of Newfoundland* (London, 1895), 494.

would pass Confederation, and E. M. Macdonald, of the *Halifax Citizen*, set off, with Patrick Power, for St. John's to rally Newfoundlanders against any further attempt to press Confederation on Newfoundland. At the Commercial Rooms in St. John's on June 26 Macdonald and Power preached against Confederation to a meeting of forty merchants and members of the Assembly. The result was a public petition that no action be taken on Confederation unless it had first been approved in an election.[74] Musgrave did not consider the petition of any importance.[75] Nevertheless E. M. Macdonald's visit had been well timed; it was just two weeks afterward, on July 10, that Governor Musgrave called a Council to reconsider Confederation. Governor Fenwick Williams of Nova Scotia, writing on the day of Howe's departure for England, July 5, had said that delegates from Nova Scotia, New Brunswick, and Canada were going to London; could the Newfoundland legislature reconsider Confederation? Failing that, could Newfoundland delegates be sent to London?[76] Musgrave hoped Council might be willing to risk one or the other. They were not. They told Musgrave there was no reasonable ground to anticipate anything but an adverse decision from the legislature should such an initiative be taken.[77] Later in the same year both the *Public Ledger* and the *Newfoundland Express*, dismayed by the depression and destitution around them, urged the appointment of delegates to London; surely no harm could result from at least conferring with the others.[78] But the *Daily News*, while sympathetic, was probably speaking for the Government when it averred that "in view of the windy declamations" of the Opposition, the Government was right to wait until public opinion allowed it to move with more impunity.[79] Musgrave was forced to admit to Governor Williams of Nova Scotia that any attempt to revive Confederation by reconvening the legislature would be doomed to failure. Nor would a dissolution help.[80]

But Musgrave was not without resource. He wrote Cardwell asking for another despatch to impress upon Newfoundland the disadvantages of remaining outside Confederation. Upon this despatch Arthur Black-

[74]St. John's *Public Ledger*, June 29, 1866.

[75]C.O. 194, Musgrave to Carnarvon, Aug. 7, 1866. Also E. C. Moulton, "The Political History of Newfoundland, 1861–1869," M.A. thesis, Memorial University of Newfoundland, 1960, 195.

[76]Miscellaneous papers of Governor's office, Williams to Musgrave, July 5, 1866 (confidential).

[77]C.O. 194, Musgrave to Cardwell, July 10, 1866.

[78]*Public Ledger*, Oct. 19, 23, 1866; *Newfoundland Express*, Nov. 1, 1866.

[79]St. John's *Daily News*, Oct. 27, 1866.

[80]Nova Scotia, Lieutenant Governor, General Correspondence Received, Musgrave to Williams, July 10, 1866 (confidential).

wood, the Chief Clerk of the North American department at the Colonial
Office, sensibly minuted, "I doubt, myself, the wisdom of writing such
very strong despatches to a weak colony. They can scarcely fail to be
construed as a menace. And upon this subject especially I should
deprecate anything like using violence." Indeed, enough force had been
used elsewhere already. Lord Carnarvon, the new Colonial Secretary,
felt compelled to add, "some pressure from home may be necessary:
but I doubt that the time for this has yet come."[81]

The result was that on January 31, 1867, while the Canadian, Nova
Scotian, and New Brunswick delegates were hard at work in London
revising the first draft of the British North America bill, the Newfoundland Legislature opened without a word about Confederation in the
Speech from the Throne. It was a significant omission. Newfoundland
was not yet ready for Confederation. It was all very well for the *Public
Ledger* to say that those who opposed Confederation wanted to keep
Newfoundland "a mere fishing station,"[82] or for D. W. Prowse to put
together a pejorative list of the opposition—"all the host of official
vampires and small fry of newspapers and reporters are dead against it,
and so are all those whose interests as merchants will, as they fear, be
affected. . . ."[83] But when the merchants of St. John's combined with
the Irish Roman Catholics and with the innate conservatism of the outports, not even the pressure of the Colonial Office, the economic devasta-
tion of 1866, or two-thirds of the St. John's newspapers could persuade
Newfoundland to join Confederation. The St. John's *Morning Chronicle*
was accurate enough, February 4, 1867: "the absence of any reference
to the subject of Confederation in His Excellency's speech on Thursday
last is tolerably certain evidence that, so far as Newfoundland is concerned, the scheme has pretty well come to grief."

Shea wrote optimistically as ever to Macdonald in May, 1867, that
a more wholesome feeling about Union was growing up in Newfoundland. Macdonald with his usual verve replied he was glad to hear it,
for Newfoundland "held the key to our front door. . . ."[84] Anthony
Musgrave went to Ottawa that October to see Macdonald and Monck;
he also witnessed the opening of the new Parliament of the Dominion
of Canada. But Shea's hopes and Musgrave's energies were to no avail.
Newfoundlanders preferred to retain the key in their own hands.
They were not ready to surrender it in 1867, in 1869, or for many

[81]C.O. 194, Musgrave to Cardwell, July 10, 1866; Blackwood's minute of
July 28; Carnarvon's minute of Aug. 11. (Cardwell gave up office on July 6, 1866.)
[82]*Public Ledger*, Feb. 5, 1867.
[83]*Newfoundlander*, Feb. 6, 1865, reporting debates of Jan. 27.
[84]Macdonald Papers, Macdonald to Shea, June 3, 1867.

years to come.[85] Governors came and went; Carter died many years later in 1900, Shea in 1905. But Newfoundland remained as she was, harried by economic storms as savage as her winter gales, devastated not infrequently by fire and famine, but resilient, tough, and to Canadians stubborn. Not even "a Light House on every Headland! !" would persuade her in 1869;[86] and by that time Newfoundlanders had become "quite impregnated with the bitter animosity of the Nova Scotians. . . ."[87]

[85]See H. B. Mayo, "Newfoundland and Confederation in the Eighteen-sixties," *Canadian Historical Review*, XXIX, 2 (June, 1948), 125–142, for the 1869 election; Harvey Mitchell, "Canada's Negotiations with Newfoundland, 1887–1895," *Canadian Historical Review*, XL, 4 (Dec., 1959), 277–93.

[86]From an election poster of 1869, enclosure in C.O. 194, Hill to Granville, Nov. 5, 1869.

[87]C.O. 194, Hill to Granville, Oct. 22, 1869 (confidential).

12. PRINCE EDWARD ISLAND

PRINCE EDWARD ISLAND, a hundred miles long by thirty wide, lay green and low in the Gulf of St. Lawrence between Cape Breton Island and the north shore of New Brunswick. The character and life of the Island, as of agricultural communities generally, was not very different in 1864 to what it is now. Even the population has been relatively static, being only about 20 per cent higher at the present time than the 87,000 of 1864. It was divided into roughly equal numbers of Roman Catholics and Protestants, the Catholics largely Irish, the Protestants mainly Scottish. It was an unstable mixture at the best of times. Like oil and vinegar the Irish Catholics and the Scottish Protestants refused to mix except when shaken by some external force, which happened occasionally in controversies with the Colonial Office. Prince Edward Island politics were surprisingly violent and rather contrasted with the placid charm of the Island landscape. In a word, Island politics were parochial. With an assembly of thirty members representing a population of some 87,000, with responsible government nine years old, the Island itself without the contact with transoceanic commerce that characterized Nova Scotia, it was a small, isolated, violent little bailiwick.

The complacency of Canada in 1865, the calm of Newfoundland in the election of 1865, have no counterpart in Prince Edward Island. There the air was filled with recriminations. The Prince Edward Island delegation to the Quebec Conference had tried to preserve a united front and had not been successful. When the delegates returned to the Island all pretence at unity was abandoned with relief and the delegates revealed themselves in their true Island colours as they began, with not a little zest, a crossfire of criticism. The politics of past years were canvassed; debates in the Quebec Conference were aired; and edifying public arguments were fought over who did or did not propose or second certain motions. The number of Island accounts of the conference and of the speeches of the delegates was evidence more of the rigour of Island politics than of the literary ambitions of its public men.

The attitudes of Island politicians to Confederation were complicated by traditions of personal bitterness. John Hamilton Gray had, for example, ousted his Conservative colleague Edward Palmer from the premiership in 1863. Palmer had been Premier since 1859 and he not unnaturally resented being so displaced. His resentment against Gray may have influenced, even decided, his view of Confederation. In fact the Island delegation to Quebec had been split across party lines. On the Confederate side was T. Heath Haviland, a Conservative though of independent mind. With Haviland stood J. H. Gray, the Conservative Premier, and W. H. Pope, the Provincial Secretary and owner of the *Islander*. To these was joined Edward Whelan, the Irish Catholic editor of the Liberal *Examiner*. On the anti-Confederate side, Edward Palmer, the Conservative Attorney General and Government leader in the Legislative Council, joined with George Coles, leader of the Opposition in the Assembly, and A. A. Macdonald, leader of the Opposition in the Legislative Council. The situation was the more curious because not all of the delegates had been consistent in their attitudes to union. Whelan rejected it in April, 1864, and supported it in October; Coles supported it in August, rejected it in November. Whelan became an enthusiastic convert, angry at the "petulance of this little place";[1] Coles rejoiced that Prince Edward Island was so firmly opposed. J. H. Gray had been a lukewarm supporter of union in April and was to resign because of it in December.

However, the truth was that no party or group could have taken up Confederation and survived. Personal recriminations, changes of heart, visions of a united British America had all to bow before the fundamental fact that the people of Prince Edward Island did not want to join any union, and they had no intention of being forced to do so.[2] Self-sufficient in an agricultural age, with her capital never more than "a day's drive"[3] away, Prince Edward Island was quite happy as she was. Maritime union had not been acceptable, and Confederation did not suit the Islanders either. Like the Acadians a century before, they simply wanted to be left alone. This local patriotism may seem extraordinary, but many of the Island's inhabitants had never been away from the Island in their life;[4] they had little opportunity to cultivate

[1]Charlottetown *Examiner*, Dec. 26, 1864.

[2]A good article covering the period 1858 to 1873 is D. C. Harvey's "Confederation in Prince Edward Island," *Canadian Historical Review*, XIV, 2 (June, 1933), 143–60.

[3]Charlottetown *Examiner*, Aug. 22, 1864, "Union Question, No. 1," quoted *supra*, 64.

[4]George Brown's impression. Brown Papers, George Brown to Anne Brown, Sept. 13, 1864.

larger loyalties. The local patriotism of the Islanders was both real and powerful.

The loyalties of the Islanders were not, moreover, weakened by the hard times such as Newfoundland was experiencing. In Newfoundland the shattered fishing economy invited the sovereign remedy that Confederation purported to supply. The principal social question in Prince Edward Island was not pauperism but the ownership of land. The effect of this question was to embitter the relations between tenants and proprietors, and inevitably, after the introduction of responsible government, the relations between the Island government and the British government. It also made the Island much less amenable to suggestions, and threats, emanating from the Colonial Office that attempted to persuade the Island to adopt Confederation.

The land of Prince Edward Island had originally been carved up into 67 lots and granted to deserving supporters of George III in 1767. Thus at its very inception as a separate province in 1769 the Island was saddled with a problem that was to remain unsolved for over a century.[5] Similar problems in the American colonies were nicely dissolved by the Revolution; in the Island, when from the time of responsible government onward successive governments tried to deal with the question, they had their legislation rather unceremoniously disallowed in London. Although there was undoubtedly a case for the proprietors, they had been given considerable, probably excessive, indulgence by the Crown. As in the case of the Newfoundland French Shore Commission of 1860, a commission appointed that same year to settle the Prince Edward Island land question only fanned the flames higher. The Commission[6] had brought in a report favourable to the Island, which the Prince Edward Island legislature promptly implemented.[7] However, the report was not only rejected by the proprietors, but to the pained surprise of the Islanders, the rejection was sustained by the Colonial Office and the Island's remedial legislation disallowed. The land question was the centre of Island politics during the sixties and it culminated in the Tenant League and its attempts to secure by extra legal means what could not be got otherwise.

Thus Prince Edward Island's principal aim was to throw off the

[5]See Frank MacKinnon, *Government of Prince Edward Island* (Toronto, 1951), 105–19, for a general summary; also Harvey, "Confederation in Prince Edward Island," 155.

[6]The Commission was composed of Joseph Howe, for the tenants; J. W. Ritchie, also of Nova Scotia, for the proprietors; and J. H. Gray, of New Brunswick, as chairman.

[7]Prince Edward Island, Assembly, *Journals*, 1862, Appendix. Also MacKinnon, *Government of Prince Edward Island*, 118–9.

incubus of old landlords, not to acquire a new one in the shape of a distant but powerful government at Ottawa. The Island had had unhappy experiences in dealing with distant governments; she liked having her own government in Charlottetown and did not propose to make a change if she could avoid it.

Edward Whelan, T. Heath Haviland, A. A. Macdonald, and Edward Palmer arrived back in Charlottetown on Wednesday, November 9, 1864.[8] The next day the *Monitor* published the Quebec Resolutions, and on Friday Palmer was out denouncing Confederation to a crowd in Market Square.[9] W. H. Pope and J. H. Gray arrived home (via New York) to learn that the public defection of one of their colleagues had occurred already.[10] George Coles, who arrived a few days later, soon followed Palmer. At once correspondence began in the newspapers with claim and counterclaim about what was or was not said and done at the Quebec Conference.

The action of Palmer and Coles followed of course from their performance there. Ambrose Shea wrote Galt, "I see old Palmer has not disappointed any of us—"[11] Shea mentioned "mercenary motives" at work. If so, jealousy of Gray was another. Whelan, who disliked Palmer for personal and political reasons, described him as "the steadfast apostle of *the stand-still, the do-nothing, the Sleepy Hollow school.* . . ."[12] Both Palmer and Coles were accused, with a little justification, of gross inconsistency. Coles' speech at Ottawa on November 1, Palmer's at Toronto two days later, were published by the indefatigable Whelan with emphasis on the sentences that tacitly approved of Confederation.[13] Palmer asserted that neither he nor Coles could have been expected to criticize Confederation at a public dinner in honour of the delegates. Criticism would have damped the enthusiasm of post-prandial hospitality. At this the Confederate press delicately suggested that Coles and Palmer had not been in a position to know or care what they said.

[8]*Islander*, Nov. 11, 1864.
[9]*Ibid.*, Dec. 9, 1864, letter of W. H. Pope of Dec. 5.
[10]*Ibid.*, Nov. 18, 1864.
[11]W. G. Ormsby, "Letters to Galt concerning the Maritime Provinces and Confederation." *Canadian Historical Review*, XXIV, 2 (June, 1953), 167–8, Shea to Galt, Dec. 15, 1864. Palmer was not that old, being 55. Shea was 46.
[12]*Examiner*, Nov. 21, 1864 (original italics).
[13]*Ibid.*, Nov. 28, Dec. 5, 1864. The following quotations are from E. Whelan, *Union of the British Provinces* (Charlottetown, 1865). Coles at Ottawa, Nov. 1: "in going for Federation the Government of Prince Edward Island were carrying out his views—views which he had entertained for many years." (page 138) Palmer at Toronto on Nov. 3: "from all that has been witnessed by the Delegates representing that Island, they will not hesitate to recommend to their people the great Union which I hope soon to see accomplished." (page 183)

Thus it was in self-defence that Palmer turned to his record at the Conference, to justify his recent utterances in Charlottetown by his past conduct at Quebec.[14]

Since Palmer was the Attorney General, J. H. Gray, the Premier, felt increasingly uncomfortable. Gray himself had published a letter in November appealing for support for Confederation. "Will you record your votes among those who are content to vegetate like Dormice?" he asked. Will the Island continue to see her legislature "slighted and thwarted, and its most solemn enactments trampled underfoot?" Confederation would end all that. It would solve the Island's land problem by giving Prince Edward Island the opportunity to make her legislation effective; it would give the Island "the protection of a strong Government under whose shield we shall command the respect of Downing Street."[15]

Mid-December, 1864, a month after the Island delegation had returned home, saw the Conservative government of the Island in chaos. The Premier and the Attorney General, the two leading figures in the government, were impugning each other's motives and actions in public. Even as cabinet government was conceived in Prince Edward Island, this could hardly go on much longer. That it was an old quarrel did not make it more gentle. The *Monitor* said on December 29 that "the recent mission to Canada has developed and matured pre-existing elements of discord." Gray vividly described his troubles in a letter to Charles Tupper:

I daresay you may have observed in the papers, that the People here are frantic on the Union question—When I returned from Canada after our happy intercourse, I found the whole community poisoned by Mr. Palmer— "we were sacrificed" ["]taxation of millions for defence" "our militia to be drafted for slaughter to the confines of Canada"—*I had sold* the Country
Such a storm, my very friends were dumb, and had to hide their heads.
Independent of all private or personal considerations, I felt Mr. P's conduct such as to demand my protest, if but out of respect to those gentlemen I had felt it an honour & credit to have been associated with.
Had I brought his conduct before the Council and insisted on his resigning or that I wd. have done so, such was the storm that I wd. have been told I sacrificed & persecuted him on account of his exposure of my treason.[16]

Gray resigned on December 16. He was a strong figure politically;

[14]The leading points of Palmer's argument have been developed, *supra*, 94–5.
[15]*Islander*, Nov. 18, 1864, letter of J. H. Gray of Nov. 16.
[16]Tupper Papers, J. H. Gray to Tupper, Jan. 7, 1865.

he was almost—but not quite—indispensable to the Conservatives. The Conservative *Monitor*, however, thought Gray was being recklessly precipitate. His resignation, coupled as it was with the resignation of James C. Pope (brother of W. H. Pope and a Conservative colleague close to Gray), threatened to undermine the position of the Conservative government, and with it the Protestant cause with which the Conservatives were largely identified.[17] *Ross's Weekly* described the whole episode with the flamboyant cheerfulness of an opposition paper on December 29:

> . . . the late frost and strong westerly winds have carried off the effluvia of the big Canadian frolic, and . . . the agitators' minds are cooling down to a consideration of the necessity of reconciling themselves to public opinion, and of the disadvantages of losing office . . . the *sham-paine* is becoming real, and the Palmer pill nauseous . . . [J. C.] Pope thinks it better to retain his resignation under lock and key. . . .

The last clause was a reference to one of the subsequent shifts of the Conservative cabinet, part of a desperate attempt to keep the Conservative ship afloat.[18] In an astonishing manœuvre, James C. Pope withdrew his resignation, took the helm and became Premier. Edward Palmer was forced out of the Cabinet in January, rumours of his imminent jettison having been circulated since mid-December.[19] Not the least astonishing event in an amazing series was Palmer's retention of the office of Attorney General despite his resignation from the Council. As if to round out the comedy, James Pope asked Gray to return as Premier.[20] Gray refused. John A. Macdonald later consoled him with the remark that his course was "only what we anticipated from a soldier and a gentleman. . . ."[21] The Conservatives finally added T. Heath Haviland to the Council, a "red-hot unionist" as Coles described him,[22] and Kenneth Henderson, an anti-Confederate. The net effect of all these manœuvres was: first, to replace a Confederate Premier with an anti-Confederate one (J. C. Pope); second, to drop a strong anti-Confederate from the Council, though not from office (Edward Palmer); third, to maintain the non-committal colour of the Government by adding two

[17]*Monitor*, Dec. 29, 1864.

[18]Another Conservative attempt in 1871 gave the Island its railway. MacKinnon, *Government of Prince Edward Island*, 133.

[19]*Monitor*, Dec. 22, 1864, noted these rumours and said that Palmer deserved better treatment from the Conservative party.

[20]*Examiner*, Jan. 16, 1865.

[21]Macdonald Papers, Macdonald to Gray, March 24, 1865.

[22]Coles' description was actually embodied in a want of confidence motion. P.E.I., Assembly, *Journals*, 1865, 7 (March 3).

new members of opposing views. Whatever else, the Conservatives were still in power, and the unhappy prospect of a Liberal, perhaps a Catholic, government was avoided.

The newspaper alignment was as strange as the political one. The Conservative and Protestant *Islander* found itself allied to the Liberal and Catholic *Examiner* on the question of Confederation. Against Confederation were the Conservative, Protestant *Monitor* and *Protestant*; the Liberal, Catholic *Herald* (formerly the *Vindicator*); the *Patriot*, in the odd position of being both Liberal and Protestant; and *Ross's Weekly*, which was sympathetic to the Tenant League. Even this proportion, five out of seven, does not fully convey the strength of the opposition.

Whelan did not exaggerate when he said that the Island was "dead set against Union in all shapes and forms."[23] The excitement was considerable,[24] but overwhelming opposition unmistakable. As early as December 30, the *Islander* wrote, "the great majority of people appear to be wholly averse to Confederation. . . . We have done our duty. We have urged Confederation—the people have declared against it. . . ." Reading this the same day, Dundas clipped it out and sent it to Cardwell. This, he wrote, "is the present state of public opinion on this subject."[25]

Edward Whelan was sadly disappointed at the turn of affairs. A convert to Confederation, Whelan had all the enthusiasm of one. Twitted on more than one occasion with having changed his mind, Whelan replied that the Quebec Conference would have changed even Joseph Howe. "I believe that if he had been at the Quebec Conference he would have acted a very different part from what he has done."[26] Clearly Quebec had changed Whelan. He had caught sight of a greater British America, and suddenly Prince Edward Island had become very small and provincial. Whelan's feelings found vent in the *Examiner*.

The cause of Confederation happily does not depend on the will of the small politicians of the small Island of Prince Edward. If the cause be fought with success on the main land, its consummation cannot be delayed through the petulance of this little place. . . . But we cannot resist smiling at the exceeding simplicity of those who think that the other Provinces

---

23Ormsby, "Letters to Galt," Whelan to Galt, Dec. 17, 1864.
24"I never saw a time when newspapers were so much sought after, and the speeches delivered at public meetings so generally read." P.E.I. Assembly, *Debates*, 1865, 11 (March 2). The reference was to Tignish, P.E.I. Cf. also the view of the Saint John *Telegraph*, Dec. 14, 1864, quoted *supra*, 106.
25C.O. 226, Dundas to Cardwell, Dec. 30, 1864.
26P.E.I. Assembly, *Debates*, 1866, 120 (May 8).

will be confederate while the British Government must go to the expense of keeping up a protectorate over this patch of sand bank in the Gulf of St. Lawrence, where the inhabitants imagine they have such a paradise as would be contaminated by alliance with their powerful, prosperous fellow subjects on the main land.[27]

It was hardly to be expected that Charlottetown could ever be anything else than "an obstacle in the path of progress.[28]

The causes of the Island's opposition to Confederation were summed up by the *Islander*. Union would bring a ruinous tariff, ruinous taxation —for an Intercolonial railway that would do the Island no good anyway —and conscription for a British American army. Islanders "would be marched away to the frontiers of Upper Canada to fight for the Canadians. . . ."[29] Probably the major reason for opposition was fear of increased taxation. As Whelan put it, "the asses of country people, who can't see an inch beyond their noses . . . are afraid they are going to be tremendously taxed . . . ."[30] J. C. Pope claimed that the Island was being asked to transfer a steadily increasing revenue to a central government in exchange for high tariffs and high taxation.[31]

The Assembly met on February 28, 1865. It promised, in the Reply to the Speech from the Throne, to give Confederation its "most earnest consideration." Earnest it was. In due course the Assembly witnessed the Premier, J. C. Pope, moving five anti-Confederate resolutions against those of his brother, the Provincial Secretary, who had urged eight resolutions in favour of Confederation. The Premier professed sympathy for the principle of union, but said that the Quebec Resolutions did not offer fair terms. This kind of argument Whelan thought quite singular. It was, he said in a homely Island metaphor, as if the Premier and his anti-Confederate friends were willing to see a field ploughed in principle, but objected to the destruction of the daisies and the mice that lived there.[32]

J. C. Pope objected particularly to the principle of "representation by population." He was not alone in this; Whelan, Palmer, Coles, A. A. Macdonald had all, in one way or another, objected to the same thing. Islanders seemed to feel that rigid adherence to this formula was unfair. Representation by population was not followed in any colony, so Pope

[27]Charlottetown *Examiner*, Dec. 26, 1864.
[28]*Ibid.*, Feb. 20, 1865.
[29]*Islander*, Jan. 6, 1865. Cf. also Gray's remarks to Tupper, *supra*, 183, and C. F. Bennett's in Newfoundland, *supra*, 167.
[30]Ormsby, "Letters to Galt," Whelan to Galt, Dec. 17, 1864.
[31]P.E.I., Assembly, *Journals*, 1865, 45 (March 24).
[32]Charlottetown *Examiner*, Jan. 30, 1865.

argued; the weight given to the country vote was well known. Why should Prince Edward Island have a smaller representation than Montreal?[33] Moreover, the greater proportionate representation in the Senate made little difference to the Islanders; four members in a Senate of 76 was not that much different from five members in a Commons of 194. In addition, the Island was small in population and would remain so, Pope believed, because it did not have the conditions of growth. Thus, the Island's representation would grow steadily less as other provinces increased in population. In short, representation by population "would deprive this Colony of any legitimate influence. . . ."[34]

As for the local legislature of the Island, it would, in Pope's view, have little or no purpose under Confederation. Its powers and duties would be negligible. And eighty cents a head was "not a liberal compensation for the surrender of a separate Government, with the independent powers it now enjoys."[35] One of J. C. Pope's supporters remarked that under Confederation, "The Local Legislature . . . would be little better than a town council; we would have this building here merely to look at."[36] George Coles, with his usual vehemence, went one better; "We would be a laughing stock to the world."[37] The supporters of Confederation did not try to defend the status of the local legislature. They had little to say about its powers and duties after Confederation. Presumably it would be like the daisies and the field mice of Whelan's figure, to be ploughed under without regret.[38] The *Islander* said that each province in united British America ought to be a municipality, the Island's position being comparable to that of the Isle of Wight in Great Britain.[39]

The debate on the two sets of resolutions continued in the Assembly

[33]To a similar argument by Palmer the Toronto *Globe* suggested that all of British North America should be divided up into states equal in size to Prince Edward Island and then represented equally! (*Globe*, Dec. 13, 1864.)

[34]P.E.I., Assembly, *Journals*, 1865, 46 (March 24).

[35]J. C. Pope's Resolution No. 4.

[36]P.E.I., Assembly, *Debates*, 1865, 64 (March 30).

[37]*Ibid.*, 67 (March 31).

[38]T. Heath Haviland, in the debates of 1866, made a belated attempt to show how the local legislature would still control much of its own affairs. "The powers . . . given to the Federal Legislature . . . neither require nor necessitate a nulification [sic] of the . . . Provincial Constitutions. . . ." Given on May 8, 1866, but appears not in the *Debates* of 1866, but as an appendix to the *Debates* of 1867, 152.

[39]*Islander*, Oct. 28, 1864, "Union of the Provinces, No. 1." The point is elaborated in the *Islander*, Dec. 30, 1864, "Union of the Provinces, No. 3": "A parliamentary union, with organized shires or municipalities, would certainly be much less likely to foment sectional discord . . . as well as decidedly more economical, central and energetic."

for a week. Finally on March 31, 1865, J. C. Pope's amendment to his brother's resolutions carried triumphantly, 23–5. Confederation was decisively rejected by the Assembly, and a few days later a similar resolution was carried unanimously in the Legislative Council.[40] The Address to the Queen at the end of the session left no room for doubt. Prince Edward Island did "emphatically reject a Union which . . . we believe would prove politically, commercially and financially disastrous."[41] This brusque treatment was repeated in May, when the Island government replied to the Nova Scotian overture for renewed discussion of Maritime union. Tupper's attempt may have been recognized for what it was: in any case all forms of union were summarily rejected by the Prince Edward Island government.[42]

But discussion continued even when it was admitted on all sides that Confederation could not be carried. The principal reason was the Colonial Office. Cardwell's despatches kept the pot boiling briskly, and as 1865 drew on, the heat was increased. Shortly after the 1865 session had begun Dundas was told that the salary of the lieutenant governor might be placed on local charge.[43] This painful exigency could be avoided by acceptance of Confederation. On April 28 Cardwell said that in view of the Island's dependence upon Great Britain for defence, great weight should be given to measures, like Confederation, that Britain thought desirable for that purpose. On June 24 an even stronger despatch went out from London.[44]

It was only a coincidence that brought the question of troops immediately to the fore. Cardwell's latest despatch had scarcely been received before trouble developed over quite a different matter. Late in July, 1865, just as Dundas was leaving to go home on leave of absence,[45] the deputy sheriff of Queens County and his bailiffs were stopped on the highway and relieved of property they had seized under a court

---

[40]P.E.I., Assembly, *Journals*, 1865, 92, and D. C. Harvey, "Confederation in Prince Edward Island," 146–8; P.E.I., Legislative Council, *Journals*, 1865, 58 (April 3).

[41]P.E.I., Assembly, *Journals*, 1865, 95–7 (April 3).

[42]The Island Minute of Council is enclosed in Nova Scotia, Lieutenant Governor, General Correspondence Received, Dundas to MacDonnell, May 30, 1865. See *infra*, 214.

[43]C.O. 227, Cardwell to Dundas, Feb. 18, 1865. In 1869, with the greatest reluctance, the Assembly agreed to provide £1,400 a year. MacKinnon, *Government of Prince Edward Island*, 86–7.

[44]C.O. 227, Cardwell to Dundas, April 28, 1865; Cardwell to Dundas, June 24, 1865.

[45]Dundas' tour of duty was up, but he was well liked in the Island and Cardwell thought his continuation there would be useful in furthering Confederation.

execution. This marked the first outbreak in a series of incidents known as the Tenant League riots. The Administrator of the Colony, the Hon. Robert Hodgson, promptly telegraphed to Halifax for troops. A contingent of eleven officers and 120 rank and file left Halifax on August 4 and arrived in Charlottetown on August 6.[46] The disturbances were suppressed almost as soon as the troops made their appearance, but only their presence deterred the League from further action.[47] Hodgson would not part with the troops, and this provoked choleric remarks from the Citadel in Halifax over British troops being used as civil police.[48] Matters were not helped by Hodgson's statement that he could not say when the need for troops would end,[49] by the record of nine deserters in the first three weeks,[50] or by references in the Charlottetown papers to the pleasant picnic the soldiers were having. The troops were not finally withdrawn for another year and a half, on June 27, 1867.[51] J. C. Pope's purchase of the Cunard estate for the Prince Edward Island government—some 212,000 acres, about one-seventh of the Island—may have helped to ease the land question, though it was not finally settled until after 1873.

Cardwell's despatch of June 24, 1865, provoked a stiff reaction from the legislature when it met in 1866. The session opened late, on April 9, doubtless with the hope that the moves toward Confederation in New Brunswick and Nova Scotia would have beneficial effects in the Island. A Confederate government was within forty-eight hours of assuming power in New Brunswick, and Confederation was to be launched the very next day, April 10, in Nova Scotia; in both provinces the Fenians were causing tremendous excitement. The effect of all these events upon Prince Edward Island was only to make her cling more tightly to her independence. The rude, cold blasts from the world, from the Colonial Office, and from the Fenians were like the north wind in the old fable, making the traveller clasp his coat more firmly. Confederation was not even mentioned in the Speech from the Throne. It was on April 16, a week later, that Premier J. C. Pope brought

[46]Military Correspondence, Nova Scotia Command, Francklyn to Military Secretary, Horse Guards, Aug. 12, 1865.
[47]Some of the Leaguers ultimately went to prison for terms up to 18 months.
[48]Military Correspondence, Nova Scotia Command, Francklyn to Military Secretary, Horse Guards, Aug. 12, 1865.
[49]*Ibid.*, Hodgson to Francklyn, Aug. 8, 1865, enclosure in Hastings Doyle to Military Secretary, Horse Guards, Aug. 31, 1865.
[50]From the official record. A week later the *Islander* reported 13 deserters in four weeks and added that none had been apprehended despite a £20 reward. (*Islander*, Sept. 8, 1865)
[51]*Ibid.*, July 5, 1867.

down the Governor's message containing the "strong and deliberate opinion" of Her Majesty's Government on Confederation. It produced a strong and deliberate answer. "Any Federal Union of the North American Colonies that would embrace this Island, would be hostile to the feelings and wishes as it would be opposed to the best and most vital interests of its people." The Premier justified the unequivocal wording on the ground that the Islanders were afraid they might somehow be manipulated into Confederation; that the Island "even againt [sic] the will of our people, might be made a member of the Confederate States or Provinces of British America."[52] The example of Nova Scotia was to prove that such suspicions were not entirely without foundation. Whelan tried to persuade the Prince Edward Island Legislature at least to recognize the principle of union, but even that was defeated.

The Premier's resolution of 1866 was more than his brother, the Provincial Secretary, could stomach, and W. H. Pope resigned office on May 28, 1866. T. Heath Haviland also resigned the solicitor-generalship, but he found leaving office altogether too great a sacrifice, and so took Pope's place as Provincial Secretary.[53]

October, 1866, brought a further inducement to the Island to enter Confederation; this time it was from Tilley and Tupper, who were then in London. It was a belated recognition of what had been suggested at Charlottetown two years before: a proposal for the Confederation to buy out the landed proprietors of the Island, the sum to be $800,000.[54] Made under other circumstances the offer might have been more graciously received than it was. Except by the *Examiner* and the *Islander*,[55] it was coldly received in the Island. Could it melt the ice out of Northumberland Straits? That was the *Herald*'s question.[56] And it was to take more than $800,000 to melt the Islanders' resistance. There was a mocking ring in the jingle published in the *Yarmouth Tribune* in Nova Scotia:

> That eight hundred thousand will surely suffice
> To buy all those Islanders up in a trice.[57]

An unenthusiastic Canadian Minute of Council did not help, and it was considered in the Island to be practically a veto on Tilley and Tupper's

[52]P.E.I., Assembly, *Journals*, 1866, 95 (May 7); *Debates*, 1866, 100–1.
[53]*Islander*, June 1, 1866; C.O. 226, Dundas to Cardwell, June 4, 1866.
[54]Memorandum in C.O. 227, Carnarvon to Dundas, Sept. 27, 1866.
[55]E.g., *Islander*, Oct. 19, 1866.
[56]Charlottetown *Herald*, Nov. 7, 1866. Cf. also *Summerside Progress*, Oct. 29, 1866.
[57]*Yarmouth Tribune*, Feb. 6, 1867, from "Quiz" of Annapolis County.

proposal.[58] J. C. Pope, the Premier, who was in London at that time, pricked up his ears at the idea;[59] but as far as the Island was concerned, the stern Resolution of May, 1866, was their last word on Confederation. Dundas wrote to Carnarvon just before the election of 1867 that "the opposition . . . to Union generally has never been more violent than at present. . . ."[60]

After eight years in power the Conservative government was defeated in the election of February, 1867. Their frantic efforts in December, 1864, had availed them only a temporary triumph. They were criticized by the Liberals with only a little justification but much success as the "corrupt confederate faction."[61] And they were still divided. The Premier wanted to keep Confederation an open question; Edward Palmer still wanted it condemned outright.[62] The Conservative ship went down with J. C. Pope and Palmer still arguing. By March George Coles was the new Premier, and he could look forward to a comfortable majority in the Assembly of about nineteen to eleven.[63]

The election brought Whelan the post of Queen's Printer, but the by-election the post required was too much. Whelan's sympathy to Confederation, his criticism of the Tenant League, lost him the by-election by 37 votes, to Edward Reilly, the editor of the *Herald*, a paper of the same political and religious colour as the *Examiner*.[64] And the Liberal victory itself brought no joy to Whelan. His Confederation sympathies fell on even stonier ground among the Liberals, and he was by this time thoroughly disillusioned with affairs in Prince Edward Island. His belief in Confederation, he said in 1866, "I will probably retain as long as I live. . . ."[65] But he had not long to live. He did not even outlive McGee. Ailing in the summer of 1867, Whelan died at Charlottetown on December 10 of that year, at the age of 43.[66]

Nothing that Whelan, or W. H. Pope, or Gray could do or say made

[58]The Canadian Minute of Council was dated Oct. 22, 1864, and was enclosed in a despatch from Monck to Dundas, Oct. 26, 1864. The $800,000 turned up in later negotiations, and it was actually embodied in the imperial Order-in-Council of June 26, 1873, that admitted the Island into Confederation.

[59]J. Pope, *Memoirs of the Right Honourable Sir John A. Macdonald* (Toronto, [1930]) 507.

[60]C.O. 226, Dundas to Carnarvon, Feb. 6, 1867.

[61]Charlottetown *Herald*, Feb. 6, 1867.

[62]*Islander*, Feb. 8, 1867.

[63]*Examiner*, March 4, 1867. In the Legislative Council, which, like the Canadian, was partly elective, six seats were contested of which the Liberals got five. They could expect a majority of about 7–5 in their favour.

[64]*Examiner*, May 6, 1867.

[65]P.E.I., Assembly, *Debates*, 1866, 121 (May 8).

[66]*Examiner*, Dec. 16, 1867.

any difference in the Island attitudes to Confederation between 1864 and 1867. "That tight little island"[67] showed no enthusiasm for union; it preferred "to stand off and watch the game for a little while."[68] Six years later, in 1873, under the stress of financial troubles, with controversies over land, religion, and schools more pressing than in the 1860's, and with Island political parties split into volatile factions, Prince Edward Island joined Confederation. But between 1864 and 1867 the first Island response to the question of Union was fear of the loss of Island independence, fear of the atrophy or the obliteration of the Island legislature. Islanders saw little hope of rescuing their local legislature intact out of the melting pot of union. It was as Cornelius Howat truly said in the 1866 debates, "a question of 'self or no self.'"[69] And for the Islanders their legislature was then, as now, the symbol of their self-respect.

[67]The Montreal *Gazette*'s phrase, Oct. 28, 1864.
[68]*Summerside Progress*, June 17, 1867. Cf. also Charlottetown *Herald*, Dec. 28, 1864: "Well, we say, let the other colonies unite if they desire to do so, and if we see that any benefits would result to this Island, we can join the Confederation afterwards."
[69]P.E.I., Assembly, *Debates*, 1866, 108 (May 7).

13. NOVA SCOTIA

IN 1864 NOVA SCOTIA had a population of about 350,000, which was distributed around the rocky perimeter of 4,500 miles of coast and along the great swale of the Annapolis Valley. Nova Scotia was part of the North American continent only by virtue of a neck of land twelve miles wide, and it was the classic *paenensula*, near island in shape, outlook, and attitudes. The long coastline—ten times the length of the province—nurtured an economy now approaching maturity and within two decades of obsolescence. Nova Scotian ships sailed the oceans of the globe. "In the ports of the Seven Seas and the waters thereof," wrote Frederick William Wallace, "the terms 'Nova Scotiamen' and 'Bluenose' were known to seamen of all nationalities during the 'sixties."[1] New Brunswick built ships and sold them: Nova Scotia built them and sailed them.[2] Wallace described one, seen in 50° South, between Cape Horn and Australia:

> . . . the stranger came storming up out of the west into plain sight. She was a big ship—a wooden three-master, black-hulled, heavily sparred, and deep laden—and she was forging through the long green seas with yards almost square. . . . This exhibition of sail-carrying in a heavy breeze, the well-set and well-trimmed masts and yards, the fautlessly stayed masts, and general spotless appearance of the ship evoked . . . murmured admiration. . . . "Hard packets these Bluenose ships. Worse than the Yankees, they say."[3]

She was a Nova Scotiaman, run like a New Englander, but flying the Red Ensign, and she was a symbol both of the origins and of the present strength of Nova Scotia.

Nova Scotia was near the zenith of her commercial prosperity. "Our province," said the *Morning Chronicle*, December 18, 1865, "is prosperous beyond example. . . . We are on the full tide of prosperity under the lowest tariff in America." The decades immediately following the mid-century provided a prosperity that Nova Scotia had not seen

[1]F. W. Wallace, *Wooden Ships and Iron Men* (London, 1924), 115.
[2]*Ibid.*, 108.　　　　　　　　　　　　　[3]*Ibid.*, 2–4 *passim*.

before or would again. The iron hull—the real nemesis of Nova Scotian shipbuilding—had not yet appeared; the steam engine and the screw propeller had not affected the basis of her carrying trade. The inshore and offshore banks provided the fisheries; larch, spruce, pine, and white oak, the wood; fifty or sixty snug harbours, the opportunity. The rest was up to human hands. These were not idle. "At no previous period in the history of this province has there ever been as much capital invested in shipping and ship-building, as at the present."[4] This was the opinion of the *Morning Chronicle* in 1863. By 1867 the tonnage of Nova Scotian-owned ships amounted to 350,000—one ton for every inhabitant—and 75 per cent more than New Brunswick, Nova Scotia's nearest rival.

Nova Scotia had at that time a major role in sea communications between Britain and the United States. Ships westward bound to New York and Boston called regularly at Halifax. Ships eastward bound to Liverpool and London also called. In fact, the south shore of Nova Scotia looked out upon the whole periphery of the Atlantic. Bermuda seemed closer than Quebec. The British empire had in consequence a meaning for Nova Scotia that it had for no other province. The empire was tangible. The forces that held it together were real and powerful. It was natural for Joseph Howe to prefer empire solidarity to visions of a continental North American domain. Where was the reality of empire in the wilderness of rock and forest that lay north and west, behind Nova Scotia? The lines of communication across the accessible ocean were broad and easy: those across the hills and distances of British North America were tortuous and remote. Surely with such a capital as London, said Howe, "we need not seek for another in the backwoods of Canada, and may be pardoned if we prefer London under the dominion of John Bull to Ottawa under the dominion of Jack Frost."[5] And, Howe asked, "Is Halifax . . . so poor an outlook for an orator. . .?"[6]

Halifax, it is true, did not have the grandeur of London. To Dr. Charles Mackay of the London *Times*, it looked like an inferior edition of Portsmouth.[7] The houses were built of wood, often painted a dingy brown, and looked to Canadians as if mechanics might be occupying them. But then a fine carriage with a liveried coachman would drive up in front of them: "you enquire as to its ownership and

[4]Halifax *Morning Chronicle*, Oct. 6, 1863.

[5]*Morning Chronicle*, June 9, 1866, reporting Howe's speech at Barrington, N.S.

[6]*Ibid.*

[7]London *Times*, Oct. 24, 1865, report of Oct. 10 from Halifax.

find that the person who is the subject of your interrogatory lives in the unpretending domicile of wood. . . ."[8] Thus Charles Belford of the Toronto *Leader*. Halifax was in fact a rich city and it had a rather Georgian character. "There is a courtly air about it . . . its bloods drive fast horses . . . its ladies dress in the height of fashion, read the latest novels as well in the language of Madame George Sand . . . as in their native tongue. . . ."[9] Like St. John's and Charlottetown, Halifax boasted a fine Georgian legislature. Other monuments added lustre: a very expensive Government House for the governor and his entourage; a handsome round church and round clock tower that had been provided by the energy and good taste of Queen Victoria's strident father. But Halifax was still a port; its Water Street differed little from others of the same ilk in St. John's and Saint John: ". . . with the exception of a few good houses, the whole range of buildings is of the most filthy and inferior description; nearly all of which are petty shops, groceries, and groggeries of the lowest sort, and frequented by innumerable hordes of soldiers and seamen. . . ."[10] The soldiers came from the companies of British artillery, infantry, and engineers who were stationed in the Citadel, a massive stone and earth fortress comprising some 50 acres which commanded the harbour and was the central point in the British defence system of the West Atlantic. Of seamen there was no end. Halifax in summer was the headquarters of both the North American and West Indian squadrons of the British Navy. A regular ship-of-the-line carried 700 men, and sometimes a dozen ships would be in port at once. The groggeries in Water Street never lacked for patrons.

Temperance legislation was still a long way in the future, and not even the Baptists—New Brunswick and Nova Scotia had the largest percentage in British North America—went so far as to advocate seriously outright abstinence in the *Christian Messenger* which was their paper. This kind of moderation was also characteristic of the religious divisions generally in Nova Scotia. They were not as sharp or as bitter as those in other provinces. J. W. Johnston, the erstwhile Premier, Tupper, the new one, and the Conservative party as a whole, had successfully cultivated the Catholic vote, and it did not appear to weaken the party with Protestant voters. Roman Catholics amounted to 25 per cent of the population; another 25 per cent were Presbyterians; Baptists, Anglicans, and Methodists, in that order, followed.

[8]Toronto *Leader*, Aug. 22, 1864, report of Aug. 12 from Halifax.
[9]*Ibid.*, Aug. 22, 1864, report of Aug. 17 from Saint John.
[10]A. L. Spedon, *Rambles among the Blue-Noses* (Montreal, 1863), 131.

Softened asperities in religion were a concomitant of Nova Scotian political life. It is fair to say that the Nova Scotian equivalent for the Canadian rebellions of 1837 was Howe's Twelve Resolutions. Some were unkind enough to suggest that the relative mildness of the Nova Scotian reaction in 1837 was the result of a lively sense of British favours, past, present, and future. There is no doubt that the British military and naval base in Halifax exercised a chastening influence upon political and social extravagance. But perhaps the differences between Canadian and Nova Scotian political life lay also in the differences between Canadians and Nova Scotians.

In Canadian and Nova Scotian newspapers one is struck by the differences in attack and in outlook. The Canadian newspapers, notably those of Canada West, have often a rough bellicosity, a kind of frontier vehemence; in Nova Scotian papers there is a greater suavity, perhaps a little more old-fashioned dignity. It was possible to sense that Halifax was closer to London than Toronto in thought and feeling. This was not to say that Nova Scotia lacked political energy: on the contrary, as the Halifax *Evening Reporter* said, public opinion in Nova Scotia was, "if anything a little too strongly developed, stronger even than in England. The reason for this is that every man here is more or less a politician. . . ."[11] But in Nova Scotia politics was sustained and controlled by a rudimentary sense of fair play. Hastings Doyle, the Major-General commanding the forces in the Maritime provinces, wrote Howe in later and more troubled years, "I hope, like a true Briton, you will not kick them [the Confederation party in Nova Scotia] when they are down!" Howe replied characteristically, "The victory has been decisive but I hope it will not be abused."[12] There is no escaping the feeling of vital political energy in Nova Scotia. Even the restlessness of Nova Scotians, their dissatisfaction with the limits of provincial horizons, their search for a new and more satisfying formula of empire, British or British American, supports this. The discussion of Confederation, once started, did not abate until long after July 1, 1867. Editorials on union in all phases and shapes filled the papers; letters to the editor, public debates, and the crowds at the Temperance Hall meetings, all attest the political vitality of Nova Scotia in more spacious days.

Richard MacDonnell, the Lieutenant Governor of Nova Scotia from 1864 to 1865, remarked upon the same thing. MacDonnell never enjoyed very good report either in London or in Halifax, but his

[11]Halifax *Evening Reporter*, Nov. 8, 1864.
[12]Howe Papers, Hastings Doyle to Howe, Oct. 1, 1867 (confidential); Howe to Hastings Doyle, Oct. 5, 1867.

despatches, though unsympathetic to Confederation, were often shrewd
and they cannot be dismissed merely as partisan opposition to a
great cause. Your ministry, he wrote Monck of Canada, early in 1865,

> . . . seem not to have cared how Canadian—selfishly Canadian, they may
> have appeared to Bluenose who is very happy as he is . . . your Ministry
> seem not to have suspected any rocks or shoals ahead whilst they were in
> reality trying to steer through a channel full of them . . . don't suppose
> that I question in any way the good faith or ability of your Lordship's
> Ministers—I simply question their politic manipulation of the subject with
> so keen a spectator as Bluenose watching the game—[13]

It was sound advice. Nova Scotians were willing to consider union;
they had been discussing the subject periodically for years, but they
were not ready to be whisked into union simply because Canada was
finding her own constitution too difficult to manage. Better reasons than
that would have to be urged. Nothing made Nova Scotians more dis-
trustful of Confederation, wrote MacDonnell to Cardwell, "than the
strange forgetfulness of Canadian statesmen that they were speaking
not merely to a Canadian Parliament but to all these Provinces."[14]
If the Canadians still read Confederation in the light of Canadian
politics, Nova Scotians could be excused for doing the same. The
old feeling of distrust for Canadians appeared again. *Timeo Danaos
et dona ferentes*: MacDonnell's quotation applied all too aptly in Nova
Scotia to Canadians bearing Confederation and the Intercolonial railway. Even Galt's Sherbrooke speech, comprehensive and searching
though it was, Tupper found too much from the Canadian point of
view.[15] Whelan in Charlottetown underlined the same point in a letter
to Galt. "There is one drawback only to the satisfaction which I
derived from the perusal of your speech: *You treat the question too
much from a Canadian point of view.*"[16]

As in Newfoundland and Prince Edward Island Confederation
crossed political boundaries. In Nova Scotia there was no coalition as
there was in Newfoundland in April, 1865; the Nova Scotian Liberals
continued to oppose the Government, notably over the Pictou Railway.[17]

[13]MacDonnell to Monck, March 20, 1865 (private). Copy in Nova Scotia,
Lieutenant Governor, General Correspondence Despatched.

[14]C.O. 217, MacDonnell to Cardwell, March 16, 1865 (confidential). An
able despatch that well sums up the Nova Scotian attitude to Confederation.

[15]W. G. Ormsby, "Letters to Galt concerning the Maritime Provinces and
Confederation," *Canadian Historical Review*, XXIV, 2 (June, 1953), 167–8,
Tupper to Galt, Dec. 13, 1864. Also quoted *supra*, 107.

[16]*Ibid.*, Whelan to Galt, Dec. 17, 1864.

[17]E.g., Nova Scotia, Assembly, *Debates and Proceedings*, 1866, 182 (March
30). The Government won, 31–20.

In Nova Scotia the position was not unlike that in Prince Edward Island before December, 1864; Liberals agreed to support a Conservative Confederation policy. The difference between Nova Scotia and Prince Edward Island was that in the former the Conservative government had, and continued to have, a Confederation policy: in Prince Edward Island it had disrupted the government and caused the resignation of the premier. The Nova Scotian Liberal leaders, Archibald and McCully, supported Confederation right to the end; and while they were prepared to vote, and did vote, against the government on other issues, they never abandoned Confederation, though under considerable pressure from a wing of their party to do so. Tupper needed such support; he could never have carried Confederation without it. At the same time Archibald and McCully themselves could not have carried Confederation, and they may have believed that they had not the power to defeat it.[18]

Adams G. Archibald, leader of the Opposition in the Assembly and Howe's political heir, was remarkably deft and subtle. He had of course the warrant of an old established family name, which counted as seriously in Nova Scotia as in Boston. He never seems to have lost the respect of his Liberal colleagues, and his position in the party survived until Confederation had been passed in April, 1866. Archibald had an air of sweet reasonableness about him which was singularly winning, if rather deceptive.[19] An eye witness described an interview, probably in 1866, between Howe and Archibald when Howe used all his considerable powers of argument and persuasion to get Archibald to break with Tupper. "I remember when Howe in his excitement, standing up appealing to Archibald as his (Howe's) son in political party faith, Archibald sat at the table with his head bowed between his hands as though bending beneath the storm, and, looking over at me, made a grimace and gave me an expressive wink."[20] It said much for Archibald's coolness. Perhaps it was contempt. In 1867 Howe said bitterly, "I loved him like a brother or a son."[21] One is left not so much with admiration for Archibald as sadness for Howe.

Jonathan McCully, leader of the Liberals in the Legislative Council, was much more volatile. McCully was a quick and agile debater; on

[18]Note the following from the *Halifax Citizen*, Nov. 5, 1864: "The [Liberal] opposition have not the power either to carry or defeat the Confederation scheme. . . ."

[19]Montreal *Gazette*, Oct. 28, 1864, commenting on Archibald at the Quebec Conference.

[20]Related by Dr. George Johnson, and quoted by E. M. Saunders, *Three Premiers of Nova Scotia* (Toronto, 1909), 371–2.

[21]*Morning Chronicle*, May 15, 1867, reporting Howe's speech at Mason Hall, Halifax, May 9.

his feet he was unbeatable for "strong, vigorous, downright dialectics."[22]
He took up causes with ease and expounded them with facility; and,
except for Howe, he was the most telling writer in the province. He
had made the *Morning Chronicle*, in the six years he had been its
editor, the most powerful paper in the province and its only daily. But
he was not much liked or appreciated and he never had the loyal
following of Howe or Archibald. He lacked the tenacity of the former
and the integrity of the latter. McCully was probably sincere in his
belief in Confederation, but he was facile. He lacked a solid foundation.
In this respect he rather resembled his fellow Nova Scotian in Vancouver
Island, William Smith—alias Amor de Cosmos—who until 1863 owned
the Victoria *British Colonist*.[23] In Windsor in 1866 Howe remarked
on McCully's conversion to Confederation. St. Paul, Howe said, was
converted by a flood of light; Danaë was changed from a virgin into a
strumpet by a shower of gold; "you, who know the man, can judge
whether McCully was converted after the fashion of Danaë or St.
Paul."[24]

It was easy to allege insincerity against all three leaders, Tupper,
McCully, and Archibald. Tupper, it was true, had lectured on Confederation in 1860, but he had been cool to the idea when it was first
broached in the summer past by the Canadians. McCully, and probably
Archibald, had been opposed. It was the events from August to October
that had changed them. On November 24, 1864, the *Halifax Citizen*
spoke of

... a few ambitious individuals, who feel our legislature too small for their
capacity; and its rewards too trifling for their acceptance; who feel
anxious to strut in embroidered court suits, plush breeches, silk stockings
and bagwigs before a Vice Roy at Ottawa, and enjoy fat salaries, far away
from the Provinces whose best interests are to be shamefully voted away
in return for a fortnight's feasting and a few private promises.

William Garvie, one of the *Citizen*'s editors, poked fun at the Nova
Scotia coalition on Confederation in *Barney Rooney's Letters*:

"Tupper, alorra," sez McCully, wid a vice as soft as a tub iv Cumberland
buther, "considher the claims iv the opposishun."
"Troth will I, McCully mavourneen," sez Tupper, as soft as another tubful
iv the same, only twice as big, "afther I look out for number one, as my way
is, ye know."[25]

22Montreal *Gazette*, Oct. 28, 1864.   23See *infra*, 318–19.
24Halifax *Morning Chronicle*, May 19, 1866, reporting Howe's speech at
Windsor of May 8.
25[William Garvie], *Barney Rooney's Letters on Confederation, Botheration and
Political Transmogrification* (Halifax, 1865), 15–16.

MacDonnell, too, was suspicious. He wrote Cardwell that he could not "allow such a measure [as Confederation] to be decided by the intrigues and influences which both Government and opposition leaders—looking for their reward to Ottawa—could bring to bear on their supporters in the present Parliament." He would have insisted on a dissolution—as Gordon was to do in New Brunswick—had he not been restrained by Cardwell.[26]

It must be said that Confederation came not inopportunely for Tupper. His school legislation of 1864 had made him unpopular. It had imposed a form of direct tax on Nova Scotians by tying school appropriations from the government to assessments levied "voluntarily" by the school districts, and, however farsighted, it was mightily resented. Confederation could serve Tupper's purpose by diverting public attention from awkward issues of provincial politics. "He would annex this Province to Canada, or to Massachusetts, or to the moon, or propose to do so," said the *Halifax Citizen*, November 5, 1864, if it would distract attention. No doubt Confederation was convenient; but it was soon clear that it would, if pressed, be a far more serious danger than the School Act of 1864. Tupper did not hesitate. There was a certain recklessness about Tupper that could be called courage. It was both physical and political, and it was one of Tupper's more endearing qualities.

To his courage Tupper joined a resolute determination and a garrulous tongue. He was an inveterate talker, and the old story of his later years—that Macdonald was the captain of the ship while Tupper supplied the wind for the sails—was only an exaggeration. The description by the Montreal *Gazette* (October 28, 1864) suited him, "forcible, keen, and emphatic," with a "suppressed temptation to sarcasm" in his voice. To Laurier Tupper seemed "the very incarnation of the Parliamentary athlete. . . ."[27] It took courage to pass the School Act; it was to take more courage to put Confederation through a dying legislature in the face of the probable opposition of at least two-thirds of the province. Tupper was a strong man: his curly black hair that framed his face—he affected a short and not unbecoming form of mutton-chop whiskers—gave him a resemblance to some audacious lion pertinaciously on its way forward.

Tupper and the other Nova Scotian delegates arrived in Nova Scotia early in November. McCully, Archibald, and Henry came via Port-

[26]C.O. 217, MacDonnell to Cardwell, Nov. 24, 1864 (confidential). MacDonnell said he would keep no copy of this despatch. Also Cardwell to MacDonnell, Dec. 8, 1864. (See *supra*, 105n)
[27]Dominion of Canada, House of Commons, *Debates*, 1916, 585.

land and Saint John, Tupper and Dickey from New York. Public opinion, as in Newfoundland, was at first quiescent not anticipating perhaps the rapidity with which the delegates were prepared to move, but by the third week in November "cat's paws" were stirring.[28] "We cannot take up a Colonial paper," said the Halifax *Evening Express* on November 14, 1864, "which is not largely occupied with . . . [Confederation] in some form or other." By early December the cat's paws had become a strong breeze.

As in Newfoundland and Prince Edward Island the newspapers of the capital functioned in some respects as a metropolitan press. In Nova Scotia the easy communications by rail to Truro and Windsor—both less than three hours away—and by sea along the south shore gave the Halifax papers an important role in the public life of the province. But as in the other two Maritime provinces the newspapers of the capital were, in respect of Confederation, distinctly misleading. In Nova Scotia there was a remarkable disparity between the Halifax papers and the country papers. The majority of Halifax newspapers supported Confederation: all but one of the country ones opposed it.

The country papers opposed to Confederation included both Yarmouth papers, the *Herald* and the *Tribune*, Conservative and Liberal respectively; the *Liverpool Transcript*, from the south shore; the *Eastern Chronicle* of New Glasgow; and the Bridgetown *Free Press* of the Annapolis Valley. Only the Pictou *Colonial Standard* supported Confederation.[29] The country papers often took the theoretical grounds for their opposition from the pages of the Halifax *Citizen*, and, by 1865, from the Halifax *Morning Chronicle*. They did not generally essay flights of constitutional argument on their own. In this respect they differed from the little Reform papers of Canada West which stood sturdily on their own two legs in any kind of argument. The real basis of the opposition of the country newspapers to Confederation was their instinctive suspicion of change, and, be it added, of Canada. The Yarmouth papers illustrate this well.

Are the people of Nova Scotia so discontented with their present system of Government that they are willing to change it at such a cost. . . ? (*Herald*, Dec. 8, 1864)

---

[28]Halifax *Morning Journal*, Nov. 23, 1864; Halifax *Sun*, Nov. 23, 1864.

[29]It is worth recording that the Reverend George Munro Grant (1835–1902), from 1863 minister of St. Matthew's Presbyterian Church, Halifax, and in 1877 Principal of Queen's University, Kingston, publicly supported Confederation. His general view was, "the sooner, the better." Like many Nova Scotians he disliked the federal principle, and even opposed control of the Crown lands by local legislatures. Pictou *Colonial Standard*, April 11, 1865, published his letter.

We have the trade of the world now open to us on nearly equal terms, and why should we allow Canada to hamper us? (*Herald*, Dec. 15, 1864)

Are the people of Nova Scotia prepared to yield up their flourishing customs revenue to a federal treasury in Canada, there to be squandered in jobbery and corruption? (*Tribune*, Nov. 9, 1864)

Confederation was thought of in Yarmouth as an evil Canadian egg being hatched by politicians in Halifax. And the Intercolonial Railway, which was a long way from many centres in Nova Scotia, offered few advantages to Yarmouth.[30]

In Halifax the situation was reversed. Halifax was in fact the centre of Confederate strength in Nova Scotia. In the 1867 election, when anti-Confederates took 18 out of 19 seats in the Dominion House of Commons, and 36 out of 38 seats in the Nova Scotian Assembly, it was estimated that the vote in Halifax City (as opposed to Halifax County) was almost two to one in favour of Confederation.[31] In favour of Confederation were most of the Conservative papers, the *British Colonist*, the *Evening Reporter*, and the *Evening Express* (Roman Catholic); two Liberal papers, the *Morning Chronicle*[32] and the *Morning Journal*; all the religious papers, the Baptist *Christian Messenger*, the Methodist *Provincial Wesleyan*, and the Presbyterian *Witness*. That left, in opposition to Confederation, only the Liberal *Citizen*, and the Liberal *Sun*, the latter feeble with the unpopularity of its civil war policy[33] and the age of its editor. The independent *Acadian Recorder* was uncertain of Confederation and eventually opposed it. The *Bullfrog* appeared late in 1864 edited anonymously by two of the garrison officers and was also opposed.

[30]The Conservative *Yarmouth Herald* had criticized the Intercolonial Railway policy of the Howe government as early as 1862: "cheapness of interest of a loan should be no inducement to undertake a railroad that cannot assuredly pay working expenses" (May 15, 1862). Its attitude to the Tupper government's Intercolonial policy was the same (Nov. 17, 1864).

[31]Halifax, county and city together, was then what it is now, a two-member constituency. The vote in the 1867 Dominion election was as follows:

	Anti-Confederation		Pro-Confederation	
	Jones*	Power*	Tobin	Shannon
Whole constituency	2381	2361	2158	2154
Halifax city	830	819	1234	1227

SOURCES: Halifax *Evening Reporter*, Sept. 20, 1867; Halifax *Morning Chronicle*, Sept. 23, 1867.
  *Elected.

[32]The *Chronicle* became anti-Confederate in January, 1865.
[33]The *Sun* supported the North, the only Halifax paper to do so.

The most conspicuous feature of the newspaper discussion in Halifax, and to some extent in the province as a whole, was the remarkable support for legislative union of British America. Nowhere, not even in the Montreal *Gazette*, were there such persuasive arguments for the beauty of legislative union and the wickedness of federation. "We seek Union," said the *Evening Express* December 9, 1864, "because we are, in reality, one people and ought to be one nationality. . . ." Upon this premise it was possible to speak, as the *Acadian Recorder* did, of "the superiority of . . . a Legislative Union, where the central power would be absolute. . . ." The *Evening Reporter* put it simply: "in this province public opinion has tended in favor of a Legislative Union. . . ." A confederation seemed to the Presbyterian *Witness* "a loose business. A legislative union . . . would be far more likely to prove permanently satisfactory."[34] Papers for and against Confederation sounded the same theme, but the heaviest orchestration came from the *Halifax Citizen*.

History has now satisfactorily proved that Legislative Union is the only lasting Union. Federation is not Union. . . . It makes no matter that it [the Quebec plan] has given these local legislatures very little to do. The Legislatures have to meet, and having met, they will find something to do, if they have to make employment—to elaborate grievances or increase taxes. . . . All this is insured by the double legislature system which keeps up the barriers between the different districts of the proposed Union as rigidly as ever and prevents . . . the fusion of the British American population in one actual indivisible nationality.[35]

No sooner had Tupper arrived home from New York than he found himself forced to defend the Quebec Resolutions against the charge of being a federation. The whole Confederate press took up the theme that Confederation was a legislative union in all but name. Tupper himself, in the *British Colonist*, November 22, denied that the term "federal" was really applicable.

We have heard of late a great deal of playing upon words in the use of the term "Federation" and other cognate expressions. People are apt to be misled by words . . . like these. . . . Consequently we, in discussing this subject, purpose dropping the use of such terms. . . . What the delegates on the Quebec Conference had to provide for was . . . a strong Central Government, a sufficiently firm consolidation of the Provinces to insure their acting as an undivided and indivisible unit *in all cases where necessary*.

But British North America, Tupper went on, comprised a vast territory with great diversity of institutions. This made concessions to local

[34]Halifax *Acadian Recorder*, Jan. 4, 1865; Halifax *Evening Reporter*, Oct. 28, 1864; Halifax *Witness*, Nov. 5, 1864.
[35]*Halifax Citizen*, Nov. 19, 1864.

governments necessary, even desirable. Local and private bill legislation would be so enormous that no general government could cope with it. Men sitting in the central parliament would not have sufficient local knowledge, nor feel sufficiently the local interest, to deal satisfactorily with local measures. The delegates were forced to make provision for local legislatures. But Tupper affirmed stoutly that,

. . . these [local] Legislatures will not be Legislatures in the sense in which we have been used to understand the term. They will be essentially Municipal bodies; for, under the proposed Constitution, their functions will be limited and clearly defined. Nova Scotia, for instance, will be a large Municipality under the Central Government; but just as clearly a municipality as the City of Halifax now is under our Provincial Government. . . .

This municipal nature of the provincial governments under Confederation would, Tupper said, guard against the "absurdity" of local governments assuming sovereign pretensions.

Several revealing analogies were used to develop this theme in the succeeding issues of the *British Colonist*, the most important of which was the New Zealand one. Two issues were devoted to a comparison between the New Zealand constitution of 1852 and the Quebec Resolutions. The pursuit of the same objects, said Tupper, had had the same results. Both constitutions had "endeavoured to secure *a strong General Government* whilst providing for the due protection and proper management of *local interests* by the establishing of subordinate, local, legislative organizations."[36]

Legislative union, Tupper argued, might have been the best thing in the world for British America. There was unfortunately one slight objection to it: it was impossible. "Lower Canada stands in the way. In no practicable way can the difficulty be removed." That being the case, "why babble about Legislative Union?" Federations were unpopular: Tupper admitted that. But federations were not the same everywhere. The principle showed astonishing variations. It could be "as strong or as weak as the people please," and if properly constructed could be "one of the strongest and most durable of States."[37]

Tupper was not alone in his defence of the Quebec Resolutions. He was supported by the *Evening Reporter* and *Evening Express*, both Conservative, and by the powerful Liberal daily, the *Morning Chronicle*.

[36]Halifax *British Colonist*, Nov. 24, 1864 (original italics). Note the use of the New Zealand analogy by McCully at the Quebec Conference, *supra*, 96, by Macdonald in support of the local constitution for Canada West, *infra*, 285, and by Sir Frederic Rogers, *infra*, 326.
[37]*British Colonist*, Dec. 3, 1864.

These followed a similar line to Tupper with variations. McCully, once he had resigned as the editor of the *Chronicle* and had created the *Unionist*, went even further than Tupper. Some people, McCully said, object that Nova Scotia would be swamped by Confederation. But of course Nova Scotia will be swamped and in the central government "we hope and believe that Nova Scotia, like each and every one of the other Colonies comprised in it will be effectually swamped; that we shall then hear nothing of any local parties; that then our public men will not be known as Canadians, and New Brunswickers, and Nova Scotians, but only as British Americans."[38]

The religious newspapers supported Confederation with striking unanimity.[39] Of these the Presbyterian *Witness* was the most outspoken. It approved of Tupper's explanations and noted with particular satisfaction the power of disallowance. It was clear from this power, said the *Witness* on November 19, 1864, that "whenever there is a collision between the General and the Local Governments, the latter must always give way." Disallowance was to the *Witness* the final assurance of complete central control. It was precisely this indiscriminate use of disallowance that Christopher Dunkin was concerned about. As described by the *Witness* its use could hardly be confined, not even within the broad limits of Cartier's "unjust or unwise legislation."[40]

The support of the clerical press, and much of the clergy, was only part of the widespread support accorded Confederation by the professional classes. The opinions of the pulpit, the Bench, and the Bar were in fact constantly used as examples by the Confederate papers. The *Acadian Recorder* complained that government papers of Confederate persuasion were continually trying "to shut your mouth by invoking the name of Archbishop Connolly, Bishop Binney [Anglican], the Clergy, the Admiral, General and Governor *and the Judges and the Bar*."[41] Even doctors were reported to anticipate an enlarged scope for their talents in Confederation.[42]

The opposition to Confederation used two arguments against it. First, Nova Scotia did not want union at all. Second, if there was to be union, federation was the worst possible kind. Howe spoke of Confederation as

---

[38]Halifax *Unionist*, Jan. 23, 1865. Similar, though not so outspoken views, appeared in the *Morning Chronicle*, Nov. 11, 12, 15, 19, 24.

[39]The Catholic paper, the Halifax *Evening Express*, was not in this sense a religious paper. While its sympathies were undoubtedly Catholic (and Conservative) its main purpose was news, not religion.

[40]*Supra*, 146.

[41]Halifax *Acadian Recorder*, April 18, 1866.

[42]Halifax *Evening Reporter*, Dec. 10, 1864, giving a rather premature opinion.

a monstrous thing, "unlike anything in heaven or on earth or under the earth. . . . neither an Empire, a Monarchy, nor a Republic."[43] McCully as well as Tupper chided the opposition with inconsistency, for saying one minute that Nova Scotia would be swamped by Confederation and the next that federation was too weak a constitution to last. But it made no difference. Both arguments were effective and both were used. Perhaps the simplest of the opposition views was that of the *Sun*. Why change? The danger it put in terms of the old saw: "I was well—I wished to be better, I took physic—and here I lie."[44]

The *Citizen* was more formidable, and its case cogent enough. Legislative union was impossible, so the *British Colonist* alleged, because of the French Canadians. But need this be? "Is everything to give place to Lower Canadian sectionalism?" Nova Scotia did not need union. She did not have to rush headlong into alliance with a province like Lower Canada which showed such unreasoning selfishness about the first principle of union. Nova Scotia could wait if these were the conditions; she could afford to wait one year or five years, until Lower Canada outgrew her prejudices.[45] Nor was Upper Canada blameless. Confederation would merely wipe off old scores between the Canadas. Upper Canada would get her "rep. by pop.," Lower Canada her "un-British" system of local autonomy. The Maritime provinces will however pay the piper.[46]

The *Acadian Recorder* preached from a similar text but with additional regrets for the loss of Maritime union. If only the Quebec Conference had brought forth legislative union, all would have been well. The *Recorder* believed that "Acadia is ready and anxious to accept it. . . ."[47] But pressure from Lower Canada for federal union was the stronger reason why the consummation of Confederation should be delayed. The division of powers seemed to the *Recorder* a peculiarly glaring example of the evils of federation. Who could have thought that British American statesmen, trained in British institutions, would have attempted "to write the duties and functions of the general government in a list," as if they were merchants making an inventory?[48] No mere stock-taking could ever be complete. The powers of responsible government were in essence unlimited, subject only in the case of the colonies, to ultimate review under the Crown.[49]

The predominant concern of the opposition, before mid-December,

[43]Halifax *Morning Chronicle*, June 9, 1866, reporting Howe's speech at Barrington, N.S. Cf. also "hydra-headed monster" in A Farmer, *Common-Sense* (Cornwallis, 1865), 26.

[44]Halifax *Sun*, Jan. 30, 1865. [45]*Halifax Citizen*, Dec. 31, 1864.
[46]*Ibid.*, Nov. 24, 1864. [47]*Acadian Recorder*, Oct. 3, 1864.
[48]*Ibid.*, Nov. 18, 1864. [49]*Ibid.*, Jan. 4, 1865.

1864, had thus been the issue of legislative union. After that time there was a noticeable shift in emphasis. In Tupper's words they took up "that peculiar line of argument which is perplexing to all and interesting to none": finance. "Every man of them crammed on arithmetic."[50] Tupper expressed contempt for financial arguments, but he knew perfectly well how powerful they were. His letters to Macdonald show plainly that he feared the effects of arguments that used the heavy Canadian debt, the high Canadian tariff, the expensive double governments of federation, to show that Confederation would bleed Nova Scotia white.[51] Tupper even went so far as to direct the argument to the safer levels of constitutional discussion in order to avoid taxation. The opposition should, he said, have laid "more stress . . . on the beauties of Legislative Union, and the evils of Federation. . . . The Opposition could have held before the people the example of the United States, and prophesied mourning, lamentation and woe. . . . The Opposition turned their backs on such resources as these, and took up Finance."[52]

The *Bullfrog* pointed the way, December 17, 1864.

The financial portion of the Confederation scheme is its most important feature. Since no real Union is in contemplation, but rather a careful bargain between Canada and the Lower Provinces—free trade and an Intercolonial line offered by the former, and a Union which will loose Canada's political deadlock by the latter—the fiscal portion of the agreement assumes a gigantic importance.

The development of this theme began in the public meetings in December in the Temperance Hall on Starr Street. The first was on Friday, December 9, at which Tupper, Archibald, and McCully all duly glorified the powers of the central government.[53] Opposition speakers tried to control a further meeting a week later, but were voted down by the audience and retired. On Friday, December 23, however, the opposition arranged a meeting, and here not only were the familiar arguments against federation recited,[54] but calculations made, and the long battles begun over the arithmetic Tupper so much dreaded—taxation, tariffs, and exports.

The suspicions of the business community were already aroused. The

[50]*British Colonist*, Jan. 17, 1865.
[51]"I knew that it would be excessively easy to excite our people on the question of taxation. . . ." Tupper Papers, Tupper to Macdonald, April 9, 1865.
[52]*British Colonist*, Jan. 17, 1865.
[53]*Morning Chronicle*, Dec. 12, 1864.
[54]E.g., A. M. Uniacke: "Often have I listened with pride and pleasure to the speeches of the Hon. Mr. Howe on this subject—(loud cheers); but who ever heard him advocate a Federal Union?" *Morning Chronicle*, Dec. 28, 1864.

Evening Reporter noticed with regret that "our capitalists are in the front rank of the opposition. . . . Many of our merchants are strenuous opponents of union because union in their estimation means more businessmen, greater competition, less profits, more trouble."[55] The leader in this issue was William Stairs, President of the Union Bank of Halifax, and he gave a major speech on the subject at the meeting on December 23. McCully in the *Chronicle* of December 28 heaped ridicule on Stairs' arguments. "He appeared before the meeting in a galaxy of figures. A Chaldean astronomer, an Egyptian astrologer, could not follow him. Gladstone would have fainted." But Stairs made his point. Basic to his argument was the Nova Scotian 10 per cent tariff that produced 80 per cent of the province's revenue. The prospect of a Canadian tariff of 20 per cent, in exchange for a mere subsidy, gave every merchant pause. Taxation and tariff was now to become too powerful to be dismissed. The *Morning Chronicle* had tried to elevate the issue on December 23: "We have no sympathy with that class of men, whose mental vision is bounded by Dartmouth on the one side, and Citadel Hill on the other. It is not the building of a Town-house we are discussing; we are engaged in laying the foundation of an Empire." But empire or not, by the end of December, joint meetings in Windsor on December 28 and Halifax on December 30 and 31—with Temperance Hall jammed with people—had raised the issue of tariff and taxation in unequivocal terms. Opposition speakers hammered away relentlessly both at these issues and at Canada's lurid financial history. It was not long before scarcely seven merchants along the whole two miles of wharves, chandlers, and brokerages that was the Halifax waterfront were in favour of Confederation.[56] Governor MacDonnell told Cardwell that the opponents of Confederation included men "of the highest social standing here, and in fact comprise most of the leading bankers and merchants, the wealthiest farmers, and the most independent gentlemen in the Province. . . ."[57]

At this point—January, 1865—the struggle going on behind the scenes for the control of the policy of the *Morning Chronicle* finally broke into the open. The *Morning Chronicle* had long been owned by

[55]*Evening Reporter*, Dec. 10, 1864. A few months later it was reported in the anti-Confederate papers, by way of warning to manufacturers, that a Canadian manufacturer of boots and shoes, visiting Saint John, N.B., offered to supply men's boots at $1.90 a pair in bond. They cost $2.75 a pair wholesale in Saint John. (*Morning Chronicle*, July 26, 1865)

[56]Howe's estimate. Howe Papers, Howe to Sir John Hay, Nov. 12, 1866. Howe here recapitulates the growth of the Nova Scotian opposition.

[57]C.O. 217, MacDonnell to Cardwell, Feb. 16, 1865.

William Annand, Liberal member for Halifax County in the Assembly and the Inspector-General in the late Howe administration. Annand had, in 1857, persuaded Jonathan McCully to take the post of editor. On July 1, 1864, Thomas Annand, a son, had turned over supervision of the paper to his brother Charles, and although the father continued, as before, to wield a strong influence, he was in England during the crucial period, August to November, 1864. It was in that time that McCully, the editor, was able to use his influence to make the policy of the paper strongly Confederate. When William Annand returned he asked McCully not to compromise the paper, and the Liberal party, any further, but the Liberal party was already compromised, and McCully, by now as "full of glory as Lucy Neal,"[58] had no intention of abandoning Confederation.[59] At the end of December when, as a result of the Temperance Hall meetings, the differences between the two men were obvious and public, Annand went to Howe and asked Howe if he should not fire McCully. Howe would not commit himself, but Annand apparently had already made up his mind.[60] On January 10, 1865, a brief notice appeared in the *Morning Chronicle* that the proprietor, Charles Annand, was resuming full control of the paper.[61] McCully was out.[62] In a matter of two weeks he had bought the moribund *Morning Journal* and made it into the *Unionist and Halifax Journal*; but from this time onward the *Morning Chronicle* was the leading opposition paper in Nova Scotia. On January 11, 1865, the first of Howe's "Botheration Letters" appeared there.

Joseph Howe was at one of the most difficult points of his long career. After three years as Premier of Nova Scotia, just when he might have been expected to enjoy affluence and power, to reap the benefit of his twenty-seven years in the public service of his province, he found his taste for local politics had palled, and he had given it up in 1863. He felt the need for something grander than the petty issues of local affairs. Had he private means he might decently have retired from public

[58]Howe's description, after meeting McCully at the time. *Morning Chronicle*, May 19, 1866, reporting Howe's Windsor speech of May 8.

[59]Much of this information is in the McCully–Wm. Annand correspondence, *Morning Chronicle*, Jan. 16, 1865.

[60]At which Howe smiled and said to Annand, "You are very like a woman. You make up your mind first and ask counsel afterwards." Howe's account of this incident is in his Mason Hall speech in Halifax, May 9, 1867, in *Morning Chronicle*, May 15, 1867. It is later quoted by William Annand for other reasons in *Morning Chronicle*, April 10, 1869.

[61]Charles Annand seems only to have handled the business side of the enterprise. The responsible editor was now William Annand.

[62]McCully later accused Howe of being responsible for the break between himself and Annand (*Unionist*, March 29, 1865).

life, but he had none. Howe had never cared much about money. He had been generous with it when he had it—few men more so. He "would give his last cent to relieve distress."[63] He was feckless, no doubt, but that was part of the best quality in him, the openness and warmth of his nature. He loved to love and to be loved, and he gave of himself and his means with his whole heart. Howe had looked to the imperial government to reward him according to his talents and his long public service, and he became Her Majesty's Fisheries Commissioner (pursuant to the Reciprocity Treaty) in 1863. But it was a post which, at £750 a year, he could hardly have believed decently commensurate with his capacity or his achievements. (His contemporary, Francis Hincks of Canada, had been made a Governor, first of Barbadoes, then, in 1862, of British Guiana.) Tired, poor, rather embittered, Howe found Confederation, coming in the circumstances it did, somewhat disconcerting. He had grown away from British North American union. He had talked about it often enough, in 1854 and in 1861. On occasion he still did, but he had grown rather disillusioned with Canadians. His attention was now directed to what he seems to have believed was the more important question of the British empire. If for no other reason than this, Howe's attitude to Confederation was equivocal. Moreover, it was being brought to Nova Scotia by a man whose capacity was below Howe's and whom Howe regarded as an upstart doctor from Cumberland whose only major asset was sheer brass. Howe was enough of an egotist to resent both Tupper and Tupper's project. There was a ring of truth in the remark attributed to him, "I will not play second fiddle to that d———d Tupper."[64] Whether he would have supported Confederation had he had an opportunity similar to Tupper's is another matter. Two contemporaries, Edward Whelan and G. M. Grant thought he would have;[65] but reasonable doubt still remains if his interest in the whole subject was not now largely exhausted and if his public support of Confederation in August, 1864[66] can be taken as anything else than alcoholic rodomontade.

[63]Rev. John Currie's recollection. John Currie (1830?–1909), a younger contemporary of Howe, was Professor of Hebrew at Pine Hill Divinity School, Halifax, from 1871 to 1908. His recollections about Howe are recorded by Archibald MacMechan, in MacMechan's copy of Chisolm's *Howe*, in Dalhousie University Library. It was Rev. John Currie who said Howe "boasted he had kissed every woman in Nova Scotia."

[64]Saunders, *Three Premiers of Nova Scotia*, 371.

[65]For Whelan see *supra*, 185. Grant's view is given in his *Joseph Howe* (Halifax, 1906), 73. This book was published after Grant's death, reprinted from articles Grant had published in 1875 in the *Canadian Monthly and National Review*.   [66]*Supra*, 71.

Howe had been in Halifax in that month and had met Governor
MacDonnell who asked him to go to Charlottetown. But Howe's official
duties prevented him.[67] Thus, while the Charlottetown and Quebec
Conferences were going on, Howe was cooped up in the little 700-ton
H.M.S. *Lily*, off the Labrador coast. He returned to Halifax in Novem-
ber to find Confederation well in train and Tupper prepared to take the
question to the legislature in the spring session. Howe, who had written
to Tupper in August that he would be very happy to co-operate on
Maritime union, found himself in November in a very different position.
The Maritime union project had been metamorphosed into British
American union, and that Howe was not really prepared to accept.
Howe still held his hand, but by the end of December, when his old
friend William Annand "had joined the opposition, and confronted the
Delegates on the platform at Temperance Hall," Howe could hold back
no longer.[68] He was still H.M. Fisheries Commissioner and could not
come out openly, but he was also Joseph Howe and could still write.
The "Botheration Letters" were the result.

Howe wrote these anonymously, but the authorship was thinly veiled,
for Howe's style was recognizable. The *Evening Express* guessed; "we
are not exactly certain who blows the literary bellows of the *Chronicle*
now, but judging from the easy style introduced, we have a shrewd
suspicion who he is."[69] The "Botheration Letters" appeared as twelve
editorials in the Halifax *Morning Chronicle* between January 11 and
March 2. In these Howe summed up the anti-Confederate arguments,
enlivened them with the warmth of his own style, and illustrated them
with reflections from his own considerable experience. Howe saw Confederation as an attempt to repeat the constitutional disasters of the
first and second empires. Great Britain had tried to work local legislatures in harmony with the imperial parliament, had found the system
impracticable, and had been forced to concede responsible government.
Any British American parliament constituted under a federal system
would encounter the same results in dealing with the local legislatures

[67]Howe's account of his role at this time is given in his Windsor speech of
May 8, 1866 (*Morning Chronicle*, May 19, 1866). Howe wrote Lord Russell, the
Foreign Secretary, asking permission to go, but no answer was received in time,
and Howe was obliged to decline, although an official invitation had already
been sent to him. As it turned out, Lord Russell's decision was against Howe
going to Charlottetown.

[68]*Evening Reporter*, Dec. 9, 1865, letter from Howe of Dec. 7.

[69]*Evening Express*, Jan. 20, 1865. Howe was invited by Annand to replace
McCully as editor of the *Chronicle* at McCully's salary. Howe said he accepted
no salary at all for the work he did. (*Halifax Citizen*, April 8, 1869, Howe's
"Letter to the Electors of Hants, No. 2.")

of the provinces. Sooner or later these legislatures would make their power felt in ways unknown to the letter of the Quebec Resolutions. "Why shall we try over again the experiment which the experience of the Mother Country condemns?" The only reason for federation, Howe alleged, was French Canadian resistance to legislative union.[70] Here, with an unerring eye, Howe assessed the French position.

Ever since the Union of the Two Provinces, the French Canadians, by sticking together, have controlled the Legislation and the Government of Canada. They will do the same thing in a larger Union, and, as the English will split and divide, as they always do, the French members will, in nine cases out of ten, be masters of the situation. But should a chance combination thwart them, then they will back their Local Legislature against the United Parliament. . . .[71]

Union was certainly not strength under circumstances such as these.

Where there are no cohesive qualities in the material, no skill in the design . . . unite what you will and there is no strength. . . . Was there strength when the new wine was united to the old bottle, or the new cloth to the old garment? Is union strength when a prudent man, doing a snug business is tempted into partnership with a wild speculator? Was Sampson much the stronger when the false Delilah got him confederated, bound him with cords and cut off his hair?[72]

In Letter No. 9 Howe spoke of the "squadron" who had helped to engineer the union of Scotland and England in 1707, and forecast a dark future for the "squadron" of Nova Scotia when they came to face the people.[73] And imperial despatches urging Confederation only compounded the felony:

We should like to have seen Dr. Tupper making such a proposal to Simon Bradstreet Robie, or Mr. McCully trying to seduce Herbert Huntingdon into a conspiracy against the existence of our Legislature, and pleading a despatch as a reason why the people should have no voice in the matter. Robie's opinion would have been delivered with unmistakable emphasis, and we much mistake the man if Huntingdon's right leg, with a heavy boot at the end of it, would not have commenced a series of gymnastic responses very edifying to behold.[74]

Let the delegates blow the trumpet of union as much as they please, Howe said, "but hereafter we trust to hear no more of Imperial Despatches commanding a Union. . . ."[75]

[70]Cf. also the views of the *Citizen* and the *Acadian Recorder, supra*, 206.
[71]*Morning Chronicle*, Jan. 13, 1865, "Botheration Letter, No. 2."
[72]*Ibid.*, Feb. 8, 1865, "Botheration Letter, No. 10." (Howe's italics)
[73]*Ibid.*, Feb. 3, 1865.   [74]*Ibid.*, Feb. 1, 1865, "Botheration Letter, No. 8."
[75]*Ibid.*, Feb. 4, 1865. Not one of the Botheration Letters, but an editorial called "Canadian Generalship," probably written by Howe.

Howe's letters were a distinct enunciation of Nova Scotian patriotism, and they rallied opinion everywhere. In the words of one person, reporting a village Confederation debate, "a non-political community had suddenly been ushered into political existence."[76] When the discussion of Confederation began in Nova Scotia the delegates controlled, as Howe rightly said, the most influential newspapers; they were familiar with the Quebec Resolutions and the arguments by which they might be sustained; yet within three months parties had been realigned, public meetings organized, public letters written. Howe described the change vividly.

Nothing illustrates more finely the high spirit and intellectual resources of Nova Scotia than the rapidity with which all this was done. . . . Men, who had taken no share in mere party disputation, jumped upon the platform and confronted these delegates. . . . To its honor be it said, one portion of the independent press [the *Halifax Citizen*] sounded the tocsin of alarm from the first, other newspapers, shaking off old trammels, came into line [the *Morning Chronicle*], and the Botheration Scheme was ventilated in every part of the Province, and so far as Nova Scotia is concerned, may now be considered as dead as Julius Caesar.[77]

With Tilley's defeat in New Brunswick, four days after this was written, Confederation was to all intents and purposes just as dead as Howe said it was.

The rout of Confederation was also seen in the Assembly. "Bluster and arrogance ruled the hour until the House met, when the pin feathers of the Delegates suddenly fell."[78] The attitude in the House and in the country was distinctly threatening, and some strategic retreat might be necessary. The Speech from the Throne was non-committal. The "encomiums" of Cardwell were duly noted,[79] but the Speech asked only that Confederation be considered with care and prudence. That was on February 9, 1865. Nothing further was heard on the subject of Confederation for a month and a half. Tupper's position was in fact extremely difficult. The *Bullfrog*, as shrewd as its name, had analysed it well enough, February 4, 1865. "The position of the ministry is precarious in the extreme: DR TUPPER has a difficult hand to play, and, although he is a cunning player . . . it is just possible he may lose the game upon the issue of which he has . . . risked his political existence. . . ." The course of Confederation in Nova Scotia was largely

76*Ibid.*, Feb. 14, 1865.
77*Ibid.*, March 2, 1865, "Botheration Letter, No. 12."
78*Ibid.*, May 9, 1865, a retrospect of the session.
79"Encomium" was not intended in any pejorative sense.

determined by events in New Brunswick,[80] though even before the news of Tilley's defeat the adoption of Confederation by Nova Scotia was highly doubtful;[81] in any case it was clear by March 6 that Confederation had been defeated. But Tupper did not intend to lose the game. A Council meeting on March 9 resolved on Maritime union resolutions as a means of staving off an adverse vote on Confederation;[82] these were tabled on March 22 and moved on April 10.

Although the resolutions referred only to Maritime union, the debate was on Confederation. Tupper himself devoted only a fraction of his speech to the former. It was a long speech; Tupper was not famous for his conciseness. He gave the background of Confederation and much of its history, making the usual obeisance to legislative union, but he introduced little that was new. Finally he came to the resolutions for Maritime union. Owing "to circumstances over which we have no control" (well might Tupper say this), it was impossible to bring in resolutions on Confederation.[83] Maritime union was desirable in any case. Tupper admitted that the chance of persuading Prince Edward Island was slim, but he felt sure that New Brunswick would receive the proposals favourably.[84]

As in the Canadian debate on Confederation, nearly every member in the Nova Scotian house had an opportunity to express his views, and did, though usually upon Confederation rather than Maritime union. Under the circumstances it could hardly be a very distinguished debate, and it reflected little that had not already appeared in the newspapers. It dragged on until April 24. On that day, when Tupper moved resumption of the debate, Archibald rose and said it would be absurd to continue it. The resolutions for Maritime union then passed without a division. The *Morning Chronicle* of May 9 concluded in its retrospect of the session that Confederation had been "quietly shelved by the unanimous vote of the House." The *Acadian Recorder* thought so too, April 26, and breathed a fervent, "Long may it rest."

By this time the Canadians were on the scene. Galt and C. J. Brydges were in Halifax on April 13, pursuant to an arrangement made with Tupper in Canada the previous October to consider the construction of

[80]So Tupper told Gordon early in June, Cardwell Papers, Gordon to Cardwell, June 5, 1865.

[81]C.O. 217, MacDonnell to Cardwell, Feb. 15, 1865 (confidential).

[82]According to MacDonnell, this was his device. C.O. 217, MacDonnell to Cardwell, March 16, 1865 (confidential).

[83]Nova Scotia, Assembly, *Debates and Proceedings*, 1865, 215.

[84]For Prince Edward Island reaction, *supra*, 188; for New Brunswick, *infra*, 248.

the Truro to Moncton section of the Intercolonial.[85] They were also, with Cartier, on their way to England. Galt and Cartier, with Tilley who was also there, drove in four-horse carriages through crowded streets to a public meeting called in their honour, one which Cartier described as "vraiment magnifique."[86] The *Morning Chronicle* of April 15, 1865, called it merely a clamorous gathering of "the great unwashed." Noting the persistence of the Canadians the *Acadian Recorder* warned, April 26, "Many a lover has succeeded by sheer dint of perseverance." As if to underline this remark the Colonial Office peremptorily ruled out Maritime union, in such terms that Macdonnell and Tupper were precluded from considering the matter any further.[87]

A mission to England by the Nova Scotian ministers, similar to that of the Canadians, would under the circumstances seem too conspiratorial if the Canadians were still in London. ". . . it would, I fear," wrote Tupper to MacDonnell, "be just now prejudicial to the cause of Confederation here."[88] Tupper and Henry did not go to England until late in June, when the Canadians had gone home, and then ostensibly to discuss only railways and reciprocity.[89] There was rough justice in the *Morning Chronicle*'s statement of July 14: "The confederation tornado which swept across the length and breadth of British America . . . has, at length, spent itself on the other side of the Atlantic."

While Confederation took Tupper and Henry eastward to London, reciprocity took Howe westward to Detroit. The abrogation of the Reciprocity Treaty, notice of which was given by the United States early in 1865, was to become effective on March 17, 1866. A variety of moves were made in the summer of 1865 to rescue the Treaty. Five hundred Americans and fifty British Americans travelled to Detroit for a convention sponsored by the Detroit Chamber of Commerce, that

[85]They were apparently to come in November, 1864, but their visit was postponed. Brydges sent an engineer instead to survey existing lines in Nova Scotia and New Brunswick. See P. B. Waite, "A Chapter in the History of the Intercolonial Railway, 1864," *Canadian Historical Review*, XXXII, 4 (Dec. 1951), 356–69.

[86]"Mon cher Langevin:— Vous avez dû, j'espère, recevoir le télégramme de Brydges envoyé d'Halifax La démonstration qui nous a été faite dans cette ville a été vraiment magnifique Elle nous aidera beaucoup dans notre Mission. . . ." Collection Chapais, Cartier to Langevin, 22 avril 1865.

There were complaints in the Assembly on April 13 about the proposed use of the Volunteers to augment the celebration. (Nova Scotia, Assembly, *Debates and Proceedings*, 1865, 238–45.)

[87]C.O. 218, Cardwell to MacDonnell, April 1, 1865.

[88]Nova Scotia, Minutes of Council, May 19, 1865, Tupper to MacDonnell, May 11, 1865.

[89]Nova Scotia, Minutes of Council, June 20, 1865.

opened on July 11, 1865. According to the *Detroit Advertiser*, "The modesty of the Canadians was in marked contrast with the arrogance of the bristly delegation from Chicago. . . . They bore more than one insulting taunt of the advocates of 'the American side' with the most exemplary forbearance. . . ."[90] Even before Howe's speech the British Americans had won many friends, but on the last day Howe swept the convention off its feet. He spoke darkly of fortifications on the American side of the border, and appealed for peace and amity on both sides. His own son, he said, had fought for the northern cause, in the 23rd Ohio Regiment. At this the cheers were deafening, and Howe himself, never much the master of his own emotions, almost broke down.[91] For British Americans, the Detroit convention was a success, and resolutions were passed favouring renewal of the Reciprocity Treaty. But they had little effect. The New York papers boasted that two years from the end of reciprocity the British North American provinces would be forced to join the United States. This kind of triumphant leer was to appear periodically for some time to come.[92] There was truth enough in the sensible, matter-of-fact chauvinism of the *New York Herald*. All the commercial and geographical interests of the British provinces lay with the United States: Canada West with Ohio, Illinois, and Michigan; Canada East with New York and Vermont; the Maritime provinces with Maine and Massachusetts. "All other connections are to them really of no value whatever. . . ."[93] And Washington remained adamant. Galt and Howland, in Washington while the Detroit convention was on, came home chastened and pessimistic.

Whatever might be the ultimate fate of reciprocity, it was highly desirable that measures be concerted by the British American provinces together. There was a feeling of irritation in the Maritime provinces over the way Canada pre-empted all negotiations. The free entry into the American market of flour, grain, livestock, fruit, lumber, fish, furs—in short, natural products—had benefited Canada rather than the Maritimes; the irony was that these benefits had been largely paid for by the gift of the Maritime inshore fisheries to the Americans. Earl Russell, the British Foreign Secretary, had suggested a "Confederate council" to furnish information to Her Majesty's Government on the

[90]Detroit *Advertiser and Tribune*, July 15, 1865, quoted in the Halifax *Morning Chronicle*, July 22, 1865.

[91]J. Howe, *The Reciprocity Treaty: Its History, General Features, and Commercial Results* (Hamilton, 1865), 14.

[92]*New York Herald*, July 18, 1865; *New York Tribune*, July 18, 1865; for later comments see *Erie Dispatch* quoted by Toronto *Globe*, Jan. 27, 1866.

[93]*New York Herald*, Jan. 17, 1866.

negotiation of commercial treaties.[94] The result was another conference at Quebec, on September 15, 1865, though on a much more modest scale than that of 1864. Ambrose Shea represented Newfoundland, R. D. Wilmot New Brunswick, J. C. Pope Prince Edward Island, and J. W. Ritchie (the Solicitor General) Nova Scotia, and they met with Brown, Cartier, and Galt. Brown held a high opinion of the work of this Council[95] and he was not altogether unjustified. One concrete result was the immediate conversion of R. D. Wilmot of New Brunswick to Confederation.[96] It may also have helped to alleviate Maritime jealousy of Canadian influences in Washington and London.

The opportunity was also taken by the Canadians to extend an invitation to the Maritimers who had entertained the Canadians so warmly in August, 1864, to come and visit Canada in September, 1865. An estimated two hundred and forty invitations were sent out. Nova Scotia set aside $5,000 to help send visitors. The Saint John *Weekly Telegraph* of September 20 called it "return match to the great intercolonial drunk of last year," but it was in the end largely a failure. Only fifty-four actually went[97] and in the different circumstances of September, 1865, not even McGee, who had charge of it, could make it a success. Confederation was at a standstill; the after-dinner speeches that rang so fervently in 1864 had a distinctly hollow note in 1865.

By this time too the Confederate cause in Nova Scotia had a hollow and empty sound. The Confederate newspapers toiled manfully at their task. The *Unionist* began a series called "Confederation Catechism" in March; the *British Colonist* a "Review of the debate on the Union of the Colonies" that occupied it through July and August; the *Evening Express*, taking a broader view, began a series on British North America from Newfoundland to Vancouver Island that lasted intermittently from July until October. The *Unionist* battled with the *Morning Chronicle* the whole summer, while the *British Colonist* took on the *Citizen* and the *Acadian Recorder*. But it was an unsatisfying business at best. On August 7 the *Express* confessed ruefully that "the feelings of a large proportion of the people of the Lower Provinces are, upon the whole, hostile to Union." The *Morning Chronicle* of Septem-

---

[94]For its constitutional significance see N. McL. Rogers, "The Confederate Council of Trade," *Canadian Historical Review*, VII, 4 (Dec., 1926), 277–86.

[95]Brown Papers, Brown to Monck, Dec. 25, 1865.

[96]*Infra*, 251–2.

[97]From Nova Scotia, 23; New, Brunswick, 28; Prince Edward Island, 3. Even the *British Colonist* criticized some of the arrangements for the visit (Oct. 10, 1865). Also Saint John *Morning Telegraph*, Sept. 16, 1865.

ber 27 commented that the "roar of artillery from the Union batteries has given place to the occasional discharge of a gun from the dismantled works."

"A nation, indeed! Say rather 'a thing of shreds and patches' " was the principal theme of the *Morning Chronicle*.[98] It elaborated this in a remarkable editorial published on October 16 called "The Binomial Theory of Government," one of the most interesting criticisms of the principle of federation. Federation was described algebraically as $(x - y)^n$, where x was the power of the general government, y the power of the local, and n the constitutional expansion. It was clear from this formula, the *Morning Chronicle* said, that the powers granted to local governments must subtract something from the simple—the otherwise simple—plenary authority of the central government. The *Chronicle* did not distinguish between the general and particular powers given to the central government in Resolution 29. It assumed, as Resolution 29, and later Section 91 of the British North America Act assumed, that the particular powers were merely explicit illustrations of a simple and comprehensive grant of legislative authority. The *Chronicle* feared the diminution of this power. Federation, it said, deranges monarchy. It "clogs the executive function" by setting up the "derivative authority of the local Legislatures against the constituted authority of a central Government." Since the local legislatures were, by the *Chronicle*'s reasoning, derived from the central government, federation became a "second term of unknown value and an unprofitable complication in government. . . ." The local legislatures the *Chronicle* regarded as insidious, republican devices mitigating the high authority of the Crown exercised by the central power. The local legislatures followed "the feelings and opinions of the masses; the federal principle is the consolidation of their authority. . . ."

Another critic who had similar views was the Governor of Nova Scotia, Richard MacDonnell. He had opposed federation from the start; and although he was a chivalrous enough adversary, he distrusted both Confederation and those who had initiated it. At Quebec he remarked to Macdonald, "You shall not make a mayor of *me*, I can tell you." It was for reasons of this kind that MacDonnell was unceremoniously transferred to Hong Kong in September, 1865, where he could be his own ministry, and thus avoid the conflicts that his wit, quick tongue, and critical propensities had caused in Nova Scotia. He had never been disposed, so the *Unionist* said, September 4, 1865, "to spare or spoil what he considered a joke, for a Minister's sake." He was

[98]Halifax *Morning Chronicle*, Oct. 21, 1865.

accused of being the very pivot of anti-Confederate influence; he may have been distrusted by his own Council, but not even the anti-Confederates seem to have regretted his departure.[99]

The new governor of Nova Scotia was altogether different. Lieut.-General Sir William Fenwick Williams was a native Nova Scotian, a soldier, and a veteran of the Crimean War in which he had won fame for an honourable defence of Kars, a city in Turkish Armenia. Since that time he had been for six years Officer Commanding Her Majesty's forces in British North America. He had no political experience. Sixty-five years of age, Williams was a fine old veteran who knew how to take orders and he was sent to Nova Scotia to put union through by every means at his disposal. The Nova Scotians were not ignorant of this purpose and they were not intended to be. On November 8, 1865, the *Royal Gazette* published Cardwell's letter to Williams, in which it was made abundantly clear that the expectation of Confederation was the reason for his appointment.

Charles Fisher's victory in the York by-election in New Brunswick in November, 1865, was a cheering note for Confederates in Nova Scotia;[100] but there was, regrettably, nothing cheerful about the by-election in Lunenburg County, Nova Scotia, on December 27. The Government bent all its efforts: road contracts were freely let to deserving supporters; there was a fresh despatch from Cardwell urging the wishes of the imperial government, and which was duly published on the eve of the election.[101] This despatch the *Chronicle* of December 27 represented as Canadian in origin—"the voice is Jacob's voice but the hands are the hands of Esau." But Lunenburg was lost. A seat that the Conservatives had won in 1863 by 509 votes was lost in 1865 by 686. With the reduced franchise of 1865 this was, as the Government admitted, defeat by a very large majority.[102] Canadian papers commiserated, but it was not a good omen on the eve of the year 1866 when so much was expected.

However, at the same time, with the steady pressure from the British government and with Fenian alarms since October, the anti-Confederates seemed to give ground a little. On November 15, the

[99]MacDonnell's remark to Macdonald is from Frances E. O. Monck, *My Canadian Leaves: An Account of a Visit to Canada in 1864–1865* (London, 1891), 211. The entry is dated Saturday, Nov. 26, 1864, and the information is probably drawn directly from Macdonald himself. For anti-Confederate feelings, see for example *Halifax Citizen*, Aug. 12, 29, 1865.

[100]*Infra*, 253–4.

[101]*Royal Gazette*, Dec. 23, 1865, quoting Cardwell to Williams, Nov. 24, 1865.

[102]*British Colonist*, Dec. 30, 1865. Legislation passed by the Howe government reduced the franchise by forty per cent. It became effective in June, 1864.

Morning Chronicle suggested the possibility of a new conference on union. Perhaps this overture was the result of the York election in New Brunswick; in any case, it was greeted cordially in the government papers.[103] And just at this point George Brown arrived on the scene from Canada, his purpose being to explore the immediate prospects for union. He had had conferences with Gordon, Tilley, and Smith in New Brunswick, and he was impressed with the progress of pro-Confederation sentiment there.[104] And in Nova Scotia Brown put this question to William Annand in a long private interview at Tupper's house about November 20.

William Annand was now the leading spirit of the Nova Scotian anti-Confederates. Although he did not command the following among the Liberals that Archibald had, he had long been a close friend of Howe, and his outspoken opposition to Confederation, expressed in the *Morning Chronicle*, had given him considerable influence in the province among Liberals and Conservatives alike. Annand had been in England in the summer of 1865 where he had met A. J. Smith of New Brunswick, and, like Smith, had had a pretty frank interview with Cardwell. Apparently Cardwell made no attempt to disguise his policy; the British government "would use every means in their power, short of coercion" to induce the Maritime legislatures to accept Confederation.[105] How far Annand was sincere in his sudden interest in union in the *Morning Chronicle* was uncertain; Brown tried to find out. The Saint John *Telegraph* suspected that the real purpose was to sow discord among the supporters of Confederation.[106] Brown tried in vain to get Annand to accept Confederation as it stood; he even said that if nothing were done soon about Confederation "Canada would seek some other mode of settling her difficulties, and leave the Maritime Provinces to their fate."[107] That Annand was much moved by this unhappy prospect was doubtful; Brown had, however, other strings to his bow. He appealed to Annand's Liberalism and held out the possibility of a British North American union under the agreeable

[103]Halifax *Evening Express*, Nov. 17, 1865; *British Colonist*, Nov. 21, 1865.

[104]Brown Papers, George Brown to Anne Brown, Nov. 18, 1865. See *infra*, 252.

[105]Annand's recollection of the conversation, given in the *Morning Chronicle*, March 2, 1869; other recollections appear *ibid.*, March 23, 1869.

[106]Saint John *Morning Telegraph*, Nov. 18, 1865, commenting on the *Morning Chronicle*'s editorial of Nov. 15.

[107]William Miller's recollection of the conversation, but at second hand, as relayed to him by Annand. Nova Scotia, Assembly, *Debates and Proceedings*, 1866, 236 (April 13). Annand at first denied the truth of Miller's version, but the next day admitted it was correct, *ibid.*, 237.

auspices of a national Liberal party. "I have always sworn by the *Chronicle* and the *Nova Scotian*," said Brown diplomatically. "We are all Liberals.[108] You and I have been personal friends, we have long acted together, and it is too bad at this period that I should be obliged to throw myself into the hands of our opponents to carry this measure. . . ."[109] Brown also intimated that any support Annand might give Confederation would not go unrewarded.[110]

Annand did not commit himself, but there remained the possibility that both Annand and Smith of New Brunswick might be persuaded to support some kind of union, one cleared perhaps of the taint of the Quebec scheme. Such a proposal was not without support even in Canada. On December 8, the Conservative Ottawa *Citizen* said that the Canadian government "are prepared to listen to any proposals for the adoption of another and a better scheme." Brown and Macdonald doubtless were willing; Cartier doubtless was not. What Annand had in mind was something rather less definite and distinctly more tortuous.

In January, 1866, Annand's colleague, William Miller, felt he could no longer persist in opposing union and believed the time had come for "effecting some compromise by which the objectionable features of the Quebec scheme could be got rid of."[111] Annand apparently agreed, and the result was a new editorial in the *Morning Chronicle* on January 24, 1866, urging that union be considered. Not all those who opposed the Quebec plan, said the editorial, were opposed to union; the Quebec scheme, "matured in a few weeks, amid exhaustive festivities, was not the measure to consolidate British America," and the necessity of some kind of union was becoming obvious. "The colonies cannot, in the very nature of things, always continue as they are."

The government papers welcomed these overtures. On February 2 the *Evening Express* agreed that the Quebec plan had met a storm of opposition from large and influential sections of all parties, and that some changes in it would be inevitable. The *British Colonist* tried to confine the issue to the Quebec plan, with changes in detail; the *Chronicle* insisted however that "the work must be commenced *de novo*."[112] By this time it was almost certain that the Nova Scotian

[108]Annand's version of the conversation, *ibid.*, 237.
[109]Miller's version, *ibid.*, 236.
[110]Annand alleged he was promised "Money, place and preferment in Canada." Tupper promptly sent off a telegram to Brown and duly read Brown's reply to the Assembly. Brown denied making such a promise (*ibid.*, 237). Annand later claimed to have been misreported and that he had only *implied* bribery.
[111]Miller's account, *ibid.*, 311 (May 1).
[112]*British Colonist*, Jan. 27, 1866; *Morning Chronicle*, Feb. 1, 1866.

government itself had abandoned hope of getting the Quebec Resolutions through the Legislature as they stood. They had taken too much of a battering. And union, after all, was the main issue. For union, plain union, with nothing of the Quebec taste in it, there was some sympathy in Nova Scotia. The Halifax *Sun* suggested the point on April 11, 1866: "Many had been strongly prepossessed in favour of Confederation before the completion and promulgation of the scheme which was intended to make it a fixed fact.—The vision of a vast country stretching across the continent from sea to sea, with but one Government and one Law, had in it something sublime which captivated at first sight." The great difficulty was to bring these sublimities to earth. Nova Scotians seemed to prefer to talk and dream rather than act. A great country from sea to sea was a grand conception, but the presentation of the practical means to realize it seemed depressing, perhaps even crude.[113] Before long Tupper had grasped this point: that the question of terms could, with great advantage, be left severely alone.

Annand, for different reasons, also avoided the question. It was possible that he was considering union: what was probable was some scheme for postponing Confederation. To propose a new convention was a useful move. Anti-Confederates had no wish to appear intransigeant or unpatriotic in the face of the known desires of the British government; Fenian threats made patriotism obligatory; some overt gesture toward union placed the anti-Confederates in a better tactical position. Annand, three years later, said that the whole scheme was a red herring. A new convention to discuss union from the beginning could be held in the confident anticipation that "the delegates would not agree when they met. . . ."[114] Whatever Annand's motive, he could be, and was, "earnestly sincere in the opinion that it is better to have a new convention."[115]

Tactics were by now of some importance. The Liberal caucus met the day the legislature opened, February 22. Annand proposed that Archibald be deposed as Liberal leader on the ground of his Confederation sympathies. An anti-Confederate party, with Annand presumably at the head, would be far more effective; it could call in Conservative

[113]A reporter for the Montreal *Evening Telegraph*, in Nova Scotia in July, 1867, reported the following conversation with what he called an "intelligent Anti": "Have you any objection to a plan of Confederation?" "No." "Well, why your objection to this one?" "I don't like it." A. G. Gilbert, *From Montreal to the Maritime Provinces and Back* (Montreal, 1867), 53.

[114]*Morning Chronicle*, March 2, 1869.

[115]E. M. Macdonald's view, contained in a letter addressed to an unknown member of the New Brunswick government at Fredericton dated March 18, 1866. Published in the *Halifax Citizen*, Feb. 25, 1869.

support, and it could propose a new union convention. But to both proposals the majority of the party appear to have been opposed. They would not depose Archibald, neither would they consider a new convention on union.[116] They were not convinced, as Annand was, of any clear and present danger from Confederation; they could not believe that anything in the nature of a *coup de main* was conceived of, and New Brunswick was surely a powerful security that nothing could be done about Confederation in Nova Scotia.

When the Nova Scotian legislature opened on February 22, to the astonishment of nearly everyone, and to the chagrin of Gordon and Monck, nothing whatsoever was said about Confederation in the Speech from the Throne. The *Chronicle* thought it extraordinary: not a syllable on Confederation in the Governor's Speech. A week later, still puzzled, it wrote, "The House of Assembly is as tranquil as a summer sea. . . ."[117]

The Assembly without a ripple on its surface belied the frantic activity going on behind the scenes. Williams, Gordon, and Monck were in close and active communication. The telegraph did yeoman work. Two days before the Nova Scotian legislature had opened Gordon telegraphed asking for a strong stand on Confederation in the Nova Scotian Speech. Williams replied that it was then too late to change the Speech and that in any case he would damage the cause of Confederation in both provinces by such a statement; he could not afford to risk the possibility of a vote against Confederation. Williams for his part mightily regretted the late meeting of the New Brunswick legislature (March 8) and wired Lord Monck that Gordon must be impressed with the fact that "Success depends in both Provinces entirely upon his prompt efforts."[118]

Gordon had in fact devised the stratagem of persuading A. J. Smith to accept a paragraph in the Throne Speech favouring Confederation, on the ground that Cardwell's despatch of June 24, 1865, left no alternative. Monck feared that the complete omission of any reference to Confederation in the Nova Scotian Speech would now strengthen Smith's hand, and his capacity to resist Gordon. This he wired rather tersely to Williams. Williams' telegram in reply was revealing: "Mr. Gordon knows we are in a minority here until Confederation is carried

[116]Nova Scotia, Assembly, *Debates and Proceedings*, 1866, 311 (May 1). (William Miller) Also *Morning Chronicle*, March 23, 1869.

[117]*Morning Chronicle*, Feb. 23, 1866; March 2, 1866.

[118]Nova Scotia, Lieutenant Governor, Telegram Book, Gordon to Williams, Feb. 20, 1866; Williams to Gordon, Feb. 21, 1866; Williams to Monck, Feb. 27, 1866.

in New Brunswick. I cannot therefore see how a hostile vote here would have helped him, while it would have prevented our success after it had been carried there."[119]

About a week later, on March 7, Annand rose in the Assembly to ask what was going on. He had seen a report in the *British Colonist* of a speech of John A. Macdonald's at Cornwall, Canada West; Macdonald had said Confederation was certain to pass in a few weeks.[120] Did or did not the Government of Nova Scotia have a Confederation policy? Tupper blandly replied that he was just as astonished as Mr. Annand at Macdonald's remarks. It would be "altogether futile for Nova Scotia to move at present." Annand refused to be put off. Why was it that Prince Edward Island and Newfoundland had both mentioned Confederation in their Speeches?[121] Why was Nova Scotia so very different? W. A. Henry, the Attorney General, came to Tupper's rescue. "The government," he said, "had no policy on the subject. . . ."[122]

This was sheer evasion. Williams and the Tupper government were in an awkward position. Nearly all the ordinary business of the session would be completed in four weeks or so; the New Brunswick legislature had not met, and when it did meet, a day later on March 8, it was almost at once locked in debate over Charles Fisher's precipitate want of confidence motion.[123] In this aggravating dilemma Williams and Tupper could do nothing. Williams could only telegraph apologetically to Gordon:

. . . am sorry that my line of operations has not helped you. Hope Anti Confederate joy will soon turn to sorrow by your measures. My total abandonment of Confederation is too much like Punch even for their sincere belief. They know what I was sent here for.[124]

The same day, March 7, Canada called out the militia against the Fenians.[125] Within a few days of the receipt of this news in Nova

[119]Williams Papers, Monck to Williams, Feb. 26, 1866; Nova Scotia, Lieutenant Governor, Telegram Book, Monck to Williams, Feb. 28, 1866; *ibid.*, Williams to Monck, Feb. 28, 1866.
[120]Ottawa *Citizen*, March 2, 1866 gives a full report of Macdonald's speech of March 1. The *British Colonist*, March 6, 1866, gave only a brief report presumably of news received by telegram.
[121]Nova Scotia, Assembly, *Debates and Proceedings*, 1866, 53–5 (March 7). Annand said Prince Edward Island, but the legislature there had not yet met.
[122]*Ibid.*, 55.
[123]*Infra*, 258.
[124]Nova Scotia, Lieutenant Governor, Telegram Book, Williams to Gordon, March 7, 1866.
[125]Note Monck's remarks: "I have called out a considerable force of Volunteers in anticipation of Fenian invasion—wh. *I* do not believe will take place. . . ." Williams Papers, Monck to Williams, March 12, 1866.

Scotia Williams telegraphed to Monck: "A great change here, if Gordon acts promptly for the Quebec scheme or otherwise. Pray read my message and urge him on. Nearly all our ordinary business done and Howe is away." That same day, March 12, back came Monck's answer. Could Williams possibly begin with Confederation without waiting for Gordon? It was now "morally certain" that Gordon could get Confederation through in New Brunswick, "but he may not be able to hurry matters."[126] Williams took the hint, and began.

As Lieutenant Governor, Lieutenant General Sir William Fenwick Williams had already made a good reputation in Halifax. He was a fine figure of a man and a military hero; he had made himself agreeable with an excellent table at Government House, and his geniality was a pleasant contrast to the tartness of his predecessor. But he was a soldier, and he not only knew how to take orders, but had some aptitude for executing them. On March 13, the day after Monck's telegram, he sent for William Annand. "If disengaged after breakfast, anytime after 10, should be glad to see you for a few moments."[127] Williams suggested that Annand should propose to Tupper, on the floor of the House, a new convention, to be held in London under the auspices of the Colonial Office, and which would work out the details of a plan of union. Annand could be confident that if he made such a move Tupper would agree to it.[128] Annand hesitated. The new convention he sought was within his grasp, but he was suspicious. He asked for time to consider, and he wanted to see Smith in New Brunswick with whom he had been for some time in agreement. The aim of both was that anti-Confederates in the two provinces should "act together, adopt a common policy, and support each other."[129] Williams believed that Annand was willing,[130] and that Smith could also be brought around. On March 19 Williams telegraphed Gordon, "Annand goes to day to confer with Smith and I have great hopes for our joint success— Communicate by telegraph daily in what way I can assist and push on your work. . . ."[131]

Annand's trip was stopped however. Gordon, for one, did not want him.[132] Gordon had his own views about how Confederation could

[126]Nova Scotia, Lieutenant Governor, Telegram Book, Williams to Monck, March 12, 1866; Monck to Williams, March 12, 1866.
[127]Williams to Annand, as published in the *Morning Chronicle*, March 23, 1869.
[128]As recounted by Annand, *Morning Chronicle*, March 2, 1869.
[129]*Ibid.*, May 25, 1866; March 23, 1869.
[130]Nova Scotia, Lieutenant Governor, Telegram Book, Williams to Monck, March 14, 1866.
[131]*Ibid.*, Williams to Gordon, March 19, 1866.
[132]*Ibid.*, Gordon to Williams, March 19, 1866.

be achieved in New Brunswick, and he was afraid Annand might stiffen Smith's resistance. In fact it was probably already too late. Smith was already dilatory and circumspect in dealing with union, and Gordon was becoming convinced that a complete change of government might be necessary. Smith, for his part, found Annand's proposal a little embarrassing;[133] and he was sure he could weather Fisher's vote of want of confidence by at least five or six votes.[134] He did not need a proposal for a new convention; union, he thought, could be defeated without recourse to that, and he was not ready to jeopardize his own position to help Nova Scotians who in any case depended heavily upon him. Besides, he was soon made aware that some of Annand's friends were not very happy about Annand's proposals. E. M. Macdonald as soon as he got wind of them promptly telegraphed a friend in the New Brunswick government to wire Annand to stay home.[135] Howe later remarked, "So earnest was Mr. Annand in this business that it took Killam, McLellan, McDonald, and some others of the more energetic of our party to choke him off and keep him at home."[136] Annand had to content himself with a letter to Smith. In this letter some of the efforts concerted by Nova Scotian and New Brunswick anti-Confederates, something of their mutual dependence, and some of the difficulties of their position are revealed.

Halifax, 20 March, 1866

MY DEAR SMITH,—

I have felt very anxious since the meeting of your Parliament, as to how you would come out of the fight, and whether you would be able to hold your ground against the enemy. We have not yet heard the result of the want of confidence motion, but I was glad to see a telegram from a member of your Government on Saturday last that the Administration would be sustained, and that you were safe for the present as regards Confederation. I had made up my mind, previous to the receipt of the telegram, to visit Fredericton with the view of conferring with you, and taking such steps as might be thought advisable in the interests of both Provinces. Like yourself, I desire no political Union with Canada, because I feel that the Maritime Provinces, in any scheme that may be matured, must be seriously injured by a connexion with a colony which must necessarily exercise a preponderating influence over all the others. But if,

---

133Letter from an unknown member of the New Brunswick government to A. G. Jones, March 24, 1866, quoted by Jones in a speech, Jan. 13, 1868, *Morning Chronicle*, Jan. 16, 1868.

134Smith to Annand, March 25, 1866, referred to in *Morning Chronicle*, March 23, 1869.

135*Halifax Citizen*, Feb. 25, 1869.

136Howe's "Letter to the Electors of Hants, No. 2," *Halifax Citizen*, April 8, 1869.

either through the exertions of the British Government, or change of opinion, or want of pluck, on the part of the people of the seaboard Provinces, it may be necessary to deal practically with the Union question, then I want to be in a position to make the best possible bargain under the circumstances for my own country.

Now, as long as you can rely upon your own people, there will be no necessity to move here. Large as is the Government following in our Assembly, upon the Confederation question, they are powerless, and will so continue as long as New Brunswick maintains her present attitude. But it is right you should know that, however universal the feeling in the country, the majority in the House is not to be relied on should your Province back down. I find a growing feeling among members in favor of union of some sort, and a proposition for a new Convention from our side of the House would be eagerly seized on by some of the government supporters. Now, if we are to have a Union, let it be one that has some more redeeming features than the Quebec Scheme. . . .

My chief object in now writing is to learn if you have an idea of proposing a new Convention, because, if that policy is to prevail in the maritime provinces I would like to be in a position to take the initiative in our Assembly. . . Let me know at your earliest convenience what your views are, and if necessary, telegraph on receipt of this. If we are to have a Union we must take care that it is a fair one, and this can only be done by Nova Scotia and New Brunswick acting cordially together. *Trusting that there may be no change in the POLITICAL CONDITION of these two Provinces for many a day to come,*   I am,   Yours sincerely,

W. ANNAND.[137]

Mistaken in tactics Annand may have been—some of his friends thought so—but his estimate of the position of affairs was remarkably accurate.

Just three days before, on March 17, Governor Williams ordered out the Nova Scotian militia to counter the Fenian danger, 8,000 men with 2,000 in reserve.[138] Three Fenian ships were said to have left New York to attack Halifax. Militia artillery companies proceeded to man the batteries in Point Pleasant Park; war materiel was sent over to George's Island and out to Macnab's at the harbour mouth. Of Fenians "nothing else was talked of during the day, and at every corner of the streets, in the principal thoroughfares, and places of public resort, anxious groups might be seen awaiting confirmation or contradiction of the news which created so much alarm."[139] On Monday, March 19, three regiments of the militia were mustered on the Common, some of them armed with

---

[137]Annand to Smith, March 20, 1866, in *Morning Chronicle*, March 2, 1869 (original italics). Annand reported in the paper that he had requested this letter from Smith for purpose of publication.

[138]Nova Scotia, Lieutenant Governor, Telegram Book, Williams to Gordon, March 19, 1866.

[139]*Morning Chronicle*, March 19, 1866.

the main available weapon—the Crimean muzzle-loader with its long sword bayonet.[140]

Joseph Howe arrived back in Halifax on March 27. Annand, who had wished Howe would come home,[141] now surrendered the reins to him, and then "there was an end to intrigue and editorials."[142] Annand had nibbled at union and backed away, but some of his followers succumbed. Before New Brunswick had dealt with Confederation, when, in fact, the constitutional manœuvres of Gordon were approaching their most precarious stage, it became clear that the "growing feeling among members in favor of union of some sort"[143] had produced some definite —and as it turned out, decisive—shifts of opinion in the Nova Scotian Assembly.

[140]*Ibid.*, March 20, 1866.

[141]Miller's report of a conversation with Annand in March, 1866. (Nova Scotia, Assembly, *Debates and Proceedings*, 1866, 311 (May 1).) Annand's reply is not in the Debates; he alleged his speech was misreported and would not give up proofs. Annand's speech is given in the *Halifax Citizen*, May 24, 1866. Annand throws doubt on other aspects of Miller's report, but does not deny this one.

[142]Howe's "Letter to the Electors of Hants, No. 2," *Halifax Citizen*, April 8, 1869.

[143]Annand's phrase, from Smith to Annand, March 20, 1866, quoted above.

14. NEW BRUNSWICK

EACH OF THE FOUR MARITIME PROVINCES had a distinctive character derived from the facts of its geography and the accidents of its history. New Brunswick's proximity to the United States, her preoccupations with lumbering and shipbuilding, her population of a mixture of Loyalist and Irish all combined to give her a racy character that was both disconcerting and fascinating. Though physically larger than Nova Scotia, New Brunswick had a smaller and less homogenous population. Nova Scotia had internal divisions of course, but sea communication tended to unite the province. New Brunswick however was divided geographically and politically in two: the North Shore and the Saint John valley.

The North Shore, more east than north, was the eastern side of New Brunswick from Baie Chaleur to Cape Tormentine. It was itself divided. The northern part, centred on the Miramichi, was dominated by the wood and lumber trade in Newcastle and Chatham; the southern, by Moncton, a growing settlement at the bend of the Petitcodiac. Between these two parts of the North Shore stretched a belt of forest that effectively separated them. Newcastle's inland communications were with Fredericton, by means of a difficult journey up the Miramichi valley; Moncton's were with Saint John by means of the five-year-old railway that went by the resounding title of the European and North American.

The European and North American railway was a symbol of the hopes and ambitions of the other section of the province, the Saint John valley. The politics and policies of New Brunswick were largely controlled by the Saint John valley, to the chagrin and often the annoyance of the North Shore. The Saint John valley contained two-thirds of the province's 267,000 inhabitants. Saint John was the largest city in the Maritimes, larger than Halifax or St. John's. Including Carlton and Portland, immediately across the river, Saint John numbered some 42,000, twice the size of Hamilton, and approaching Quebec or Toronto. Saint John was an ambitious and aggressive city, and its people were vivacious and active. The Charlottetown *Examiner* spoke of them as "the lively inhabitants of that 'fast' city."[1] Visitors were often struck by the differences between Halifax and Saint John. Halifax had then, and retained for many years to come, its class consciousness and with it a certain stiffness of manner. Saint John people called the Nova Scotian capital "sleepy Halifax,"[2] and Saint John was more open and affable. It had a bustling American character that visitors found agreeable.[3] J. W. Carman, the editor of the Kingston *British American*, observed New Brunswickers in August, 1864:

. . . they are more American [than Can]adians are—more democratic in [their ta]stes—have more of the "free [and easy"] swagger in their manners than the [peopl]e of this Province. In St. John you see [mor]e big men loosely dressed, with their [hat]s at a declination of forty-five degrees on the backs of their heads, smoking segars [sic] in Hotels on the Sabbath, talking politics, than in Canada—more flash-dressed ladies at Theatres and Concerts than in Canada—[4]

Saint John was, said Charles Belford of the Toronto *Leader*, a strictly commercial city. "Its people . . . go about their business as if their business were all of life to them. . . ."[5] It was not a beautiful city. Like many ports in the Maritimes, including Halifax and St. John's, its geography was the most attractive part of it. And, like Halifax and St. John's also, its houses were built largely of wood; if of brick, then "the brownest of bricks," while the wooden houses were usually painted in "the most *ochrish* of fashions."[6] "Halifax brown" it was sometimes called in Halifax, but it was well nigh universal in Maritime cities: an unusually disagreeable mixture of tan and chocolate. Saint John's public streets were hardly in keeping with her ambitions either; even a Saint John paper admitted that the sidewalks and wharves were in shocking condition. Pretty King's Square was run down and neglected.[7] Altogether Saint John had a "rather sombre aspect" that belied the geniality of the place, a curious juxtaposition that may obtain even now.

Saint John was not the capital of New Brunswick, though it certainly thought it should be. Fredericton, eighty-five miles up river, had been chosen the capital from motives of defence and sheer pique. Fredericton, the "Celestial City" as it was called in Saint John with undisguised

[1]Charlottetown *Examiner*, Sept. 19, 1864.
[2]Saint John *Weekly Telegraph*, Aug. 2, 1865.
[3]A. L. Spedon, *Rambles among the Blue-Noses* (Montreal, 1863), 134.
[4]Kingston *Daily British American*, Aug. 19, 1864, "The Parliamentary Excursion, V." (Part of this report is torn away.)
[5]Toronto *Leader*, Aug. 22, 1864, report of Aug. 17 from Halifax.
[6]*Ibid.*, Aug. 12, 1864, report of Aug. 6 from Saint John.
[7]Saint John *Weekly Telegraph*, Aug. 2, 1865.

sarcasm,[8] was about the size of Charlottetown, with a population of 6,200. Half-hidden from the river by its elms and maples,[9] Fredericton was a somnolent little town, lulled by the river and the spacious landscape into a bucolic materialism that made it both agreeable and enervating.

The Saint John river valley was quite the loveliest in the lower provinces. The route from Rivière du Loup to Fredericton was well known for the "beauty of the scenery, the excellence of the road, the goodness of the post-horses, and the comfort of the little inns that stand at intervals of forty or fifty miles. . . ."[10] Dr. Mackay of the London *Times*, travelling up to Fredericton from Saint John, remarked on the beauty of the river, "as lovely as Windermere or grand as Loch Awe."[11] Arthur Gordon, the Governor, loved it, as he loved much of New Brunswick.[12] It appealed to his Scottish nature. Gordon was fond of hunting and canoeing, both of which he did often with Indian guides. Gordon's youthful enthusiasm (he was only thirty-five in 1864) was refreshing. He liked to travel by sleigh in winter, "lightly skimming over the rock-hard snow roads,—over the frozen lakes,—over the ice bound rivers. . . . Out in the clear keen air . . . the tinkle of sleigh bells . . . whisked along under the still sunlight or the frosty starlight. . . ."[13] Other sides of New Brunswick life Gordon liked less. He thought Harry Moody, his young aide-de-camp, was making a mistake in marrying a "through the nose speaking ill educated unmannered native girl,"[14] even though she was a judge's daughter. As for New Brunswick politics, Gordon thought them deplorable. Even to Nova Scotians New Brunswick politics had a crude flavour, though it was not surprising that Nova Scotians should think so, prejudiced as they were. Gordon's strictures on the subject were exhaustive and formed a perennial theme in the quantity of despatches, public and private, with which he favoured Cardwell.

New Brunswick politics followed the American orientation of her people. There was a vigorous Jacksonian licence about New Brunswick

[8]*Ibid.*, May 10, 1865. Reputedly because the Anglican bishop had his seat there.

[9]Toronto *Leader*, Aug. 16, 1864, report of Aug. 8 from Fredericton.

[10]London *Times*, Oct. 11, 1865, report of Sept. 21 from Fredericton.

[11]*Ibid.*

[12]J. K. Chapman, "The Career of Arthur Gordon, 1st Lord Stanmore," Ph.D. thesis, University of London, 1954, 21–3.

[13]Stanmore Papers, Gordon to William Wood, Feb. 12, 1868; also Chapman, "Career of Gordon," 22–3.

[14]Stanmore Papers, Gordon to Waterfield, Nov. 11, 1862; also in Chapman, "Career of Gordon," 24n.

politics that may have outdone even Maine. Members of the Assembly were sufficiently ill-educated and ill-mannered that to be one was almost disqualification from polite society—at least by Gordon's definition of society.[15] Gordon's view may have been determined by the more austere rectitude of his own society in Britain, but a description by the Saint John *Telegraph* suggests that there was more to Gordon's attitude than prejudice.

There they sit day after day, quietly pocketing the $4 and other perquisites, eating and sleeping and drinking at the public expense, but never, except probably once in the term, are they found opening their lips in the interests of the people whom they represent. This is the sort of thing which has lasted long enough. . . . We have seen a member of the Legislature before now, not only ignorant, possessing information of no higher grade than that afforded by an Engine House education, but filthy in personal appearance, squirting tobacco juice on every side of him. . . .[16]

Members of the Assembly were too often those who could find a place nowhere else. The Speaker of the Assembly found a post as keeper of a county gaol and duly resigned to take the more lucrative and apparently more promising position.[17] Some members of the Tilley ministry, Gordon complained, administered public office in such a way as to "convert their posts into sinecures by habitual absence from the seat of Government," or worse, "to divert from their proper uses"[18] the sums of public money that passed through their hands. They were, in short, "utterly incapable and inefficient."[19] Strong as Leonard Tilley was politically—and he was considered by the semi-independent *Telegraph* to wield more influence than any other New Brunswick politician, past or present—he was criticized for surrounding himself with men who were "quite incapable of filling the positions which they hold."[20] Gordon admitted candidly that the unpopularity of the Smith ministry late in 1865 was largely because they refused to act with the partiality required by their supporters. Government in New Brunswick presents the picture of a robust little corporation for the private aggrandizement of its members and the incidental conduct of public business.

Thus politics in New Brunswick often turned on questions of more direct concern to pocketbooks or personalities. "Party politics," wrote Charles Belford, "do not run high. There are no great questions dividing

[15]Gladstone Papers, British Museum Add. MSS 44320, Gordon to Gladstone, Jan., 1864.
[16]Saint John *Weekly Telegraph*, Jan. 25, 1865.
[17]Gladstone Papers, Gordon to Gladstone, Jan., 1864.
[18]C.O. 188, Gordon to Cardwell, May 8, 1865 (confidential).
[19]*Ibid.*, April 10, 1865 (confidential).
[20]Saint John *Morning Telegraph*, April 14, 1864.

parties and the battles of Parliament are mainly of a personal nature, except when railway matters are introduced."[21] Patronage and railways, these were the issues that divided New Brunswick, not Liberal and Conservative. Party labels were rather meaningless, for there were no questions to give them vitality. The Tilley government was nominally Liberal, but the Opposition was a heterogenous collection of ex-Liberals and quondam Conservatives. The Smith government of 1865 was this mixture. Smith himself was the former Liberal Attorney General; J. C. Allen, Smith's Attorney General, was a Tory. A. H. Gillmor, the Provincial Secretary, was "never much of anything except as a standing candidate for Auditor-Generalship."[22] This description fitted all too many politicians. The personal touch was well illustrated in 1860 when a new issue of New Brunswick postage stamps was ordered from New York. There appeared, in the series with Queen Victoria and the Prince of Wales, no less a personage than the lumber merchant from Woodstock who happened to be the Postmaster General. The face of Charles Connell was beautifully engraved, in rich brown, on the five-cent stamp. This was more than even the New Brunswick government was prepared to stand for, and Charles Connell was hastily jettisoned and the stamp precipitately abandoned.[23] Political life was rather gamey, and politicians seemed content to have it so. But as the Saint John *Telegraph* remarked, "New Brunswick, however, is not peculiar in the production of political vermin."[24] Of both Fredericton and Charlottetown Goldwin Smith's unrepentant aphorism is not altogether inappropriate: "The smaller the pit, the fiercer the rats."[25]

The ferocity of politics in New Brunswick goes far to explain the curious history of Confederation there. Confederation, like Western Extension, was a bone of contention that temporarily distracted politicians from more personal issues. For a time Confederate and anti-Confederate became a convenient substitute for other political labels. Even this was only temporary. The new government in 1865 might have taken up Confederation if by doing so it had been confident it would stay in power. In other provinces Confederation became either an open question, as in Prince Edward Island and Newfoundland, or the basis

[21]Toronto *Leader*, Aug. 16, 1864, report of Aug. 9 from Saint John.
[22]Saint John *Weekly Telegraph*, May 10, 1865.
[23]The stamp was probably never issued. Mint copies are now worth about $1000.
[24]Saint John *Morning Telegraph*, Dec. 31, 1864.
[25]Quoted by G. M. Wrong, "Creation of the Federal System in Canada," in Wrong, Willison, Lash, and Falconer, *The Federation of Canada, 1867–1917* (Toronto, 1917), 17.

THE LIFE AND TIMES OF CONFEDERATION

of an agreement between Liberals and Conservatives as in Canada and
Nova Scotia. In New Brunswick it was neither. It was a complication of
all existing issues, public and personal, that precariously divided the
"ins" from the "outs."

In the beginning New Brunswick was indifferent or even hostile to
political union. The point was made by a New Brunswicker who sat
beside the Toronto *Leader*'s correspondent at dinner. "We, in New
Brunswick, do not want an union with Canada or Nova Scotia. We have
nothing to gain. . . . What is required is a more intimate commercial
connection with you. We want the Intercolonial railway. . . ."[26] This was
ultimately to be Joseph Howe's position. It was reasonable that commercial ties should precede political ones. But the political union of the
British American provinces could not have been created this way. The
natural lines of geography and trade were all against it. If commercial
ties had to precede political ones the Dominion of Canada would
probably never have been created at all. Indeed this suggests why, to the
rationale of the businessman or trader, Confederation must often have
seemed so visionary.

New Brunswickers had always had a sharp eye on the "crucial problem of hard cash," as Professor Bailey put it,[27] and the discussion of
Confederation in New Brunswick tended to have this primeval character.
Leonard Tilley had risen to power on his financial ability, and it was
probably for this reason that his peculiar views on temperance were
forgiven him. Tilley's speeches on Confederation were heavily freighted
with the profit and prosperity that would come to New Brunswick with
union. The pages of the *Morning Freeman* were largely taken up with
financial comment, and the *Morning News*, which reflected Tilley, was
not very different.

Leonard Tilley was rather an inscrutable figure. He was forty-six
years of age in 1864, a Saint John businessman who had been a member
of the Assembly for the past fourteen years. Gordon considered him
very intelligent; the *Morning Telegraph* spoke of "his wonderful tact in
governing, his unceasing application to the duties of his office . . . [and]
the strong personal friendship he is capable of inspiring. . . ."[28] Tilley
was the rare example of a politician who knew when not to talk. He
had not been a frequent speaker at the Quebec Conference, but he was
always clear and to the point. "The unpardonable sin in Mr. Tilley's
mind, would seem to be, surplusage. . . . Any ordinary man can open

[26]Toronto *Leader*, Aug. 16, 1864, report of Aug. 9 from Saint John.
[27]A. G. Bailey, "The Basis and Persistence of Opposition to Confederation in
New Brunswick," *Canadian Historical Review*, XXIII, 4 (Dec., 1942), 377.
[28]Saint John *Morning Telegraph*, April 14, 1864.

an argument; most men can keep one up, but Mr. Tilley always knows where his matter ends. . . . The condensation of his style is no bad index to the tenacity of his character."[29] Of his personal character less is known. His smiling, rosy-cheeked face was the reflection of an agile, if sanguine, mind. Tilley usually knew his own limitations; he lacked the ruthless realism necessary to distinguish those of others. Tilley was unblushingly pedestrian; he had little imagination. Like the apothecary he was, he had a better head for details than for principles. He was "just what a man possessing moderate abilities, a good memory, and some natural aptitude for ordinary business . . . might be expected to become."[30] But he was clever; he was like a fox, quick, resourceful, persistent, and at times courageous. "Mr. Tilley is never so dangerous, so fertile in expedients . . . as when his adversaries think they have him cornered."[31] In 1855 Tilley had been largely instrumental in bringing a prohibition act into a province whose consumption of spirit was about three gallons per capita per year. It kept him out of office for two years. He was sensible enough to see that his experiment with such reform legislation was premature, but he never abandoned his belief in its necessity. It was so with Confederation. With the Intercolonial Railway it was, he thought, economically feasible, and the state of New Brunswick politics made it politically desirable. Tilley never mentioned the latter, and the *Morning News* never made the savage comments on the state of New Brunswick politics that the Saint John *Globe* and Saint John *Telegraph* did. Tilley was aware of it well enough; it was entirely characteristic of him that he accepted it as it was and used it to his own advantage.

J. H. Gray was four years older, and a weaker man. Gray had pretensions to be an orator, and he was indeed a more finished speaker than Tilley. Gray's fault was a rich redundance of expression which made him effective at one time, boring at another. He had made a good impression in Canada, but it was not surprising that at his first public meeting after his return to New Brunswick he said "nothing worthy of serious refutation."[32] Whatever his weaknesses on the platform, Gray was a staunch and determined friend of Confederation. Other "friends" of Confederation were less scrupulous, notably Charles Fisher and W. H. Steeves. The Duke of Newcastle once called Fisher "the worst public man in British America,"[33] though this was, perhaps, unfair.

[29]Montreal *Gazette*, Oct. 28, 1864.
[30]Saint John *Daily Evening Globe*, Sept. 27, 1865, letter on Tilley's career by "Ivan."
[31]Saint John *Morning Telegraph*, April 14, 1864.
[32]*Ibid.*, Nov. 19, 1864.
[33]Cardwell Papers, Gordon to Cardwell, Nov. 20, 1865.

The New Brunswick delegates arrived in Saint John by the Portland boat on November 8, 1864. A week later in Fredericton the adoption of the Quebec Resolutions was discussed in Cabinet, and after two days discussion it was agreed to adopt the report from Quebec, though in the face of some opposition, notably from G. L. Hatheway, Tilley's Minister of Public Works, and one of the four members for York County.[34] On Thursday, November 17 the first public meeting was held in the Mechanics Institute in Saint John with speeches by Tilley and Gray and some 1500 people present. Neither Tilley nor Gray were in good form, and the general consensus was that the meeting was a failure.[35] Gray needed "more rehearsal."[36] And Tilley of all people, commented the *Telegraph*, ought to have given some kind of comprehensive financial analysis of the scheme—just the kind that Galt was about to do in Sherbrooke, and which the *Telegraph* duly praised.[37] But Tilley "did not study up." None of the New Brunswick delegates had,[38] and there was some questioning of the right of the New Brunswick delegates to take up Confederation at all. A. J. Smith told the electors of Westmorland in round New Brunswick style that "the ministry are a mere creation of the people . . . and are delegated with no power to alter or change the political relations of the people. . . ."[39] It could fairly be alleged, said the *Weekly Telegraph* on November 30, that the delegates "were not fairly off with the 'old love' [Maritime union] before they were 'on with the new [Confederation].' " Tilley wrote Brown of difficulties and prejudices to be overcome. He expected to be successful, but he felt public opinion was at the moment against him and Gordon's attitude was often embarrassing.[40] But the meetings soon went better. The day after his letter to Brown Tilley had a most successful evening at the Saint John Mechanics Institute, when he had the audience stamping its approval at the end of his speech. The *Evening Globe*, not very favourable to the Tilley government, noted, "Mr. Tilley at the present moment is 'master of the situation'. . . ."[41]

"Confederation," said the *Weekly Telegraph* on November 30, "is the name of a new play recently introduced on the political stage." Charles Fisher was performing the same piece in York County while

[34]Hatheway to Gordon, Jan. 7, 1865, published in the Fredericton *Head Quarters*, Jan. 25, 1865, and Saint John *New Brunswick Courier*, Jan. 28, 1865.
[35]*New Brunswick Courier*, Nov. 19, 1864; C.O. 188, Gordon to Cardwell, Dec. 5, 1864.
[36]Saint John *Morning Telegraph*, Nov. 28, 1864.
[37]*Ibid.*, Dec. 5, 1864; also Dec. 19, 1864.
[38]*Ibid.*, Dec. 8, 1864; Dec. 19, 1864.
[39]*Ibid.*, Nov. 29, 1864; Chatham *Gleaner*, Dec. 3, 1864.
[40]Brown Papers, Tilley to Brown, Nov. 21, 1864.
[41]Saint John *Daily Evening Globe*, Nov. 24, 1864.

the North Shore was being entertained by Johnson and Mitchell. "Mr. Smith has already begun to arrange the scenery in Westmorland County. . . ." The same play, the *Telegraph* went on—newspapers could never let a good metaphor go—"is having a great run in the principal cities and towns in Canada. . . . No dramatic performance ever attracted so much attention throughout British America, or became so widely diffused in so short a time."

The Saint John papers were evenly divided on Confederation. The *Morning News* and the *New Brunswick Courier*, both government papers, favoured it. The *Morning Freeman* and *Evening Globe* opposed both the Government and Confederation. The influential and independent *Morning Telegraph*, a daily with a remarkable circulation of 12,000,[42] was cautious, but its support for Confederation gradually increased, and late in January it came out in support of it. The Fredericton papers were similarly divided, the government *New Brunswick Reporter* in favour, and the *Head Quarters*, which was anti-Tilley, opposed. In the smaller centres, in Woodstock, Chatham, Sackville, for example, the newspapers were generally opposed. None of the New Brunswick papers seem to have altered their customary allegiances as a result of the Confederation question.

The Saint John *Evening Globe* was not unsympathetic to the idea of union, but gradually went against Confederation. With the Fredericton *Head Quarters* it believed New Brunswick was being pushed into union by Canadians whose powerful exigencies drove them on, and by the Colonial Office. It also disliked federation on principle. The *Globe*'s belief in legislative union was not shared by many New Brunswickers; but J. C. Allen, Smith's Attorney General, agreed with its views, and so did Gordon. Part of the *Globe*'s criticism of federation stemmed from a mighty suspicion that the New Brunswick legislature was bad enough already and that if the leading members of it went to the House of Commons in Ottawa, the remainder left in Fredericton would beggar description.

Conceive, if you can, the style of men that will offer themselves for seats in the local legislature . . . pettifogging politicians whose statesmanship will consist in engineering situations for themselves and their friends, and whose patriotism will be developed in filling their own pockets at the expense of the State. . . . A Legislative Union of the Colonies would have swept local bodies away altogether, and this could have been done with great advantage to the public welfare.[43]

---

[42]The *Telegraph* claimed a circulation of 12,000, the largest in New Brunswick, and no one disputed it. The Halifax daily, the *Morning Chronicle*, was reported in 1869 to have a circulation of 3,000.

[43]Saint John *Daily Evening Globe*, Oct. 17, 1864.

There was some public support for legislative union, though in New Brunswick it was nothing like so powerful or so well articulated as in Nova Scotia. But one public meeting, on December 6, was largely given over to this theme. Confederation, said J. W. Lawrence, the leading speaker, was a rickety structure thrown together without a plummet or a line and would crumple in the first gale. Besides, what use would British America have of "seven Governments and seven Legislatures?"[44]

The *Morning Freeman* made gestures in the same direction. The *Freeman* was edited by a Roman Catholic Irishman, Timothy Anglin, who had come from Ireland after 1848. Anglin was described by Gordon as a man of some ability, but of singularly narrow mind and editor of "a cheap paper."[45] Like the opposition papers in Nova Scotia, the *Freeman* took delight in pointing out what it regarded as the expensive complexities of the Quebec scheme. It was simply a legislative union with the useless and expensive machinery of local legislatures added.

Their very first session will prove them worthless, and when they have served the purpose of deluding some of the people with a show of Federal Union, they will be abolished. If this Union must be, it would be better to abolish the local Legislatures at once in appearance as well as reality than to set up such expensive shams.[46]

It was almost as if the *Freeman* were reading Macdonald's mind.

But the truth was that few people, certainly not Timothy Anglin or A. J. Smith, believed New Brunswick was ready to give up her legislature. The *Freeman*, like the Chatham *Gleaner* which had similar arguments,[47] was using legislative union largely as a weapon. The *Morning News* ridiculed this opposition interest in legislative union. If the New Brunswick delegates had actually proposed such a thing, "what would Mr. Smith and his friends have said? Would they not have denounced with torrents of indignation the men who could thus seek to rob the people of their rights, and remove from their control the management of their local affairs? Certainly they would, and with good cause too."[48] Had legislative union been the basis of deliberation, said the Fredericton *Reporter*, "we have no hesitation in saying the whole project must prove a failure."[49] And though the *Evening Globe*, like the Halifax *Citizen*, was in earnest about legislative union, it is impossible to take seriously

[44]Saint John *Morning Freeman*, Dec. 8, 1864.
[45]C.O. 188, Gordon to Cardwell, April 10, 1865 (confidential). Anglin in later years became Speaker of the House of Commons (1874–1877). Roman Catholics, mainly French and Irish, comprised some 30% of the New Brunswick population.
[46]*Morning Freeman*, Nov. 3, 1864.
[47]Chatham *Gleaner*, Sept. 24, Dec. 10, 1864.
[48]*Morning News*, Feb. 3, 1865.
[49]Fredericton *New Brunswick Reporter*, Oct. 28, 1864.

most other protestations. Legislative union was merely a convenient stick with which to beat the Government.

Tilley extracted what advantage he could from the federal principle. Confederation could still give New Brunswick, he said, the privilege of dealing with its own local affairs; there would be a legislature at Fredericton after Confederation as before. This was his theme at a Saint John public meeting on December 16, at which Tilley arrived with a pile of books under one arm, looking for all the world like "a New England preacher with his bundle of com[m]entaries. . . ." Tilley used them to demolish arguments on legislative union by Timothy Anglin, J. W. Lawrence, and A. J. Smith, but he never allowed the books to impede him. He also "plied the *argumentum ad homines*, as Mr. Tilley knows how."[50] The government and Confederate papers followed Tilley's line. Like their cohorts in Halifax they defended the *modus vivendi* arrived at by the Quebec Conference, though they drew some characteristic New Brunswick conclusions. The Saint John *New Brunswick Courier* of January 7, 1865, said the people of New Brunswick would insist on the retention of the local legislatures. Besides, legislative union would require municipal institutions; municipal institutions would require direct taxation; and everyone knew how impossible that was. The *Courier*'s view is interesting for it revealed, as did Shea's in Newfoundland, the prevalent assumption of Confederation supporters that the local governments would manage their affairs from the basic eighty-cent-a-head subsidy provided by the central government.[51] Direct taxation seemed outside discussion. What Musgrave called the "morbid apprehension" against it in Newfoundland was also true of New Brunswick, and Tupper's school legislation showed how distasteful it was in Nova Scotia.[52] The Quebec plan was plainly interpreted by the Confederate papers as a redistribution of the available revenue. It had to be so interpreted. It could never have been passed otherwise. The lively fear of increased taxation that existed in all four Maritime provinces was not based upon a chimera; it had been aroused not only by the higher Canadian tariff but also by the latent suspicion that the local legislatures could not survive on the allotment given them by the Quebec Resolutions, and that other forms of taxation might be necessary.[53]

These suspicions had quickly made their presence felt in the other Maritime provinces, and Tilley was not long in feeling their effects in New Brunswick. By the beginning of January, 1865, the question of

[50]Saint John *Morning Telegraph*, Dec. 17, 1864.
[51]Resolution 64 of the Quebec Resolutions.
[52]C.O. 194, Musgrave to Cardwell, July 19, 1865. *Supra*, 169 and 200.
[53]E.g. *Morning Freeman*, Dec. 27, 1864: "an increase of taxation must be an inevitable consequence of a Union of the Provinces on the plan proposed."

legislative union had been wholly submerged by more material issues. The comparison with Nova Scotia is obvious. In New Brunswick these issues developed even earlier and with more effect. "New Brunswickers, it appears, are in the estimation of their delegates, such a money-loving, money-seeking, money-making people, that they can understand nothing but money, or, if they can, nothing else will interest them." This from the *Morning Telegraph* on December 8, 1864. The *New Brunswick Courier* said quietly on December 10: "The financial part of the project has received the most attention." The Fredericton *Head Quarters* began this theme as early as October and was still at it in December. Tilley's main purpose was to satisfy his audiences that Confederation would not increase their taxation, and the *Morning News*, in issue after issue in December, made the same point. The *Evening Globe*, December 5, was struck by the way New Brunswick clung grimly to the financial issue. Nova Scotia and Canada had not done so. It was all too natural; "for years past our local politics have turned almost wholly upon some question of taxation. . . ." It was in fact difficult to direct New Brunswickers toward more lofty concerns. But these should not be burked; Confederation was something more than a question of taxation.

That our people are not satisfied with our present position and status can not be denied. There are in our hearts . . . deep aspirations urging us towards nationality. These may be vain; but they exist. . . . They may originate only in our imagination . . . but imagination governs the world, (according to Napoleon) and it is a much more powerful agent for the promoters of Confederation scheme to operate upon than all the columns of figures they have yet arrayed. . . .

The mature and lofty *Telegraph*, February 6, 1865, also disparaged "this paltry hobby of taxation" as matter of minor concern; but the March elections showed how taxation was used at the hustings, with what effect Tilley was the best judge. An election placard in York County said Confederation would impose a direct tax on every cow, ox, or sheep, and Canadian competition would ruin New Brunswick farmers. "Do you wish Canada Oats, Beef, Pork, Butter etc., to come into this country at one half the price you are now receiving? Do you wish the whole Revenue of this country to be handed over to . . . the dishonest Statesmen of Canada? If you wish these things, then vote today for Fisher, Street and Dow."[54]

By mid-December Tilley had been a month at work in Saint John County, and after Christmas he set out to stump the southern half of

[54]*Weekly Telegraph*, March 8, 1865. Cf. also William Needham's speech to the tanners and foundrymen of York County, Fredericton *Head Quarters*, Dec. 14, 1864. Also quoted in A. G. Bailey, "Opposition to Confederation in New Brunswick," 380.

the province. With Charles Fisher he addressed a meeting in Fredericton on January 5, with E. B. Chandler one in Sackville on January 11. He was with J. Steadman at another in Moncton on January 12 (the largest ever seen there), and again in Shediac on January 13. He was back in Fredericton on January 19 speaking with Steadman in Temperance Hall. Something was up and it was soon clear what this was: it was the dissolution of the New Brunswick Assembly and a general election.

About this election there has been much discussion, then and since. The newspapers seemed staggered. "Why has the Government resolved to dissolve the Assembly? This question is frequently asked. . . ."[55] Even the Saint John *Weekly Telegraph* confessed on January 25 that it was "unable to imagine the reason, unless the government was divided; upon no other ground that we can conceive of would they have the hardihood and assurance to embroil the country in a General Election at this unseasonable period of the year." A. J. Smith even called the dissolution an act of tyranny.[56] The *Telegraph* was right; the Government was divided. It was divided within the Ministry and it disagreed with Gordon. Some of the Council (and doubtless many in the Assembly) wanted the session to be held in the usual way, without Confederation being discussed at all. This would ensure that members of the Assembly would nicely pocket their four dollars a day before being put to the chances of an election.[57] But early in November, before Tilley had returned, the *Morning News* had assumed that Confederation would be put through the existing legislature.[58] That was the course that the Canadians and Nova Scotians wanted. But it was not that simple. Tilley soon discovered that such a proceeding would arouse great opposition. In any case his hand was forced, both by Gordon and by the public. In a speech in Carlton on November 21 he was pressed into admitting that Confederation would not be pushed through the legislature until after a general election. He made this commitment "very hesitatingly," and in oblique language; but he made it.[59] What was more, he was held to it. Gordon probably had a hand in Tilley's action.[60]

[55]Fredericton *Colonial Farmer*, Jan. 30, 1865.
[56]Saint John *Weekly Telegraph*, Feb. 8, 1865.
[57]C.O. 188, Gordon to Cardwell, Jan. 16, 1865 (confidential).
[58]Saint John *Morning News*, Nov. 7, 1864.
[59]*Morning Telegraph*, Nov. 25, 1864.
[60]". . . our Governor informed me shortly after my return that he would not consent that the measure or address should be submitted to the House for their action until after an election; and that he had ascertained that he could find a ministry who would take the responsibility for advising that course." Macdonald Papers, Tilley to Galt, undated.

By January, 1865, Tilley was in a quandary. Confederation would not, perhaps could not, go through the existing Assembly. That much was clear. The alternatives were not very happy. One was to avoid discussion of Confederation in the spring session—simply to table the correspondence—and have a dissolution in June. This was the alternative Tilley preferred, and the one that most of the newspapers seemed to expect. The other was to dissolve at once. This was Gordon's view. Since the Assembly had not been elected on the Confederation issue Gordon maintained that the scheme should "be put 'squarely' before the people."[61] Moreover Cardwell, though he may not have wanted a dissolution very much, liked even less any postponement of the question by New Brunswick; Nova Scotia and Canada were proposing to bring Confederation at once before their legislatures. Finally, complicating Tilley's difficulties, G. L. Hatheway, the Minister of Public Works, resigned on January 4 because of his opposition to Confederation.[62] Hatheway was influential, and his resignation, though not made public at once, undoubtedly weakened the Government. It also weakened its capacity to resist Gordon. Gordon urged dissolution upon his divided councillors and in the end Tilley reluctantly acquiesced. Within a fortnight he was regretting it.[63]

The dissolution caused considerable excitement. The government men threw up their hats at the news and cheered lustily for Tilley and Confederation. "All through the week just closed," wrote the Saint John *New Brunswick Courier* on Saturday, February 4, "not only in this city, but in the country, Confederation has formed the all absorbing topic. Knots of people debating on the streets corners, clusters in the hotels and public places, visitors at home, all enter into earnest discussion, and some become sufficiently interested even to get angry." The issue was joined at once. The *Morning News* boldly took up the glove thrown down by the *Morning Freeman*: "The issue of the coming election is, as the *Freeman* . . . very fairly puts it, 'Confederation or no Confederation'. . . ."[64]

[61]H. Moody, "Political Experiences in Nova Scotia, 1867–9," *Dalhousie Review*, April, 1934, 65. Despite the title, Moody, who was Gordon's aide-de-camp, was also reviewing some of the events in New Brunswick.

[62]Hatheway to Gordon, Jan. 4, 7, 1865, in Saint John *New Brunswick Courier*, Jan. 28, 1865. Hatheway said in his nomination speech on Feb. 24 that if he had not resigned Tilley would not have dissolved. (Fredericton *Head Quarters*, March 1, 1865.)

[63]Cardwell Papers, Gordon to Cardwell, Feb. 8, 1865. Another explanation of Tilley's dissolution was that it was forced upon him by his own Cabinet, it was said by a vote of 5–4, Tilley being in the minority. (Saint John *Daily Evening Globe*, Oct. 10, 1865, letter signed "Ivan.")

[64]Saint John *Morning News*, Jan. 25, 1865; Saint John *Morning Freeman*, Jan. 24, 1865.

But there was more to the election than Confederation. The Government had been in power, with but one brief interruption, for almost ten years, and power had sapped whatever character it might originally have possessed. Gordon had not a good word to say about any of the ministers but Tilley and Mitchell. The *Telegraph* echoed these sentiments.[65] One suspects that Tilley's interest in Confederation was like Tupper's, not only because it was in itself worthwhile but also because it was a convenient smokescreen. In Nova Scotia it offered cover from the School Act of 1864, in New Brunswick from the accumulated weaknesses of nearly ten years of office. But even those who opposed Confederation were embarrassed by the support of worn-out politicians; "They will spring up like mushrooms after a smart rain shower. Without honor or principle . . . utterly reckless as to the means employed in conducting an election,—purchasable as no doubt many of them will be —these political guerillas will haunt every hustings. . . ."[66] Still, the opposition weakness was not so notorious. It was possible that the corruption of the Government may have been a contributing cause to Tilley's defeat. Smith's government was, in Gordon's eyes at least, much more reputable.[67]

Western Extension was also an issue in the election of 1865.[68] Almost every government from 1854 onward had been deep in railways. In New Brunswick, one is tempted to think, politics were railways. The modest success of the railway from Saint John to Shediac increased the pressure from the south generally, and from Saint John in particular, for the extension of the line west to the Maine border, thence to link up with a projected American line to Bangor and Portland. This was Western Extension and it was the darling of the Saint John businessmen. But the North Shore counties were not ready to sit idly by and see large sums spent again upon railways for the southern section of the province. The existing European and North American was quite enough. In 1864 the Tilley government had straddled the issue. It passed the Railway Facility Act—nicknamed the Lobster Act, for going in so many directions at once—that offered a subvention of $10,000 a mile toward construction of railways in several specified sections of the province. The eighty-three miles from Saint John to the American border were estimated to cost $30,000 a mile, nearly $2.5 million. With the government subvention, this left about $1 million

[65]C.O. 188, Gordon to Cardwell, April 10, 1865 (confidential); *ibid.*, May 8, 1865 (confidential); *Weekly Telepraph*, Jan. 16, 1865.

[66]*Weekly Telegraph*, Jan. 25, 1865.

[67]C.O. 188, Gordon to Cardwell, May 8, 1865 (confidential).

[68]A. G. Bailey, "Railways and the Confederation Issue in New Brunswick. 1863–1865," *Canadian Historical Review*, XXI, 4 (Dec., 1940), 367–83.

to be raised in stock and the rest on mortgage.[69] Strenuous efforts were made to sell stock in the Western Extension Company in 1864, but the calls were not paid, and the question soon lay dormant. By January, 1865, prospects for Western extension were anything but promising.

At this point Confederation came on the scene and with it came the promise of the Intercolonial Railway. The Intercolonial was the really concrete advantage that Tilley could promise from Confederation, and he was at pains to secure it. To be effective it had to have firm support not only from Canada but from Nova Scotia, and Tilley was watchful in both directions.[70] When the Saint John *Globe* picked up a remark of Macdonald's that appeared to compromise the Intercolonial,[71] Tilley wired Macdonald to reiterate the Canadian promise, and Macdonald's reassuring reply was duly read out to a meeting in Portland.[72] But there were ways of sabotaging even the Intercolonial, and it did not take A. J. Smith long to discover what they were.

At Saint John, on January 31, 1865, Smith delivered a two-hour broadside against Confederation to a vast assemblage packed so tightly that reporters could hardly get in.[73] Smith made the points he had made at Sackville on January 20[74]: the wickedness of federation, the jobs promised. "It was thought that the Conference would break up, when it was proposed that the Governors of the Provinces should be appointed by the General Government. This acted like a charm, all was at once Love Purity and Fidelity. (Laughter) He hoped none would understand him to mean that any of the Delegates had thoughts or hopes for themselves, but of their friends left at home. (Renewed laughter)."[75] Smith also asked, "which would they prefer, Western Extension or the Intercolonial?" It was a question that seemed to admit of only one answer. "Western Extension was worth ten Intercolonials."[76] Two days later, at the Institute, with hundreds turned away, Tilley stoutly denied that Confederation comprised Western Extension at all. Western Extension was a fixed fact, Confederation or not. But

[69]The *Morning News'* analysis, Sept. 19, 1864.

[70]Canada, Minister of Finance, Papers, Tilley to Galt, Jan. 27, 1865 (telegram), related to Nova Scotia and the Intercolonial.

[71]Macdonald made it the day the Confederation debate opened in Canada, Feb. 3 (*Confederation Debates*, 18). See also D. G. Creighton, *John A. Macdonald: The Young Politician* (Toronto, 1952), 404–5.

[72]*Weekly Telegraph*, Feb. 22, 1865.

[73]*Ibid.*, Feb. 1, 1865.

[74]Sackville *Borderer*, Jan. 27, 1865.

[75]*Weekly Telegraph*, Feb. 1, 1865.

[76]These exact words are not in the reported version of Smith's speech but Mitchell's quotation of them. *Weekly Telegraph*, March 15, 1865.

the result was that although the Intercolonial did not become a liability to Tilley, it was not the supreme advantage he hoped it would be. Of course if the Intercolonial should follow the Saint John valley, it would be better, but no one knew the answer to that. Tilley could not say it would follow the Saint John valley, but he would not admit it would go by the North Shore. From the precincts of York County G. L. Hatheway derisively asked him,

> Mr. Tilley will you stop your puffing and blowing
> And tell us which way the Railway is going?[77]

It was evidence of Tilley's sense of humour that he quoted this for the benefit of the Saint John audience, but all he could say was that he favoured the central route, whatever that might be.[78] Smith's gambit had been remarkably successful; Peter Mitchell, extracting what advantage he could for the North Shore tacitly revealed it.

> Look at the canvass of these men in York, St. John, and Westmorland. What was the burden of their song? It was this: "The Intercolonial Railway will go by the North Shore." . . . Read the speeches at their public meetings . . . the placards scattered through the country districts, and they never cease to wring [sic] changes on the Railway by the North Shore.[79]

The North Shore might enjoy the prospect of the Intercolonial as much as it pleased, but the political power lay in the south-west. Smith, giving up a pawn, had got a bishop.

The elections began on February 28 in Kent County in the east and continued until March 18 when Northumberland voted.[80] This arrangement was general practice but for Tilley it had a supreme disadvantage: the results in one county affected others. The defeat of Tilley candidates in York on March 2 powerfully influenced the vote in Saint John County on March 3 and in Saint John City on March 4. In the end Tilley lost his own seat in Saint John, and his supporters dwindled to eleven in a House of forty-one. Tilley resigned on March 27, 1865. This sharp defeat, the rout of Tilley supporters "horse, foot and artillery" as the *Evening Globe* had it on March 27, was caused so Canadian government papers suggested, by the liberal use of American funds. They drew the lesson that "the alternative of Confederation

[77]Fredericton *Head Quarters*, Feb. 1, 1865; also quoted by A. G. Bailey, "Opposition to Confederation in New Brunswick," 379.
[78]*Weekly Telegraph*, Feb. 8, 1865, report of Feb. 2.
[79]*Ibid.*, March 15, 1865, reporting Mitchell's speech of March 7, in Newcastle.
[80]Some of the dates of polling were as follows: Kent, Feb. 28; York, March 2; Saint John County, March 3; Saint John City, March 4; Kings, March 14; Northumberland, March 18. (*Weekly Telegraph*, March 1, 1865)

or Annexation is more than ever confirmed when we see how completely American influence can control elections of the Provinces."[81] As in the old fable of the blind men and the elephant, each interpreted Tilley's defeat by his own preoccupations. Gordon said it was because of repeated acts of bad faith by the Canadians and because Confederation was not a legislative union. J. H. Gray attributed it to the Saint John bankers and merchants who feared Canadian competition. The *Morning News* blamed the Roman Catholics who had been beguiled by the *Morning Freeman*. In conversation with Gordon, Tilley blamed the Roman Catholics and Western Extension, and, he added pointedly, the lack of time to prepare New Brunswickers for the change.[82]

However Tilley's defeat was not so shattering as might at first be supposed. Tilley lost Saint John City by 113 votes; Queens County was lost by only 40 votes; at least nine seats were lost by less than 300 votes in each. The *Telegraph* made a complex calculation of the total New Brunswick vote as 15,556 for the Tilley government, and 15,949 against.[83] When A. J. Smith formed his government, he did not dare appoint members from marginal constituencies to portfolios, for their re-election was anything but certain. A. R. Wetmore would probably have been made Attorney General had it not been for the fact that he was the new member for Saint John City. R. D. Wilmot and Timothy Anglin, both from Saint John County, were in the Cabinet, but they were without portfolios. Not without reason did J. H. Gray write George Brown that the defeat was only temporary and would be reversed. Whatever else, Gray wrote, Brown and the Canadians must stick to their guns.[84]

The Toronto *Globe* had been philosophical after the defeat of Tilley in New Brunswick, but when Tupper in Nova Scotia proposed Maritime union again, the *Globe* lost patience. "It is impossible," it said on March 24, 1865, "that Canada can delay its constitutional reforms for an indefinite period." There were hints that the Reform party now wanted to abandon Confederation altogether.[85] It was this reaction that J. H. Gray doubtless anticipated in his letter to Brown,

[81]Quebec *Morning Chronicle*, March 6, 1865.

[82]Cardwell Papers, Gordon to Cardwell, ·March 13, 1865; C.O. 188, same; Macdonald Papers, J. H. Gray to Macdonald, March 13, 1865; *Morning News*, March 10, 1865; C.O. 188, Gordon to Cardwell, May 22, 1865 (confidential).

[83]Complex because the New Brunswick constituencies were multi-member ones. The *Morning Freeman* arrived at 27,509 for Tilley, 46,268 against him (March 30, 1865). This was a riposte to the *Telegraph*'s calculation of March 29. The *Telegraph*'s table was quoted by the London *Times*, April 28, 1865.

[84]Brown Papers, Gray to Brown, March 27, 1865.

[85]Toronto *Leader*, April 3, 1865; Montreal *Transcript*, April 10, 1865.

and the *Globe*'s state of mind was temporary. Even so, the *Globe* was criticized as the "very foremost skedaddler in a political Bull Run."[86] Like Bull Run, the New Brunswick defeat caused some panic in government circles in Canada and Nova Scotia. It had produced remarkably quick footwork in Halifax. The opposition to Confederation in both provinces cheerfully concluded that the end of the noxious scheme was in sight.

Though the Smith government was not necessarily opposed to union, it was opposed to the Quebec form of it. Opposition to the Quebec scheme was in fact the one thing that held together the eclectic group of men comprising the Smith ministry. R. D. Wilmot found personal relations most unsatisfactory, and Wilmot's growing distaste for the situation in which he found himself was to have important consequences; he was to resign early in 1866 for personal reasons and because of union. About union the ministry was divided; united against the Quebec plan, they were in varying degrees in favour of or opposed to union. Three of the leading members, Wilmot, Allen, and Smith, all professed themselves in favour of union "in the abstract." A. H. Gillmor said politely that "abstract union was abstract nonsense";[87] but it was not necessarily a shibboleth. J. C. Allen's view, seen at least through Gordon's despatches was toward legislative union; he believed that the Quebec plan made impossible the "more substantive" union.[88] Smith toyed with union until his resignation in April, 1866. T. W. Anglin, despite occasional references to legislative union in the *Freeman*, was essentially an isolationist. G. L. Hatheway had broken with Tilley over Confederation and was probably opposed to union; so was Richard Hutchinson, a North Shore lumber merchant. A. H. Gillmor and Bliss Botsford were largely nonentities.

The *Weekly Telegraph* of April 5, 1865, predicted a short and unhappy life for the Smith régime. "Singular in its conception—marvellous in its birth—its life, perhaps will be brief and bitter, and its death may not be lamented." The *Telegraph* ridiculed the odd collection of Liberals and Tories. When Joseph Howe arrived from Nova Scotia on May 6 to visit Smith and others, it commented that if the members of the New Brunswick government were strangers to Howe, they were equally so to one another. "The best opposition that can be offered to the Government is to let it alone. It cannot hang together,

[86]Quebec *Morning Chronicle*, March 27, 1865.
[87]Saint John *Morning Freeman*, March 27, 1866, reporting Assembly debates of March 23. Gillmor was replying to a remark of R. D. Wilmot's.
[88]C.O. 188, Gordon to Cardwell, Feb. 9, 1865 (confidential).

and must fall to pieces of its own weight."[89] It was a good description of what became Tilley's policy.

The new Nova Scotian proposal for Maritime union was thus a little unsettling. In Saint John it "excited the utmost surprise"[90] and in Fredericton some alarm. On March 31, 1865, the Fredericton *New Brunswick Reporter*, in an excess of resolution, cried, "Electors of York, to arms!" to oppose that most wicked enterprise, Maritime union, that would "remove to Halifax every public office in Fredericton. . . ." The Smith government was cautious, though the alarm had died down somewhat when the legislature met on April 27. Smith moved a resolution similar to Nova Scotia's, but it was largely *pro forma*. In supporting the Maritime union resolution Smith contented himself with commonplaces, such as "babes must creep before they can walk."[91] Smith probably knew how sincere were Tupper's latest Maritime union proposals, and if he had not surmised it, Howe's visit doubtless enlightened him. And it may have been Howe who was indirectly responsible for the adroit attempt to embarrass the Nova Scotian government by actually appointing delegates to a Maritime union conference. MacDonnell, with Tupper, went over to Fredericton and told Gordon how impossible it would be for Nova Scotia to respond to such a move.[92] Few in New Brunswick were surprised or dismayed, however, when Maritime union was repudiated by Downing Street.

The real issue of the 1865 session was Western Extension. A new, anti-Smith paper, the *Morning Journal*, appeared on May 3, its avowed purpose being to press for Western Extension. The people of Saint John, it said, were "disappointed, deceived, betrayed" by the lack of action by the Smith government. The legislature took the matter up at some length; eventually it was agreed that it should be undertaken as a Government work. With this in hand, Smith and Allen left for London after the session was over, to sound out the prospects for financial support. They were also to contract for the Moncton-Sackville section of the Intercolonial. Finally they were to put directly to the Colonial Secretary the New Brunswick government's dislike of Confederation and of imperial pressure to effect it.

Already the New Brunswick government had revealed its sensitiveness on this subject. An editorial in the London *Times* in April, which

[89]*Weekly Telegraph*, May 10, 1865.   [90]*Ibid.*, March 29, 1865.
[91]Fredericton *New Brunswick Reporter*, June 2, 1865, reporting debates of May 25.
[92]C.O. 217, MacDonnell to Cardwell, June 7, 1865 (confidential). MacDonnell also conferred with leaders of both Government and Opposition on the Intercolonial Railway, *ibid.*, June 8, 1865 (confidential).

said merely that Confederation was progressing favourably, was enough to needle the Smith government into sending a note to Cardwell. It was not a very gracious note: it implied that Gordon's despatches might not have sufficiently enlightened Mr. Cardwell on the state of opinion in New Brunswick, and it offered the unpalatable home truths that Prince Edward Island had rejected Confederation, that Newfoundland had postponed it, and that in Nova Scotia only a group in Halifax were in favour of it.[93]

To imperial pressure New Brunswick was even less willing to submit than Prince Edward Island. Her loyalty to Great Britain was perhaps weaker than that of any other North American colony save the western ones of Vancouver Island and British Columbia. New Brunswick was not prepared to knuckle under to anyone, least of all the Colonial Secretary. Corruptible she might be, but she would not be pushed. Not even newspapers sympathetic to Confederation were prepared to tolerate the possibility that Confederation be imposed upon New Brunswick by the Canadians and the Colonial Office. "There is not room for a difference on this point," wrote the *Telegraph* firmly. "Any outside attempts to settle our destiny, come from what quarter they may, would be the means of postponing a union with Canada indefinitely. . . ."[94] But the Canadians had been at work already. The result was embodied in the stiff despatch of June 24, 1865, which almost enjoined Confederation. This reached New Brunswick early in July, and the New Brunswick Cabinet, under the temporary leadership of Wilmot and Anglin replied in a terse and cutting Minute of Council, on July 12. "From the language of this despatch it would be natural to infer that it related to some scheme for effecting an entire Legislative and Administrative Union of the British North American Provinces . . . but the words used . . . lead the Committee to conclude that it is intended to refer to the [Quebec] Resolutions. . . ." These resolutions, said the Minute, had been rejected by New Brunswick, for the simple reason that there was nothing in them "that gave promise of moral or material advantage." And, the Minute went on, surely the British government did not "share the ignorance . . . of the Federal scheme which appears to prevail among the British public. . . ." Confederation was a product of Canadian difficulties; its purpose was not to unite but to separate.[95]

[93]C.O. 188, Gordon to Cardwell, May 22, 1865, enclosing Memorandum of Council. Also in New Brunswick, Legislative Council, *Journals*, 1866, 63 (April 3). The issue of the *Times* referred to was probably that of April 28, 1865, mentioned *supra*, 246n.   [94]*Morning Telegraph*, June 3, 1865.
[95]New Brunswick, Executive Council, *Minutes*, July 12, 1865.

This remarkable Minute was couched in language that Smith and Allen might not have used, though Smith read it in Downing Street and told Cardwell he fully approved of it. He remarked later that "he felt proud of his colleagues." And Smith himself was by no means backward when it came to asserting his views to officials in Downing Street. He told Cardwell that members of the British government, not having been in New Brunswick, "were not in a position to know what was for the benefit of, or what suited the Province." Nevertheless the Minute was strong medicine even in New Brunswick, and it was to damage Smith in 1866, for it was used throughout the Province, as he admitted, "from school house to school house," to brand the Government disloyal.[96] The Confederate newspapers objected not only to the tone but to the suggestion that New Brunswick had rejected Confederation. The *Morning News* devoted several issues to showing that New Brunswickers had not rejected the Quebec plan and the Minute had no right to say they had. The *New Brunswick Reporter* published similar protests.[97] Even the Fredericton *Head Quarters* and the *Woodstock Acadian*, both of whom supported the Smith government, were reported dubious about the wisdom of the Minute.[98] It was, however, welcomed in anti-Confederate circles in Charlottetown and the praise for it there was echoed by the anti-Confederate *Patriot* of St. John's, Newfoundland.[99] The Toronto *Globe* joined in the fray and was duly taken to task by the *Freeman*.[100] Two years later the *Freeman* remarked that there had never been a state paper in New Brunswick that had caused so much feeling. Or one so misrepresented. To correct this the *Freeman* eventually printed the Minute on April 23, 1867, showing the parts written by Timothy Anglin, and the rest attributed to Arthur Gordon, who was by that time, safely out of the way in Trinidad. Anglin said that he and others had struck out of Gordon's draft a statement declaring union could be formed on terms acceptable to New Brunswick, and replaced it with the declaration that the province was opposed to any closer political connection with Canada.

It was shortly before the original publication of the Minute that Gordon left for England. It was widely rumoured that he was leaving

[96]Saint John *Daily Evening Globe*, March 15, 1866, reporting Smith's speech in the Assembly, March 13.
[97]Saint John *Morning News*, Aug. 25, 28, 30, 1865; Fredericton *New Brunswick Reporter*, Sept. 8, 15, 22, 1865.
[98]Though so alleged by the *Morning News*, Sept. 6, 1865.
[99]*Supra*, 172–3.
[100]Toronto *Globe*, Sept. 2, 1865; *Morning Freeman*, Sept. 12, 1865.

the province. The *Morning News*, August 16, 1865 doubted he would ever return. The *Weekly Telegraph*, the same day, spoke of "that unfortunate reserve that for the last three years, has chilled the walls of Government House. . . ." Tilley would probably have been pleased to see Gordon go away.[101] Gordon, for his part, had offered to resign in January.[102] He was offered Hong Kong in March and had accepted it, but after Tilley's defeat decided to remain to see Confederation through.[103] Gordon was in fact going to England to get married, which he did on September 20, and his honeymoon terminated with a not very pleasant interview with Cardwell at the Colonial Office.[104] What Cardwell wanted was a governor who would execute Colonial Office orders: what New Brunswick preferred was what Trollope called the Canadian *beau idéal* of a governor, "a faineant Governor, a King Log, who will not presume to interfere with us; a Governor who will spend his money and live like a gentleman and care little or nothing for politics."[105] Gordon was neither type. He was conscientious, high-spirited, fastidious, and probably to some of his New Brunswick contemporaries, rather a prig. He was not altogether happy in New Brunswick nor was he much liked, and perhaps it would have been wise if he had not returned in September, 1865. But return he did, to everyone's astonishment and placed for the first time in four years a mistress in Government House, Fredericton. He was also instructed to "further the cause of Union by every means within his power. . . ."[106]

As in Prince Edward Island and Nova Scotia, the debate in the newspapers was not stopped by the setback to Confederation, though the heat somewhat abated. Throughout the spring and summer of 1865 almost every issue of the *Morning News* had an editorial on Confederation. So also the *New Brunswick Reporter*. At the end of June, 1865, the *News* ran a series called the "Growing feeling in favour of Confederation." These met with derisive denials from the *Freeman*, which referred to the *News'* exercises in whistling in the dark.[107] But by the autumn there was a change in mood. The Ministry itself was changing. R. D. Wilmot had been appointed the New Brunswick delegate to the Quebec Conference on reciprocity, held on September 15, and had

[101]Macdonald Papers, Tilley to Galt, undated.
[102]Cardwell Papers, Gordon to Cardwell, Jan. 2, 1865.
[103]*Ibid.*, Gordon to Cardwell, May 22, 1865.
[104]Chapman, "Career of Gordon," 66.
[105]Anthony Trollope, *North America* (New York, 1862), 85.
[106]Monck's description. Macdonald Papers, Monck to Macdonald, Oct. 26, 1865. Also in J. Pope, ed., *Correspondence of Sir John Macdonald* (Toronto, 1921), 29.
[107]Saint John *Morning Freeman*, July 4, 1865.

returned from Quebec a supporter of Confederation. Wilmot still
believed legislative union preferable, but his trip to Quebec had convinced him that it was impracticable. French Canadians were a
powerful antidote to wishful thinking on that subject; furthermore, the
work of the Conference had impressed upon Wilmot, "most forcibly,
the necessity of union on some terms. . . ."[108] The *Woodstock Acadian*,
opposed to Confederation, sympathized with Wilmot; "but," it said,
"union is one thing and the Quebec Scheme is quite another. . . ."[109]
Wilmot, however, had been impressed with the readiness of Canadian
Ministers to meet objections to the Quebec scheme, and this conquest
the Canadians followed up by sending George Brown to New Brunswick early in November. Brown arrived in Saint John on Friday,
November 10, met R. D. Wilmot at the Waverley Hotel, and the next
day they both went up to Moncton to see A. J. Smith. Brown was also
able to effect a meeting in Saint John between Wilmot and Tilley.
After this remarkable week-end's work Brown went up to Fredericton
on Monday, where he stayed for three days with Gordon. Gordon
described Brown's visit in a private letter to Cardwell:

Mr. Brown was with me for some days last week. Though I have not a
good opinion of him, I am very ready to admit his ability and energy; and
we get on capitally together. We confidentially settled the whole course of
operations to be pursued here, and found ourselves almost perfectly
agreed. I am convinced I can make (or buy) an union majority in the
legislature.

Brown's view was that a considerable change had taken place in New
Brunswick and that even the Smith government would take up union if
they could do so decently.[110] Not unnaturally Wilmot believed the
Smith government should reconsider its views about Confederation,
or at least state its objections. Wilmot did not resign; apparently with
Gordon's blessing he tried to bring his colleagues around to his view.
    This kind of activity made Timothy Anglin uneasy. Anglin had,

[108]Wilmot to Gordon, Feb. 21, 1866, published in Saint John *Morning News*,
March 14, 1866; Fredericton *New Brunswick Reporter*, March 16, 1866.
    Wilmot's speeches in Canada in September, 1865, also reveal his change of
heart. At London, C.W., Sept. 21, 1865, he said that if the wooing between
Canada and the Maritimes had been a little protracted, "the courtship would
certainly end in marriage . . . a union would take place. . . ." (*London Evening
Advertiser*, Sept. 22, 1865)
[109]*Woodstock Acadian*, quoted by the Saint John *Morning Journal*, Oct. 11,
1865.
[110]Cardwell Papers, Gordon to Cardwell, Nov. 20, 1865; Brown Papers,
George Brown to Anne Brown, Nov. 13, 1865; *ibid.*, Brown to Monck, Dec. 25,
1865; Saint John *Morning Journal*, Nov. 13, 1865.

however, an additional grievance: Western Extension. All through the autumn the *Freeman* had been pressing for more aggressive measures. Anglin wanted Western Extension undertaken as a government work. But the Government dallied. Smith and Allen had received no help in London. Financial troubles in the form of decreased revenue and the discount of provincial debentures in London made any major financial commitment difficult, if not unwise. Private enterprise was therefore necessary. There were great hopes in mid-summer when an announcement was made by the Western Extension Company that a contract had been signed with an American firm; the first sod was officially turned on November 8, 1865, with speeches by both Smith and Tilley.[111] But snow fell all that day, and it suggested the wintry prospects for Western Extension. A few men were put to work; but they were laid off again, and nothing was done.[112]

Thus a good deal of the unpopularity of the Smith government that developed in 1865 can be laid at the door of its railway policy. It may well have been that a more aggressive policy was impossible; fading hopes for reciprocity made it even begin to seem—*horribile dictu*—less desirable. But Timothy Anglin felt that the reluctance of the Cabinet to begin Western Extension was the measure of their support for Confederation. As a result, shortly after the ineffectual sod-turning, Timothy Anglin resigned. His resignation removed from the Government the most determined isolationist and left it more than ever open to persuasion from Wilmot and from Gordon.[113]

An indication of a change in popular feeling was perhaps the victory of Charles Fisher in the York County by-election. The significance of this victory was widely debated, then as now. Fisher accepted nomination only at the last moment. He professed noble regret that duty should call him to endure once more political contest. His address to the electors of York was a mixture of metaphors not altogether inappropriate: "The strong feeling evinced for me . . . leave[s] me no honourable alternative but to step into the arena and throw myself upon you, my fellow subjects." (Gordon found this too good to resist and sent it to Cardwell.)[114] Fisher also said the Quebec scheme would have to be changed. He even accused the Smith government of manufacturing a special brand of Confederation themselves.[115] John Pickard, the

111Saint John *Daily Evening Globe*, Nov. 9, 1865.
112A. W. Bailey, "Railways in New Brunswick, 1827–1867," M.A. thesis, University of New Brunswick, 1955, 210.   113*Infra*, 256–7.
114*New Brunswick Reporter*, Nov. 3, 1865, reporting Fisher's speech of Oct. 25; C.O. 188, Gordon to Cardwell, Nov. 6, 1865.
115*New Brunswick Reporter*, Nov. 3, 1865, reporting Fisher's speech of Oct. 25.

Government candidate, said many people were opposed to Confederation, but, he added with unabashed equivocation, many were also in favour of it. Pickard's speech was a good index to the state of mind of the Smith government. Newspapers supporting Pickard said Confederation was not the main issue, but like Pickard's speeches they did not want to commit themselves. The *Evening Globe*, though it supported Smith, said "The real issue is Confederation." The Confederate papers agreed.[116] They were probably right. It is difficult to believe that colonial union of some kind was not the main issue in the York election; the Canadians put up some $8,000 or more believing it was. As for the Quebec scheme both Tilley and Mitchell found occasion to impugn it in the next few months,[117] and Fisher was being politic in stating it had to be re-cast.

Fisher won the election, by 1927 to 1218.[118] Whatever the cause of Fisher's victory, whether Confederation, Fenianism, or some thousands of Canadian money, it was hailed by the Confederate papers as a triumph for their cause, and its psychological effect was considerable. "Un triomphe éclatant," cried *Le Courrier de St. Hyacinthe* on November 10. A lively debate followed in Canada East over whether Fisher's victory was for Confederation or not.[119]

The Smith ministry was thus put more and more on the defensive. Wilmot was converted to Confederation. The support of the Roman Catholics and those who wanted Western Extension was weakened by the defection of Anglin. The Ministry had lost an important by-election. Added to this, it was becoming unpopular among its own supporters because it was, in Gordon's view, too honest.[120] Gordon was confident he could make or buy a union majority in the legislature when the time came. And if he could not persuade his Government to agree to Confederation he could force them to resign, very much as Manners-Sutton had ejected the Fisher government a decade before. By the third week in November, Gordon was optimistic about prospects for union. His great hope just at this point was to get rid of Smith altogether, by making him Chief Justice. The incumbent, Robert Parker, was mortally ill, and on November 17, the day after George

116Saint John *Daily Evening Globe*, Oct. 28, 1865; *Morning News*, Nov. 8, 1865; Fredericton *New Brunswick Reporter*, Nov. 10, 1865.

117Saint John *Morning News*, April 25, 1866, said that neither Tilley nor Mitchell was committed to the Quebec scheme as it was.

118*New Brunswick Reporter*, Nov. 10, 1865.

119*Le Journal des Trois Rivières* was especially involved in this debate, e.g. 21 nov. 1865. Also *Le Pays*, 14, 18 nov. 1865.

120C.O. 188, Gordon to Cardwell, Dec. 4, 1865.

Brown left Fredericton, Gordon had a long talk with Smith, with the aim of persuading him to take the position. Smith was at that time willing, and had Parker been dead, Gordon said, Smith could have been sworn in as Chief Justice then and there. The trouble was Parker did not die until November 28; and although it was publicly expected that Smith would be appointed,[121] Smith had in fact been stiffened by his friends in the interval and consequently declined the chief justice-ship when it was offered.[122] And by the New Year, 1866, the setback to the Nova Scotian government in the Lunenburg by-election, and the uncertainty of Confederation in Newfoundland, seemed to damp the ardour of the Confederates and to increase the resistance of the Smith government; nevertheless Gordon retained, and continued to retain, complete confidence in his ability to carry union.

A. J. Smith was an honest and stubborn man with a hot temper and a caustic tongue. He was convinced that the Quebec scheme would be unfortunate for New Brunswick. He was too down-to-earth to believe in the high-flown glories that animated some of his opponents; like Timothy Anglin, he was a New Brunswicker first and last and would not stand by and see New Brunswick extinguished, as he believed it would be, by the Quebec scheme. Yet he probably believed some form of union was useful, perhaps even inevitable. Gordon thought well of him—a feeling Smith did not reciprocate—and it was probably Gordon's confidence in Smith's integrity that made him believe Smith's general remarks about union could be converted into concrete terms. So they were: but they were terms that no Canadian minister could have accepted.[123] In the debate on Maritime union in 1864 Smith had said that it was a scheme good or bad depending on details; as the Fredericton *Head Quarters* remarked at the time, there was a world of fighting in details.[124] It was so with Smith and Confederation.

Wilmot was more tractable. It may have been that Wilmot was perfectly genuine in his conversion to Confederation. But if so, it was not his main motive. With Wilmot perquisites usually triumphed over policies, and his manœuvres in 1866 have to be considered with these

[121]Saint John *Daily Evening Globe*, Nov. 29, 1865.
[122]Brown Papers, Gordon to Brown, Dec. 21, 1865 (private).
[123]Such terms as these: 1) abandonment of representation by population; 2) each province to have an equal number of senators; 3) the Maritime provinces to be exempt from taxation for Canadian canals; 4) the federal revenue collected in each province to be kept for local application. From Smith's résumé of events from March 3 to April 10, dated April 13. In New Brunswick, Assembly, *Journals*, 1866, 217–20; also Saint John *Daily Evening Globe*, April 19, 1866.
[124]Fredericton *Head Quarters*, April 13, 1864.

elemental facts in mind. Wilmot had several grievances. His cousin, L. A. Wilmot, had been passed over in the appointment of the new Chief Justice.[125] Wilmot would have resigned when the appointment was made, but he was persuaded, perhaps by Smith, or by Gordon, to withhold his resignation. Wilmot also wanted the office of Auditor General for himself; it was a nice sinecure, but the Assembly had been unkind enough to reduce the salary of the office by $400. This, said the Minute of Council in reply to Wilmot's complaints, had given Mr. Wilmot no little dissatisfaction. Wilmot also resented the appointment of A. J. Smith as delegate to Washington on the reciprocity negotiations when he, Wilmot, had gone to Quebec the previous September on this very subject. These matters of patronage bulked large in Wilmot's eyes and may have determined his course. But Wilmot also wanted to be Premier and he saw in Confederation the means.[126] By making the grounds of his resignation from the Government its failure to bring in Confederation, Wilmot hoped to put Gordon in the position of having to agree with his sentiments and calling upon him to form a government. Gordon for his part had no great liking for Wilmot or his grievances, but Wilmot was useful. Gordon refused to accept Wilmot's resignation when it was first tendered in January and waited until Smith had returned from Washington on February 14. It was then accepted, but in circumstances which made it almost inevitable for Smith to consider union in some form. "His Excellency had put it to them pointedly: I must test Confederation through Mr. Wilmot or through you; I prefer it with *you*; choose which course you will adopt."[127]

Gordon now turned his attention to persuading Smith to state his objections to the Quebec scheme in concrete terms. Smith's terms for union were really impossible without a new conference, and Smith must have known they were. Nevertheless Gordon said he thought them reasonable and that the Canadians would accept most of them,[128]

[125]It was an example of the shrewdness of a French-Canadian newspaper that it remarked that Justice Parker's demise would cause difficulties for the New Brunswick government, *Le Journal des Trois Rivières*, 15 déc. 1865. L. A. Wilmot, R. D. Wilmot's cousin, was the senior judge on the New Brunswick bench, but he was an ardent supporter of Confederation and the Smith government therefore appointed W. J. Ritchie. (New Brunswick, Executive Council, *Minutes*, Wilmot to Council, Dec. 2, 1865; Minute of Dec. 29, 1865.)

[126]The administration formed after the fall of the Smith government was sometimes called the Mitchell-Wilmot one, but Mitchell was premier. R. D. Wilmot became a Senator in 1867.

[127]Mitchell's account, given in his speech in the Legislative Council April 14 and 16. Reported in the Saint John *Morning Telegraph*, April 24, 1866.

[128]Smith's account in his résumé of April 13. Saint John *Daily Evening Globe*, April 19, 1866.

and took them with him when he set off for Canada about February 20. This trip was of course public knowledge, and it was assumed by some that Gordon would concert with Monck measures to apply further pressure for Confederation.[129] By March 3 Gordon was back in Fredericton and on that day had a long meeting with Smith. Canada was willing, Gordon said, to make concessions, though he did not specify what these were. He did say, however, that his instructions from the Colonial Office, notably the despatch of June 24, 1865, obliged him to include Confederation in the Speech from the Throne. If Smith found that impossible to accept, he had only one course: Gordon was prepared for that. If on the other hand Smith accepted the Speech, then Gordon was clearly in a good position; Smith had then either to put Confederation through or, if he ultimately backed down, be weakened, perhaps fatally, in any opposition he might make to those who would undertake the task.[130] Monck thought Gordon's effort in getting Smith to agree to Confederation in the Throne Speech was, in the difficult circumstance of Nova Scotia's entire silence on the subject, masterly.[131]

But Gordon was too confident. He believed he dominated his Council[132] and he closed with Smith not only because he trusted him but because he was sure he could persuade him and guide him. In this Gordon was mistaken. He placed more reliance on his own powers than was justified, more confidence in Smith than circumstances warranted. Yet, it was not easy to discern a better alternative. Fisher would not have been prepared to accept responsibility for putting through the Quebec scheme;[133] Mitchell was not even in the House, but in the Legislative Council; Tilley was not in any House, but hovered uncertainly in and out of the ex-member's gallery in the Assembly. The difference in the type of union measure that Fisher or Smith would take responsibility for was perhaps less significant than the differences between the men themselves, one in, the other out, of office. Gordon doubtless believed that changes in the Quebec scheme were inevitable, and the choice between Fisher or Wilmot out of power, and Smith in, was an obvious one. What Gordon failed to anticipate was the animus of the Opposition in being robbed of Confederation and its attendant honours, Smith's stubborn determination to stick to the kind of union

---

[129]Ibid., Feb. 21, 1866.
[130]C.O. 188, Gordon to Cardwell, March 25, 1866 (confidential).
[131]Williams Papers, Monck to Williams, March 12, 1866.
[132]Council "members do *nothing* and look to me to write their minutes and dictate their measures." Stanmore Papers, Gordon to Waterfield, Jan. 15, 1866.
[133]The Quebec scheme never passed the New Brunswick Assembly, and Fisher had avoided all commitments to the Quebec scheme in the York by-election.

measure he thought best, and the extent of the reluctance of Smith's supporters to follow him in a union programme of any kind.

Gordon was not, however, wholly ignorant of Smith's difficulties and he sought to mitigate these by some form of agreement with the Opposition. About March 5, just before the legislature was to meet, Smith found himself at dinner at Government House with Peter Mitchell, one of the leading members of the Opposition; they had been invited by Gordon to see if some union programme could be agreed to by Government and Opposition. Mitchell was apparently willing though suspicious and he was nervous of his colleagues' reaction.[134] Smith was not very comfortable either, and in any case the arrangement did not survive more than a week of the violence of politics and the stresses and strains of the Session. Gordon had, however, succeeded in persuading Smith to agree not only to a paragraph on union in the Speech, but also, apparently, to the appointment of a select committee to consider details.[135] In return Gordon toned down the strength of his remarks on union.

Still union was in the Speech, and the result was that Smith's supporters were surprised, even pained.[136] Among Confederates there seemed to be general surprise.[137] The Smith ministry alienated not a few supporters by manifestly inclining toward union in the Throne Speech. Anglin's influence over the Roman Catholics through the anti-union *Morning Freeman* did not help. At the same time the Government did not take up Confederation with sufficient force to entitle it to the forbearance of the Opposition.[138] Not that the Opposition was prepared to be very forbearing; Charles Fisher and his friends had no wish to see Confederation brought in by others than themselves.[139] And the indecent haste with which the want of confidence motion was launched indicated the Government were going to get no quarter. "The Government will have to stand shoulder to shoulder . . . and the people, if they are yet opposed to Confederation, will have to back them up manfully; for

[134]Mitchell related that his political friends were angry when they learned of this interview. " 'Mitchell, you have destroyed, you have ruined our party,' and left me in anger." Saint John *Morning Telegraph*, April 24, 1866, reporting Mitchell's speech in the Legislative Council of April 14.
[135]Mitchell said that even the names of the committee had been decided, nine in all, with a government majority. The committee included Smith, Chandler, Fisher, and Mitchell.
[136]Peter Mitchell, "Secret History of Canadian Politics," in Toronto *Evening News*, Feb. 15, 1894.
[137]Fredericton *New Brunswick Reporter*, March 9, 1866.
[138]C.O. 188, Gordon to Cardwell, March 25, 1866 (confidential).
[139]Suggested by Fredericton *New Brunswick Reporter*, Feb. 23, 1866.

never, I think, was such a combined effort made against any Government in this country. . . ." Thus the Fredericton correspondent of the Saint John *Evening Globe*.[140]

Gordon for his part was disposed to honour his agreement with his Council and to avoid embarrassing them. If Confederation would be more acceptable to Smith's supporters with the glosses that Smith chose to put upon it, that was reasonable in view of the difficulties the Government was having. Union was the thing, and as long as that was accomplished Gordon much preferred leaving Smith to pick his own means.

But Smith's speeches in the House made it increasingly apparent that he was moving away from any concrete union policy whatever. The select committee was not appointed, and Smith's replies in the debate began to disturb Gordon. On March 12 Smith said he was willing to consider any union scheme that would benefit New Brunswick, but "he would never go for the Quebec Scheme, which gives up our independence forever to the control of the people of Canada. . . ."[141] That was not unexpected. But two days later, on March 14, Smith said categorically that the Government had no scheme for union in train at all.[142]

Somehow Smith had slipped away from Gordon and from union. There seems little doubt that he was now persuaded that the kind of union he had in mind had no hope of realization, that the cold truth was that he was to be the means by which the Quebec scheme, or a disguised form of it, was to be placed before the New Brunswick legislature. At what point Smith became convinced of this is impossible to say. Tilley and Mitchell said that they suspected all along that Smith was insincere in accepting the principle of union, but these statements were made afterward.[143] The Saint John *Morning Telegraph*, as soon as the Speech was out, said that some people suspected "ruses, resorted to by His Excellency's advisers for the purpose of more thoroughly defeating Union."[144] Gordon believed Smith had accepted the Throne Speech with some misgivings but in all sincerity. The whole truth will perhaps never be known, for Smith's papers were burnt after his death. His change of heart may well have been the result of trouble with his own supporters; but it is not difficult also to suspect the hand of the Nova Scotians in stiffening Smith's resistance to union. It was on March 13 that Governor Williams of Nova Scotia suggested to William Annand

140Saint John *Daily Evening Globe*, March 15, 1866, report of March 14.
141*Ibid.*, March 14, 1866, reporting Smith's speech of March 12.
142*Ibid.*, March 16, 1866, reporting Smith's speech of March 14.
143Mitchell, "Secret History of Canadian Politics"; Macdonald Papers, Tilley to Macdonald, April 14, 1866.
144Saint John *Morning Telegraph*, March 10, 1866.

that he propose a new union conference. Annand and his friends were definitely in communication with the Smith government by March 17. The Nova Scotian anti-Confederates, who had so much to lose if Smith gave way, had made sure that he was fully alive to his responsibilities.[145]

If union was then to be resisted, the want of confidence motion became a positive advantage. It helped to rally government followers; best of all, it delayed, and perhaps it might even derail, Confederation. Smith became convinced he could survive the want of confidence motion by five or six votes.[146] Thus there was everything to be gained by delay.[147] So the debate dragged on. On April 4, when the Order of the Day began, there was not even a member of the Opposition ready to speak, and the Government was happily obliged to call upon its own supporters.

Gordon had now become acutely uneasy; he was convinced that the Government was deliberately delaying the debate to forestall Confederation. He thought the Smith ministry might be defeated if given time. But whether it could or could not be defeated, there was no time. The session of the Nova Scotian legislature had begun six weeks before, on February 22; as early as March 12 Gordon received a telegram from Williams saying that New Brunswick would soon have to deal with Confederation, because all the ordinary business in Nova Scotia would soon be finished.[148] Pressure from Nova Scotia mounted, and Gordon resolved to take the first opportunity of putting the Smith government on the horns of the dilemma: union or resignation.[149]

Smith clung stubbornly to office, and Gordon began to feel that the opportunity of dismissing the Smith government with any propriety was rapidly escaping him. At this point Smith seems to have been out-manoeuvred. Perhaps he had not expected Gordon to force the issue of Confederation with the want of confidence motion still pending, or suspected Gordon's sharp device of using the Legislative Council as the means. There were two addresses by the Legislative Council. The first, presented to Gordon on April 2, was merely a general union resolution which Gordon replied to in the usual form.[150] The second was specific,

[145]See especially Annand's letter to Smith, March 20, 1866, quoted *supra*, 226–7.

[146]Smith to Annand, March 25, 1866, referred to in Halifax *Morning Chronicle*, March 23, 1869.

[147]Some were puzzled, however, by Smith's tactics. The Saint John *Daily Evening Globe*, March 22, 1866: "We cannot see what the Government is about. Why do they not press the question to a vote, push through the public business, send the Legislature home. . . ."

[148]Nova Scotia, Lieutenant Governor, Telegram Book, Williams to Gordon, March 12, 1866.

[149]C.O. 188, Gordon to Cardwell, April 23, 1866 (confidential).

[150]New Brunswick, Legislative Council, *Journals*, 1866, 33–4 (April 2).

asking for union on the basis of the Quebec scheme. As the *Morning Journal* remarked, the first resolution was for *a* confederation: the second, for *the* Confederation.[151] It was the second one that did the business. How far Gordon influenced it is difficult to tell. It is impossible to believe he could have been unaware of it. It began in the Legislative Council on April 3. That was the day of William Miller's Confederation speech in the Nova Scotian Assembly, which Governor Williams announced triumphantly to Gordon by telegram. It may have been just this that persuaded Gordon to act.[152] Monck wrote Williams the next day, "I heard from him [Gordon] yesterday that his Upper House will adopt the resolutions. . . ."[153] And the Quebec Resolutions were adopted, two days later on April 6. The Legislative Council of New Brunswick was the only House in the Maritime provinces to officially request union on the basis of the Quebec scheme.[154]

On Saturday morning, April 7, 1866, Gordon made ready to receive the address from the Legislative Council with expressions of great satisfaction. These expressions Smith, who had called at Government House at 11 o'clock, advised against. Gordon then postponed decision. But at noon he had made up his mind. After some delay in reaching Smith, for which either Gordon or Smith can be suspected of being deliberately responsible, Gordon informed him that he was going to go through with his reply. Smith protested. Gordon then suggested Smith should consult his colleagues, but in the time available before the arrival of the Legislative Council, now down to half an hour, and with the want of confidence debate still on the stretch in the Assembly, Smith refused the suggestion. Gordon then played the only card he could. He said he would reply to the Legislative Council anyway; Mr. Smith could now do whatever he thought best. Three days later, April 10, 1866, with the want of confidence motion still unresolved, the Smith government resigned.

[151]Saint John *Morning Journal*, April 13, 1866.
[152]"Today at 3 P.M. Miller the violent Anti Quebec scheme member moves the Resolution for Confederate union to be passed by Act of Imperial Parliament assisted by delegates." Nova Scotia, Lieutenant Governor, Telegram Book, Williams to Gordon, Williams to Monck, April 3, 1866. See *infra*, 269.
[153]Williams Papers, Monck to Williams, April 4, 1866 (private and confidential). From the same letter, "I was delighted to get your telegram last night. . . . Your proceedings in the Union matter ought materially to help Gordon."
[154]New Brunswick, Legislative Council, *Journals*, 1866, 78–9 (April 6). The Council resolution contained two parts: 1) "That a Union of all the British North American Colonies, based on the Resolutions adopted at the Conference . . . held at Quebec . . . is an object highly to be desired. . . ."; 2) "That the Legislative Council should concur in any measure which may be necessary to carry such a Union into effect." The resolution passed 12–5. An Address to the Queen was then presented and passed.

The whole transaction caused Gordon the "deepest mortification."[155] Echoes of it reverberated in Newfoundland, Prince Edward Island, Nova Scotia, and Canada. The Toronto *Globe* vigorously supported Gordon. The Montreal *Herald* could not understand why the *Globe*, so outraged with Sir Edmund Head in 1858, could justify Gordon in 1866. But the *Globe* boldly drew a parallel, and added pointedly that Mr. Wilmot and his Confederate colleagues in New Brunswick would doubtless get a dissolution if they asked for it.[156] In New Brunswick the coup was followed by bitter recriminations in the newspapers that supported the Smith government.[157] Gordon had, so he said, attempted to do his duty with as much impartiality and justice as possible; he had ended up with "a thousand groundless misrepresentations and . . . a miserable personal wrangle. . . ."[158] Even Gordon's private relations with Mitchell, Wilmot, and Tilley over the past months were aired in the *Morning Freeman*. "It is now evident that for months past the secrets communicated by the Governor to his unconstitutional advisers were by them used in the preparation of numberless newspaper articles which seemed to be such an extraordinary mixture of truth and fiction, fact and fancy, and which bore a strange air of authority."[159]

Five days after the Smith government had resigned, amid the accusations and arguments of the "constitutional crisis," came on April 15 word of the first Fenian raid on New Brunswick.

155C.O. 188, Gordon to Cardwell, April 23, 1866 (confidential).
156Toronto *Globe*, April 19, 1866; Montreal *Herald*, April 21, 1866; Toronto *Globe*, April 24, 1866.
157Particularly the Saint John *Morning Freeman*, April 14–May 1, 1866.
158C.O. 188, Gordon to Cardwell, April 23, 1866 (confidential).
159Saint John *Morning Freeman*, April 24, 1866.

15. THE FENIAN INVASIONS
AND THEIR EFFECTS

THE WEEK THAT FOLLOWED the resignation of the Smith government in New Brunswick, April 10 to 17, 1866, decisively influenced the fate of Confederation. Before April 10 Confederation was in an uncertain, not to say precarious, position: after April 17 a Confederate government was in office in New Brunswick and a Confederation resolution had passed the Nova Scotian legislature. The Fenians could not themselves have effected these changes, but they did produce conditions that made them possible. With the Fenians Gordon's action in dismissing Smith seemed less reprehensible; with the Fenians Tupper could carry Confederation in the Nova Scotian House. In Canada, too, the Fenians had their effect in that they tended to dissolve further resistance to Confederation. The Fenians are indisputably part of British American union; much more is owed to them than is generally realized, and they cannot be taken lightly.

The Fenian movement had begun in 1858 to liberate Ireland, and since that time had grown and prospered. By 1866 part of the movement in the United States had taken up aims directly consistent with American continental ambitions: the conquest of British North America. In other words, the Fenians were prepared to strike a blow for Ireland not only by sending aid across the sea but also by direct action in North America.[1] They had more than their share of internecine quarrels; they were often discounted as a heterogenous collection of wild-eyed Irishmen whose aims were as naive as their execution of them was inept. They were, in short, easy to ridicule. But their threat was taken seriously by British North Americans; Macdonald, who had a cool head, was not disposed to underrate them. "I am watching them very closely. . . ." he wrote to Monck. "The movement must not be despised, either in America or in Ireland. I am so strongly of that opinion that I shall spare no expense

[1]W. D'Arcy, *The Fenian Movement in the United States, 1858–1886* (Washington, 1947).

in watching them. . . ."[2] Joseph Howe, who arrived in Halifax late in March, 1866, straight from Washington and New York, used similar words. He told people that the Fenians were "formidable and not to be despised."[3]

There were good reasons for taking their threats seriously. The Union army of 800,000 was being disbanded, and for $6 a soldier could take his gun and accoutrements with him. Arms were cheap and easy to get. Many of the Fenians were battle-tried veterans of the Union army; feckless perhaps, reckless certainly, but properly commanded and led they could be a formidable fighting force. They had also acquired considerable funds and not a little sympathy. That they failed to achieve more than they did was evidence not so much of their weakness as of their internal feuds, and what ruined the Fenians was the enforcement of American neutrality, belated and reluctant though it was, by President Johnson. But few in British North America knew what President Johnson would do.[4] He was an unknown, and for all practical purposes he was like Lincoln or Seward, neither of whom were much liked or trusted north of the border. The American government was in fact in an awkward position. Sir Frederick Bruce, the British minister in Washington, reported President Johnson's view that the American government, while it was determined to put down every overt act by the Fenians, was at the same time experiencing great difficulty in suppressing Fenian agitation, and that the radicals in the Republican party would be quick to exploit any collision between the Administration and Irish feeling.[5] Moreover, Fenian ambitions were openly shared by many Americans, and there was little evidence to show that Americans would not support the Fenians or would try to prevent them from being effective. The *New York Herald*, though extreme, was not uncharacteristic:

it will be well for our government to watch this confederation movement in Canada, and see whether it does not portend evil. . . . It will, however, only be necessary to utter a word of encouragement to the thousands of Fenians who are eagerly awaiting an invitation to invade Canada, for our government to settle the question of a Canadian monarchy with an English Guelph upon the throne, promptly and forever.[6]

---

[2]Macdonald Papers, Macdonald to Monck, Sept. 18, 1865. Also D. G. Creighton, *John A. Macdonald: The Young Politician* (Toronto, 1952), 421.

[3]Letter from Howe to the people of Nova Scotia, *Morning Chronicle*, April 10, 1866.

[4]A. J. Smith of New Brunswick who was in Washington in February, 1866, had personal assurances from President Johnson.

[5]F.O. 5, Bruce to Lord Clarendon, April 17, 1866 (secret and confidential).

[6]*New York Herald*, March 15, 1866. Also quoted by the Ottawa *Citizen*, March 21, 1866.

In the House of Representatives in June, 1866, there were two resolutions proposed, one that the Fenians be recognized as lawful belligerents, the other that "this House does heartily sympathize with all true Irishmen in their holy struggle for freedom. . . . That we remember with gratitude that many brave Irishmen . . . mingled their blood with the patriots of the Union Army. . . ."[7] And a considerable fifth column existed, at least potentially, in Canada and New Brunswick, where about 10 per cent and 12 per cent, respectively, were Irish born.[8] The *Irish Canadian* of Toronto, the organ of the most militant Irish, was probably annexationist in sympathy.[9]

The menace of the Fenians had been growing steadily since the autumn of 1865. Lord Monck was warned by the British Consul in New York as early as September, 1865.[10] Fenian conventions in January and February, 1866, filled the air with sound and fury. St. Patrick's Day, March 17, was considered the danger point. On March 7, 1866, the Canadian militia were called out. In Canada this mobilization of 10,000 volunteers caused a sensation, and it was not without effects elsewhere.[11] On March 17 Nova Scotia followed. But the threat did not materialize, and the anti-Confederate papers said the whole thing was an *ignis fatuus* to lead the provinces into Confederation.[12] Within a fortnight, however, the situation grew rapidly more threatening. On March 27 Williams urgently requested Cardwell to arrange to have 10,000 rifles shipped from Liverpool by the next packet.[13] On April 5 the New York *World*'s Halifax correspondent reported wild rumours of heavy firing off Yarmouth, and later that Yarmouth had been captured! On April 8 the Washington *Sunday Herald* reported that a Fenian expedition had positively sailed.[14]

The real threat was not on the coast of Nova Scotia but of New

[7]United States, 39th Congress, 1st Session, *Congressional Globe*, 3085–6 (June 11, 1866). The two resolutions were not reported out of the Committee on Foreign Affairs.

[8]The proportion was significantly higher in cities: in Montreal, 20 per cent; in Saint John, 25 per cent; in Toronto, 30 per cent.

[9]*Irish Canadian*, May 17, 1865, sympathizing with the *Galt Reporter*, see *supra*, 157.

[10]P.A.C., Series G, Archibald to Monck, Sept. 16, 1865.

[11]*Supra*, 224–5.

[12]In Nova Scotia, the Halifax *Morning Chronicle* and the *Halifax Citizen*; in New Brunswick, the Saint John *Morning Freeman*; in Canada, Montreal *Pays* and *Union Nationale*.

[13]C.O. 217, Williams to Cardwell, March 27, 1866 (confidential). The rifles were sent about April 20.

[14]New York *World*, April 9, 1866, report of April 5 from Halifax. These rumours seem to have been pure fabrication.

Brunswick. On April 7 Fenians arrived in Portland with 500 rifles.[15] In a few days Portland's streets were filled, so it was said, with "knots and coteries of suspicious looking Americanized Irishmen, carrying revolvers and long dirk knives in their pants' belts. . . . They all appear to have plenty of money, which is spent with great profuseness." Eastport, where the Fenian "convention" was to be held, was the main rendezvous, and it was reported "full of Yankee skippers, eager and anxious to offer their services and schooners to transport a Fenian army."[16] These newspaper reports were probably exaggerated—the Toronto *Globe*'s correspondent said they were, and so did the British Consul in New York[17]—but they had their effect in New Brunswick and Nova Scotia. By this time the New Brunswick militia was out in the border towns. H.M.S. *Pylades* from Halifax reached Campobello on April 9.[18] H.M.S. *Niger* followed. On April 11 it was reported from Eastport that "two large English warships are here now, with steam constantly kept up, port-holes [gun-ports] open, and everything ready. The Americans are wild and consider it a challenge. American veterans are joining [the Fenians]. . . ."[19] So were some Canadians. Michael Murphy, president of the Hibernian Society of Toronto, and six others were arrested by Canadian authorities at Cornwall; they had been on their way to Eastport.[20] Boarding houses in Eastport were reported "crammed" with Fenians,[21] who were, at this stage at least, a well-disciplined group totalling about 500.[22]

Undoubtedly some of the Fenian excitement was simply manufactured. E. M. Archibald, the British consul in New York, considered some of the New York papers, notably the *World*, to be subsidized by

[15]*Ibid.*, April 9, 1866, report of April 8 from Portland.

[16]*Ibid.*, April 9, 14, 1866.

[17]Toronto *Globe*, April 25, 1866, report of April 16 from Eastport; F.O. 5, E. M. Archibald to Lord Clarendon, April 10, 1866.

[18]Halifax *Morning Chronicle*, April 12, 1866; New York *World*, April 11, 1866. H.M.S. *Pylades* was a corvette, 21 guns, 1278 tons.

[19]New York *World*, April 12, 1866, report of April 11 from Eastport.

[20]Toronto *Leader*, April 10, 11, 1866; Montreal *Transcript*, April 11, 1866. Early in September, 1866, Murphy and the others tunnelled their way out of Cornwall prison and escaped to the United States. (Ottawa *Citizen*, Sept. 3, 1866.) A full account of the whole incident is in C. P. Stacey's "A Fenian Interlude: The Story of Michael Murphy," *Canadian Historical Review*, XV, 2 (June, 1934), 133–54.

[21]New York *World*, April 11, 1866, report of April 10 from Eastport. Note however E. M. Archibald's comment, ". . . neither do I believe that Eastport Hotels are crammed with Fenians. . . . I am rather confirmed in my supposition that the whole proceeding is a pretentious one on the part of O'Mahony and Killian. . . ." Archibald to Bruce, April 11, 1866, enclosure in F.O. 5, Bruce to Clarendon, April 12, 1866.

[22]Military Correspondence, Nova Scotia Command, Major-General Hastings Doyle to Military Secretary, May 7, 1866.

the O'Mahony and Killian faction to make popular their cause, and that the whole purpose of the Campobello enterprise was to stimulate the recruitment of men and funds. ". . . it was designed," wrote Archibald to Clarendon, "to create a *sensation*. . . ."[23] There was in short much smoke but little fire.

The Indian Island escapade gave just enough touch of flame to give a semblance of truth to reports of the menace of the Fenians. At midnight on Saturday, April 14, five Fenians made their way to New Brunswick territory, Indian Island in the St. Croix estuary, presented their revolvers to the head of the deputy collector of customs, and made off with the British flag.[24] Gordon promptly wired Halifax for reinforcements. The British government, already warned by the threats of March had sent from Malta H.M.S. *Tamar* with part of the King's Own Regiment and H.M.S. *Simoon* with the 22nd Cheshire Regiment, though both were still some days' steaming time distant.[25] On April 17 the imposing H.M.S. *Duncan*, the Halifax flagship of 81 guns and 3727 tons, sailed from Halifax for St. Andrews with companies of the Royal Artillery, Royal Engineers, and the 17th Yorkshire East Regiment, totalling 32 officers and 682 men.[26] The same day General Meade and his staff sailed from Philadelphia.[27] A cheerful expansionism appeared to prevail in New York; at a mass meeting at the Cooper Institute, A. L. Morrison, senator for Missouri, asked if the cheers from the crowd meant that "the green flag shall be unrolled on British territory?" He was answered by cries of "Yes," "Every man do his best."[28]

Two days later, on April 19, the Toronto *Globe*'s correspondent observed H.M.S. *Duncan* off Eastport as she patrolled the bay, half covering it with a huge cloud of black smoke and looking "a very Triton among minnows."[29] General Meade and 300 American soldiers also arrived at Eastport on April 19. General Hastings Doyle met Meade on board the U.S.S. *Regulator* at 2:30 P.M. that day. The contrast between them was like that between Grant and Lee the year before; Meade was in civilian clothes, Doyle in the full dress uniform of a British general.[30] With Meade determined to enforce American neutrality, with five British warships in the vicinity, and some 5000 British and New Brunswick

[23]F.O. 5, Archibald to Clarendon, April 24, 1866 (secret).

[24]Saint John *Morning Journal*, April 16, 1866; New York *World*, April 17, 1866.

[25]*Simoon* reached Saint John on April 18; *Tamar*, Halifax on April 20.

[26]Military Correspondence, Nova Scotia Command, Hastings Doyle to Secretary of State for War, April 21, 1866.   [27]New York *World*, April 18, 1866.

[28]*Ibid.*, April 19, 1866. Cf. also Schuyler Colfax's speech, *infra*, 316n.

[29]Toronto *Globe*, April 26, 1866, report of April 19 from Eastport.

[30]New York *World*, April 27, 1866, quoting Boston *Advertiser*, April 21, 1866.

troops available, the Fenians understandably hesitated. There were two other minor incidents,[31] but the Fenians realistically abandoned their expedition. By April 26 the great Eastport convention was over; when 200 Fenians left for Portland on that day, they left behind unpaid bills and unpleasant memories.[32] It had cost the Fenians thousands, and the arms captured by Meade were reported to be 1,500 rifles and 100,000 cartridges together with other weapons.[33] The whole affair was nothing less than a fiasco.

But it had effected a great change in the orientation of Confederation in New Brunswick and Nova Scotia. The truth was, as Howe so plainly said, that "when message after message is rushing over the wires to inform us of the gathering of raiders upon our frontiers—every ship, like a bloodhound on the leash . . . when every soldier and militiaman awaits the summons . . . it has been determined to launch this Confederation scheme. . . ."[34] The Smith government was turned out of office in New Brunswick; Tupper launched Confederation in Nova Scotia.

In Nova Scotia, even before the actual foray against Indian Island, the Fenian menace had caused shifts of opinion. This was particularly noticeable among the Roman Catholics. There is an instructive letter written to Tupper by the Catholic Bishop of Arichat—a Cape Breton diocese—on April 12, 1866:

In reply [to your letter], I am happy to be able to say that your views respecting the great topic, the Union of the Colonies, under their new phase have been very favorably received here. Altho' no admirer of Confederation on the basis of the Quebec Scheme, yet owing to the present great emergency and the necessities of the times, the union of the Colonies, upon a new basis, we receive with pleasure.[35]

The Bishop of Arichat also sent a pastoral letter in a similar vein and which was published in the Halifax *Evening Express* on April 16:

Current events and all reliable sources of information within our reach point to one conclusion, that, namely, British aid and protection in the hour of danger and emergency can be secured on one condition only—and that condition is the UNION OF THE NORTH AMERICAN BRITISH PROVINCES. We allude not to the Quebec Scheme of Union which our own and a neighboring Legislature have already rejected. . . . We cannot withold the encouragement and approval of our sanction from the plan of Union now before our Legislature.

[31]H. A. Davis, "The Fenian Raid on New Brunswick," *Canadian Historical Review*, XXXVI, 4 (Dec., 1955), 330–1.

[32]Military Correspondence, Nova Scotia Command, Hastings Doyle to Military Secretary, May 7, 1866.   [33]Halifax *Morning Chronicle*, April 30, 1866.

[34]*Ibid.*, April 12, 1866, letter from Howe to the people of Nova Scotia.

[35]Tupper Papers, Colin F. Mackinnon to Tupper, April 12, 1866.

The effect of these events was seen in Assembly, particularly in two Catholic members who had opposed Confederation; William Miller, Liberal member for Richmond, and Samuel Macdonnell, Conservative member for Inverness—both Cape Breton constituencies—now supported union, though not on the basis of the Quebec Resolutions. Miller rose in the House on April 3. No person, he said, could fail to recognize the signs of the times. "I need not remind hon. gentlemen that the whole aspect of things around us have been changed within one short year." American designs on British North America were only too obvious. If the Government would publicly abandon the Quebec scheme and support a new measure that would be drawn up under "the arbitrament of the Imperial Government," Miller would agree to it.[36]

This was of course nothing less than what William Annand had been asked to do, three weeks before. There was thus some rough justice in the derisive remark later, *William Miller made William Annand's motion.*[37] It seems reasonable to suppose that Miller had been subjected to the same influences as Annand from Government House and had finally accepted the invitation of the Governor to make an offer to Tupper.[38] There is a ring of truth in the account given many years later by Samuel Macdonnell: "Miller came to me one day and told me he had learned on the very best authority that Annand and other leaders of the Anti-Confederates were negotiating with the other side and planning to accept Confederation . . . and we . . . had better get into line or we should be left out in the cold and lose all chance of obtaining any good positions. I could not believe him. But two days later Miller again came to me, assured me he knew Annand was making terms with the enemy. . . ."[39]

[36]Miller had urged British American union in the Maritime union debate of March, 1864 (*supra*, 57), but had opposed the Quebec scheme. Miller's speech of April 3, 1866, is in Nova Scotia, Assembly, *Debates and Proceedings*, 1866, 185–90.

[37]Letter from "Elector" of March 6, 1869, in *Halifax Citizen*, March 13, 1869. In the letter the passage quoted above is italicized. "Elector" was alleged to be A. W. McLelan, who voted against Confederation, 1866.

[38]Note the tense in the following telegram, Nova Scotia, Lieutenant Governor, Telegram Book, Williams to Monck, April 3, 1866: "Today at 3 P.M. Miller the violent Anti Quebec scheme member moves the Resolution for Confederate union. . . ."

[39]G. Patterson's version of a conversation with Samuel Macdonnell and quoted in G. Patterson, "An Unexplained Incident of Confederation in Nova Scotia," *Dalhousie Review*, VII, 4 (Jan., 1928), 445. Also reprinted in his Studies in Nova Scotian History (Halifax, 1940), 110–12. As to the truth of Macdonnell's story Patterson says, "None who knew MacDonell [sic] would question his word." At the same time Patterson doubts Miller's story of Annand's role. There is however no reasonable doubt of what Annand was doing. (See *supra*, 220–7.)

To Miller Tupper replied, with unintended irony, "I am not at all surprised at the statements made by the hon. member—";[40] he added, "the last twelve months have been pregnant with circumstances that must give an importance and an urgency to this question of Colonial Union such as it has never obtained before."[41] He professed caution; but the *Morning Chronicle* of April 4, 1866, was probably right when it alleged that Tupper had only produced "a very pretty piece of acting." Williams telegraphed to Monck and Gordon in triumph. "Miller spoke beyond an hour. Annand dead against the measure. My advisers preparing a resolution course being clear—"[42] The course was not quite clear yet. Miller's speech was followed by a violent but brief debate that lasted two days. There were insinuations that Miller and Macdonnell had been subjected to influence, which Miller hotly denied.[43] Members of the House seemed, however, surprised at Miller's speech. The *Halifax Citizen* was outraged.

> Go, deceiver, go
> 'Twere folly to upbraid thee,
> Hate can't make thee worse
> Than thine own shame hath made thee.[44]

By this time—Friday, April 6—the work of the session seemed to be running out. Little business was transacted on that day; there was no Saturday meeting at all; Monday's business was done in an afternoon. It must have been with a sigh of relief that Tupper received the news from Fredericton. On Tuesday, April 10, the day Smith resigned, Tupper moved the resolution for Confederation.

Tupper's resolution asked for the appointment of delegates to arrange

[40]Tupper denied then, and afterward, that a single word had passed between himself and Miller on the subject of place or preferment (Nova Scotia, Assembly, *Debates and Proceedings*, 1866, 204). While this may possibly be literally true, it is altogether unlikely that Tupper was not fully informed of Williams' negotiations both with Annand and with Miller.

[41]*Ibid.*, 190 (April 3).

[42]Monck replied both by telegram and letter. The following is from the letter, Williams Papers, Monck to Williams, April 4, 1866 (private and confidential): "I was delighted to get your telegram last night informing me that the Union resolution was to have been moved yesterday under such favourable circumstances—I trust I shall soon hear that you have been completely successful—"

[43]Nova Scotia, Assembly, *Debates and Proceedings*, 1866, 190–1, 193, 204. Ironically, accusations were made by William Annand.

[44]*Halifax Citizen*, April 3, 1866. The *Citizen* was misquoting Thomas Moore. *Poetical Works of Thomas Moore* (Philadelphia, 1844), 337:
> Go—go—'tis vain to curse,
> 'Tis weakness to upbraid thee,
> Hate cannot wish thee worse
> Than guilt and shame have made thee.

"a scheme of union" that would "effectually ensure just provision for the rights and interests of Nova Scotia."[45] The speeches that followed were extensive and fierce, but the most powerful argument for union was the call to arms:

The whole police [sic] of the United States has been acquisition of territory. Their ambition is insatiable. . . . If we remain disunited . . . the time may come when we shall have the British flag lowered beneath the stars and stripes, and the last gun fired from the Citadel as a British fort.[46]

Tuesday, April 17, 1866 was the last day of debate. It was on that day that the troops from the Citadel marched to the Dockyard to board H.M.S. *Duncan* to go to the front. Thus, "while the Bay of Fundy was alive with ships of war, and the frontier bristling with bayonets,"[47] the Nova Scotian Assembly, weary from almost fifteen hours of debate, finally divided at 2:30 in the morning of Wednesday, April 18. Four Conservatives voted with the Opposition: but five Liberals voted with the Government. The result was 31–19 for Confederation.[48]

"A wretched intrigue," Howe called it,[49] rushed "through at black midnight."[50] Anti-Confederates looked darkly on the whole enterprise. The Fenians had, said the *Morning Chronicle*, given time for the British Minister in Washington to send to the West Indies and Malta for the Fleet, and while it was possible that the Canadian, Nova Scotian, and New Brunswick authorities were quite innocent, one thing was certain: "the proceedings from beginning to end, were the very best possible to subserve the ends of the Confederates. The Fenians made their appearance at Eastport, and forthwith the Confederation resolution was tabled in our House of Assembly. A few days after the resolution was carried, and presto! the Fenians had evaporated and gone."[51]

[45]Nova Scotia, Assembly, *Journals*, 1866, 60 (April 10).

[46]Nova Scotia, Assembly, *Debates and Proceedings*, 1866, 257 (April 11).

[47]Letter from Howe to the people of Nova Scotia, *Morning Chronicle*, April 19, 1866.

[48]Nova Scotia, Assembly, *Journals*, 1866, 70 (April 17). The *Morning Chronicle*, Jan. 30, 1867, referred to the five Liberals as "those whiskered rats who crossed the floor in the direction of the Premier last winter." The Confederation resolution passed the Legislative Council by a vote of 13–5 on April 16, Legislative Council, *Journals*, 1866, 45. Williams had asked for, and received, authority from Cardwell to create additional Legislative Councillors, should it have been necessary to swamp the Legislative Council (C.O. 218, Cardwell to Williams, March 17, 1866 (confidential)). A private letter emphasized, "You can not be too *secret* in respect to this document. . . ." (Williams Papers, Cardwell to Williams, March 17, 1866.)

[49]Letter from Howe to the people of Nova Scotia, *Morning Chronicle*, April 19, 1866.

[50]*Ibid.*, May 19, 1866, reporting Howe's Windsor speech of May 8.

[51]*Ibid.*, May 8, 1866; also *Halifax Citizen*, May 3, 1866.

An immense agitation began in Nova Scotia against Confederation. Howe set off to stump the province and made a tremendous impression.[52] A monster petition to the British House of Commons was begun. Howe, Annand, and their cohorts in the anti-Confederate newspapers— the *Morning Chronicle*, the *Halifax Citizen*, the *Acadian Recorder* of Halifax, and almost every country paper from Sydney to Yarmouth— began the long and bitter campaign against the *coup de main* that would impose Confederation. "We of the Maritime Provinces," wrote the *Yarmouth Tribune* on June 27, 1866, "are required to give up, not only . . . self-government won nearly thirty years since from the officials of Downing Street, but rights and powers . . . which we have enjoyed for more than a century. . . . The loss of self control will be as total and complete as the loss of revenue." Howe covered Confederation with ridicule. British America is to be a nation, he mocked, "without an army or a navy—without a King or President, or a Foreign Office,—with no capital but debts clubbed together, and a frontier of four thousand miles. (Laughter.)"[53] The sturdy independence of the province found ready, even violent, expression on the theme stated by an anonymous poet in the *Yarmouth Tribune* the year before (January 4, 1865).

> Shall we yield our independence—
>   Fling our dearest rights away?
> Shall we link our fate with a bankrupt State,
>   And our native land betray? . . .
>
> From broad TOOWAUBSCOT's wave, that moans
>   With restless ebb and flow—
> From each and all, in trumpet-tones,
>   Rings forth the answer—No!

Her Majesty's Government concurred in the gratification expressed by Governor Williams that Confederation was "warmly supported by eminent men of both parties"; the despatch was published in the *Royal Gazette* on May 23. But it had a hollow sound. Williams himself admitted that "every man who voted for the measure felt that he was exhibiting to the Queen the highest proof of his loyalty and devotion. . . ."[54] The *Acadian Recorder* intimated on May 30, 1866, that

---

[52]Howe's speech in Liverpool on June 5, for example, where the crowds overflowed the Court House and stood outside to listen, *Liverpool Transcript*, June 7, 1866. It was reported that his speech at Digby, on May 17, drew people all the way from Saint John, N.B., *Halifax Citizen*, June 2, 1866.

[53]*Morning Chronicle*, June 9, 1866, reporting Howe's speech at Barrington, N.S.

[54]C.O. 217, Williams to Cardwell, April 26, 1866.

the only reason Confederation passed was the Fenian invasions. That, one is tempted to think, was the truth of the matter.

II

In New Brunswick the fall of the Smith government caused almost as much excitement as the passage of Confederation in Nova Scotia. It was alleged that in Fredericton personal encounters took place in the streets between partisans of each side. The edge of the constitutional issue was, however, blunted by Smith's earlier acceptance of union in the Throne Speech, and the Fenians ruined the anti-Confederate cause. Killian's speeches at the Eastport convention seemed diabolically calculated to do the greatest damage to the anti-Confederates. Killian said that the Fenians were out to defeat Confederation. A Fenian proclamation in Saint John, on April 16, at the height of the alarm said that republican institutions were now a necessity for New Brunswick. "English policy, represented in the obnoxious project of Confederation, is making its last efforts to bind you in an effete form of Monarchism."[55] Statements like this were disastrous for the anti-Confederates. "It was an unlucky hour for the anti-Confederates when Mr. Killian put forth his manifesto declaring against Confederation. Nothing could have been done equal to it to carry Confederation."[56] The Saint John *Morning Freeman* said mournfully on April 21, "If Mr. Killian were in the pay of the Canadians and Mr. D'Arcy McGee himself wrote his speech for him, he could not have said anything better suited to the purposes of the Canadian party."

But Gordon was doubtful of success. Monck wrote to Williams:

What is to be the result of the late events in New Brunswick? I am afraid they are not so sanguine of success there as they were some time since— It will be very vexatious, when we have gone so very near success if we shall fail there a second time—Do you think you can do anything there privately amongst your friends?[57]

Williams could, and did.[58] Tilley assured Macdonald that with sufficient

[55]Saint John *Morning Telegraph* April 17, 1866. It was claimed by the Charlottetown *Patriot*, April 21, 1866 (quoted by *Halifax Citizen*, May 3, 1866) that this proclamation was bogus; but it is also quoted from Fenian sources by Davis, "Fenian Raid on New Brunswick," 322. It is probable that the proclamation was Fenian, but that its distribution in Saint John could have been "assisted" by Confederation sympathizers.
[56]St. Stephen *Charlotte Advocate*, quoted in *New Brunswick Reporter*, April 27, 1866.
[57]Williams Papers, Monck to Williams, April 23, 1866.
[58]Cardwell Papers, Williams to Cardwell, June 21, 1866 (private): "my nephews carried all four members from Kings County in which my sisters live:

means New Brunswick could be carried.[59] Smith was compromised by his acceptance of union, and his attempt to win the elections of May and June, 1866, by concentrating on the constitutional issue did not help much, in a time of crisis, to strengthen his cause. Probably Gordon, Tilley, and Smith all underestimated how powerful the effects of the Fenians were. And it may well have been that it was easier to defend the Governor than the Quebec scheme.

As in Nova Scotia it was found politic in New Brunswick to pass over the Quebec scheme. And, as in Nova Scotia also, the support of the Roman Catholic church was successfully procured. The *Morning Freeman*, which, as the Bishop of Chatham said, had "come to be generally regarded as the exponent of Catholic feeling," as such was now discredited.[60] And though Timothy Anglin dutifully published the Bishop's pastoral letter praising Confederation, he vigorously dissented from the opinions expressed. Anglin charged Bishop Rogers of Chatham, Bishop Mackinnon of Arichat, and Archbishop Connolly of Halifax with using tactics more resembling those of the Orange Order than Roman Catholic bishops. For this he was publicly rebuked by the New Brunswick bishop.[61]

Both sides in the election drew on funds supplied from outside the province. Votes usually went for ten dollars each, and Tilley used Canadian means to the extent of some $40,000, possibly more.[62] There was help for Smith from Nova Scotia. Howe himself may have been asked to go in person to New Brunswick;[63] and the Halifax *Unionist* of June 1, 1866, charged that Nova Scotian funds were being sent over to bribe the New Brunswick electors. Patrick Power, a Roman Catholic Liberal and a supporter of Howe,[64] had recently been to New Brunswick and had seen Anglin; he denied any bribery had taken place, but he admitted that "certain expenses incidental to every elec-

---

and John Gray has proved a tower of strength throughout the Province." Williams' home was Sussex, N.B.

[59]Macdonald Papers, Tilley to Macdonald, April 20, 1866.

[60]James Rogers to J. M. Johnson, May 22, 1866. Printed in Great Britain, House of Commons, *Accounts and Papers*, Vol. 10, "Correspondence Respecting the Proposed Union," 443.

[61]Saint John *Morning Freeman*, May 22, 24, 26, 1866; Saint John *Morning Journal*, June 1, 1866, letter from Bishop Rogers of May 26.

[62]Creighton, *Macdonald: The Young Politician*, 434–5.

[63]Halifax *Witness*, June 2, 1866, said Howe would be paid to go to New Brunswick and campaign for Smith. Howe replied in a telegram to Garvie of the *Citizen*, "No money was offered to me to go to New Brunswick. . . ." *Halifax Citizen*, June 5, 1866.

[64]Power was elected to the House of Commons for Halifax County in 1867.

tion" were being supported by Nova Scotians.[65] In fact an appeal had gone forth from the Anti-Confederate Association of Saint John to the Anti-Confederation League in Nova Scotia. A subscription was at once opened in Halifax, and on May 29 some $2200 was remitted to Saint John.[66]

But it made no difference. Tilley and Mitchell swept the province. They inflicted a worse defeat upon Smith than they themselves had sustained in 1865. Then they had taken eleven seats: Smith took only eight in 1866. The eight seats were all in eastern counties—Westmorland, Kent, and Gloucester—furthest from Fenian alarms. The outcome of the election was determined by the shift of the southwestern counties, where the Fenians had caused the greatest sensation. The change in Charlotte County, in the extreme southwest, was striking. It returned four anti-Confederates in 1865 and four Confederates in 1866, in both cases by substantial margins. And Western Extension was no longer an issue; the prospects of reciprocity were nil, and the Fenians completed the ruin of the western railway. The *Freeman* surveyed the graveyard of its hopes: "the public almost ceased to talk or think of western extension, having grown indifferent about it."[67]

Confederation was thus triumphant in the New Brunswick legislature. A brief session—less than three weeks—began on June 21, 1866. As in Nova Scotia, the Address was not on the basis of the Quebec Resolutions. It was remarkably similar to the Resolution in Nova Scotia, except that New Brunswick, true to her interests, made the Intercolonial Railway an indispensable condition. Union was to be arranged "upon such terms as will secure the just rights and interests of New Brunswick, accompanied with provision for the immediate construction of the Intercolonial Railway. . . ."[68] Four days after it was introduced, the Address passed the Assembly on a straight government vote, 31–8.[69]

The contrast between New Brunswick and Nova Scotia from this point on was remarkable. In New Brunswick the anti-Confederates, after the crushing defeat in the elections, were shattered and demoralized;[70] in Nova Scotia, they proceeded from strength to strength. E. M. Macdonald of the *Halifax Citizen*, with Patrick Power sailed

[65]Power to Editor of *Citizen*, June 2, 1866, in *Citizen* of that date; Saint John *Morning Telegraph*, June 12, 1866.
[66]Patterson, *Studies in Nova Scotian History*, 117–18.
[67]*Morning Freeman*, July 10, 1866. The railway was finally completed in 1869.
[68]New Brunswick, Assembly, *Journals*, 1866, 145 (June 26).
[69]*Ibid.*, 153 (June 30).
[70]G. L. Hatheway was reported, however, in Summerside, Prince Edward Island, speaking against Confederation there. Charlottetown *Patriot*, June 16, 1866, quoted in *Halifax Citizen*, June 23, 1866.

for St. John's on June 20 to rouse the Newfoundlanders.[71] Annand and Howe set off for London in July, but, unlike the summer before when Annand met Smith in London, there were no anti-Confederate representatives there from New Brunswick.

III

Despite the majority in the Canadian legislature in 1865 for Confederation, there was still much uneasiness about it in Canada East. The very means that Tupper and Tilley used to make Confederation acceptable to the legislatures of Nova Scotia and New Brunswick sent a current of alarm through the French Canadians. The abandonment of the Quebec scheme by the two Maritime provinces seemed to put everything at hazard once more. The attitude of the Nova Scotians to the federal principle was well known, and there was suspicion in Canada East that changes would be made to the Quebec Resolutions in London not only to make Confederation financially more attractive to Nova Scotia and New Brunswick, but also to make it more centralized.[72] Tupper's remarks in the Nova Scotian legislature were not reassuring. "The Imperial Government," he said, ". . . will have an opportunity of largely improving that scheme. . . ."[73] William Miller had spoken of the "arbitrament of the Imperial Government,"[74] and, despite the assurance of *Le Journal de Québec* and other ministerial papers, the issue of "l'arbitrage impérial" threatened to be awkward and possibly to become dangerous.

It swept *Le Canadien* out of the Confederation orbit altogether. "Nous accusions nos ministres de nous trahir et de vouloir mettre les droits du Bas-Canada à la merci d'une convention siégeant à Londres, délibérant sous l'influence du bureau colonial et décidant sans appel."[75] *Le Canadien*, once so frightened of "le gouffre américain" now became afraid of "le gouffre de la confédération."[76] The contagion spread further. It caused the resignation of two of the editors of *Le Courrier de St. Hyacinthe*, Paul DeCazes and Honoré Mercier. *Le Canadien* had sometimes leaned in a Liberal direction, but *Le Courrier de St.*

---

[71]St. John's *Public Ledger*, June 29, 1866. *Supra*, 176.

[72]And proposed by Governor MacDonnell as early as January, 1865. MacDonnell to Monck, Jan. 2, 1865 (confidential) in C.O. 42, Monck to Cardwell, Jan. 20, 1865 (confidential).

[73]Nova Scotia, Assembly, *Debates and Proceedings*, 1866, 222 (April 10).

[74]*Ibid.*, 189 (April 3). Cf. Macdonald Papers, Macdonald to Peter Mitchell, April 10, 1866, "The Imperial Government is now the arbiter. . . ." Also in J. Pope, ed., *Correspondence of Sir J. Macdonald* (Toronto, 1921), 31–2.

[75]Quebec *Canadien*, 18 mai 1866.

[76]*Ibid.*, 22 mars 1865; 19 sept. 1866.

Hyacinthe was staunchly Bleu. It believed that "la population cana-
dienne-française est et doit rester conservatrice. . . ."[77] But DeCazes
and Mercier believed that the Bleu leaders had betrayed French-Canadian interests; they had "trop compté, dans ces derniers temps, sur leur
propre force, et pas assez sur leurs devoirs comme chefs et comme
membres d'une nationalité. . . ."[78] They had failed to resist "la politique
adoptée maladroitement" by Nova Scotia, a policy which had opened
the way to new and dangerous concessions. DeCazes and Mercier
resigned on May 24, 1866.

The criticism by DeCazes and Mercier was on the whole moderate,
but it was significant because it was moderate—and Conservative.
As it turned out, this break was decisive for Mercier, and he separated
definitely from Cartier at this point.[79] The Rouges were of course far
more vehement. They were sympathetic to Smith and they saw in
the actions of Gordon in New Brunswick and Tupper in Nova Scotia
both determination and ruthlessness. On May 10, 1866, *L'Union
Nationale* spoke with a shudder of "les trames odieuses, ourdies par nos
gouvernants pour anéantir d'un même coup notre nationalité et nos
libertés politiques." Joseph Cauchon in *Le Journal de Québec* (May
29, 1866) replied that French Canadians had nothing to fear; their
ministers would never allow any sacrifice of French rights in London.
La Minerve even said that the Quebec scheme could not be amended
and the London Conference would thus have little to do.[80] And
Cartier's attitude in London, seven months later, certainly showed
that he was well aware of the possibility of a Bleu revolt if he conceded too much.[81]

Though the issue of "l'arbitrage impérial" definitely detached some of
the Bleus from Confederation, and alarmed others, the Fenian invasions
stopped this movement before it had gone far enough to threaten
Cartier's control of Canada East. The Fenians even weakened the
opposition to Confederation of the moderate Rouges. *L'Ordre* was an
example. In 1865 *l'Ordre* had believed that there was more protection

[77]*Le Courrier de St. Hyacinthe*, 26 avril 1866.
[78]*Ibid.*, 24 mai 1866, letter of DeCazes and Mercier.
[79]L. O. David, *Souvenirs et biographies, 1870–1910* (Montréal, 1911), 109.
David was one of the editors of *L'Union Nationale*.
[80]Montreal *Minerve*, 15 mai 1866. This remark was quoted pointedly by the
anti-Confederate *Halifax Citizen*, May 22, 1866.
[81]"The French delegates were keenly on the watch for anything which
weakened their securities. . . ." G. E. Marindin, ed., *The Letters of Frederic
[Rogers], Lord Blachford* (London, 1896), 301–2. There was also a report
that at one point Cartier threatened to resign, a report which Groulx believes
must be taken *cum grano salis*. L. Groulx, *La Confédération canadienne: ses
origines* (Montréal, 1918), 82.

for French Canadians in the American union than in Confederation.[82] Under the impress of Fenianism, however, its views began to shift. *Le Pays* said that Cartier was deliberately exaggerating the danger of the Fenians for this very purpose. "Son intérêt exige que la peur redouble, que l'on mette tout espoir dans la confédération comme dans une barque de salut."[83] *L'Ordre* too was at first inclined to minimize the danger of the Fenians; but after the events in New Brunswick in April it turned against the United States, and after the Ridgeway invasion in June it apologized for ever having suspected the Government of exploiting Canadian fears of the Fenians, and blazed with a militant patriotism:

> Mais aujourd'hui les cris de "sang!" de "guerre!"
> Ont retenti sous la voûte des cieux.
> A votre père, à votre tendre mère,
> A vos amis faites donc vos adieux. . . .
>
> En avant, courageux soldats,
> Volez au triomphe, à la gloire!
> Dans tous vos chaleureux combats
> Remportez une éclatante victoire!![84]

The Fenian threat of May, 1866, was not taken seriously by the Canadian government. There had been so many alarms before. The one of March 17 had come to nothing; the Campobello affair in April had been a failure; and the prospects of a successful attack being mounted across the Niagara river seemed so remote that the volunteers were disbanded after the end of April. Thus, despite warnings of invasion, the volunteers were not again called out until May 31. That same night, shortly after midnight, Col. John O'Neill, a veteran of eight years in the American army,[85] with 1500 men, crossed the Niagara river without being molested either by American or Canadian troops. By noon the next day the Fenians were in Fort Erie, Canada West. The road between Frenchman's Creek and Chippewa, as one report had it, was thronged with Fenians, "Fenians mounted two deep upon horses; Fenians in lumber wagons, carrying boxes of ammunition; Fenians on foot, whistling bayonets about their heads, frantically leaping mud-puddles, and shouting 'Come on'. . . ."[86] On Saturday, June 2,

---

[82]Montreal *Ordre*, 9, 12 juin, 7 juillet 1865.

[83]Montreal *Pays*, 24 mars 1866.

[84]*L'Ordre*, 12 mars, 16 avril, 6 juin, 1866.

[85]O'Neill became president of the "Canadian" wing of the Fenians in 1867 and led two further attempts, one in May, 1870, from Vermont, the other in October, 1871, from Minnesota.

[86]New York *World*, June 2, 1866, telegraph report from Frenchman's Creek, C.W., 1:30, Friday, June 1.

they turned back at Ridgeway some Canadian volunteers who had unluckily pressed too far and too fast; the Canadians drew off with six dead and thirty or more wounded, some fatally.

In Toronto the wildest excitement prevailed.[87] The *Globe* and *Leader*, on Saturday, June 2 and the following days were given over completely to war news, and the Montreal and Quebec papers were much the same. Not even the Trent crisis approached the stir caused by the war in Niagara. There had in fact been nothing like it for thirty years. On June 2 the *New York Herald* headlined, "WAR. Revolution in Canada." And it added, "Give the Fenians a foothold in Canada for twenty days and their little detachment of occupation may be swelled into an army of thirty thousand men. . . ." The next day it suggested helpfully, "Now, Killian, is the time for Campobello." However, support for the Fenians failed to arrive, and they retreated to the Niagara River, where, on June 4, in recrossing to the American side, some four hundred were taken into custody by the Americans.

The Niagara enterprise may have been intended as a feint, for shortly after the Ridgeway invasion alarms began on the Lower Canada border. On June 7 an estimated 1300 Fenians crossed the border north of St. Alban's and camped a few miles inside Canada waiting for reinforcements. "Fenianism," wrote the Quebec *Morning Chronicle* that day, "continues to be the all absorbing topic of the day. Nothing else is heard on any side. In the hotels, in the streets, on the public promenades, groupes [sic] of persons may be seen seriously discussing the situation." But the excitement was subsiding. Reinforcements for the Fenians at Pigeon Hill, C.E., never came; President Johnson had proclaimed officially the enforcement of American neutrality on June 6;[88] and, as at Eastport and Buffalo, Fenian supplies were seized by General Meade. By June 11, even the hopeful *Herald* had to admit the war was over. "The expeditionary forces, baffled and disappointed at every turn, demoralized and disheartened, have been recalled, disbanded and dispersed."

It was probably President Johnson who defeated the Fenians in June rather than the Canadians. At Campobello the British and the New Brunswickers put up a good show in their own defence, but at Niagara and Pigeon Hill the Canadians were less well prepared. It was the *New York Herald*'s boast that "had Mr. Seward adopted the late neutral policy of Lord John Russell the Fenians ere this would have

[87]C. P. Stacey, "Fenianism and the Rise of National Feeling in Canada at the time of Confederation," *Canadian Historical Review*, XII, 3 (Sept., 1931), 252

[88]For which he was roundly criticized by some New York papers, notably the *World* and the *Tribune*.

been in occupation of Montreal."[89] This was a gross bit of blarney, but unquestionably the greatest enemy of the Fenians was the enforcement of American neutrality, which, while too late at Ridgeway to prevent Canadian dead and wounded, nevertheless effectively destroyed the military power of the Fenians. But their political power remained. Sir Frederick Bruce warned Monck that "nothing but the President and his advisers stand at this moment between us, and a most serious movement."[90]

A less militant but equally blatant attempt to acquire British North America appeared a month later in Congress. The American Congress had not been unsympathetic to the Fenians,[91] and a bill appeared in the House of Representatives on July 2, 1866, purporting to do peacefully what the Fenians wished to accomplish by force. This was "an Act for the admission of the States of Nova Scotia, New Brunswick, Canada East and Canada West, and for the organization of the territories of Selkirk, Saskatchewan, and Columbia," on terms remarkably similar to those proposed by the Quebec Resolutions, though slightly more generous to Canada, Newfoundland, and Prince Edward Island.[92] It was introduced by the chairman of the Foreign Affairs Committee, General N. P. Banks, and after second reading it was referred to committee without a division.[93] It provoked a wide reaction. On July 12, 1866, the *New York Herald* said cheerfully that it was an excellent medicine for the ills of Canada. It would "keep off the Fenian chills, the Confederation cramps . . . the Reciprocity itch . . . and all other political distempers which have afflicted feeble little Canada. . . ." The Toronto *Globe* dismissed the bill on July 5; "so silly a bit of impudence" might have been expected from J. W. Taylor of Minneapolis, who, the *Globe* correctly noted, was behind it. Even papers opposed to Confederation felt as annoyed as the *Globe*.[94] There was indignation even in Nova Scotia.[95] Charles Skinner of New Brunswick was reported to have proposed a bill in the New Brunswick Assembly for the admission of Maine, Massachusetts, New York, and

[89]*New York Herald*, June 4, 1866.

[90]Bruce to Monck, June 18, 1866 (confidential) enclosure in F.O. 5, Bruce to Clarendon, June 18, 1866.   [91]*Supra*, 265.

[92]The full text of the bill is given in the New York *World*, July 4, 1866. Partial references and full discussion of the American aspects of the bill are in T. C. Blegen, "A Plan for the Union of British North America and the United States, 1866," *Mississippi Valley Historical Review*, IV, 4 (March, 1918), 470–83. See also, L. B. Shippee, *Canadian-American Relations, 1849–1874* (New Haven, 1939), 192–3.

[93]United States, 39th Congress, 1st Session, *Congressional Globe*, 3548.

[94]E.g. Montreal *Pays*, 12 juillet 1866.

[95]The New York *World*'s Halifax correspondent described it as "pretended indignation." *World*, July 19, 1866, report of July 9.

others into Confederation.[96] Although the Banks bill was finally buried in committee, it showed British North Americans, if they did not already know it, which way the wind was blowing below the border.

All these events weakened opposition to Confederation in Canada East. "L'arbitrage impérial" after its first impact in May, 1866, gradually faded into the background, although *Le Canadien* continued its warnings,[97] and Cartier and his colleagues never lost sight of the dangers latent in it. That the Fenian troubles stimulated the rise of a national feeling there can be no doubt. The Toronto *Daily Telegraph* expressed the prevailing sentiment of Canada West, "the covenant of our nationality has been sealed with blood."[98] The main effects were, however, felt in a negative fashion, that is, in the undermining of provincial loyalties just at a time when Confederation needed all the powers its friends could muster. How well they took advantage of their opportunities was graphically illustrated in Nova Scotia and New Brunswick. The Fenians threw into sharp relief the dangers of isolation and disunion just at the time when Confederation was losing its impetus in the Maritimes.

But Fenianism could not of itself create a British American national identity. That was not to be the product of Irish agitators, or, for that matter, of two glittering months of constitution-making in 1864. A national identity was a slower and more painful creation, and long after the Intercolonial Railway became a reality in 1876, Canadian national identity remained as weak and sickly as the *New York Herald* had described Canada, attenuated by four thousand miles of frontier and the vast distances and disparities that still remained to be conquered. The effects of the Fenian invasion were direct and immediate, but like all negative effects, once removed the elements in British North America tended to revert to their original state. The federal principle allowed this, within limits, and the suspicion that such was the case was the basis of the Nova Scotian and Canadian criticisms of the principle; still, no system was capable of making Nova Scotians, New Brunswickers, English and French Canadians one if they were resolved to be as they were. Legislative union was the greatest illusion of all. And how difficult some relations within the new state were going to be was illustrated in the debate that developed in Canada in the summer of 1866 over the constitutions for the future provinces of Ontario and Quebec.

[96]Saint John *Morning Telegraph*, July 6, 1866.
[97]*Le Canadien*, 15 août 1866; also 19 sept. 1866, 28 déc. 1866.
[98]Toronto *Daily Telegraph*, June 11, 1866. Also Stacey, "Fenianism and the Rise of National Feeling in Canada," 238–61. Cf. also the view of the Toronto *Globe*, June 6, 1866, in Stacey's article, p. 252.

16. NEW PROVINCES, OLD POLITICS

OTTAWA IN 1866 was an unimposing city of about 18,000 inhabitants. Howe called it "a shabby imitation of Washington," but it was not yet even an imitation. It retained its "turbid river full of slabs and sawdust"[1] and its lumber trade atmosphere. Its only glory was the new Parliament, and splendid the buildings were in Victorian Gothic with their studied grandioseness of manner, high above the river. It was said in Nova Scotia that the Canadian Parliament could count its plaster by the acre and its cornices by the mile, but even when half-finished the buildings satisfied Anthony Trollope's taste, and Lord Monck found them, when completed, remarkably attractive.[2] So did others, after they had got over the shock of the change from the civilized and mature Quebec to the rudeness of Ottawa. The Assembly found its new home at first rather cavernous and missed the intimacy of the unlovely old place at Quebec. Brown said that at first everyone was ready to pack up and go to Montreal but even he found after a time that Ottawa was not so bad after all.[3]

It was in Ottawa that the legislature of the province of Canada met for the last time on June 8, 1866. Lord Monck noted the occasion in the Speech. The main work of the session was to prepare the province for Confederation. There was to be a reduction in the 1859 Canadian tariff—the 20 per cent items were to drop to 15 per cent, a concession to Maritime opinion; but the principal task was the provision of local arrangements for the sections of the province when they were finally divided by Confederation. The establishment of constitutions for the two new provinces of Canada East and Canada West (Ontario and Quebec as they were to become) was not especially difficult. The

[1]Halifax *Morning Chronicle*, June 9, 1866, reporting Howe's speech at Barrington, N.S. The Ottawa *Citizen* much disliked Howe's remarks, but did not deny turbidity, slabs, or sawdust. (June 19, 1866.)

[2]Anthony Trollope, *North America* (New York, 1862), 67; Brown Papers, Monck to Brown, May 17, 1866.

[3]Brown Papers, George Brown to Anne Brown, June 14, June 23, 1866.

Halifax Citizen was a little surprised it had not been done at Quebec.[4] One obstacle in the Canadian divorce was the division of assets and liabilities. But in 1866 there was a more perplexing question, that of timing.

Monck and Macdonald disagreed about this. Monck had wanted to call the Canadian legislature together early in May, without waiting for the New Brunswick elections; and he continued to exhibit impatience with Macdonald's casual, at times bibulous approach. He wrote a stern letter to Macdonald on June 21 in which he said that since he could hardly dismiss his ministers (because of Confederation), he might have to ask for his own recall unless the Canadian legislative programme were developed more energetically.[5] As for Macdonald, he gave different reasons at different times for the slow pace of legislation. In June he told Lord Monck that it was the temper of the Canadian House and the necessity for dealing with financial provisions first that had occasioned the delay.[6] Later to Tilley he gave additional explanations. He said that local constitutions for Quebec and Ontario could not be presented safely until New Brunswick had approved of Union; that he would not risk awkward questions in the Assembly on the differences—all too patent—between the Union resolution passed in Nova Scotia and the Quebec resolutions passed in Canada.[7] The truth is more difficult. There is no doubt that Macdonald had plenty to do, with the Fenian trouble and the manifold problems of the Canadian separation; but it has to be added that Macdonald's incapacity at various times in June (and in August) was notorious. The *Globe*, after the session was over and the legislation passed, tried to make political capital of it, to the embarrassment not only of Monck but of Carnarvon.[8] Even the Ottawa *Citizen*, government paper that it was, admitted sadly that Macdonald had "at times indulged a little too freely."[9]

Whatever the reasons for the Canadian delay, New Brunswick had soon to finish with Confederation, if the British Parliament were to pass the British North America bill that same summer. Williams in Nova Scotia hoped that New Brunswick would make "short work of it."[10] New Brunswick did, in four days, the final vote being on Saturday, June 30,

[4]*Halifax Citizen*, July 10, 1866.
[5]J. Pope, *Memoirs of the Right Honourable Sir John Alexander Macdonald* (Toronto [1930]), 316–18.
[6]*Ibid.*, 318–20.
[7]Macdonald to Tilley, Oct. 8, 1866, *ibid.*, 323–7.
[8]Toronto *Globe*, Aug. 17, 22, Sept. 5, 1866. See D. G. Creighton, *John A. Macdonald: The Young Politician* (Toronto, 1952), 448–9.
[9]Ottawa *Citizen*, Sept. 1, 1866.
[10]P.R.O., Cardwell Papers, Williams to Cardwell, June 21, 1866 (private).

1866. It was on the following Tuesday, July 3, that Macdonald tabled the resolutions on the local constitutions in the Canadian legislature, and the debate on them began on July 13, four days after the New Brunswick session had been prorogued.

The Canadian delegation to England was to be on its way by July 21. Toward the end of June Tupper and Archibald had come up from Nova Scotia for the very purpose of making such an arrangement, and it had been so agreed. Whether the Canadian government could have finished its legislation is not certain. Monck estimated that it probably would; but just at this critical juncture came the news from England of the resignation of the Russell government. This was, to say the least, disconcerting. Nevertheless, Lord Carnarvon, the new Colonial Secretary, was ready, indeed anxious, to put a British North America bill through the existing session of Parliament, and between July 7 and July 28 was working on just such a bill, with the support of Cardwell, the late Secretary. The Maritime delegates sailed as agreed on July 19. But the Canadians had developed a sudden and apparently inexplicable determination not to go. Lord Monck had precipitately assumed that the fall of the Russell government meant Confederation would have to be postponed until the spring of 1867, and it seems probable that before Monck was disabused of that theory by Carnarvon, Macdonald had persuaded him that the Canadians not only *should* stay home, but, with the excuse so opportunely given, *could* do so, both with profit and impunity. Delay was altogether convenient. It allowed the relaxation of the now headlong press of important legislation. The Fenians, it is fair to say, were still threatening. And Macdonald, who was never one for haste, had had a timetable that required the local constitutions, the Lower Canada education bill, together with the British North America bill in England, to be sandwiched between July 3 and the forthcoming prorogation of the British Parliament. It was too much. To the surprise of Carnarvon, and to the dismay of Tupper and Tilley, the Canadians stayed home, and did not leave Canada for another four months.

Macdonald's resolutions for the local constitutions projected a single chamber legislature of 82 members for Canada West, while Canada East received a bicameral legislature consisting of an Assembly of 65 members and a Legislative Council of 24. Legislative Councillors were appointed for life by the Crown. The legislatures of both provinces were to be administered by the lieutenant governors on "the well understood principles of the British constitution."[11]

The two provincial constitutions suggested the differing attitudes of

11Canada, Assembly, *Journals*, 1866, 141–2. Compare the phrase with "the well-understood principles of federal government," *supra*, 110–11.

the two sections of Canada toward the future role of the local governments in Confederation. The organization proposed for Canada West (Ontario) suggested Macdonald's view of what a local government should be; the full-scale bicameral legislature for Canada East (Quebec) suggested the views of the Bleus. It was a nice question whether a bicameral legislature would be more effective in guarding provincial rights than would a unicameral one, but many of the Bleus seemed to think so. Ottawa's *Le Canada* said, "Plus on simplifiera la législature locale plus on amoindrira son importance et plus on courra risque de la voir absorber par la législature fédérale. Naturellement, le Haut-Canada, qui préférerait une Union législative, ne redoute guère cette absorption."[12]

Macdonald was largely concerned with justifying the constitution for Canada West. In his words, "Were this a sovereign legislature there might be two chambers, but for a subordinate legislature one was enough."[13] Even more revealing was Macdonald's comparison of the local government for Canada West with those of New Zealand whose provincial councils and superintendents were clearly subordinated to the central government. It was suggestive of Macdonald's hopes for British North America that in 1876 the provincial system of New Zealand was abolished and replaced with 66 counties.[14] The Conservative *St. Catharines Constitutional* heartily approved of the new constitution for Canada West and Macdonald's exposition of it. The central government will thus clearly have "full power to superintend all legislative enactments of the Local Parliaments, and to veto such proceedings as might prove hurtful to the public welfare." The Hamilton *Spectator* said much the same. The Ottawa *Times*, also Conservative, did not like the one-chamber system very much, but it consoled its readers with the thought that the veto by the central government would check any anomaly.[15]

Cartier, seconding Macdonald's motion, avoided any reference to Macdonald's remark that one chamber was enough for subordinate legislatures. He neither affirmed nor denied the proposition. The reason for a two-chamber legislature for Canada East was, he said, that "the people were more monarchical in interests. . . ."[16] If Canada West wanted a single chamber on grounds of economy, let her have it,

[12]Ottawa *Canada*, 17 juillet 1866.
[13]Toronto *Leader*, July 14, 1866, reporting debates for July 13.
[14]Compare Macdonald's remarks to M. C. Cameron, *supra*, 123. Also Sir Frederic Rogers' view, *infra*, 326.
[15]*St. Catharines Constitutional*, Aug. 2, 1866, July 5, 1866; Hamilton *Spectator*, July 6, 1866; Ottawa *Times*, July 5, 1866.
[16]Toronto *Leader*, July 14, 1866, reporting debates for July 13.

but Canada East did not consider these grounds sufficient to justify abandonment of the cherished system of two houses. "Ce n'est pas pour £15,000 à £20,000 que nous aurions voulu refuser de donner plus de respectabilité à tout notre système d'institutions."[17] The Toronto *Leader* thought this justification inadequate and said the stronger reason for two chambers in Canada East was to give better representation to the English minority,[18] which in fact Cartier had hinted at. This explanation was the more plausible since the legislative councillors of Quebec were appointed for life. *Le Canadien* remarked that the legislative council of Canada East was the means by which "la garnison anglaise tiendra nos forces en échec."[19]

George Brown frankly disliked having responsible governments at the local level at all. He thought them inconsistent with the limited purposes of such governments. They should not be trammelled by having the executive responsible to the Assembly.[20] A similar constitution for Canada East had already been suggested by the Bleu *Courrier du Canada*.[21] The purpose of Brown's plan, and *Le Courrier*'s, was to render the local government emphatically executive in character, with a minimum of legislative control.[22]

A. A. Dorion moved an amendment that the local legislature for Canada East should be composed of one chamber only.[23] Speaking to his motion he said that, judging from the Quebec Resolutions, and from Macdonald's remarks, there was no necessity for a second chamber in Canada East. Why need there be, if "the duties of the local Legislatures would be of a municipal nature only?"[24] Dorion was supported by

[17]Montreal *La Minerve*, 17 juillet 1866, reporting debates for July 13.
[18]Toronto *Leader*, July 17, 1866.
[19]Quebec *Canadien*, 18 juillet 1866.
[20]Toronto *Globe*, Aug. 3, 1866, reporting debates for Aug. 2. The reason for the two-week interval between the first part of the debate and the second was the promise of the Canadian government that before the provincial constitutions were passed the Lower Canada education bill would be introduced. For the fate of the education bill, see *infra*, 288–90.
Brown suggested a plan for the local governments whereby the Assembly would be elected for three years, and the executive heads of departments, also elected, would be responsible to the Lieutenant Governor, not to the legislature.
[21]Quebec *Courrier du Canada*, 6 juillet 1866. It had already suggested this plan in its series, "La Confédération" (16 jan. 1865).
[22]Cf. also Alpheus Todd's *Brief Suggestions in Regard to the Formation of the Local Governments* (Ottawa, 1866), the aim of which was to establish a system "strengthening . . . the Executive authority, and affording due facility to the Government for exercise of a legitimate control over the Legislative Chambers." (p. 13)
[23]Canada, Assembly, *Journals*, 1866, 274–5 (Aug. 2).
[24]*Globe*, Aug. 3, 1866, reporting debates for Aug. 2.

Brown, Holton, and J. H. Pope. The Montreal *Herald* agreed. It had not believed that the Legislative Council of Quebec would be any protection for the English minority.[25] Here was the dilemma for the English Protestants: to support a unicameral legislature in the hope that the provinces would be firmly subordinated to the central power, or to plump for the bicameral legislature as insurance against the chance they would not? *Le Courrier du Canada*'s view was that the second chamber could by no means be relied upon by the English Protestants for protection.[26] Despite this, most of the English-speaking members from Canada East supported Cartier's bicameral legislature, and Dorion's amendment was defeated 69–31.

Hardly had this been done when John Hillyard Cameron of Canada West proposed an amendment giving Canada West a bicameral legislature. This was also defeated, 86–13.[27] Still, it represented a significant section of Conservative, and to a lesser extent, of Reform opinion. Both Christopher Dunkin and Richard Cartwright supported it. The Toronto *Leader* was especially conspicuous in supporting the bicameral system for Canada West. The *Leader* believed, as did Christopher Dunkin, that a single chamber was inconsistent with parliamentary institutions. There was no ballast in such a system. It would "outdo the United States in democracy" and would produce "the rankest and worst kind of a Republic." The *Leader* also criticized Macdonald's allusions to the New Zealand system. A local government in New Zealand, remarked the *Leader* sensibly, did "not legislate for a million and a half people. . . ."[28] The Reform *Newmarket Era* agreed in principle with the *Leader*. The unicameral system for Canada West looked suspiciously like "a huge County Council."[29]

But behind the unicameral system for Canada West there was generous, if often inarticulate, Reform and Conservative support. Brown, though he would have preferred a more strictly municipal type of constitution, supported Macdonald's measure, and the *Globe* followed. With the *Globe* went the great mass of Reform opinion in Canada West. The truth was that the local constitutions were not a major issue. The Toronto *Leader*, that critical and reluctant supporter of Macdonald, tried to persuade Canada West that the local constitution was of major importance.[30] Canada West was not persuaded. Nor was Canada East

25Montreal *Herald*, July 5, 1866.
26Quebec *Courrier du Canada*, 9 juillet 1866.
27Canada, Assembly, *Journals*, 1866, 275–6 (Aug. 2).
28Toronto *Leader*, June 27, 1866; July 16, 1866.
29*Newmarket Era*, July 5, 1866.
30Toronto *Leader*, Aug. 7, 1866.

much troubled. It seemed far less concerned than Canada West. The English Protestants seemed satisfied with the two-chamber system, and it gave the French the illusion that their local government would be more independent of central control than it was intended to be. In fact, the local constitutions were a bore, in the House and out of it. That July in Ottawa had been scorching, and the combination of constitutions and heat produced in the House a sleepy *ennui* that seemed to affect reporters and legislators alike.[31]

The reason for the lack of interest in the local constitutions was not far to seek. The local governments were to be subordinate, and it was natural that most of the members of the Canadian legislature would prefer to take their seats in the Dominion parliament, in the same house and with many of the same associates and party lines that had existed in the past. The local governments seemed clearly of a lower order; to become a member of them would be to take a step down. Most of the members of the legislature of the province of Canada did in fact become members of the legislature of the Dominion of Canada.[32] Nor was the province of Canada unique in this respect. The Maritime legislatures lost many of the familiar faces. Thus in 1866 the Canadian legislators were creating governments in which they expected to take little part. The Toronto *Leader* had good cause to complain, August 7, that "this question of local constitutions is very much underrated." It was indeed underrated, and the debate in the Canadian Assembly reflected it. The Halifax *Evening Reporter* of April 23, 1867, would caution against a similar attitude in Nova Scotia. "We hope that the importance of the Local Legislature will not be overlooked. It is just as necessary to send able men to that body as to the House of Commons. We say this because we have seen a tendency in some quarters to underrate the work and duties of the Local Assembly."

The thorny issue in the summer session of 1866 was not that of the local constitutions, but one more concrete and one which touched more closely the lively and tender prejudices in Canada East and West. This was the educational privileges of the minorities. The provision of constitutional protection to religious and cultural minorities was a far more intractable problem than that of the local constitutions,

31Barrie *Northern Advance*, July 18, 1866.

32About twenty members of the Dominion parliament from Ontario and Quebec also sat in the provincial legislatures until this dual representation was abolished. Nova Scotia and New Brunswick had prohibited it before 1867. Ontario passed an act prohibiting it in 1872. The Quebec Assembly passed a similar measure, but it was thrown out by the Quebec Legislative Council. A Dominion Act abolished it in 1873.

and in 1866 it turned out to be only less so than it was to be thirty years later. It provoked a sharp debate in the House, the resignation of Galt from the Ministry, and an intemperate discussion in the news-papers, all of which vigorously aroused the quick passions of Protes-tants and Catholics.

In his Sherbrooke speech of November 23, 1864, Galt had promised that the Government would bring in an amendment to the existing school laws that would extend the privileges of the Protestant minority in Canada East. He appears to have reiterated this in the form of an unofficial but real commitment to the Protestant M.P.P.'s from Canada East, on March 7, 1865, just before the vote was taken on Confedera-tion in the Canadian legislature.[33] A bill to amend the existing education law was introduced into the Canadian assembly in the summer session of 1866. At first all appeared to be well. Then came a sudden and largely unforeseen reaction from the Catholics of Canada West.[34] They introduced a bill on August 3 to amend the existing Separate School Act of 1863 of Canada West to give "to the Roman Catholic minority in Upper Canada similar and equal privileges to those granted by the Legislature to the Protestant minority in Lower Canada. . . ."[35] A Protestant member from West Middlesex, Thomas Scatcherd, promptly moved the six months' hoist. At this juncture Cartier and Galt managed to secure an adjournment of debate. The excitement was considerable, both in the legislature and out of it. Even Bleu journals like *Le Journal de Québec* and *Le Courrier du Canada* now objected to giving Protes-tants in Canada East privileges that were being withheld from Catholics in Canada West. The Catholic *Canadian Freeman* of Toronto was furi-ous with Scatcherd. This was the kind of justice that Catholics could expect from a local legislature after Confederation![36] Finally the Government was forced to drop altogether the offending clauses in the Lower Canada education bill. As a result Galt resigned on August 7. Galt's resignation came apparently as a stunning surprise. It took Montreal "by the ears last night," said the *Gazette* on August 8. And it echoed in other provinces.[37] That it was only temporary was, how-

---

[33]So alleged by Dorion in the Remonstrance against Confederation signed by him and nineteen other French-Canadian M.P.P.'s, to the Earl of Carnarvon, dated Montreal, Oct., 1866.

[34]Macdonald was warned privately in 1865 that changes in the Protestant privileges would have this effect. Macdonald Papers, J. O. Reilly to Macdonald, Feb. 8, 1865.   [35]Canada, Assembly, *Journals*, 1866, 281 (Aug. 3).

[36]*Le Journal de Québec*, 4, 6 août 1866; *Le Courrier du Canada*, 6 août 1866; Toronto *Canadian Freeman*, Aug. 9, 1866.

[37]E.g., Saint John *Morning Journal*, Aug. 13, 1866; Charlottetown *Patriot*, Aug. 25, 1866.

ever, suspected. "Some sort of 'shuffle' performance, either double or single . . . seems to be expected," reported the *Sarnia Observer*.[38]

Of course the Protestants of Canada East constituted a much more powerful minority than the Catholics of Canada West. Although roughly comparable in the proportion they bore to the population of each section, the two minorities could not be compared in economic or political significance. (One difficulty was that Catholics in Canada West were scattered and found it difficult to elect one of their own religion; they were, in consequence, much under-represented.) This does not justify the disparity in privilege: it does make it understandable. It is perhaps fair to say also that the French Canadians were a more tolerant majority than the Protestants of Canada West. Brown and the Reform party were dedicated, even militant, Protestants. The establishment of conditions that would perpetuate, perhaps extend, the privileges of the Catholic minority in Canada West was not something they could contemplate with equanimity. At the Quebec Conference Brown had fought, so he said, to prevent minority guarantees of any description.[39] In 1866 he believed that "to bind down a majority in any country with iron constitutional fetters to protect a minority was a most inconvenient and inexpedient device." There was a better way to protect minorities, Brown said with some naïveté, and that was to leave "the majority free to act according to their own sense of what is right and just. . . ."[40]

To this McGee replied that Brown's confidence in the honesty and good intentions of the majority was all very well, but it was not enough. "A majority may be honestly wrong as well as honestly right. . . ." McGee thought it unfortunate that the claims of both minorities should not be settled finally before Confederation took place.[41] But they were not, and McGee was determined that the central power in Confederation should exercise its full power to maintain such rights. McGee empha-

[38]*Sarnia Observer*, Aug. 24, 1866. George Brown wrote his wife that Galt was very indignant (Brown Papers, Aug. 8, 1866); but Galt, who was in a better position to know, wrote to his wife that he parted on the best of terms with his colleagues (O. D. Skelton, *The Life and Times of Sir Alexander Tilloch Galt* (Toronto, 1920), 404).

[39]Note, however, Resolution 43, subsection 6, of the Quebec Resolutions, which guaranteed existing rights and privileges of the Protestant and Catholic minorities "as to their Denominational Schools at the time when the Union goes into operation."

[40]*Globe*, Aug. 8, 1866, reporting debates for Aug. 7. A. A. Dorion put forward a similar argument in opposition to the Lower Canada education bill.

[41]*Ibid*.

sized this in a speech in London, Canada West, a month after the session was over.

The minorities east and west have really nothing to fear beyond what always existed, local irritations produced by ill-disposed individuals; the strong arm and the long arm of the Confederate power will be extended over them all, and woe be to the wretch on whom that Arm shall have to descend in anger. . . . Localism must be taught to know its proper place; sectionalism must be subordinate. . . .[42]

Throughout the autumn of 1866 the whole question of the function of the central government in the protection of minorities received protracted and bitter discussion in Canada and, to a lesser degree, in the Maritimes. Archbishop Connolly of Halifax thought guarantees would be useful in keeping the support of Roman Catholics in Nova Scotia and New Brunswick. "Go in for the rights of minorities, Protestant as well as Catholic," he wrote Tupper.[43] The Toronto *Globe* took up the wickedness of separate schools, and it thus enjoyed the hearty vituperation of the *Canadian Freeman*.[44] On November 17 the government Ottawa *Times* said Brown's recalcitrant attitude to Catholic schools was now threatening the position of the Protestants in Canada East. McGee, before he left for England, did the best he could to calm things down. He remained in Canada until January, 1867, writing letters private and public against attempts by the Rouges and others to exploit the issue, and to allay fears such as those of *Le Canadien* which was still fretting about "l'arbitrage impérial."[45] It was not until the end of January, 1867, that McGee sailed from Boston in the *Asia*, and he still had time to stop in Halifax and encourage his co-religionists there.[46]

It was fully expected that there would be a clause in the British North America Act providing for appeal to the central government when minority educational privileges were compromised. The *Sarnia Observer* on November 9 copied an apparently authentic report that the school difficulty would be solved by allowing appeals from the local legislatures—and liked it not at all. On October 30 Cartier said in Montreal, "I also solemnly give you my word (loud cheers) that the Catholic

[42]Toronto *Canadian Freeman*, Sept. 27, 1866, reporting McGee's speech at London, Sept. 20, 1866.
[43]Tupper Papers, Connolly to Tupper, n.d., but early in 1867.
[44]Toronto *Globe*, Oct. and Nov., 1866, *passim*; *Canadian Freeman*, Dec. 13, 20, 1866.
[45]Montreal *Gazette*, Jan. 12, 1867; *Le Canadien*, Feb. 8, 1867. See also R. Rumilly, *Histoire de la Province de Québec*, I. *Cartier* (Montreal, n.d.) 53–5.
[46]Halifax *Evening Express*, Feb. 1, 1867.

minority of Upper Canada will be protected like the Protestant minority in Lower Canada. All apprehensions upon this subject are as absurd as they are false. Do not listen to them. I tell you all will be well."*La Minerve* emphasized this a few days later.[47] Many supported such a clause not only for the obvious reason but because it would be another means of controlling local governments. On November 17, 1866, the Quebec *Morning Chronicle* wrote: "It strikes many people that the most obvious deficiency of the [Quebec] scheme is that it contains no such provision, thereby giving full scope to that very element of state rights that has wrought so much mischief under the American system." The right of appeal was a useful weapon against the arbitrary sway of local powers. The *Chronicle* was even prepared to see the right of appeal extended against all acts of the local governments. Constitutional guarantees were vital to the English-speaking Protestants of Canada East. They had accepted Confederation upon the condition that central control would be strong enough to prevent them from falling under the domination of the French majority, or the far larger Catholic majority.[48] The Protestants of Canada East had no real alternative to Confederation by 1866. Dissolution of the Union was political suicide. They had to support Confederation whether they liked it or not, but truly the old Union upon which so many of their hopes had rested had fallen upon evil days. Some of the Protestants were very pessimistic, especially after Galt's resignation. J. W. Dawson, the Principal of McGill, was one of these. He could only hope that by some good fortune "we shall after all escape out of the hands of the confederationists, Fenians, French priests, American Democrats, and all other enemies of British institutions. . . ."[49] Lord Monck hoped fervently that Macdonald would weather the storm in Canada. "Any schism in Canada coming on top of Howe's agitation *might* be attended with serious consequences."[50]

In Nova Scotia Achbishop Connolly of Halifax was more confident. He wrote to Tupper in London that, given minority guarantees, "I stake my character on it that neither Howe nor any one of his Kinsmen will succeed . . . in any Catholic Constituency in either of the Maritime provinces."[51] Whatever the good Archbishop's character he was wrong in his opinion. By this time Howe's campaign had been in full

[47]Montreal *Gazette*, Nov. 1, 1866; *La Minerve*, 12 nov. 1866.
[48]The French-English ratio was 3–1; the Catholic-Protestant ratio was 6–1.
[49]Howe Papers, J. W. Dawson to Howe, Nov. 15, 1866.
[50]Macdonald Papers, Monck to Macdonald, Oct. 22, 1866.
[51]Tupper Papers, Connolly to Tupper, Oct. 25, 1866.

swing for some months, and an ably written petition was going the
rounds in Nova Scotia. On October 25, 1866, William Garvie of the
Citizen reported 40,000 names. Destined ultimately for the House of
Commons in London, the petition sums up the Nova Scotian case
against the Quebec plan. "It s[e]cures neither the consolidation, dignity
and independent power of Monarchy, nor the checks and guards which
ensure to the smaller states self-government . . . in the neighbouring
Republic."[52] Howe in London published, late in September, the
summary of his main criticisms, *Confederation Considered in Relation
to the Interests of the Empire.*[53] It was an effective piece. Howe was
struck by the disparity in size and resources between Canada and the
Maritime provinces. This disparity was not compensated for, as it was
in the United States, by equal representation of each province in the
Senate. There was no possible way that they could ever secure "a fair
share of influence over the administration." The Maritime provinces
would not only be swamped politically; they would also be so economically. Canada was so powerful that ultimately the Maritimes would
be mere shells, subordinated to the politics and the economy of the
St. Lawrence, bereft of any native vitality.

Howe's *Confederation* appeared in the newspapers from Canada
West to Newfoundland. It may not have fallen in Charlottetown like
a bombshell, as the Charlottetown *Herald* said it did (October 10),
but it was powerful enough to cause the Saint John *Morning News* to
spend two weeks, October 3–17, 1866, commenting on and criticizing
it. In London Tupper duly replied,[54] and in British North America the
Confederate press took up Tupper's cause.[55] Annand followed Tupper,
and McCully and Archibald followed Annand.[56] The Nova Scotians in
London spared not themselves or their pens. But by this time as far as
Nova Scotia was concerned, the arguments on the merits of the case
were over and done with. The real question was, as the *Yarmouth
Herald* said on November 22, 1866, "not Mr. Howe's consistency or

[52]From the *Yarmouth Herald*, July 5, 1866.
[53]For convenience citation is made to J. A. Chisholm's *Speeches and Public
Letters of Joseph Howe* (2 vols., Halifax, 1909), where it is reprinted, II,
468–92.
[54]C. Tupper, *Letter to the Rt. Hon. Earl of Carnarvon* (London, 1866).
[55]E.g., Charlottetown *Islander*, Nov. 16, 1866; Toronto *Globe*, Nov. 12, 1866.
[56]William Annand, *Confederation; A Letter to the Rt. Hon. Earl of Carnarvon* (London, 1866); A. G. Archibald, *Letter to the People of Nova Scotia*
([London] 1866); J. McCully, *British America: Arguments against a Union of
the Provinces Reviewed: With Further Reasons for Confederation* (London,
1867).

inconsistency—not even the advantages and disadvantages of Confederation—but, whether the people of Nova Scotia should have Confederation forced upon them without their consent. . . ."

On this question there were gnawing doubts in Nova Scotia about the attitude of the British government. The London *Daily News*, September 21, 1866, commenting on the Nova Scotian petition, remarked, "It may be necessary in the general interest to override the opinions of particular bodies of colonists. . . ." Other London papers were not encouraging, and the Nova Scotian papers published the extracts with gloomy forebodings. The London *Times'* thoughts about British America taking her place among the independent nations of the earth were quoted by the *Citizen* in a tone something like a dirge.[57] And the British government set its face like flint against remonstrances from Nova Scotia. Nothing Howe or his friends could do made any difference. Lord Carnarvon heard Howe's views and arguments; "do Justice," Howe said, "though the Heavens fall." But Carnarvon, though not perhaps unmoved, remained unshaken.[58] After the British North America bill was signed, on March 29, 1867, Howe had no alternative but to return to Nova Scotia, cured, as he said, "of a good deal of loyal enthusiasm,"[59] and bitter against the Canadians. "We must submit of course," he wrote John Young, "because we cannot fight the British Government, but if the Queen's troops were withdrawn I would die upon the Frontier rather than submit to such an outrage. . . . Our first duty will be to punish the rascals here who have betrayed and sold us. If then convinced that the Canadians are disposed to act fairly, we may try the experiment. . . ."[60] This was generally the view of the anti-Confederate newspapers in Nova Scotia. As long as the British North America bill was a bill every constitutional mode of opposing it was pursued; when it became an act it might have to be accepted. "Mortifying and humiliating as the fact is to the people of Nova Scotia . . . there remains, at present, but one course to pursue, that is, to make the best of circumstances, and submit patiently to the yoke. . . ."[61] Even in Prince Edward

[57]*Halifax Citizen*, Nov. 27, 1866. The best example of this theme in the *Times* was Feb. 21, 1867: "we look forward to the time when the new Dominion shall be self-subsisting—united to us by the tie of a common descent, but as completely self-governed as the United States themselves."

[58]C.O. 217, Howe to Carnarvon, Dec. 10, 1866, and Minute of Carnarvon thereon, Dec. 13, 1866; Howe Papers, Howe to Carnarvon, Jan. 21, 1867; Carnarvon to Howe, Jan. 29, 1867.

[59]Howe Papers, Howe to Lord Stanley, April 25, 1867.

[60]*Ibid.*, Howe to Young, May 11, 1867.

[61]*Yarmouth Herald*, April 11, 1867. The *Herald* was however a Conservative paper.

Island the anti-Confederate papers thought this the correct course for Nova Scotia, to give the new Dominion "a fair and candid trial."[62] So said also the anti-Confederate Chatham, N.B., *Gleaner* on June 8. To a vast throng in Temperance Hall, Halifax, on the Queen's Birthday, 1867, Howe, too, said the fact of union had to be faced. If Nova Scotia became like Ireland, reduced to milk and potatoes, then "we will take up our rifles"; but in the meantime, however apprehensive of the future, "we will . . . do our duty like men and Nova Scotians. . . ."[63]

There is something sad about Howe in these days. Young Ross Robertson's new Toronto *Daily Telegraph* had been unkind enough to say of him, with the contempt reserved by the young for the old, "His day has gone by, and he babbles of the past as if he were fighting over again the battles of responsible government."[64] There was enough truth in it. Howe could not forbear reminding his audiences of the great days in 1835 when the young printer had defended himself and the freedom of the press. He had fallen prey to his own vanity. In the bitter quarrels of 1869 Howe's colleagues on the *Morning Chronicle* were savage: "This old man vanity-struck. . . ."[65]

The old Nova Scotian legislature met for the last time in March, 1867. A final attempt was made to stop Confederation in the Reply debate, but it was defeated 32–16 by the Government majority. The *Acadian Recorder*, March 20, 1867, listed the names of the thirty-two gentlemen responsible. The legislature wound up its business on May 7, 1867, and the *Yarmouth Herald* wrote a doleful *finis*. In Saint John the *Morning Freeman* performed the same office for the New Brunswick legislature on June 15: "Died—At her late residence, in the City of Fredericton the 20th May last, from the effects of an accident which she received in April, 1866, . . . the Province of New Brunswick, in the 83rd year of her age."[66] A suggestive despatch came from the new Colonial Secretary to Governor Williams of Nova Scotia; it asked him

[62]Charlottetown *Herald*, June 26, 1867.

[63]Halifax *Morning Chronicle*, May 29, 1867, reporting Howe's speech of May 24.

[64]Toronto *Daily Telegraph*, May 30, 1866. Ross Robertson (1841–1918) founded the paper in May, 1866. It later became the Toronto *Evening Telegram*.

[65]Halifax *Morning Chronicle*, Feb. 25, 1869.

[66]In the "funeral" procession was a smiling Tilley in a court suit with the editor of the *Morning News* carrying Tilley's cocked hat; the member for St. John (perhaps A. R. Wetmore who had changed sides) whose little sons were singing,

> I have no country now,
> Mr. Tilley sold my Country, Tow, Row, Row.

Then followed "the hungry swarm," in order of rank and station, and headed by R. D. Wilmot.

to ship home to the Colonial Office all the confidential despatches to and from Nova Scotia. Only that despatch was to be found in Nova Scotia afterward.[67]

In Canada manœuvring preliminary to the new *métier* had already begun. Holton and Brown had begun to look to the mending of old Liberal fences. Like Howe, Holton did not like the new constitution or the means used to carry it, but it was the constitution, and as such, he told Brown, "we must therefore live under it, [and] work it. . . ."[68] The Montreal *Herald* which often reflected Holton, said, "it is the duty of all to give the system a fair trial. . . ."[69] But there was more to the Liberal moves than the mere acceptance of Confederation. They were looking now to both policies and power.

In June, 1867, A. A. Dorion began a series in *Le Pays* called "Le parti libéral et la Confédération," which while providing a *raison d'être* for liberalism, also suggested some lines of Liberal policy. It was to be expected that Dorion would condemn the centralization inherent in Confederation, and he believed that in the future some modification in the relations of the central government with the local ones would be necessary. Under the circumstances, "le parti libéral devra chercher à donner plus d'élasticité au lien fédéral, et à repousser les éléments de centralisation dans la distribution des pouvoirs. . . ."[70] Surprisingly, the Toronto *Globe* soon developed sympathy with this view. Only three weeks after the inauguration of Confederation, it was already complaining of Macdonald's interference in provincial affairs and of what it called "the tyranny of the Confederate cabinet." The *Globe*'s new attitude to the central government went hand in hand with its new political *démarche*; it now asserted theories of federation it would never have done before. "Local Governments under a Federal system," said the *Globe* without a blush on July 25, "are essentially independent of the general authority. If they were not independent their existence would be useless."

The *Globe* and Brown were thus clearly out against the Government. The reason was frankly political. McGee and other members of the Government were saying that the government party was the party of Union, that coalition was essential and should continue. Galt, in a compelling speech at Lennoxville in May, 1867, said, "My view is, sir,

[67]C.O. 217, Buckingham and Chandos to Williams, May 4, 1867 (confidential); Nova Scotia, Lieutenant Governor, General Correspondence Received.
[68]Brown Papers, Holton to Brown, May 5, 1867.
[69]Montreal *Herald*, March 27, 1867. Also quoted with approval by the *Quebec Daily Mercury*, March 28, 1867.
[70]Montreal *Pays*, 4 juin 1867.

that the Government of the New Dominion must practically be a continuation of the Quebec Convention."[71] To this both Brown and the *Globe* were vigorously opposed. The question was not, in the *Globe*'s view, who were for and who against union. That was a gross and unwarrantable distortion. The real issue was, how to make the union work the best.[72] From the *Globe*'s viewpoint the honest policy was to break up the Coalition completely and give the Reformers, who had stood loyally behind the Government on Confederation, a chance to form a government themselves. The union was not in danger in any event. "Time for Reformers to Move" was the title of an editorial in the Reform *Newmarket Era* as early as December 7, 1866. This sentiment grew, and by the spring of 1867 the *Globe* had thrown all its strength behind it.

Elsewhere there was some surprise and even indignation at the *Globe*. Brown, said the Quebec *Mercury*, "must needs play the demagogue." Brown's attitude was just obstructionist. The Saint John *Telegraph*, not unsympathetic to Liberalism, thought it was wrong to split the union party; in New Brunswick, it said, such a thing would be madness.[73] It was not at all clear it was wise even in Canada. The Liberal party had many different elements in it, and it was not easy to discern the common ground on which a Liberal government might be formed. Brown had done some promoting when in New Brunswick and Nova Scotia in November, 1865. His conversations with William Annand in Nova Scotia revealed Brown's dislike for the Coalition and the hope of forming a new national party, but Annand was not prepared to co-operate in a union policy.[74] Perhaps, too, by 1867, the Nova Scotian Liberals, at least the anti-Confederate ones, found it even more difficult to forgive Brown the Coalition of 1864. The Liberals in Nova Scotia, New Brunswick, and Canada had tended to think of themselves as one party, and Brown's joining the Conservatives in 1864 seemed to the rest only second in perfidy to the abandonment of the Intercolonial by Canada in 1863.[75] Nor were the Rouges in 1867 apt to be sufficiently elastic to accept the new constitution—or Brown—at once.[76] *L'Ordre*, it was true, was philosophical on March 27, 1867: "La tâche de l'Opposition doit

---

[71]*Quebec Daily Mercury*, May 25, 1867, reporting Galt's speech of May 22.
[72]Toronto *Globe*, May 15, 1867.
[73]*Quebec Daily Mercury*, April 20, 1867; May 1, 1867; Saint John *Morning Telegraph*, April 9, 1867.
[74]*Supra*, 220–1.
[75]Macdonald makes this point in a letter to the editor of the Toronto *Telegraph* in 1868, enclosing a copy of the *Halifax Citizen* Dec. 22, 1868, for "manipulation." Macdonald to Morrison, Dec. 30, 1868, in J. Pope, ed., *Correspondence of Sir John Macdonald* (Toronto, 1921), 81.
[76]Brown Papers, Holton to Brown, May 1, 1867.

s'arrêter ici; ayant noblement rempli son devoir, il ne lui reste plus qu'à accepter le fait accompli." But *L'Ordre*'s views were not Dorion's and Dorion was the real leader of the Rouges. In other words, the hopes of a new Liberal party on a national, or even on a Canadian basis, were probably unrealistic. Brown could perhaps unite the Reformers of Canada West, and it was with this in mind that the Reform Convention of 1867 was called to meet on June 27 in the Music Hall in Toronto, but to this proceeding not even the Reformers of Canada West were agreed. A correspondent in the Reform Woodstock *Sentinel* put it that he could see "no probable advantage of any magnitude likely to result. . . . The convention has already created disunion among Reformers." Not a few Reform papers took a similar attitude.[77] The Reform *Hastings Chronicle* of Belleville noted that there were only 30 representatives at the convention from east of Cobourg, while Brampton village alone sent 19.[78] On the other hand the militants in Toronto and the west believed in it. Party issues must exist, said the *Sarnia Observer*. "We don't care a straw which of the two parties takes hold first. Let the Tories take the bats first . . . and let us see how long they can stay at the wickets. It will be our innings when the 'stumps' are drawn." And old Upper Canadian Reformers will have still to watch the French Canadians, for they will profit if they can from whatever administration takes power. "The old fox will be around the hen-roost, watching his chances. . . ."[79]

The Convention opened in Toronto with some six hundred present. The British North America Act, though it was said to have some defects, was nevertheless enthusiastically endorsed. Howland and McDougall, still Reform members of the Government, urged Reform support of the Coalition. McDougall criticized Brown for deserting the Confederation ship before it had safely entered port and concluded with a stirring appeal for unity among Reformers and continued support of the Government. Joseph Rymal—who had been one of the few Reformers originally

---

[77]Woodstock *Sentinel*, quoted by the Toronto *Leader*, July 9, 1867; also *London Free Press*, St. Catharines *Journal*, Oshawa *Vindicator*, Owen Sound *Comet*, *Stratford Beacon*. The Hamilton *Times* said if there were going to be any convention it ought to be of all the Liberals in British North America, not just the Canada West wing of them. "If the Reformers of the Maritime Provinces adopt one platform, those of the Province of Quebec another, and the Reformers of Ontario a third, how is it possible there can be unity of party action over the whole Dominion? A convention of the Reformers of Upper Canada alone cannot accomplish it." Hamilton *Times*, quoted in *Stratford Beacon*, June 14, 1867.

[78]Belleville *Hastings Chronicle*, July 3, 1867.

[79]*Sarnia Observer*, March 13, March 1, 1867.

opposed to Confederation—replied that Brown ought to have nothing to do with "the dirty crew in the coalition ship." It was a pirate anyway. If Howland and McDougall, or any other Reformers, wanted to be Tory let them go; Rymal hoped "the tories would keep them and make the most of them."[80] Brown made a long and argumentative speech. An unfriendly critic described the scene in a letter to Macdonald:

It would take pages to describe the proud strut of the conquering hero, as he appeared that night; sometimes pensively pacing the platform before the whole audience, now with arms akimbo, now with uplifted head & chest expanded by force of the attitude, while in his terrible mood you might see him rushing to & fro in more violent passion than Richard when he comes upon the stage exclaiming, "My kingdom for a horse." . . .[81]

In the end a resolution, sufficiently mild to raise only three dissenting votes, was passed condemning coalitions for ordinary administrative purposes. But the Reform Oshawa *Vindicator* (July 3) put the result fairly enough: "the convention of 1859 fought for a principle, while that of 1867 fought for power. . . . Anti-coalition may be the decision of the convention, but it was not the decision of the people." This was soon borne out, in the constituency of South Ontario at least; a "Coalition" supporter, T. N. Gibbs, defeated Brown by a vote of 1292–1223.[82]

The Conservatives were at first uneasy about Reform attempts to break the Coalition, but gradually the division in the Reform party appeared and the Conservatives rejoiced. Their policy was simple. They had merely to plead for an end to party spirit, preach the wickedness of partisan violence, and rally people behind a "Union" government.[83] This was the theme of James Beaty, the editor of the Toronto *Leader*, in his speech to the electors of East Toronto, "you have seen [it] working in the United States. . . . Party has done all that—party, which is more powerful over the mind of people than the love of the national interests of the country."[84] Said the Bleu *Journal de Québec*, on April 1, 1867, "C'est le temps ou jamais de se tendre la main, d'oublier les luttes du passé." This was the theme of government papers generally,

[80]*Globe*, June 29, 1867, report of June 27 and 28. Rymal's view of Confederation quoted *supra*, 37.

[81]Macdonald Papers, [Alex?] Cameron to Macdonald, June 29, 1867 (private and confidential).

[82]The official figures for the elections of 1867 are given in Canada, House of Commons, *Sessional Papers*, 1868, No. 41.

[83]The Barrie *Northern Advance*, Aug. 1, 1867, even quoted George Washington to this effect.

[84]Toronto *Leader*, Aug. 24, 1867.

as well it might be at the beginning of what many hoped would be a new era in politics. The elections results of August and September, 1867, showed how successful an appeal it was. The Coalition carried 67 out of the 82 Ontario seats in the new House of Commons.

There was another shaft in the ample quiver of the Conservatives: the Roman Catholic bishops of Canada East. Cartier and McGee had gone to Rome from England in March, 1867. Whether they obtained for Confederation the high sanction of the Vatican is not known. What is known is that in June, 1867, four of the five bishops of Canada East, Quebec, Rimouski, Trois Rivières, and St. Hyacinthe followed the New Brunswick and Nova Scotian example of the year before and issued pastoral letters enjoining acceptance, even support, of Confederation. These were read from French-Canadian pulpits on two successive Sundays in mid-June and published in large print in the Bleu papers. Even Liberal or Rouge papers, like the *True Witness* and *L'Ordre*, felt obliged to print them. How devastating they were for the Rouges can be judged from the words of C. F. Baillargeon (Administrator of the Archdiocese of Quebec). "What should reassure us, Dearly Beloved Brethren, is that the new form of Government just given has been prepared with care by men as well known for their patriotism as for the services which they have rendered to their country."[85] Thomas Cook, Bishop of Trois Rivières, criticized the violence of some who opposed Confederation:

. . . il est toujours répréhensible de manquer de modération. . . . Nous avons surtout regretté les efforts qui ont été faits pour jeter l'alarme parmi vous. . . . Oh! comme nous serions heureux, N[os] T[rès] C[hers] F[rères], si . . . nous voyions les hommes de tous les partis se rallier sincèrement et marcher comme un seul homme sous le même drapeau pour travailler . . . à promouvoir la prosperité et assurer le bonheur de notre commune patrie.[86]

This letter, said the Bleu *Canada* (June 19, 1867) devoutly, "est l'évène-ment du jour. C'est . . . une pièce historique dont nos annales garderont mémoire. . . ." Ignace Bourget, Bishop of Montreal, for the moment held his peace, but a month later, in July, his pastoral letter, a model of gentle resignation, was published in *L'Ordre*. Bourget made no attempt to praise Confederation. The Church had, he said, submitted to the Union of 1840 and "prêcha à ses enfants l'obéissance à l'autorité

[85]Montreal *True Witness*, June 28, 1867, pastoral letter of Baillargeon of June 12, 1867. Baillargeon had been co-adjutor bishop to P. F. Turgeon, Arch-bishop of Quebec (1850–67).
[86]*Le Journal des Trois Rivières*, 11 juin 1867; *Le Courrier de St. Hyacinthe*, 11 juin 1867, letter dated June 8, 1867.

constituée. Aujourd'hui, elle accepte sans réplique le Gouvernement fédéral parcequ'il émane de la même autorité."[87]

As the Toronto Convention split the Reformers, so the pastoral letters of the bishops split the Rouges. *L'Ordre* represented the moderate Rouges who were close to the Church. *L'Ordre*'s purpose was the increasingly difficult one of reconciling liberalism and catholicism and of demonstrating that such an alliance was possible.[88] A. A. Dorion through *Le Pays*, J. B. E. Dorion in *Le Défricheur*, others in *L'Union Nationale*, were committed, however, to the full limit of their liberal ideas. To follow a course the Church considered wrong was not desirable, but sometimes it was necessary. In 1867 *L'Ordre* stood by the clergy; the others remained in varying degrees in opposition to Confederation and the Church. *Le Pays* was the most militant and on September 21 pilloried the four bishops who had virtually ordered their flock to vote for candidates who supported Confederation. The bishops had praised Confederation as a work nearly perfect; they had exalted the patriotism of its supporters, but "ceux qui n'acceptent pas de bonne grâce le renversement de nos institutions ne peuvent conduire qu'à l'anarchie, *à la trahison.* . . . Et tout cela, pour quelle raison? Parce que c'est une LOI, adoptée pas les autorités constituées!!" The clergy had rights as citizens and as clergy. No quarrel could be taken with their right to their opinions as citizens, but, *Le Pays* continued, "Ce que nous censurons sans réserve . . . c'est l'intervention du prêtre dans un ordre politique, où il n'a rien à voir, comme prêtre." This proposition was condemned by *L'Ordre* the following day, September 22. It had warned as early as July that some papers were more zealous for party than for the church. Now its direst prophecies were fulfilled. But *Le Pays* was not to be halted by the expostulations of its milder colleague.

Ainsi nous avons eu le spectacle de quatre évêques, qui ont rompu avec toutes les traditions de l'épiscopat pour venir faire les petites affaires d'un parti, condamné au mépris des honnêtes gens. . . .

Eh, bien, nous offrons la tribut de notre admiration à la sagesse . . . qui a inspiré la zèle, digne des temps primitifs de l'église, aux apôtres qui ont dépensé tant d'onction et de malédictions de notre intègre parti *bleu.*[89]

Le Canada of Ottawa consigned *Le Pays* to perdition as "l'organe de

[87]Montreal *Ordre,* 29 juillet 1867. The reasons for Bishop Bourget's coolness to Confederation are partly suggested by his coolness to Cartier. This had arisen because of an ecclesiastical quarrel in which Cartier had espoused the cause of the Sulpicians against the bishop. R. Rumilly, *Histoire de la Province de Québec: I. George Etienne Cartier* (Montreal, n.d.), 47–8, 117.

[88]*Le Pays*' description, 30 nov. 1865.

[89]*Le Pays,* 24 sept. 1867, Cf. also *L'Union Nationale,* 3–10 oct. 1867.

l'Institut Canadien de Montréal. . . ."⁹⁰ It was in fact a quarrel that went beyond the immediate issue of Confederation. The end of it was not in sight in September, 1867; it was to continue with increasing bitterness in the years to come. Laurier's speech on political liberalism in Quebec City in 1877 was only the continuation of the position *Le Pays* had stated so uncompromisingly in 1867.

In the elections in 1867 Langevin, Cauchon, Galt, and J. H. Pope all won their seats by acclamation. Cartier carried Montreal East by 2431 to 2085, against Médéric Lanctot, one of the editors of *L'Union Nationale*. A. A. Dorion only won Hochelaga by 23 votes, and the Rouges and English Liberals between them took only twelve seats of the province's sixty-five. Dorion had good cause to be bitter against clerical interference.

In New Brunswick, Charles Fisher, J. H. Gray, and Charles Connell,⁹¹ were all in by acclamation. Tilley and Johnson won decisive victories in Saint John City and Northumberland County respectively. Though T. W. Anglin of the Saint John *Morning Freeman* was in Parliament for Gloucester, one of the North Shore French counties, and A. J. Smith won easily in Westmorland, only four, perhaps five, of the 15 members for New Brunswick could be classed as anti-Confederate. But in Nova Scotia the result was crushing. "The battle has been fought and lost," said the Confederate Halifax *Express* forlornly on September 20, "and never before, we believe, was defeat so thorough." Tupper managed to defeat William Annand in Cumberland County by 97 votes, but Archibald and Henry went down to defeat in Colchester and Antigonish, along with every other Confederate candidate in Nova Scotia. Jonathan McCully and William Miller, to whom the Confederate cause owed not a little, were, happily for them, Senators.

The Conservative government of Macdonald and Cartier, aided by Coalition Reformers from Ontario, Liberals from New Brunswick, and a lone Conservative from Nova Scotia, settled into office with the happy expectation that when the first Dominion parliament convened in November they would meet it with a comfortable majority of about 130–51. The opposition was hopelessly divided. Between aggressive Brown Reformers, angry Nova Scotians, and recalcitrant Rouges, what could be a common policy? Not even anti-Confederation. Howe was to call the new nationality a man on stilts, but for all that, and despite the difficulties Macdonald had in cabinet-making, the new government was proceeding smoothly. Already Macdonald was getting letters about jobs

⁹⁰*Le Canada*, 27 sept. 1867.
⁹¹Of stamp fame; see *supra*, 233.

and he knew well how to deal with those. By November the Parliamentary waters swarmed "with all sorts of loose fish, the ravenous sharks, ready to swallow the largest and fattest prizes, while the more modest minnows nibble at the crumbs left. . . ."[92] Soon enough would the Conservative power be consolidated.

Dorion was struck by the irony of it all. "C'est du vol de cette somme d'argent [$100,000]qu'est incontestablement sortie la confédération."[93] The Conservative party from so parlous a condition in June, 1864, was now in the swelling full tide of its strength. The new government was just the old one, a little larger and much stronger. The familiar faces of Canadian politics soon were dominant in the politics of the new Dominion. Howe himself said, "the centre of power and influence will always be in Canada. It can be nowhere else."[94] Macdonald took the Maritimes casually. They offered him more room for manœuvre but, once Confederation was passed, they were not in themselves a serious concern. It was Tilley who had to warn him in 1868 that Nova Scotia could not be allowed to go on as she was. Macdonald was first and last a Canadian who usually read politics in the light of Canadian experience. In Canada he had had a hard apprenticeship; because of it Conservatism rested not insecurely on those all too experienced shoulders. Confederation had not originally been Macdonald's idea, but no man made better use of it. For those who supported Union and Macdonald all was well: Tupper, McCully, Tilley, Cartier, Langevin, all duly received their rewards, political and personal. Brown, who had had the courage of his convictions in June, 1864, found in 1867 that he had been outmanœuvred once again. Macdonald had stolen the Coalition and with it the spoils of power.

[92]Newcastle (N.B.) *Union Advocate*, Nov. 28, 1867.
[93]*Le Pays*, 17 sept. 1867.
[94]J. Howe, *Confederation*, in Chisholm, *Speeches and Letters of Howe*, II, 433.

17. THE WEST

FOR CONFEDERATION THE AMERICAN PURCHASE of Alaska was a significant flanking movement. The Queen signed the British North America Act on March 29, 1867. In Washington that same night the American Secretary of State, William Seward, and the Russian Minister were up until the small hours completing the agreement for the purchase of Alaska. It was signed then and there—about 3 o'clock in the morning on March 30, 1867. It went to the Senate a few hours later. The remarkable concurrence between the signing of the British North America Act and the American purchase of Alaska, accidental though it was, underlined the essential connection between the two events. Alaska, said the London *Morning Herald* on April 2, was the American riposte to Confederation; Americans regarded the creation of a union to the north of them as a kind of grievance. It seemed to them an aggravating agglomeration of British colonies whose main purpose was to frustrate American ambitions. J. L. Chamberlain, the governor of Maine, said as much, at the opening of the Maine legislature in January, 1867. "If it [Confederation] is successful, the result cannot but be injurious to us. The friends of this country in the Provinces are earnestly opposing the scheme."[1] The Maine Senate protested that the monarchical consolidation to the north was a violation of the Monroe doctrine.[2] So did the United States Congress.[3] It is almost certain that objections such as these caused Lord Stanley, the British Foreign Secretary, to suggest, indeed to urge, the famous change of name from "Kingdom of Canada" to "Dominion of Canada."[4] Charles Sumner urged the Senate to ratify

[1]Montreal *Gazette*, Jan. 9, 1867; Halifax *Evening Express*, Jan. 11, 1867, and quoted from *Maine Legislative Documents*, 1867, 32. See Alice R. Stewart, "The State of Maine and Canadian Confederation," *Canadian Historical Review*, XXXIII, 2 (June, 1952), 148.

[2]Halifax *Evening Express*, March 18, 1867; Ottawa *Citizen*, April 2, 1867; also Stewart, "Maine and Confederation," 150.

[3]United States, 40th Congress, 1st Session, *Congressional Globe*, 392 (March 27, 1867).

[4]F.O. 5, Bruce to Stanley, March 2, 1867, raises this question.

the purchase of Alaska on the ground that it was a "visible step in the occupation of the whole North American continent."[5] The Senate did ratify the Treaty, by a vote of 37–2.[6] The American newspapers gave some indication of how Americans felt. Alaska may or may not have been the "sucked orange" that the New York *World* said it was, but the justification for its purchase was often the hope of gaining the territory between Alaska and the United States. The *World* consoled itself with the belief that Alaska was "an advancing step in that manifest destiny which is yet to give us British North America." The New York *Sun* agreed.[7] English papers recognized the same logic. The *Morning Post* said the reason for the American purchase was not the intrinsic value of Alaska but the hope of acquiring the territory south of it. Sir Frederick Bruce, the British Minister in Washington, wrote in exactly that vein to Lord Stanley.[8]

In British North America Alaska seemed a long way off and only a few were yet thinking on this scale. British Columbia had many of its own problems to think about; it did not so much resent the acquisition of Alaska as envy the energy displayed by its new owner.[9] British Columbia newspapers were regretful but philosophical. Great Britain could have had Alaska in the Crimean War, said the New Westminster *British Columbian* on April 27, but "the old sleepy British Lion" was not so disposed. The Americans however were mulcted of seven millions "for the doubtful luxury of an Arctic preserve in which to cool the ardour of their 'manifest destiny' aspirations. . . ."[10] J. S. Helmcken was less sanguine. Americans, he wrote later, were boasting that "they had sandwiched B. Columbia and could eat her up any time."[11] To Macdonald and many of the Conservatives in Canada the Alaskan purchase only underlined what a vast and unmanageable inconvenience the British west was. The Montreal *Gazette* (April 1, 1867) said the Americans were welcome to Alaska. The Toronto *Globe* kept up its usual lively

[5]The Senate considered the Alaska Treaty in Executive Session, and consequently there is no report of the debates. Sumner's speech was afterwards published. This version is from the *New York Tribune*, May 28, 1867.

[6]E. L. Pierce, *Memoirs and Letters of Charles Sumner* (4 vols., London, 1893), II, 325. The purchase was officially proclaimed by President Johnson, June 20, 1867.

[7]New York *World*, April 1, 1867; New York *Sun*, April 1, 1867.

[8]London *Morning Post*, April 2, 1867; F.O. 5, Bruce to Stanley, April 2, 1867.

[9]See *infra*, 320.

[10]New Westminster *British Columbian*, July 3, 1867.

[11]J. S. Helmcken, *Reminiscences*, V, 67–9, quoted in W. E. Ireland, "A Further Note to the Annexation Petition of 1869," *British Columbia Historical Quarterly*, V, (1941), 68.

trade in Northwest affairs without dwelling very much on Alaska. Galt however pointed out the danger suggested by the new American move. Alaska was the American answer to Confederation, said Galt at Lennox-ville on May 22. It could not be ignored. British North America could not allow the West to go by default. "If the United States desire to outflank us on the West, we must . . . lay our hand on British Columbia and the Pacific Ocean. This country cannot be surrounded by the United States—we are gone if we allow it. . . . We must have our back to the North."[12]

It needs here to be recalled that the northern border of the province of Canada, and that of the Dominion of Canada of 1867, was only the watershed of the rivers flowing into the Great Lakes and the St. Lawrence. The boundary line, along the height of land between the St. Lawrence and Hudson's Bay systems, was unmapped, untrodden, and largely unknown. This boundary began at the Labrador; from thence it ran westward, some two hundred miles to the north of Ottawa, one hundred miles to the north of Lake Huron, and it met the American border about a hundred miles west of Fort William. Thus the Canada of 1867 was curled up, so to speak, in the St. Lawrence valley and the Great Lakes. Northward and westward across this unsurveyed border lay the chartered territory of the Hudson's Bay Company, in its pos-session for nearly two hundred years. In 1867 there was not much danger about the territory north of the Canadian border, but westward the danger was real and it was steadily becoming worse. This was the territory that Galt was worried about. Its cession to the United States was from a British North American point of view unthinkable, but it was also possible. The American purchase of Alaska threw into sharp relief all the anachronisms in the British possessions in the West, not just the Hudson's Bay Company territory but the colony beyond the Rockies, British Columbia. On April 2 the London *Times* declared it quite possible that British Columbia might join the United States and contemplated the prospect without regret.

The Toronto *Globe* had long urged the cause of the Northwest (as it was called) in Canada. It kept up a continuous and often informed commentary on events in Red River and British Columbia. In its attitude to the West the *Globe* was the Canadian counterpart of the ambitious *New York Herald*. The theme is best illustrated perhaps in Brown's speech to the Reform Convention of 1859. "What true Canadian," Brown asked, "can witness the tide of immigration . . . into the vast territories of the North-West . . . who does not feel that to us rightfully

[12]Montreal *Gazette*, May 24, 1867; *Quebec Daily Mercury*, May 25, 1867.

belongs the right and the duty of carrying the blessings of civilization throughout those boundless regions, and making our own country the highway of traffic to the Pacific?"[13] In 1864 the *Globe* was still preaching this gospel though insofar as the Pacific colonies were concerned it had won few converts; Canada in 1864 was not very interested in the Pacific coast. The arduous trek of the Overlanders of 1862 to British Columbia was not the vanguard of further emigration; when the gold diggings fell off the reports coming back to Canada discouraged further enterprises of the kind.[14] It was interesting that the Reform *Stratford Beacon*, whose editor, William Buckingham, had spent two years in Red River setting up the *Nor'Wester*, was not altogether happy about the prospect of Canadian acquisition of the Northwest. Like Edward Ellice, Buckingham was concerned about having to assume "the responsibility and expense of governing an immense territory hundreds of miles from our western confines. . . ."[15]

It was for reasons such as this that the Conservative party had opposed all western adventures. In 1858 Edward Bulwer-Lytton, the Colonial Secretary, discussed the West with Cartier, Ross, and Galt, and report had it that he was ready to cede the whole region to Canada but that Cartier refused to consider it. This report was published in the *Nor'Wester*[16] and when it reached Toronto it made the *Globe* positively savage. The *Leader* was philosophical. Bulwer-Lytton, who might soon have "the miserably good luck of the man who won the elephant," could keep his prize: Canada ought to leave the Northwest well enough alone. Besides, the *Leader* continued, annexation of the Northwest by Canada would in any case be ridiculous: "a little reflection would serve to show that the great North-West can never be governed by a central government of which the seat would have to be on the banks of the Ottawa."[17] John A. Macdonald, for his part, wished heartily he could forget the West. "I would be quite willing, personally," he wrote Edward Watkin in 1865, "to leave that whole country a wilderness for the next half-century, but I fear if Englishmen do not go there, Yankees will. . . ."[18] Hence the brief session of the Canadian parliament in August, 1865,

[13]Toronto *Globe*, Nov. 16, 1859, reporting Brown's speech of Nov. 10. Also quoted in the Red River *Nor'Wester*, Feb. 14, 1860.

[14]Victoria *Weekly British Colonist*, Oct. 18, 1864, "Letter from the East," of Aug. 16.

[15]*Stratford Beacon*, Oct. 20, 1865.

[16]*Nor'Wester*, Dec. 28, 1859, quoting a letter from [A. K.] Isbister of London to Donald Gunn of Red River, reporting an interview of the former with Bulwer-Lytton. Also in W. L. Morton, *Manitoba, a History* (Toronto, 1957), 107.

[17]Toronto *Leader*, Jan. 27, 1860.

[18]Macdonald Papers, Macdonald to Watkin, March 27, 1865 (private).

ineffective though it was in other respects, brought to the attention of the Legislature the concern of the Canadian government with the Northwest. The Government had in fact proposed to Great Britain that all British territory east of the Rockies "should be made over to Canada— subject to such rights as the Hudson's Bay Company might be able to establish."[19]

Red River was in a dangerous position. Minnesota, just fifty miles south of Winnipeg, had been made a state in 1858; by 1865 it had a population of some 300,000.[20] Communication northward, down the Red River, had developed considerably. Equally significant was the establishment of new American territorial governments further west along the forty-ninth parallel, Dakota in 1861, Idaho in 1863, Montana in 1864. The Americans were moving toward the vacuum of the British West, and the Hudson's Bay Company, though recently re-organized, seemed less certain of its position than before. The settlements themselves, along the Red and the Assiniboine rivers, were humble enough, a straggling collection of river lot farms, managed desultorily by the Métis whose real interest was in the more exciting and more remunerative occupation of hunting buffalo. The total population of the colony, not including Indians, was only about 8,000. At the forks of the Red and the Assiniboine was what the *Nor'Wester* in 1865 grandiloquently called the "Town of Winnipeg"[21] a rather imposing name for a village that doubtless looked as stark as the little fortnightly itself. The population of "Winnipeg" consisted largely of traders and storekeepers, some Hudson's Bay officials, and a few articulate Canadians, two of whom ran the *Nor'Wester*.

The *Nor'Wester* had been founded in 1859, its type and press being hauled in laboriously from St. Paul on a Red River cart. After the adventures of its two owners in getting to Fort Garry,[22] they had some reason to publish the congratulations from leading Conservative and Reform papers in Canada West.[23] In 1860 James Ross was added to the staff and with Ross came a demand for a Crown colony for the British Northwest. Even proposals for a British North American federation were entertained.[24]

[19]Canada, Assembly, *Journals*, 1865 (2nd Session), 12 (Aug. 9).

[20]In 1860 Minnesota had a population of 172,023; in 1870, 439,706.

[21]The change from "Red River Settlement" was made between Aug. 3 and Sept. 22, 1865 on the *Nor'Wester*'s front page.

[22][Bone, Clark, Colquhoun, Mackay], *A History of Canadian Journalism* (Toronto, 1908), 27.

[23]*Nor'Wester*, Dec. 28, 1859. The papers included, the Toronto *Leader*, Hamilton *Spectator*, Conservative; Toronto *Globe*, *Perth Courier*, Reform.

[24]*Nor'Wester*, Feb. 14, 1860; Feb. 1, 1861.

But in the next years prospects for Red River grew less hopeful. A depression set in in 1861 and the departure of the Royal Canadian Rifles on August 6, 1861, to Canada added to the gloom. The creation of Dakota Territory south of the border in that year only pointed up the anomalies of the British Northwest. "Americanism," said the *Nor'Wester* on February 5, 1862, "has become rampant with all classes. . . . Even old Scotchmen and Englishmen . . . now join in the general outcry against the British connection. . . . What is the use—say they—of being connected with Britain. . . ? It is a mere name, an empty sound. . . ." And during the summers the whistle of the American river steamer from Georgetown, Minnesota, mocked the silence of the British government. American energy and enterprise, said the *Nor'Wester*, "throws into the shade the slow-going do-nothing Britons . . . . the people of Red River now say to England—Do something for us at once or forever give us up and let us shape our own destinies."[25] William Buckingham, comfortably re-established back in Canada, made the position of the people in the Northwest abundantly clear: "Shut out from the rest of the world by physical barriers . . . and apparently abandoned to their fate by their fellow-subjects, their chief intercourse has been with American citizens. To them they are indebted for whatever acts of kindness they may have received; and the Americans themselves are not insensible to the value of the country."[26]

As a result of meetings held in Red River in January, 1863, Sandford Fleming was appointed to present petitions to both the Canadian and the British governments on the future of Red River. At Quebec the Sandfield Macdonald government were not very enthusiastic, and their organ, the *Quebec Daily Mercury*, was absolutely opposed, to any attempt by Canada to acquire the Northwest. Fleming left for London on May 13, 1863.

That spring the telegraph brought word that the International Finance Company had bought out the Hudson's Bay Company and hopes were again raised in Red River; any change in the Company seemed for the better. And in the fall of 1863 came rumours from the east about a British North American union. "From Halifax to Huron," said the *Nor'Wester* with not a little exaggeration, "the question of the Confederation of the British North American provinces is being discussed. . . . The question, therefore, which we hear every day [is]—'Is there to be any change in the government of Red River?' "[27]

[25]*Ibid.*, May 28, 1862.   [26]*Stratford Beacon*, Jan. 25, 1867.
[27]*Nor'Wester*, Nov. 11, 1863. Some discussion of Confederation was engendered by the Intercolonial railway issue in 1863. *Supra*, 54–5, 66.

Apparently there was not. Fleming reported that his mission to Great Britain had not been very successful. T. F. Elliott, the deputy Under-Secretary for Colonies, was solicitous, even hopeful, but Newcastle, the Colonial Secretary, made it clear that the imperial government was reluctant to assume the cost of opening up the Northwest. As for the Canadian government, it was quite as reluctant as Newcastle was. Fleming added that he had hoped to come out to Red River, but his new duties on the Intercolonial survey postponed that indefinitely.[28]

A year later the Quebec Conference seemed to offer some further hope of a salutary change. The *Nor'Wester* deplored the fact that no delegates had been sent from the Northwest, that Red River was "voiceless at a most critical juncture."[29] But it was not altogether voiceless. James Ross, who until recently had been part owner of the *Nor'Wester*, was in Toronto at the reception for the Quebec Conference delegates and, in fact, replied to the toast to the Northwest. Ross extolled the Northwest's resources, doubled its population and pleaded for more immigration to it from Canada.[30] And in Red River Confederation still showed vitality in December, 1866, when at a public meeting in Fort Garry the following resolution was passed: "That in consequence of the great political changes which the British North American Provinces are now on the eve of undergoing . . . no further delay should take place in creating the Red River a Crown Colony, with the view to joining Confederation under conditions which may be submitted for the approval of the people. . . ."[31] Had Red River been created a Crown Colony many difficulties might have been obviated. The demand in 1864 for a role in the Quebec Conference, the suggestion in 1866 that conditions for joining Confederation should be submitted to the people, the reiterated demand from 1859 for the creation of a Crown Colony, all pointed to the difficulties that were to arise with the transfer of 1869, when no specific reference was made to the wishes or opinions of Red River people. William Buckingham warned in the *Stratford Beacon* (January 25, 1867) that Red River should be made a province. "The control of their local affairs, with a representation in the general Parliament of the country, would, we have reason to know, prove more satisfactory to them than 'annexation'

[28]Fleming's report is dated Oct. 29, 1863, and was published in the *Nor'-Wester*, Dec. 7, 1863.

[29]*Ibid.*, Oct. 17, 1864. Also quoted in the Saint John *Morning Telegraph*, Nov. 25, 1864.

[30]E. Whelan, *Union of the British Provinces* (Charlottetown, 1865), 183–5.

[31]*Nor'Wester*, Dec. 29, 1866, quoted by the New Westminster *British Columbian*, Feb. 27, 1867.

to Canada. . . ." It was significant that when rumours appeared in British Columbia in April, 1867, that the purchase of that colony was being contemplated by the United States, the objections of the *British Columbian* were not so much to becoming part of the United States (though that was objected to), but rather to the method proposed to effect the change. Being "sold like slaves" was not something to be tolerated.[32] This attitude was to be expected in a Crown Colony like British Columbia, but it was not unreasonable in a chartered one like Red River. Still, the helplessness of the country, its uncertain even precarious drift, may have persuaded Canadians that outright annexation to Canada would have been acceptable to Red River people. For helpless Red River certainly was. There was no more pathetic illustration than the question asked so often of the editor of the *Nor'Wester*: "Have you heard anything lately as to what is to be done with this country?"[33]

Westward across the thousand miles of prairie lay the western border of the Hudson's Bay Territory, the Rockies, and beyond was the colony of British Columbia, modest in everything but territory, ambitions, and debt. The great days of Barkerville and Soda Creek were passing; the miners had started the fruitless search for the mother lode in the vast upper reaches of the Columbia and the Fraser. The carefree life of placer mining was rapidly drawing to a close and with it the burgeoning prosperity was arrested, the climate of buoyant expansion suddenly changed, and the two Pacific colonies began to slip toward bankruptcy.

The mainland colony had been created in 1858 in an understandable burst of optimism by the Governor of Vancouver Island, James Douglas, who saw a colonial establishment on the mainland as essential prerequisite to what would shortly become a colony of 100,000 and one of the jewels of the Crown. The consequences of the Californian gold rush probably persuaded Douglas that similar ones would follow the British Columbia one. But as so often in Canadian history American analogies, if not altogether false, were misleading. New Westminster, the capital of the mainland colony, was in its name, its creation, and its decline the symbol of the hopes and the fortune of the colony itself. It was established on an impressive scale, but it was, when Governor

[32]*British Columbian*, April 27, 1867. Note that in November, 1867, a resolution was put forward in the American House of Representatives for the "purchase and annexation" of British Columbia. It was referred to committee and not reported out. United States, 40th Congress, 1st Session, *Congressional Globe*, 813 (Nov. 30, 1867).

[33]*Nor'Wester*, Feb. 6, 1865.

Frederick Seymour saw it in 1864, only the measure of how far short of realization were the hopes under which it had been founded. Victoria called New Westminster "the City of Stumps," and Victoria was prejudiced no doubt;[34] but as Seymour—who was disposed to be sympathetic to British Columbia—described New Westminster, the Victoria epithet was not without truth. "I had not seen, even in the West Indies," he wrote Cardwell, "so melancholy a picture of disappointed hopes as New Westminster presented on my arrival." Thousands of trees had been cut down to prepare the way for the great capital that would arise on the banks of the Fraser, but the blight came early. Houses were soon left untenanted; the largest hotel was to let; "decay appeared on all sides, and the stumps and logs of the trees blocked up most of the streets. Westminster appeared, to use the miner's expression, 'played out.' "[35] The whole mainland colony in 1865 had a settled population of only 5,000; in addition there were some 3,000 miners and an estimated 40,000 Indians, the administration of both of which was both troublesome and expensive.

Vancouver Island, that "other Eden," the Prince Edward Island of the west coast, was like her eastern counterpart, contemptuous of the mainland. The population of Vancouver Island was in 1865 about 7,000, of whom, as in British Columbia, about 75 per cent were male. Victoria, the capital, had perhaps a total of 1,500 and attained to the rough dignity of its nineteen years of existence, which New Westminster could hardly expect to emulate. Indeed, in the winter those who could came over from New Westminster to enjoy what Seymour called "the good living, the theatre, the fiddling, dancing and tippling of Victoria."[36] With its free port and its position at the front door of both colonies, Victoria had monopolized the business of both, a state of affairs mightily resented in New Westminster. But so precarious was Victoria's prosperity that even the possibility of New Westminster becoming an important commercial centre created consternation in Victoria. If the price of town lots in New Westminster rose, those in Victoria fell.[37] Not a little of the energy in both places was vented in futile but heated arguments about the virtues or defects of navigation to Victoria or New Westminster. Every ship that ran aground at

[34]Victoria *Weekly British Colonist*, Aug. 14, 1866.
[35]C.O. 60, Seymour to Cardwell, March 21, 1865. This despatch was later printed for Parliament, and by a series of accidents was ultimately tabled, rather to Seymour's discomfiture, in the Vancouver Island Assembly. It was published in the *Weekly British Colonist*, Aug. 14, 1866.
[36]C.O. 60, Seymour to Cardwell, April 29, 1865.
[37]*Ibid.*

the entrance to Victoria was the occasion for smiles in New Westminster, and if a ship grounded in the entrance to the Fraser it caused
happy chuckles in Victoria.

The decline of prosperity was felt in Victoria in proportion to her
commercial dominance. The year 1865 opened on a doleful note.
"Never since Vancouver Island has had an existence as a Colony have
its inhabitants experienced a greater depression than is now felt."[38]
One by one the newspapers died. The Victoria *Times* and *Evening
Express* fell in 1865; in 1866 the able Victoria *Daily Chronicle* succumbed and was amalgamated with its old arch enemy, the *British
Colonist*. A new paper in 1866, the *Evening Telegraph*, lasted six
months, then it too went to its grave. By 1867 all that was left was the
British Colonist and the annexationist *Morning News*, and the latter
went by the board in that year.

The sovereign remedy suggested in Victoria for the manifold troubles
was union with the mainland colony. Amor De Cosmos—once plain
William Smith of Windsor, Nova Scotia—the mercurial former editor
of the *British Colonist*, proposed unconditional union with British
Columbia. This he moved in the Island Assembly, and on January 27,
1865, the resolution passed by a vote of 8–4 for "immediate union of
this colony with British Columbia under such Constitution as Her
Majesty's Government may be pleased to grant."[39] Such a plea for
union unaccompanied by any conditions whatsoever seemed to the
Victoria *Chronicle* (which reflected Dr. Helmcken, the Speaker)
opposed to the best interests of Victoria.[40] But when De Cosmos and
C. B. Young, in a form of parliamentary duel, both resigned their seats
to test public opinion, Young was defeated, and Leonard McClure,
one of the editors of the *Colonist* and a supporter of union, was elected.
Governor Kennedy of Vancouver Island took the view that union of the
two colonies was absolutely essential.[41]

In New Westminster this self-immolation by the Island met with
much amusement and no sympathy. The *North Pacific Times* heaped
sarcasm on the proposal. "Eight members of the Vancouver Island
Legislature have settled the question of Union finally, and the fifteen
or twenty thousand ciphers composing the populations of the two
Colonies, are called upon by the Victoria press to render a cheerful
acquiescence to the decision of the mighty eight."[42] New Westminster

[38]Victoria *Weekly Chronicle*, Jan. 3, 1865.
[39]C.O. 305, Kennedy to Cardwell, March 21, 1865 (separate) (No. 14.)
[40]Victoria *Weekly Chronicle*, Jan. 24, 1865.
[41]C.O. 305, Kennedy to Cardwell, March 21, 1865 (separate) (No. 16.)
[42]New Westminster *North Pacific Times*, Feb. 1, 1865.

feared the loss of the capital; besides there was considerable distaste for the activities of Victoria in the seven years since British Columbia had been a colony. The hopes for union that filled the Vancouver Island press met with a chilling reception from the *British Columbian* (March 2, 1865). "The most appropriate reply to their long leaders and great swelling words may, after all, be given in four plain words: mind your own business." Governor Seymour alleged it would be impossible to govern the Cariboo from Victoria.[43]

To such considerations the Colonial Office was less than sympathetic. Blackwood minuted, "If Gov. S. has no stronger reasons to advance against joining the 2 colonies than these that he has advanced in his despatches I must confess that I, for one, see nothing but harm in postponing the Event."[44] British Columbia was not to be allowed to hinder union. Unlike Vancouver Island it did not have the full apparatus of representative institutions. It had only a Legislative Council, consisting of eight members nominated by the Crown and seven elected by the people. It could be persuaded and it was. Seymour left for England on September 7, 1865, and was gone for a year. In that time he was married and was successfully urged to accept another marriage—that of British Columbia and Vancouver Island—by Cardwell, and a despatch embodying Seymour's views was duly forwarded, not inappropriately, from Rue de la Paix, Paris.[45] The bill making the two colonies one passed the British Parliament in July, 1866.

In the meantime the Vancouver Island legislature had decided to suggest conditions after all, and amongst other things it recommended in December, 1865, the grant of responsible government. On the confidential despatch accompanying this request T. F. Elliott, the deputy Under-Secretary for Colonies, sensibly minuted that responsible government in "a little Community like Vancouver [Island] would be a mockery and a scramble, it seems to me."[46] The little community was now, on the eve of union, in parlous condition. On May 31, 1866, its overdraft in the Bank of British North America stood at $79,567 (on which it was paying 12 per cent interest) and the bank positively refused further advances unless authorized by the London directors.[47] "Nothing

[43]C.O. 60, Seymour to Cardwell, April 29, 1865. Governor Kennedy of Vancouver Island replied to this argument, C.O. 305, Kennedy to Cardwell, Sept. 7, 1865 (private).

[44]Minute of Oct. 23, 1865 on Kennedy to Cardwell, Sept. 7, 1865 (private).

[45]C.O. 60, Seymour to Cardwell, Feb. 17, 1866. This despatch was confidentially printed for Parliament but by accident was made public and was published widely in British Columbia.

[46]C.O. 305, Kennedy to Cardwell, Dec. 16, 1865 (confidential), Minute of Elliott, Feb. 14, 1866.   [47]*Ibid.*, June 1, 1866, enclosure.

can be worse," minuted Elliott, "than this Assembly's measure of borrowing money at 12 per cent to meet public services for which it neglects to provide the ways and means. From beginning to end the Assembly of Vancouver Island has shown its total unfitness for its duties. But happily its existence is rapidly drawing to an end."[48] On November 19, 1866, the union of Vancouver Island and British Columbia was officially proclaimed in Victoria and the Legislature of Vancouver Island came to its inglorious conclusion. Victoria lost her free port and her only compensation was the privilege of sending part of eight Island members to the twenty-three member Legislative Council of British Columbia. Even the capital went to New Westminster, though this was temporary. The *British Colonist* lamented on August 14, 1866, that the Act would "close the doors of our warehouses for ever. . . ." Other Victorians, who were less changeable than the *Colonist*, were philosophical or rude, according to their lights. But with or without union things could hardly be worse. As the *British Columbian* had remarked (August 4, 1866), "Beggars can't be choosers."

But British Columbia was not long reaching beggary itself. Within six months of the union it too was on the edge of bankruptcy. The funded debt of the colony was about $1.5 millions added to which was a current loan by the Bank of British Columbia of $280,000, the interest rate apparently going up with the amount. The Governor himself was paying 18 per cent for the privilege of his overdraft. By April 1, 1867, the principal public officers had been without salary for four months.[49] The Governor pleaded for help from London: "Can no assistance of any kind be furnished to us?"[50] In November, 1867, he was forced to cable for an emergency grant of £50,000.[51] Houses in New Westminster were being boarded up, and people were returning to San Francisco. British Columbia, with wonderful resources, with abundant supplies of land, timber, fish, was, in the depression after 1865, the classic example of the land corrupted by gold. The gold brought little but transient miners out for the quickest returns; most of them were not prepared to work in the ordinary way. As Seymour said, gold had "turned people's heads." Perhaps the greatest difficulty of all was British Columbia's "own belief in the uncertainty of its political future."[52]

It was not easy to discern what that future would be. Changes in

[48]C.O. 305, Kennedy to Cardwell, July 12, 1866, Minute of Elliott.
[49]C.O. 60, Seymour to Carnarvon, April 17, 1867 (secret).
[50]C.O. 60, Seymour to Buckingham and Chandos, Sept. 25, 1867 (secret).
[51]C.O. 60, Seymour to Buckingham and Chandos, Nov. 28, 1867 (telegram).
[52]C.O. 60, Seymour to Buckingham and Chandos, March 17, 1868 (separate).

communication had ambivalent effects. The telegraph with Washington territory had been opened in April, 1865, just in time to bring New Westminster the news of Lincoln's assassination. Britain on the other hand was two month's distance by mail. Perhaps that was the reason when the Atlantic cable was landed at Heart's Content, Newfoundland on July 28, 1866, it occasioned a public celebration in Victoria.[53] British Columbia was a British colony, but it was becoming like Oregon before the Treaty of 1846: full of Americans, envious of American power and energy, ready to fall into the lap of the United States. For British subjects who had been in the colony for more than a few years British and American were distinctions of decreasing significance. For Dr. Helmcken and Dr. Tolmie, two of the most respected men in the Island, who had been in the country for thirty years, national distinctions had ceased to have any meaning. Dr. Helmcken, in particular, the son-in-law of James Douglas and the Speaker of the old Island Assembly, revealed in his speeches and in the newspaper that he influenced a realism unclouded by nationalism. "Nationalty," he had said in the Assembly, "was a matter of hearts and homes. . . ."[54] The Victoria *Chronicle*, reporting the Canadian reaction to the British defence debate of 1865 on May 9, said that the cost of the British connection seemed to come pretty high. "This is a utilitarian age," it warned, "and even the finest sentiments frequently find themselves put in the stock market." For those who had long been on the west coast the American connection was becoming one of sentiment; for those newly arrived it was soon one of hard cash. And more: "The literature of Boston and New York is on every shelf, the tools and implements of Connecticut, on every farm and in every workshop and the politics of Washington on every tongue. Perhaps these things are not Americanizing the British Colonies and paving the way for annexation, but we are not so sure of it."[55] The Fourth of July was as much a holiday as the Queen's Birthday; shops were closed and fireworks set off.[56] Annexation was not the terrible word in British Columbia that it was in the east. It seemed to not a few to represent comfort and solace in a bewildering and unfriendly world. The visit of Schuyler Colfax, the Speaker of the American House of Representatives, in July, 1865, seemed a symbol of what might come to pass.[57] The *Morning*

[53]Victoria *Weekly British Colonist*, Aug. 7, 1866.
[54]Victoria *Daily British Colonist*, Dec. 16, 1865, reporting debates of Dec. 15.
[55]Victoria *Weekly Chronicle*, May 2, 1865.
[56]*Weekly British Colonist*, July 11, 1865.
[57]In 1866 Schuyler Colfax gave some remarkable speeches in support of the Fenians. He condemned President Johnson for the neutrality proclamation of

News in Victoria regularly urged annexation, and Leonard McClure, once an editor with the *Colonist,* became converted to annexation and founded a new journal, the *Evening Telegraph,* to urge it. The Victoria Theatre was the scene, on September 29, 1866, of a tumultuous meeting at which resolutions were passed in favour of annexation to the United States.[58] British Columbians sighed for a change; even annexation was better than continuing in a state of poverty and wretchedness. By 1867 the loyal *British Colonist* had to admit it.

In writing thus, we know we speak the mind of nine out of every ten men in the Colony—men who after struggling for years to awaken the Home Government to a sense of the wrongs under the weight of which we are staggering, have at last sat down in despair at the gloomy prospects before them. . . . The people—disgusted, disheartened and all but ruined —are loud in their expression of a preference for the stars and stripes. The sentiment is heard on every street corner—at the theatre—in the saloons . . . and the feeling is growing and spreading daily.[59]

Even C. B. Adderley, the Parliamentary Under-Secretary for Colonies, admitted in 1867 that "It seems to me impossible that we should long hold B.C. from its natural annexation."[60] There was solid sense in the remarks of J. S. Helmcken in 1870. "The United States hem us in on every side; it is the Nation by which we exist . . . which has made this Colony what it is. . . ."[61] This was not treason, it was truth. The British Columbians wanted, in short, a country. They wanted to be rescued from the colonial isolation in which they lived not with economic palliatives but by the solid hope of a better and more ample future, by a sense of national dignity. Something more tangible and less remote was going to be needed than the cool and disdainful shrugs of shoulders that Seymour received from the Duke of Buckingham and Chandos, something more broadminded than the imposition by the British Treasury of £10,700 upon British Columbia to pay for the useless

---

June 6 and for the stationing of the American army on the border, but for which, he said, "the green flag would now be waving all over Canada." *New York Herald,* Aug. 16, 1866.

[58]Victoria *Weekly British Colonist,* Oct. 2, 1866. See also D. F. Warner, *The Idea of Continental Union* (Kentucky, 1960), 129–31.

[59]*Weekly British Colonist,* April 30, 1867.

[60]He added however, "Still we should give and keep open for Canada every chance and if possible get Seymour to bridge over the present difficulties till we see what Canada may do." C.O. 60, Seymour to Buckingham and Chandos, July 15, 1867, Minute of Sept. 16. Also quoted in W. E. Ireland, "Pre-Confederation Defence Problems of the Pacific Colonies," Canadian Historical Association, *Report,* 1941, 53.

[61]British Columbia, Legislative Council, *Debates on Confederation,* 1870, 8 (March 9).

barracks in New Westminster that had been left behind by the Royal Engineers.

The reasons that argued change argued Confederation. In the east "annexation or Confederation" was a political shibboleth: in British Columbia it was a vital alternative. Confederation discussion had begun remarkably early in some quarters, notably in the *British Colonist*. The movements of eastern politics in 1864 the *Colonist* had noted at once and it hailed Confederation as the beginning of "the regeneration of the hitherto apron-stringed colonists. With a federation of colonies from one ocean to the other, what limits can be placed to our material greatness, and what to our political aspirations?"[62] A British American union was essential to collect and concentrate colonial energies and initiative. "We shall ultimately send ambassadors and consuls to every part of the world."[63] By 1867 the *Colonist* had talked Confederation long enough so that, however unrealistic it may have appeared, it was not new. There was in addition support from papers in New Westminster although they were more cautious. In any case by the spring of 1867 the depression was so bad that a resolution for Confederation in the Legislative Council could hardly do any harm and might do some good. It was in this mood of quiet, even morose, desperation that the British Columbia Legislative Council on March 18, 1867, passed unanimously a resolution for Confederation: "that his Excellency . . . take such steps without delay as may be deemed by him most desirable to ensure the admission of British Columbia into the Confederacy on fair and equitable terms. . . ."[64] Two enthusiasts, F. J. Barnard and Amor De Cosmos, promptly telegraphed the happy news to the Toronto *Globe*;[65] Seymour cabled Carnarvon asking that provision be made in the British North America bill for ultimate admission of British Columbia;[66] but, as Seymour said later, the Resolution was "the expression of a despondent community longing for a change."[67]

The trouble with De Cosmos and his advocacy of Confederation was that he was half prophet, half opportunist. He saw visions of the future and wanted to translate them into reality. He threw out ideas and projects with alarming profuseness and centrifugal velocity; and he

62Victoria *Weekly British Colonist*, Aug. 16, 1864.
63*Ibid.*, Aug. 30, 1864.
64British Columbia, Legislative Council, *Journals*, 1867, 50.
65Toronto *Globe*, March 20, 1867.
66C.O. 60, Seymour to Carnarvon, March 11, 1867 (telegram). Provision had already been made in Section 146.
67*Ibid.*, Seymour to Buckingham and Chandos, Sept. 24, 1867 (separate).

was thought by some to be only a political adventurer. He joined a vivid imagination to a consuming ambition; he would be orator, statesman, economist, all at once. He was devoted to Confederation, but he never realized that reckless advocacy was as perilous to a cause as relentless opposition.

Even after De Cosmos' retirement as editor,[68] the Victoria *Colonist* shared much of his enthusiasm for Confederation and some of his weaknesses. The *Colonist* had an unlovely reputation among other papers as a "political weathercock" and its editor as "General Bombastes";[69] and while such remarks can be ascribed to the ordinary canons of newspaper invective, they were not without justification. One ebullient editorial on the prospects of immediate union with Canada concluded with, "Hurrah for Confederation and the Overland Railway!"[70] The soberer pen of John Robson of the New Westminster *British Columbian* made the point, May 29, 1867: "The unquestionable advantages of Confederation are not . . . hastened a single day by the manufacture of sensational articles about imaginary despatches."

Nor was De Cosmos deterred by the difficulties in the way of Confederation. He came east and spoke with unimpaired enthusiasm at the Reform Convention in Toronto in June, 1867. British Columbia, he said, could and should come into Confederation now. "If the people of the United States can govern a territory on the Pacific Ocean, why cannot four millions of British Americans do the same thing?"[71] The theme was re-echoed at an enthusiastic Confederation back in Victoria in January, 1868, and at the Yale "Convention" in September. But it was easier said than done, even with the proposed wagon road that De Cosmos added to his conditions. More realistic British Columbians saw very well the difficulties in the way of realizing Confederation. J. S. Helmcken noted the "poverty of Canada" and its "distance from British Columbia"; Confederation seemed to him "like another leap in the dark. . . ."[72] As a critic wrote to the Victoria *Colonist*, "To give consent now for Confederation, and to be extatic [sic] over the forthcoming glories of it, to hear the busy tramp of men marching from Canada westward, filling up the tremendous chasm between them

[68]De Cosmos gave up the editorship and sold the paper in October, 1863, to a group largely composed of the staff. See W. N. Sage, "Amor De Cosmos, Journalist and Politician," *British Columbia Historical Quarterly*, VIII, 1944, 189–212.
[69]New Westminster *British Columbian*, June 15, 1867; Victoria *Weekly Chronicle*, Feb. 14, 1865.
[70]Victoria *Weekly British Colonist*, May 28, 1867.
[71]Toronto *Globe*, July 1, 1867, reporting De Cosmos speech of June 28.
[72]Helmcken, *Reminiscences*, V, 67–9, in Ireland, "A Further Note on the Annexation Petition of 1869," 68.

and us with towns and villages . . . is what I should denominate as a
'Fool's Paradise.' "[73] There was no really practical benefit that could
result to either party by the immediate admission of British Columbia,
said John Robson's *British Columbian*. Robson's emphasis was on the
necessity of making haste slowly. There had to be consideration of
terms. The Hudsons' Bay Company territory had to be dealt with. "We
must not 'throw ourselves away' while smarting under the effects of
a temporary depression."[74] There seemed to be no point in establishing
union merely to send delegates to Ottawa and receive in exchange a
Canadian ministerial appointee as governor. That would not satisfy
British Columbia.[75]

But something had to be done. The American purchase of Alaska
ultimately brought home all the basic weaknesses of British Columbia
to British Columbians themselves. The sovereign might of the republic
became by 1868 plainly evident: troops were being sent to Alaska,
Sitka was being opened up, and the vitality of the United States seemed
an unpleasant contrast with the supineness of the British government.
When the cession of Alaska was first announced the American merchants and tavern keepers hung out their American flags in triumph,
the flags seemed to mock British Columbians with the uncertainty of
their own future. They did not care much about Alaska, but they felt
keenly the power that its new owner possessed and his willingness to
do something positive and energetic about taking possession of it.
There was one hope of keeping British Columbia British: "Give the
colonist a country and a nation of which to be proud. . . ."[76] That
was a tall order, but the new government of the Dominion of Canada
was to set about it with commendable determination.

And through the new Dominion of Canada there was a stir of ambition about the West. The Halifax *British Colonist* was optimistic.[77] Even
Whelan in Charlottetown found this hope consoling in the midst of the
depressing determination of the people of Prince Edward Island "to
shut their eyes to whatever advantages Confederation may possess."[78]
In 1868 Cartier and McDougall were sent to London to negotiate the
Hudson's Bay Company transfer, and in the short time of four years
from July, 1867, both Rupert's Land and British Columbia were
included in Confederation. But the legal form was only a shell. It

[73]Victoria *Weekly British Colonist*, Aug. 20, 1867, Letter II of "Publicola."
[74]*British Columbian*, June 1, 1867.
[75]C.O. 60, Seymour to Buckingham and Chandos, Sept. 24, 1867 (separate).
[76]Victoria *Weekly Chronicle*, May 2, 1865.
[77]Halifax *British Colonist*, July 14, 1867.
[78]Charlottetown *Examiner*, July 29, 1867; June 17, 1867.

was true that one of the first results of Confederation would be, as the *British Columbian* had predicted on October 10, 1866, that "the iron horse shall traverse the continent, from Halifax to New Westminster"; but it was 1885 before that was done. Dr. Helmcken in his tough, unsentimental fashion spoke the truth:

The people of this Colony have, generally speaking, no love for Canada; they have but little sentimentality, and care little about the distinctions between the form of Government of Canada and the United States. Therefore no union on account of love need be looked for. The only bond of union outside of force—and force the Dominion has not—will be the material advantage of the country and pecuniary benefit of the inhabitants. Love for Canada has to be acquired by the prosperity of the country, and from our children.[79]

It could hardly be otherwise. Confederation in the east rested upon a sense of collective identity, which, however rudimentary, managed to survive and, slowly, even to grow; but westward from Lake Superior the old complex pattern of the fur trade had long since gone. The explorations of Mackenzie and Fraser and Thompson, the concomitant of the North West Company's lust for furs and empire, were only memories, and the domination of Montreal had been almost forgotten. The word "Canadian" in the west had to develop new associations after half a century of neglect. Given railways, men might be drawn away from the narrow identities around which swung tight old loyalties. Railways were to expand horizons, and in so doing change society, its orientation and its allegiances, slowly but finally. As they effected the gradual destruction of village independence and the extension of metropolitan influences, so also would they make possible more comprehensive political combinations. The Canadian Pacific Railway was to become the symbol of the new meaning of Canadian, even as the long and arduous canoe route, four thousand miles from Fort McLeod to Montreal, was the symbol of the old.

[79]British Columbia, Legislative Council, *Debates on Confederation*, 1870, 11 (March 9).

18. CONCLUSION

MONDAY, JULY 1, 1867, dawned clear and warm. "With the first dawn of this gladsome midsummer morn," began the Toronto *Globe*, "we hail this birthday of a new nationality. A united British America . . . takes its place among the nations of the world." "From Halifax to Sarnia," said the *New Brunswick Reporter* (July 5) from Fredericton, "we are one people,—one in laws, one in government, one in interests." Summerside, Prince Edward Island, offered its congratulations to the new Dominion thus "launched upon the sea of history; and though we do not admire the build of the craft, we cannot find in our heart to wish her other than a prosperous voyage." Even in Charlottetown some bunting appeared, as if to grace an occasion that most Islanders were glad to ignore.[1] And it was an occasion. The Toronto *Leader* rested from its quarrels with the *Globe* to say, "This is the most important day for the Provinces of British North America on which the sun has yet risen . . . our public men . . . [must] rise to the height of our new destiny. . . ." "Our new destiny" was the theme of many newspapers from Halifax to Sarnia, and even in Newfoundland and British Columbia the "memorable day for British North America" did not pass unnoticed.[2] Reports from the west coast had arrived of the unanimous resolution for Confederation; there was a swelling nationalism in eastern speeches and public demonstrations. The Northwest would soon belong, all of it, to the Dominion of Canada. The bright plumage of parade uniforms; the booming of guns in Halifax, Fredericton, Quebec, Toronto, and Ottawa; the swelling sails of the yachts in Halifax harbour and Toronto Bay; the brilliant summer day itself: who could fail to read the national barometer "set fair?"

There were some who failed to do so. In Fredericton on July 3 the *Head Quarters* said sombrely, "The future may be full of hope . . . but it is useless to shut one's eyes to the fact that in New Brunswick there

[1]*Summerside Progress*, July 1, 1867; Charlottetown *Herald*, July 3, 1867.
[2]Victoria *Weekly British Colonist*, July 2, 1867.

is discontent and indignation smouldering in many places, while in Nova Scotia these feelings are afire and in action." There was black *crêpe* in Yarmouth and Halifax; on July 1 the *Acadian Recorder* came out in black, and the Halifax *Morning Chronicle* published a bitter epitaph. "Here, alas!" said the *Examiner* in Charlottetown that same day, "the great public of Prince Edward Island treat the thing with feelings akin to contempt." The very next day, July 2, plain George Cartier was sitting down to write his angry letter to Lord Monck on the K. missing from his C.B.[3] The history of British North America between 1864 and 1867 can be written as a paean of triumphant nationality; it can also be written as a bitter comment on the machinations of Canadians and the ruthlessness of Downing Street. More than one bitter essay came from Nova Scotia and New Brunswick criticizing the selfishness of the Canadians. As the London *Times* had remarked, however, "Half the useful things that are done in the world are done from selfish motives under the cover of larger designs."[4] Whether "useful" could be applied to Confederation was a matter of debate; the British certainly thought so. The ruthlessness of Downing Street was the natural expression of the current climate of British colonial policy. Cardwell used to say it was necessary to look out of the window: this meant reading the newspapers. The editorials in the *Times* were not only a gloss on the policy of the Colonial Office but sometimes a forecast of it. Surveying the scene in New Brunswick on April 13, 1865, the *Times* to its comment on the uses of selfishness added that Confederation was so desirable that "the House of Commons ought to have the courage, if necessary, to enforce it upon the Colonies."

Confederation was not, except in Canada West, what is usually referred to as a popular movement. It was imposed on British North America by ingenuity, luck, courage, and sheer force; its story has often been told in terms of political coalitions and colonial office despatches. That was the way it happened. But Confederation had a vital public existence; as one correspondent wrote in July, 1864, "During a thirty years' residence in Canada I have never seen a period like the present."[5] The crowds at the Temperance Hall meetings in Halifax, at the Mechanics Institute in Saint John, those who welcomed the Quebec Conference to Toronto with bands and torches, who filled more humble meetings in Newcastle to hear Peter Mitchell or Market Square in

[3]Cartier to Monck, July 2, 1867, in Canada, *Sessional Papers*, 1868, No. 64.
[4]London *Times*, April 13, 1865.
[5]Victoria *Weekly British Colonist*, Aug. 23, 1864, "Canada Letter," dated July 13, 1864.

Charlottetown to listen to Edward Palmer, who waited in their thousands on the wharf in Saint John of a fine August evening to see a hundred Canadians: Confederation had a popular side besides a parliamentary one, and the newspapers tell its history.

Like the Victorians themselves, the newspapers saw politics as the central focus of society. Politics was life itself, demanding loyalties, commanding convictions. All too often it roused passion and exalted prejudice. The issues of the day usually carried with them a lively and sensitive public. The public supported many newspapers, and their very existence shows the strength and the variety of political opinion. The continuous, almost exhaustive, treatment that Confederation received in the newspapers reflected, however imperfectly, popular interest in the subject. This very imperfection suggests the main danger of the newspapers as sources of history. The newspapers of St. John's and Halifax were not an accurate guide to opinion in the two cities, still less to opinion in the provinces as a whole. Newspapers informed, but they also advocated. Their duty as they saw it was not so much to please as to encourage: to point issues, to shape policies, to forward causes. Confederation was in these circumstances a natural preoccupation. It was a great, even a challenging issue; it aroused all the natural instincts of editors to instruct, to illustrate, to promote. Here, too, the newspapers should be used with caution. They were often ready to alter their constitutional principles to suit their politics. The Toronto *Globe* was prepared to accept before July, 1867, a municipal relationship between the local and the federal government; afterward it found the local government a useful lever against the wickedness of the party in power in Ottawa. Newspapers did not always follow the ideas they expressed. Ideas were weapons, not axioms. Macdonald was especially adept at offering timely suggestions to his newspaper friends, and his request to the Hamilton *Spectator* in 1854 for a particularly steep and outrageous political turn elicited an all too characteristic reply: "It's a damned sharp curve, but I think we can take it."[6]

For all their weaknesses, however, the newspapers provide a broad study in the origins and character of the Canadian constitution. In Nova Scotia and in English Canada there is revealed, again and again, the desire for legislative union. Even after Confederation, the Attorney General of Nova Scotia still spoke of the desirability of "an incorporation of the colonies into each other . . . to be of one flesh and bone, having one head and one heart," and he summed up in a sentence the

6[Bone, Clark, Colquhoun, Mackay], *A History of Canadian Journalism* (Toronto, 1908), 29.

popular prejudice against federation: "whatever renders a legislative union impossible must make a federal union fatal. . . ."[7] At the same time the newspapers show how essential federal union was to French Canadians, Prince Edward Islanders, and some New Brunswickers. Though the fundamentally empirical character of Confederation was dictated largely by the temper of the men who shaped it and by the immediate circumstances that gave rise to it, the newspaper suggestions for Confederation, and comments upon it, reveal why it came to be what it was.

The empirical method need not have prevented a comprehensive and systematic constitution, but it made it distinctly less likely. As one New Brunswicker complained, "the scheme was never sketched by one master mind. . . ."[8] Similar comments were made by Christopher Dunkin and others. But such a constitution was the last thing Macdonald wanted. The Quebec Resolutions and their embodiment in the British North America Act he did not consider more than a blueprint, the details and the working of which would be left to be decided in the course of practical experience. The justification for empiricism in Macdonald's view was this need for elasticity. And since he personally anticipated the atrophy of the provincial system, he doubtless hoped ultimately to shake out the federal devices altogether. His memorandum on disallowance in June, 1868, suggests this same policy.[9] How much he had reason to hope was forcibly illustrated by the recurrence of the theme of legislative union in the newspapers. But the pull of old provinces and the North American environment was too strong even for Macdonald's administration of the British North America Act. How soon the new provincial identities would begin to crystallize was seen in the Toronto *Globe* in July, 1867. Party politics tended to make the local governments a weapon against the central government; this was so in Nova Scotia, and if Brown had his way it would be so in Ontario. Party established the nucleus about which would soon cluster the old provincial loyalties.

What was sought by the Quebec Conference and later by the Colonial

[7]M. I. Wilkins, *Confederation Examined in the Light of Reason and Common Sense and the British North America Act Shown to be Unconstitutional* (Halifax, 1867), 8–9.

[8]London *Times*, April 5, 1865, letter from "Union" in New Brunswick, dated March 13, 1865.

[9]". . . the General Government will be called upon to consider the propriety of allowance or disallowance of Provincial Acts much more frequently than Her Majesty's Government has been with respect to Colonial enactments." Canada, *Sessional Papers*, 1870, No. 35. Macdonald's memorandum was dated June 8, 1868, and was approved by Cabinet for transmission to the provincial governments on June 9, 1868.

Office was a mean between the federation of the United States and the legislative union of Great Britain. The New Zealand Act of 1852 was indicative of what they wanted to accomplish. Sir Frederic Rogers, the Permanent Under-Secretary of State for the Colonies, offered a suggestive reflection on this point to his colleagues:

It appears to me that throughout our whole Colonial Empire the great political problem wh. has to be solved is that wh. the N Zealand Constitution Act has attempted to solve without success indeed, but witht. that total failure wh. discredits the attempt—the problem of establishing bodies politic wh. shall be more than municipal corporations but less than confederate states—bodies possessing such large powers and above all such valuable sources of revenue as shall render them content to be subject to the central authority in matters of general concern—The question rises in Canada—VCI [Vancouver Island]—the Cape of Good Hope & N.S. Wales.[10]

There were three attempts to strike such a balance and all of them proved to be unstable. New Zealand went in the direction of a centralized state; so did South Africa, perhaps unfortunately. Canada tended in the direction suggested by the American federal system. In Canada's case the difficulty was that the very elasticity that Macdonald wanted made possible disagreements about the nature of the constitution. Whatever may be the purpose of the British North America Act, warned the editor of the Montreal *Herald*, once there were local governments in existence, with constitutional power, then American constitutional principles would become influential. The ultimate consequence would be that the province would become like the American state. "Canada is saturated with American literature, especially of the political kind, and . . . whatever may be the letter of a Federal Constitution, men on this continent will look for its interpretation to that country where precedents have been made, and where the State is as real a power as the Confederation."[11]

The general view was that the new central government at Ottawa would be the old colonial legislatures rolled into one, with a few more powers added. To Canadians the government at Ottawa would be a familiar one, but it was a type that all the provinces had known before. It would control the main sources of revenue, it would carry out the

[10]This minute was written on the back of a note from Elliott to Cardwell reporting an interview with a member of the Vancouver Island legislature. Rogers' minute is dated Oct. 17, [1866]. C.O. 60, Vol. 25, folio 434, is the reference in the British Columbia despatches.

[11]Montreal *Herald*, Jan. 18, 1867. Published as a separate pamphlet by the editor, E. G. Penny, *The Proposed British North American Confederation: Why It should Not Be Imposed Upon the Colonies by Imperial Legislation* (Montreal, 1867), 16.

main functions of a responsible colonial government; it was, in short, just the old government of the provinces writ large. It was the local governments that were new. They were the uncertain quantity. Much of the confusion about the way the new federal system would work stemmed from the fact that the role of the local governments was extraordinarily obscure. Everyone knew roughly how the government at Ottawa would work, but what of those "simulacres de gouvernements"[12] at Toronto, Quebec, Fredericton and Halifax? Shea's explanations to the Newfoundland Assembly were cloudy and complicated.[13] The debates in the province of Canada in 1866 on the local constitutions showed the difficulties in the way of a concrete understanding of the function of the local governments. Just what would they do? No one had much to go on. The existing colonial system seemed to have little or no application to the circumstances of the local governments. American state governments were not any help either. They were sovereign. Most British Americans did not consider that sovereignty was an attribute of the local governments. In French Canada there were people and newspapers who did think so, but the basic dichotomy at the heart of the federal principle eluded most commentators. The truth probably was, as Professor Brady has suggested, that a federation has never been easy to understand by people who have never lived under it.

Perhaps the most remarkable, and certainly the most pervasive characteristic of British Americans was their passionate desire for a place in the world. Galt's sensitivity to the patronizing in London and the colonists' resentment at the ignorance about them in England are of a piece. "Colonial" was not yet a word generally resented; some were even proud of being "British colonists," but it was not enough. There were some, it is true, like the Halifax *Bullfrog*, who were contemptuous of an "empire stretching from the Atlantic to the Pacific" and who believed that the "boundaries of England's Empire are wide enough for the ambition . . . of our people."[14] But the *Bullfrog* was run by two officers of the British garrison and was not quite representative. The anti-national position was better represented by Howe, and Howe was sufficiently equivocal to have a foot in both kinds of empire, British and British American. The *Globe* was not far amiss in 1863 when it said, "The union of all British America is not a question of gain with us; it is one of political *prestige* and nationality."[15] The Halifax *Morning*

[12]The phrase occurs in the resolutions of the electors of the County of St. Jean, held Dec. 20, 1864 at St. Jean, reported in *Le Pays*, 27 déc. 1864.
[13]St. John's *Newfoundlander*, March 2, 1865. Also *supra*, 169–70.
[14]Halifax *Bullfrog*, Feb. 4, 1865.
[15]Toronto *Globe*, Nov. 25, 1863 (original italics).

Chronicle also: "Let these Provinces . . . be organized into one vast Confederation . . . and we should soon possess all the prestige and command all the respect to which our numbers and our position would entitle us."[16] This kind of pride had a fine ring about it, but it could be narrow and puerile. Colonials still had some of the characteristics of the name. Galt, for all his talk of British North American independence, was crestfallen at the cavalier treatment the British North America bill received in Parliament. In this respect the British Parliament reflected the *Times*, which was happy to see the colonies going forth into the world, and did not feel that members of Parliament had the right to object to terms that the colonists themselves had decided.[17] It was being cast off in this summary fashion that British North Americans resented. They wanted to be grown up, but they felt hurt at being pushed out of the house. They wanted the trappings of nationality, but they were rather like the young folk of the *St. John's Daily News*, staggering about the world with grown-up clothes on, only just able to put one foot before the other.[18] "Responsibility," warned the *Times*, "goes with power, and the [British American] colonies being now powerful, are also responsible."[19] British North Americans were purposive yet hesitant, surer of what they wanted than they were of themselves. They were still adolescent with high dreams and fancies; nationality was the most golden of them all. July 1, 1867 was the beginning of a long and difficult maturity.

The diversity of the colonies, from Newfoundland to British Columbia was as remarkable as the distance between them. The reality of 1867 was frightening. It showed how naïve the dreams of the colonists were: Newfoundland, its population clinging precariously to a living wrested from the Labrador current and a hard land; Prince Edward Island, complacent, defiant, parochial; Nova Scotia, afloat on seven oceans, proud of herself and jealous of Canada; New Brunswick, half-American in politics and attitude; Quebec, determined to get every jot and tittle of privilege with or without Ottawa; Ontario, sleek, bigoted, and stentorian; a thousand miles from Toronto, at Red River, 9,000 mixed settlers and the Hudson's Bay Company trying to keep the northwest from the Americans; in distant British Columbia, a dying gold rush with two small and hostile towns holding the mortgage. This was the reverse of the glory arguments that resounded in the speeches of 1864. One was the stubborn and almost intractable reality: the other was a

16Halifax *Morning Chronicle*, Sept. 22, 1864.
17London *Times*, March 1, 1867.
18*St. John's Daily News*, Dec. 1, 1866, quoted *supra*, 164.
19London *Times*, Jan. 11, 1867.

political dream of wonderful audacity. There were many noble statements of this dream, by Howe, by McGee, by Brown; even Cartier on
coming home in 1867 said, "Henceforth we shall rank among the
nations."[20] But no one knew, not Cartier, not even Macdonald, what
really was involved in the creation, administration, and maintenance of
a transcontinental state. An empire of this size had been created before;
it could be done—that was the great example the Americans provided.
But it had been done by a rich and powerful nation of twenty millions.
The contemplation of the same thing by a struggling group of still discordant provinces, with a population of four millions, was surprising;
perhaps it was absurd.[21] The railway that might have given such a union
a semblance of reality did not yet exist. Union of the colonies was
achieved in 1867; but it was hardly more than a beginning. The railways at Rivière du Loup and Truro that stared into the empty miles
between marked a cause not yet won, a nationality not yet realized.
These still lay in the difficult years ahead.

[20]Montreal *Gazette*, May 18, 1867, reporting Cartier's speech of May 17.
[21]*New York Tribune*, May 25, 1867; London *Times*, Nov. 22, 1867.

Bibliographical Note

THE PRINCIPAL SOURCE for this book has been the newspapers of the time. These are widely scattered; some large collections are, however, worthy of note. The most imposing of all the collections is that of the British Museum, London. Its holdings of all colonial papers are considerable. British North American governors usually sent copies of the most important papers home, often in a weekly edition if such were available, and while some of these are still in the Public Record Office files, many have been sent to the British Museum. This collection has newspapers that are not always available even in Canada, and in some particular cases has proved extremely useful. In Canada the largest collection of newspapers is in the Parliamentary Library, Ottawa, and it is the most important for the newspapers of the Province of Canada. It is usefully supplemented by collections in the Legislative Library, and the Archives, of Ontario, and the Archives publiques de Québec. For. Newfoundland the newspaper collection in the Gosling Memorial Library in St. John's is the only major source on this side of the Atlantic. Some files of Newfoundland papers, including a few not in Newfoundland, are in the British Museum. The Charlottetown Public Library has a good collection of most of the leading Prince Edward Island papers; the New Brunswick Museum and the Public Library in Saint John perform the same office for New Brunswick ones. The Nova Scotia Archives has a comprehensive range of Nova Scotian papers. The British Columbia Archives has a fine collection of British Columbia papers; there is a less comprehensive but good collection in the British Museum. University libraries are also useful: Mount Allison, Laval, Queen's, Western Ontario, and British Columbia have small, but in many cases unique, collections of some particular newspapers. Once these resources have been explored, there remains the more arduous search of smaller libraries and newspaper offices. In fact the discovery of nineteenth-century newspapers is still going on. In this respect the work of the Canadian Library Association in microfilming newspapers is of considerable value.

The history of a great political movement like Confederation is not in newspapers alone. Public despatches and private letters allow one behind the scenes and these are, therefore, of the greatest value. The Colonial Office despatches to and from the governors of the British North American colonies are a mine of information; more than one generation of Canadian historians has quarried these despatches, and they remain still the greatest single source for British North American political history. Foreign Office despatches have also been useful for relations with the United States. Indeed, F.O. 5, as the American despatches are called, is so large that for the purpose of this book at least, it has not been possible to exhaust it. The principal collections of private papers have been the Macdonald, Howe, Tupper, and Brown Papers in the Public Archives of Canada; the Langevin Papers in the Archives publiques de Québec; the Stanmore Papers in the University of New Brunswick; the Cardwell Papers in the Public Record Office, London; and the Gladstone Papers in the British Museum.

The printed material for the Confederation period is very considerable. Some attempt has been made here to give an annotated list of useful contemporary pamphlets, even at the cost of duplicating in part the list in W. M. Whitelaw's *The Maritimes and Canada before Confederation*. The journals and debates of the colonial legislatures, the British Parliament, and the United States Congress are invaluable. As for secondary works these are now so large that an exhaustive bibliography is impossible here, but some attempt has been made to cover the ground and to set forth a useful working list of significant books and articles.

The following abbreviations have been used:

P.A.C.	Public Archives of Canada
P.A.N.S.	Public Archives of Nova Scotia
A.P.Q.	Archives publiques de Québec
P.A.O.	Public Archives of Ontario
N.B.M.	New Brunswick Museum
L.P.	Library of Parliament
B.M.	British Museum
P.R.O.	Public Record Office, London

PRIMARY SOURCES

1. MANUSCRIPTS

(a) Public Documents

Colonial Office

British Columbia: C.O. 60, Despatches from; C.O. 398, Letter Books to.
Canada: C.O. 42, Despatches from; C.O. 43, Letter Books to.
New Brunswick: C.O. 188, Despatches from; C.O. 189, Letter Books to.
Newfoundland: C.O. 194, Despatches from; C.O. 195, Letter Books to; C.O. 199, Blue Books of.
Nova Scotia: C.O. 217, Despatches from; C.O. 218, Letter Books to.
Prince Edward Island: C.O. 226, Despatches from; C.O. 227, Letter Books to.
Vancouver Island: C.O. 305, Despatches from; C.O. 410, Letter Books to.

Foreign Office

United States: F.O. 5, Originals from Minister in Washington

Canada, Province of

Governor General

G1, Despatches from the Secretary of State for Colonies
G2, Additional Despatches from Secretary of State for Colonies
G4, Despatches Sent to Executive Council
G6, Despatches from British Minister in Washington
G7, Despatches from Lieutenant Governors
G11, Drafts of Despatches to British Minister in Washington
G12, Letter Books of Despatches to Secretary of State for Colonies
G13, Telegrams
Minister of Finance, Letters Received (P.A.C.)
Minutes of Council (P.A.C.)

New Brunswick
Lieutenant Governor, Despatches Sent (Photostats) ⎫ (University of
Lieutenant Governor, Despatches Received ⎬ New Brunswick
(Microfilm) ⎭ Library)
Minutes of Council (Clerk of Council's Office, Fredericton).

Newfoundland (Newfoundland Archives)
Lieutenant Governor, Miscellaneous Papers and Despatches
Minutes of Council

Nova Scotia (P.A.N.S.)
Lieutenant Governor
Despatches from Secretary of State for Colonies
Despatches to Secretary of State for Colonies
General Correspondence Sent
General Correspondence Received
Telegram Book
Military Correspondence, Nova Scotia Command
Minutes of Council (Typescript)

Prince Edward Island (P.A.C.)
Lieutenant Governor
G33–36 Despatches from Secretary of State for Colonies
G53 Despatches to Secretary of State for Colonies
G62 Despatches from Lord Monck
G63 Despatches from Lieutenant Governors

(b) Private Papers

Allen Papers. A few letters written to J. C. Allen. N.B.M.
Bright Papers. Correspondence with Charles Sumner. B.M., Add. MSS 44390.
Brown Papers. With the kind permission of Professor J. M. S. Careless. P.A.C.
Cardwell Papers. P.R.O., 30/48.
Cartwright Papers. Toronto Public Library
Chamberlin Papers. P.A.C.
Galt Papers. P.A.C.
Gladstone Papers. Cardwell B.M., Add. MSS 44118; Gordon B.M., Add. MSS 44319, 44320; Letter Books B.M., Add. MSS 44534, 44535
Howe Papers. P.A.C.
Kirby Papers. P.A.O.
Langevin Papers. A.P.Q.
John A. Macdonald Papers. P.A.C.
Sandfield Macdonald Papers. P.A.C.
MacDougall Notes. In his copy of Confederation debates. (University of Toronto Library)
Monck Papers. P.A.C.
Russell Papers. P.R.O., 30/22
Shanly Papers. P.A.O.
Stanmore Papers. University of New Brunswick Library.
Tupper Papers. P.A.C.
Williams Papers. N.B.M.

2. NEWSPAPERS

THE FOLLOWING LIST OF NEWSPAPERS is not a comprehensive list of all the newspapers in British North America for 1864–7. It is a list of the newspapers used for this book. And although most of the newspapers extant for this period have been read, there are a few which have been missed, either because they did not seem sufficiently important or because knowledge of their existence came too late to the attention of the author. And new files still keep turning up.

Nor has it been possible to list all the repositories for the newspapers that have been used. The British Columbia list does not include the holdings of the Archives of British Columbia.

The newspapers have been arranged by provinces, in the order of the chapters dealing with the respective provinces, that is, Canada West, Canada East, Newfoundland, Prince Edward Island, Nova Scotia, New Brunswick, and the West.

The following order is observed in setting out the individual references:

    (a) Place where newspaper is published
    (b) Title (Front-page masthead is italicized)
    (c) Frequency of issue
    (d) Political allegiance, where meaningful
    (e) Issues of the newspaper available, 1864–7
    (f) Where files were read

Canada West

Aurora. *Aurora Banner*. Weekly. Reform. Incomplete file. P.A.O.
Barrie. *Barrie Examiner*. Weekly. Reform. A few issues. P.A.O.
———— *Northern Advance*. Weekly. Conservative. Nearly complete file. Microfilm, P.A.O.
Belleville. *Hastings Chronicle*. Weekly. Reform. Incomplete file. Office of the *Ontario Intelligencer*, Belleville, Ont.
———— *Intelligencer*. Weekly (Daily in 1867). Conservative 1864–5; 1867. Office of the *Ontario Intelligencer*, Belleville, Ont.
Galt. *Galt Reporter*. Weekly. Independent. June–December, 1867. P.A.O.
Goderich. *Semi-Weekly Signal*. Semi-weekly. Reform. Jan., 1864–Aug. 1865; Jan. 1866–Nov. 1866. P.A.C.
Hamilton. *City Enterprise*. Weekly. Independent. Published June–December, 1864. Complete file. Hamilton Public Library.
———— *Daily Spectator*. Daily. Conservative. Complete file on microfilm. Office of Hamilton *Spectator*, Hamilton.
Kingston. *Daily British American*. Daily. Reform. 1864. Office of the *Ontario Intelligencer*, Belleville, Ont.
———— *Daily News*. Semi-weekly. Conservative. Complete file. Queen's University Library.
Kitchener. *Berliner Journal*. Weekly. Independent Reform. Complete file. Kitchener Public Library.
London. *London Evening Advertiser*. Daily. Independent Reform. Incomplete file, 1865–7. University of Western Ontario.
———— *London Free Press*. Daily. Liberal. Complete file. University of Western Ontario Library.

Newmarket. *Newmarket Era*. Weekly. Reform. Complete file. P.A.O.

Niagara. *Mail*. Weekly. Reform, then Conservative. Nearly complete file. P.A.O.

Oshawa. *Vindicator*. Weekly. Reform. Complete file. Office of Times Publishing Co., Oshawa, Ont.

Ottawa. *Le Canada*. Tri-weekly. Bleu. A few issues. L.P.

———— *Citizen*. Semi-weekly, daily after May, 1865. Conservative. Complete file. Microfilm, P.A.C. Original in Ottawa Public Library.

———— *Times*. Daily. Conservative. Jan. 1866–June 1867. L.P.

———— *The Union*. Daily. Independent Reform. Published July, 1864–Oct. 1865. Complete file. L.P.

Owen Sound. *Comet*. Weekly. Reform. 1866–7, incomplete file. P.A.O.

Perth. *Perth Courier*. Weekly. Independent Reform. Complete file. P.A.C.

St. Catharines. *Evening Journal*. Daily. Reform. Nearly complete file. P.A.C.

———— *St. Catharines Constitutional*. Weekly. Reform. A few issues. P.A.O.

St. Thomas. *Weekly Dispatch*. Weekly. Conservative. Complete file. University of Western Ontario Library.

Sarnia. *Sarnia Observer*. Weekly. Reform. Complete file. Microfilm, P.A.O.

Stratford. *Stratford Beacon*. Weekly. Reform. 1865–7. Stratford Public Library.

Toronto. *British Constitution*. Weekly. Independent Reform. A few issues. P.A.O.

———— *Canadian Freeman*. Weekly. Conservative, Irish-Catholic. Nearly complete file. P.A.C.

———— *Daily Telegraph*. Daily. 1866–7 (begun May 21, 1866). Incomplete file. Toronto Public Library; P.A.O.

———— *Globe*. Daily. Reform. Complete file. Legislative Library of Ontario.

———— *Irish Canadian*. Weekly. Anti-Confederate. 1864–1866 only. P.A.C.

———— *Leader*. Daily. Conservative. Complete file. Legislative Library of Ontario.

Canada East

Montreal. *Gazette*. Daily. Conservative. Complete file. L.P.

———— *Herald*. Daily. Liberal. Complete file. L.P.

———— *La Minerve*. Tri-weekly. Bleu. Complete file. L.P.

———— *Montreal Daily Transcript*. Daily. Conservative. Complete file. P.A.C.

———— *L'Ordre*. Tri-weekly. Moderate Rouge. Complete file. L.P.

———— *Le Pays*. Tri-weekly. Rouge. Complete file. L.P.

———— *True Witness and Catholic Chronicle*. Weekly. Liberal. Nearly complete file. P.A.O.

———— *L'Union Nationale*. Daily. Rouge. Complete file. L.P.

———— *Witness*. Daily. Liberal. Complete file of semi-weekly edition. Queen's University Library.

Quebec. *Le Canadien*. Tri-weekly. Moderate independent Bleu. Complete file. L.P.

———— *Le Courrier du Canada*. Tri-weekly. Bleu. Complete file. A.P.Q.

———— *Le Journal de Québec*. Daily. Bleu. Complete file. L.P.

———— *Morning Chronicle*. Daily. Conservative. Complete file. L.P.

———— *Quebec Gazette*. Tri-weekly. Conservative. Complete file. L.P.

———— *Quebec Daily Mercury*. Daily. Liberal. Complete file. L.P., B.M.
———— *Quebec Daily News*. Daily. Conservative. 1864, part of 1865. P.A.C.
St. Hyacinthe. *Le Courrier de St. Hyacinthe*. Semi-weekly. Bleu. Nearly complete file. Laval University Library.
Sorel. *La Gazette de Sorel*. Weekly. Bleu. Nearly complete file. P.A.C.
Trois Rivières. *Le Journal des Trois Rivières*. Semi-weekly. Bleu. Complete file. A.P.Q.

Newfoundland

Harbour Grace. *Standard*. Weekly. Anti-Confederate. Complete file. Gosling Memorial Library, St. John's.
St. John's. *Courier*. Semi-weekly. Independent. 1864, 1866, 1867. Gosling Memorial Library. Complete file. B.M.
———— *Day-Book*. Daily. Conservative. Anti-Confederate. 1864–Aug. 1865, when name changed to the *Morning Chronicle*. Complete file. Gosling Memorial Library, St. John's.
———— *Newfoundlander*. Semi-weekly. Liberal. Confederate. Complete file. B.M., Gosling Memorial Library, St. John's.
———— *Newfoundland Express*. Tri-weekly. Conservative. Confederate. 1864, 1866, 1867. Gosling Memorial Library, St. John's.
———— *Patriot*. Weekly. Anti-Confederate. 1864–1866, B.M. 1865–1867. Gosling Memorial Library, St. John's.
———— *Public Ledger*. Semi-weekly. Conservative. Complete file. Gosling Memorial Library, St. John's.
———— *St. John's Daily News*. Daily. Conservative. Confederate. Complete file. Gosling Memorial Library, St. John's.
———— *Telegraph*. Weekly. Conservative. Confederate. 1865 only. Gosling Memorial Library, St. John's.
———— *Times*. Semi-weekly. Conservative. Complete file. B.M., Gosling Memorial Library, St. John's.

Prince Edward Island

Charlottetown. *Examiner*. Weekly. Liberal. Confederate. Complete file. B.M., Legislative and Public Library, Charlottetown.
———— *Herald*. Weekly. Liberal. Anti-Confederate. 1866–1867. Legislative and Public Library, Charlottetown.
———— *Islander*. Weekly. Conservative. Confederate. Complete file. B.M., L.P.
———— *Monitor*. Weekly. Conservative. Anti-Confederate. 1864 only. Legislative and Public Library, Charlottetown.
———— *Patriot*. Semi-weekly. Anti-Confederate. A few issues, 1864–5, B.M. July–Dec., 1867. Legislative and Public Library, Charlottetown.
———— *Protestant*. Weekly. Conservative. Anti-Confederate. 1864–5. Legislative and Public Library, Charlottetown.
———— *Ross's Weekly*. Weekly. Liberal Independent. 1864–5. Legislative and Public Library, Charlottetown.
———— *Vindicator*. Weekly. Anti-Confederate. 1864. Legislative and Public Library, Charlottetown.
Summerside. *Summerside Progress*. Weekly. Anti-Confederate. 1866–7. Legislative and Public Library, Charlottetown.

Nova Scotia

Bridgetown. *Free Press.* Weekly. Single copy. B.M.

Halifax. *Acadian Recorder.* Tri-weekly. Independent. Anti-Confederate. Complete file. P.A.N.S.

———— *British Colonist.* Tri-weekly. Conservative. Confederate. Complete file. P.A.N.S.

———— *Bullfrog.* Weekly. Anti-Confederate. A few issues. B.M., P.A.N.S.

———— *Christian Messenger.* Weekly. Baptist. Confederate. Complete file. P.A.N.S.

———— *Halifax Citizen.* Tri-weekly. Liberal-independent. Anti-Confederate. 1864–1866 (1865 only in weekly edition). P.A.N.S.

———— *Evening Express.* Tri-weekly. Conservative. Confederate. Roman Catholic. 1864–7, P.A.N.S.

———— *Evening Reporter.* Tri-weekly. Conservative. Confederate. 1864–7, P.A.N.S.

———— *Morning Chronicle.* Daily. Liberal. From Jan. 1865, anti-Confederate. Complete file. P.A.N.S.

———— *Morning Journal.* Tri-weekly. Confederate. June-December, 1864 only. See *Unionist.* P.A.N.S.

———— *Provincial Wesleyan.* Weekly. Methodist. Confederate. Complete file. Mount Allison University Library, Sackville, N.B.

———— *Sun.* Tri-weekly. Liberal. Anti-Confederate. 1864–1866. Legislative Library of Nova Scotia.

———— *Unionist and Halifax Journal.* Tri-weekly. Liberal. Confederate. 1865–7, P.A.N.S.

———— *Witness.* Weekly. Presbyterian. Confederate. 1864–1865. P.A.N.S.

Liverpool. *Liverpool Transcript.* Weekly. Liberal. Anti-Confederate. Complete file. P.A.N.S.

New Glasgow. *Eastern Chronicle.* Weekly. Liberal. Anti-Confederate. 1866 only. P.A.N.S.

Pictou. *Colonial Standard.* Weekly. Conservative. Confederate. 1864–1865. P.A.N.S.

Yarmouth. *Yarmouth Herald.* Weekly. Conservative. Anti-Confederate. Nearly complete file. P.A.N.S.

———— *Yarmouth Tribune.* Weekly. Liberal. Anti-Confederate. Complete file. P.A.C.

New Brunswick

Chatham. *Gleaner.* Weekly. Anti-Confederate. 1864–5, University of New Brunswick Library. 1866–7, N.B.M.

Fredericton. *Colonial Farmer.* Weekly. Confederate. July-December, 1864. P.A.C.

———— *New Brunswick Reporter.* Weekly. Confederate. Complete file. N.B.M.

———— *Head Quarters.* Weekly. Anti-Confederate. Complete file. Saint John Public Library.

Newcastle. *Union Advocate.* Single copy. B.M.

Sackville. *Borderer.* Weekly. Independent. 1865–1867. Mount Allison University Library, Sackville.

Saint John. *Daily Evening Globe.* Daily. Anti-Confederate. 1864, 1865 (July-Dec. only), 1866, 1867. Saint John Public Library.

———— *Morning Freeman.* Tri-weekly. Anti-Confederate. Nearly complete file. L.P.

———— *Morning Journal.* Tri-weekly. Confederate. Complete file. N.B.M.

———— *Morning News.* Tri-weekly. Confederate. Complete file. Saint John Public Library.

———— *Morning Telegraph.* Tri-weekly, daily in June, 1864. 1864, N.B.M.; 1865–7, Saint John Public Library.

———— *Weekly Telegraph.* 1864, Saint John Public Library; 1864–5, B.M.

———— *New Brunswick Courrier.* Weekly. Confederate. 1864–1865. University of New Brunswick Library, Fredericton.

———— *True Humourist.* Weekly. Confederate. A few issues. N.B.M.

Woodstock. *Woodstock Acadian.* Weekly. Anti-Confederate. A few issues. N.B.M.

Red River Settlement

Winnipeg. *Nor'Wester.* Fortnightly. 1859–65. Legislative Library, Winnipeg; Microfilm, McGill University Library.

British Columbia

New Westminster. *British Columbia Examiner.* A few issues, 1867–8. B.M.

———— *British Columbian.* Semi-weekly. Complete file. B.M.; University of British Columbia Library.

———— *North Pacific Times.* Semi-weekly. January-May, 1865. B.M.

Victoria. *British Colonist.* Daily. A few issues, 1865–8. B.M.

———— *Weekly British Colonist.* Weekly. Complete file. B.M.

———— *Daily Chronicle.* Daily. A few issues, 1864–6. B.M.

———— *Weekly Chronicle.* Weekly. 1864–1866, when publication ceased. B.M.

———— *Evening Express.* A few issues, 1864–5. B.M.

———— *Vancouver Daily Evening Post.* Daily. A few issues, 1865–6. B.M.

———— *Vancouver Times.* A few issues, 1864–5. B.M.

Great Britain

London. *Daily News.* Daily. Complete file. B.M.

———— *Morning Herald.* Daily. Complete file. B.M.

———— *Morning Post.* Daily. Complete file. B.M.

———— *Daily Telegraph.* Daily. Complete file. B.M.

———— *Times.* Daily. Complete file. B.M.

United States

New York. *New York Herald.* Daily. Complete file. B.M.

———— *New York Times.* Daily. Microfilm. B.M.

———— *New York Tribune.* Daily. Complete file. B.M.

———— *Sun.* Daily. Complete file. B.M.

———— *World.* Daily. Complete file. Institute of Historical Research, London.

3. SERIALS

Hamilton. *Canadian Quarterly Review and Family Magazine.* Quarterly. "National politics and family literature." 1864–6. Toronto Reference Library.

Montreal. *British American Magazine.* Monthly. Literature, science, and art. 1863–4. University of Toronto Library.

———— *L'Echo de la France.* Monthly. Extracts from French periodicals in Europe. 1865–7. Toronto Reference Library.

———— *L'Echo du cabinet du lecture paroissial.* Monthly. Family magazine, with generally uncritical approval of Confederation. 1864–6. Toronto Reference Library.

———— *Le Foyer canadien.* Monthly. Little comment on contemporary events. 1864–6. University of Toronto Library.

———— *La Revue canadienne.* Monthly. The best of the serials in British North America. It gave an able analysis of the news, and though of Bleu sympathies, it maintained an objective tone. 1864–7. Legislative Library of Ontario.

Quebec. *Les Soirées canadiennes.* Monthly. "Recueil de littérature nationale." 1864–5. University of Toronto Library.

Edinburgh. *Edinburgh Review.* Quarterly. Complete file. B.M.

London. *Macmillan's Magazine.* Monthly. Complete file. B.M.

———— *Saturday Review.* Weekly. Complete file. B.M.

———— *Westminster Review.* Quarterly. Complete file. B.M.

———— *Spectator.* Weekly. Complete file. B.M.

4. PAMPHLETS

ACADIAN. *A Letter to the Electors of Nova Scotia, Being a Reply to "Confederation Considered on Its Merits,"* Halifax, 1867. British North America is not yet fit for national life, being neither wealthy nor populous enough to undertake such a rash experiment as Confederation.

ALISON, A. *The Independence of Canada,* London, 1865. Advocates separation from Great Britain to avoid war with the United States. Confederation would only inaugurate "treble government."

ANNAND, WM. *Confederation: A Letter to the Right Honourable the Earl of Carnarvon . . .* London, 1866. An answer to Tupper's pamphlet.

ARCHIBALD, A. G. *Letter to the People of Nova Scotia,* London, 1866. Answering Annand.

B——, ALPHONSE. *Contre-Poison: la confédération c'est le salut du Bas-Canada,* Montreal, 1867. Anti-Rouge pamphlet that attempts to rally the French to the Bleus and to condemn Dorion for his anti-clericalism.

BARNEY ROONEY [WM. GÁRVIE]. *Barney Rooney's Letters on Confederation, Botheration and Political Transmogrification,* Halifax, 1865. A famous satire on the Quebec Conference and the Nova Scotian coalition.

BATCHELER, G. *Unification of North America,* n.p., 1866 [?]. The manifest destiny of British North America.

BELLINGHAM, S. *The Proposed British North American Confederation: A*

Reply to Mr. Penny's Reasons . . . Montreal, 1867. A point by point refutation of E. G. Penny (q.v.).

BOLTON, E. C., and WEBBER, H. H. *The Confederation of British America*, London, 1866. Anti-Confederate pamphlet by two members of the British garrison in Halifax, intended for British consumption.

BOURINOT, J. G. *Confederation of the Provinces of British North America*, Halifax, 1866. Analogies between the United States in 1787 and British North America in 1866.

BRITISH AMERICAN. *Dawn of a New Empire: Being a Reply to a Nova Scotian*, Halifax, 1864. (See NOVA SCOTIAN, *Remarks upon the proposed federation* . . .) Nova Scotia will be the Rhode Island of British North America, and by joining with Lower Canada and the other Maritime provinces can hold the balance of power against Upper Canada.

BUCHANAN, ISAAC. *The British American Federation a Necessity*, Hamilton, 1865. Letters and addresses emphasizing future economic advantages to Canada and the Maritimes.

CAUCHON, JOSEPH. *Etude sur l'union projetée des provinces britanniques*, Quebec, 1858. See *supra*, 144–5.

———— *L'Union des provinces de l'Amérique britannique du nord*, Quebec, 1865. See *supra*, 145.

CHERRIER, C. S., LABERGE, C., CLERK, G. E. *Discours sur la confédération*, Montreal, 1865. The views of the Rouge group of *l'Union Nationale*.

COLONIST, A. [S. E. DAWSON]. *A Northern Kingdom*, Montreal, 1864. A powerful plea that the times call for Confederation. See also *supra*, 114–15.

DORION, A. A. *La Confédération couronnement de dix années de mauvaise administration*, Montreal, 1867.

DOUTRE, G. *Le Principe des nationalités*, Montreal, 1864. Lecture at l'Institut canadien, Montreal. Nationality is determined not by language or race but by common soil and common interests. It is not impossible, though difficult, for French Canadians to live with English in a united British America.

FARMER, A. *Common-Sense*, Cornwallis, 1865. Anti-Canadian, anti-Confederate.

GALT, A. T. *Speech on the Proposed Union of the British North American Provinces*, Montreal, 1864. Galt's Sherbrooke speech.

GILBERT, A. G. *From Montreal to the Maritime Provinces and Back*, Montreal, 1867. Nova Scotia in July, 1867.

HAMILTON, PETER S. *Union of the Colonies of British North America*, Montreal, 1864. Three papers on union published between 1854 and 1861 reprinted. Hamilton argues for legislative union and opposes federal union.

———— *British American Union: A Review of Hon. Joseph Howe's Essay Entitled Confederation*, Halifax, 1866. Claims Howe's scheme of 1838 epitomizes Quebec Resolutions. Selections from Howe's later speeches follow.

———— *Repeal Agitation and What Is to Come of It?* Halifax, 1868. Tries to show folly of repeal agitation.

HOWE, JOSEPH. *Confederation Considered in Relation to the Interests of the Empire*, London, 1866. Howe's anti-Confederation arguments. *Supra*, 293.

———— *Reciprocity Treaty: Its History, General Features and Commercial Results*, Hamilton, 1865. Howe's Detroit speech.

———— *A Speech on Union of the Colonies and Organization of the Empire*, Pictou, 1855. Howe's speech in the Assembly asking for more Colonial Office patronage and more attention to the colonies. Hincks's reply is included.

JOHNSTON, J. W. *Speech Introducing Confederation Resolutions in the Nova Scotia Assembly*, Halifax, 1854.

McCULLY, JONATHAN. *British America: Arguments against a Union of the Provinces Reviewed: With Further Reasons for Confederation*, London, 1867. Countering Wm. Annand.

McGEE, THOMAS D'ARCY. *Letter of the Present American Revolution*, London, 1863.

———— *The Crown and the Confederation: Three Letters to the Hon. John Alexander McDonald by a Backwoodsman*, Montreal, 1864.

———— *Notes on Federal Governments Past and Present*, Montreal, 1865.

———— *Union of the Provinces*, Quebec, 1865. Two speeches on union, one at Cookshire and the other in the Canadian Assembly.

———— *The Irish Position in British and in Republican North America*, Montreal, 1866.

———— *The Mental Outfit of the New Dominion*, [Montreal], 1867.

MORRIS, ALEXANDER. *Nova Britannia*, Montreal, 1858. Gives the history as well as the industrial and economic background of the British North American provinces.

NOVA SCOTIAN. *Confederation Considered on Its Merits*. Halifax, 1867. The benefits Confederation would give to Nova Scotian economic life.

NOVA SCOTIAN. *On the Proposed Confederation of the British North American Provinces*, London, 1866. There would be more jealousies with Confederation than without it. As for the means used to effect it, Bismarck at least gave the people of North Holstein a choice.

NOVA SCOTIAN. *Remarks on the Proposed Federation of the Provinces*, Halifax, 1864. Demolishes four arguments for union, mutual defence, increased commerce, Intercolonial Railway, and nationality. Intercolonial is a bait, and federation could never produce a national state.

NOVA SCOTIAN IN CANADA. *The Union of the British North American Provinces and the Hon. Joseph Howe*, Montreal, 1866. Refutes Howe, and also Bolton and Webber (q.v.).

ONE OF THE PEOPLE. *An Enquiry into the Merits of Confederation*, Halifax, 1867. In part a refutation of NOVA SCOTIAN, *Confederation Considered on its Merits*.

PENNY, EDWARD GOFF. *The Proposed British North American Confederation: Why It Should Not Be Imposed upon the Colonies by Imperial Legislation*, Montreal, 1867. See *supra*, 326.

POPE, W. H. *Observations upon the Proposed Union of the British North American Provinces* . . . [Charlottetown], 1865.

———— *The Confederation Question Considered from a Prince Edward Island Point of View*, Charlottetown, 1866. An attempt to persuade the Islanders to accept Confederation.

RICHEY, M. M. *A Plea for Confederation of the Colonies of British North America Addressed to the People and Parliament of Prince Edward*

Island, Charlottetown, 1867. The same purpose as Pope's pamphlets, by one who believes in the "fundamental principles and noble object" of Confederation.

RYERSON, EGERTON. *The New Canadian Dominion: Dangers and Duties of the People in Regard to Their Government*, Toronto, 1867. A plea for the abolition of party spirit in the new Canada.

SMITH, GOLDWIN. *The Empire*, London, 1863. Letters from the *Daily News*. See *supra*, 19.

———— *The Proposed Constitution for British North America*, London, 1865. From *Macmillan's Magazine. Supra*, 110.

TACHÉ, J. C. *Des Provinces de l'Amérique du nord et d'une union fédérale*, Quebec, 1858. See *supra*, 143–4.

THOMPSON, T. P. *The Future Government of Canada*, St. Catharines, 1864. Argues for a republican British North America and particularly against McGee's ideas of monarchy.

THRING, HENRY. *Suggestions for Colonial Reform*, London, 1865. Reflections induced by Confederation. Urges separation of Empire into independent communities.

[TICKLE, P. I.] *The Future of British America: Independence! How to Prepare for It*, Toronto, 1865. Opposition to Confederation on the ground that it should not be a federation but a "consolidation."

TODD, ALPHEUS. *Brief Suggestions in Regard to the Formation of Local Governments for Upper and Lower Canada*, Ottawa, 1866. The parliamentary librarian advocates non-responsible local governments, similar in principle to those advocated by George Brown.

TUPPER, CHARLES. *Letter to the Right Honourable Earl of Carnarvon*, London, 1866. Reply to Howe's *Confederation*.

———— *Letter to the People of Nova Scotia*, London, 1866.

WILKINS, M. I. *Confederation Examined in the Light of Reason and Common Sense and the British North America Act Shown to Be Unconstitutional*, Halifax, 1867.

5. OFFICIAL SOURCES

British Columbia
    Legislative Council, *Debate on the Subject of Confederation with Canada*, Victoria, 1870.
Canada, Dominion of
    Sessional Papers, 1867–70
Canada, Province of
    Legislative Assembly, *Journals*, 1864–7
    Legislative Council, *Journals*, 1864–7
    Legislature, *Parliamentary Debates on the Subject of the Confederation of the British North American Provinces*, Quebec, 1865.
    Legislature, *Sessional Papers*, 1862–7
Great Britain
    Colonial Office, *Question of the Federation of the British Provinces in America*, London, 1858.

Colonial Office, *Correspondence Relative to a Meeting at Quebec of Delegates Appointed to Discuss the Proposed Union* . . . London, 1865.
Colonial Office, *British North American Provinces: Correspondence Respecting the Proposed Union* . . . London, 1867.
Parliament, *Hansard's Debates*, third series
Parliament, *Accounts and Papers*, 1865–9
New Brunswick
  Legislative Assembly, *Journals*, 1864–7
  Legislative Assembly, *Reports of Debates*, 1867
  Legislative Council, *Journals*, 1864–7
  Legislative Council, *Speeches Delivered . . . on Confederation . . . 1866*
  Legislature, *Correspondence Concerning Proposals for Inter-Colonial Union, Legislative and Federal*, Fredericton, 1865.
  Legislature, *Report of the Delegation to England*, Fredericton, 1867.
Newfoundland
  Legislative Assembly, *Journals*, 1864–7
  Legislative Council, *Journals*, 1864–7
Nova Scotia
  Legislative Assembly, *Debates and Proceedings*, 1864–7
  Legislative Assembly, *Journals*, 1864–7
  Legislative Council, *Journals*, 1864–7
Prince Edward Island
  Legislative Assembly, *Debates and Proceedings, the Parliamentary Reporter*, 1864–7
  Legislative Assembly, *Journals*, 1864–7
  Legislative Council, *Debates and Proceedings*, 1864–6
  Legislative Council, *Journals*, 1864–7
United States
  Congress, *Congressional Globe*, 1st Session, 37th Congress to 1st Session, 40th Congress
  Congress, *Papers Relating to Foreign Affairs*, 1864–7

6. OTHER PRINTED SOURCES

[BLACHFORD, FREDERICK ROGERS]. *Letters of Frederic, Lord Blachford, Under-Secretary of State for the Colonies, 1860–1871*, G. E. MARINDIN, ed., London, 1896.
[BRITISH NORTH AMERICAN ASSOCIATION]. *Confederation of the British North American provinces*, London, 1865. Extracts from speeches of delegates to the Quebec Conference given on various public occasions.
[CARTIER, G. E.]. *Discours de Sir Georges Cartier*, JOSEPH TASSÉ, ed., Montreal, 1893.
CARTWRIGHT, R. J. *Memories of Confederation* . . . A speech given to the Ottawa Canadian Club in 1906 and published by them.
——— *Reminiscences*, Toronto, 1912.
FLEMING, SANDFORD. *The Intercolonial: A Historical Sketch*, Montreal, 1876.
GRAY, J. H. *Confederation: or the Political and Parliamentary History of Canada from . . . October 1864 to . . . July 1871*, Toronto, 1872.

Hodgins, J. G. *A School History of Canada and Other British North American Provinces*, Montreal, 1865. A new school history prepared at Lovell's request for use in British North America.

Howe, Joseph. *Poems and Essays*, Montreal, 1874.

[————]. *Speeches and Public Letters of Joseph Howe*, J. A. Chisholm, ed., 2 vols., Halifax, 1909.

Hutchinson's *New Brunswick Directory for 1865–6*, Montreal, 1865.

Hutchinson's *Newfoundland Directory for 1864–5*, St. John's, 1864.

Hutchinson's *Nova Scotia Directory for 1864–5*, Halifax, 1864.

Hutchinson's *Prince Edward Island Directory for 1864*, Charlottetown, 1864.

Langevin, Hector. *Le Canada, ses institutions, ressources, produits, manufactures, etc.*, Quebec, 1855.

———— *Sir Hector Langevin*, Montreal, 1886.

Lovell's *Canada Directory for 1857–1858*, Montreal, 1858.

Lovell's *Canadian Dominion Directory, 1871*, Montreal, 1871.

[Macdonald, A. A.]. "Notes on the Quebec Conference," A. G. Doughty, ed., *Canadian Historical Review*, I, 1 (March, 1920), 26–47.

[Macdonald, J. A.]. *Correspondence of Sir John Macdonald*, J. Pope, ed., Toronto, 1921.

Mitchell, Peter. "Secret History of Canadian Politics, Political Reminiscences of the Last Thirty Years," Toronto *Evening News*, Feb. 15, 1894 (Photostat in N.B.M.).

Monck, Frances E. O. *My Canadian Leaves: An Account of a Visit to Canada in 1864–1865* (London, 1891).

Monro, Alexander. *New Brunswick, With a Brief Outline of Nova Scotia and Prince Edward Island*, Halifax, 1855.

Moody, H. "Political Experiences in Nova Scotia, 1867–1869," *Dalhousie Review*, XIV (April, 1934), 65–76. Includes some useful insights into New Brunswick politics. By Gordon's private secretary.

Notman, W., and Taylor, F. *Portrait of British Americans*, 3 vols., Montreal, 1865–8.

Ormsby, W. G. "Letters to Galt Concerning the Maritime Provinces and Confederation," *Canadian Historical Review*, XXXIV, 2 (June 1953), 167–8.

Pope, J., ed. *Confederation: Being a Series of Hitherto Unpublished Documents Bearing on the British North America Act*, Toronto, 1895.

Ross, G. W. *Getting into Parliament and After*, Toronto, 1913.

Russell, W. H. *Canada: Its Defences, Condition and Resources*, Boston, 1865.

Sleigh, Lt. Col. [B. W. A.] *Pine Forests and Hacmatack Clearings; or, Travel, Life, and Adventure in the British North American Provinces*, London, 1853.

Spedon, A. L. *Rambles among the Blue-Noses*, Montreal, 1863.

[Taylor, Henry]. *Autobiography of Henry Taylor*, London, 1885.

Trollope, Anthony. *North America*, New York, 1862.

Tupper, Charles. *Political Reminiscences*, London, 1914.

———— *Recollections of Sixty Years in Canada*, London, 1914.

Whelan, Edward. *The Union of the British Provinces*, Charlottetown, 1865.

Young, James. *Public Men and Public Life in Canada*, Toronto, 1902.

SECONDARY SOURCES

1. UNPUBLISHED THESES

BAILEY, A. W. Railways in New Brunswick, 1827–1867, M.A. thesis, University of New Brunswick, 1955.

CAMPBELL, R. H. Confederation in Nova Scotia to 1870, M.A. thesis, Dalhousie University, 1939.

CHAPMAN, J. K. Relations of Maine and New Brunswick in the Era of Reciprocity, 1849–1867, M.A. thesis, University of New Brunswick, 1951.

———— The Career of Arthur Hamilton Gordon, 1st Lord Stanmore, to 1875, Ph.D. thesis, University of London, 1954.

CORNELL, P. G. The Alignment of Political Groups in the United Province of Canada, 1841–1867, Ph.D. thesis, University of Toronto, 1955.

GOULD, E. C. The United States and Canadian Confederation, Essay submitted for the All Soul's Historical Prize, 1934, University of Toronto Library.

MACINTOSH, A. W. The Career of Sir Charles Tupper in Canada, 1864–1900. Ph.D. thesis, University of Toronto, 1960.

MOULTON, E. C. The Political History of Newfoundland, 1861–1869, M.A. thesis, Memorial University of Newfoundland, 1960.

TOUPIN, R. *Le Canadien* and Confederation, 1857–1867, M.A. thesis, University of Toronto, 1956.

SELLERS, G. J. Edward Cardwell at the Colonial Office: Some Aspects of His Policy and Ideas, B.Litt. thesis, University of Oxford, 1958.

WALLACE, C. M. The Life and Times of Sir Albert James Smith, M.A. thesis, University of New Brunswick, 1960.

WILKINSON, J. M. Maritime Union, M.A. thesis, Dalhousie University, 1939.

2. BOOKS

[L'Action Française] *Les Canadiens-français et La Confédération canadienne*, Montreal, 1927.

BAKER, G. E., ed. *The Works of William H. Seward*, 5 vols., Boston, 1884.

BECK, J. M. *The Government of Nova Scotia*, Toronto, 1957.

BIGGAR, C. R. W. *A Biographical Sketch of Sir Oliver Mowat*, 2 vols., Toronto, 1905.

BODELSEN, C. A. *Studies in Mid-Victorian Imperialism*, Copenhagen, 1924.

BOURINOT, J. G. *Federal Government in Canada*, Baltimore, 1889.

BOYD, JOHN. *Sir George Etienne Cartier, Bart*, Toronto, 1914.

BRACQ, J. C. *The Evolution of French Canada*, New York, 1924.

BRADY, ALEXANDER. *Democracy in the Dominions*, Toronto, 1952.

BURPEE, L. J. *Sandford Fleming*, London, 1915.

CAMPBELL, D. *History of Prince Edward Island*, Charlottetown, 1875.

Canada. Royal Commission on Dominion-Provincial Relations. I. *Canada, 1867–1939*. Appendixes:D. G. CREIGHTON, *British North America at Confederation*; J. A. CORRY, *Difficulties of Divided Jurisdiction*; E. M. SAUNDERS, *Economic History of the Maritime Provinces*.

Canada. Senate, *Report . . . Relating to the Enactment of the British North America Act, 1867 . . .* (O'Connor Report), Ottawa, 1939.

CARELESS, J. M. S. *Brown of* The Globe. I. *The Voice of Upper Canada, 1818–1859*, Toronto, 1959.

CREIGHTON, DONALD G. *John A. Macdonald: The Young Politician*, Toronto, 1952.

—— *John A. Macdonald: The Old Chieftain*, Toronto, 1955.

D'ARCY, W. *The Fenian Movement in the United States, 1858–1886*, Washington, 1947.

DAVID, L. O. *L'Union des deux Canadas, 1841–1867*, Montreal, 1898.

—— *Souvenirs et biographies, 1870–1910*, Montreal, 1911.

DAVIS, H. A. *An International Community on the St. Croix, 1604–1930*, Orono, 1950.

DENT, J. C. *The Last Forty Years: Canada Since the Union of 1841*, 2 vols., Toronto, 1881.

ERICKSON, A. B. *Edward T. Cardwell: Peelite*, Philadelphia, 1959.

FARR, D. M. L. *The Colonial Office and Canada, 1867–1887*, Toronto, 1955.

GROULX, LIONEL. *La Confédération canadienne, ses origines*, Montreal, 1918.

HAMMOND, W. O. *Confederation and Its Leaders*, Toronto, 1917.

HANNAY, JAMES. *The Life and Times of Sir Leonard Tilley*, 2 vols., Saint John, 1897.

—— *The History of New Brunswick*, 2 vols., Saint John, 1909.

HARVEY, D. C. *The Centenary of Edward Whelan*, Charlottetown, 1926.

——, ed. *Edward Whelan's Union of the British Provinces*, Charlottetown, 1927.

KERR, D. G. G. *Sir Edmund Head: A Scholarly Governor*, Toronto, 1954.

MACDONALD, HELEN G. *Canadian Public Opinion on the American Civil War*, New York, 1926.

MACKENZIE, ALEXANDER. *The Life and Speeches of the Hon. George Brown*, Toronto, 1882.

MACKINNON, FRANK. *The Government of Prince Edward Island*, Toronto, 1951.

MARTIN, CHESTER. *The Foundations of Canadian Nationhood*, Toronto, 1955.

MORTON, W. L. *Manitoba: A History*, Toronto, 1957.

MUNRO, W. B. *American Influences on Canadian Government*, Toronto, 1929.

ORMSBY, MARGARET A. *British Columbia: A History*, Toronto, 1958.

PATTERSON, GEORGE. *Studies in Nova Scotian History*, Halifax, 1940.

PIERCE, E. L. *Memoir and Letters of Charles Sumner*, 4 vols., London, 1893.

POOR, LAURA E. *The Life and Writings of John A. Poor*, New York, 1892.

POPE, JOSEPH. *Memoirs of the Right Honourable Sir John Alexander Macdonald, G.C.B.*, 2 vols., London, 1894.

PROWSE, D. W. *A History of Newfoundland*, London, 1895.

ROY, JAMES A. *Joseph Howe: A Study of Achievement and Frustration*, Toronto, 1935.

ROYALE, JOSEPH. *Histoire du Canada: 1841 à 1867*, Montreal, 1909.

RUMILLY, R. *Histoire de la province de Québec*. I. *George Etienne Cartier*, Montreal, n.d.
SALMON, L. M. *The Newspaper and the Historian*, Oxford, 1923.
SAUNDERS, E. M. *Three Premiers of Nova Scotia*, Toronto, 1909.
―――― *The Life and Letters of the Rt. Hon. Charles Tupper*, 2 vols., London, 1916.
SHIPPEE, L. B. *Canadian-American Relations, 1849–1874*, New Haven, 1939.
SKELTON, ISABEL. *The Life of Thomas D'Arcy McGee*, Gardenvale, 1925.
SKELTON, O. D. *The Life and Times of Sir Alexander Tilloch Galt*, Toronto, 1920.
SMITH, H. A. *Federalism in North America, a Comparative Study of Institutions in the United States and Canada*, Boston, 1923.
STACEY, C. P. *Canada and the British Army, 1846–1871*, London, 1936.
THOMSON, DALE C. *Alexander Mackenzie, Clear Grit*, Toronto, 1960.
TROTTER, R. G. *Canadian Federation*, Toronto, 1924.
TURCOTTE, L.-P. *Le Canada sous l'union, 1841–1867*, Quebec, 1871.
WADE, MASON. *The French Canadians, 1760–1945*, Toronto, 1955.
WALLACE, F. W. *Wooden Ships and Iron Men*, London, 1924.
WARNER, D. F. *The Idea of Continental Union*, Kentucky, 1960.
WEBSTER, A. P. *The True Story of Confederation*, n.p., 1926.
WHEARE, K. C. *Federal Government*, New York, 1947.
WHITELAW, W. M. *The Maritimes and Canada before Confederation*, Toronto, 1934.
WILLISON, J. S. *Sir Wilfrid Laurier and the Liberal Party*, 2 vols., Toronto, 1905.
WINKS, R. W. *Canada and the United States: The Civil War Years*, Baltimore, 1960.
WRONG, G. M. *et al. The Federation of Canada*, Toronto, 1917.

3. ARTICLES

ALLIN, C. D. "The Genesis of the Confederation of Canada," American Historical Association, *Report*, 1911, 239–48.
BAILEY, A. G. "Railways and the Confederation Issue in New Brunswick, 1863–1865," *Canadian Historical Review*, XXI, 4 (Dec., 1940), 367–83.
―――― "The Basis and Persistence of Opposition to Confederation in New Brunswick," *Canadian Historical Review*, XXIII, 4 (Dec., 1942), 374–97.
BECK, J. M. "The Party System in Nova Scotia," *Canadian Journal of Economics and Political Science*, XX, 4 (Nov., 1954), 514–30.
―――― "The Nova Scotia 'Disputed Election' of 1859 and its Aftermath," *Canadian Historical Review*, XXXVI, 4 (Dec., 1955), 293–315.
BLEGEN, T. C. "A Plan for the Union of British North America and the United States, 1866," *Mississippi Valley Historical Review*, IV, 4 (March, 1918), 470–83.
BONENFANT, J.-C. "La Genèse de la loi de 1867 concernant l'Amérique du Nord britannique," *Culture*, IX, 1 (mars 1948), 3–17.
―――― "Les Canadiens français et la naissance de la confédération," Canadian Historical Association, *Report*, 1952, 39–45.

BROWN, G. W. "The Grit Party and the Great Reform Convention of 1859," *Canadian Historical Review*, XVI, 3 (Sept., 1935), 245–65.

BURPEE, L. J. "Joseph Howe and the Anti-Confederation League," Royal Society of Canada, *Transactions*, 3rd series, vol. X, s. 2 (1917), 409–73.

CARELESS, J. M. S. "The Toronto *Globe* and Agrarian Radicalism, 1850–1867," *Canadian Historical Review*, XXIX, 1 (March, 1948), 14–39.

——— "Mid-Victorian Liberalism in Central Canadian Newspapers, 1850–1867," *Canadian Historical Review*, XXXI, 3 (Sept., 1950), 221–36.

——— "George Brown and the Mother of Confederation," Canadian Historical Association, *Report*, 1960, 57–73.

COFFEY, AGNES. "The *True Witness and Catholic Chronicle*," Canadian Catholic Historical Association, *Report*, 1937–8, 33–46.

COOPER, JOHN A. "The Fenian Raid of 1866," *Canadian Magazine*, X, 1 (Nov., 1897), 41–55.

COOPER, J. I. "The Political Ideas of George Etienne Cartier," *Canadian Historical Review*, XXIII, 3 (Sept., 1942), 286–94.

CORNELL, P. G. "The Alignment of Political Groups in the United Province of Canada, 1854–1864," *Canadian Historical Review*, XXX, 1 (March, 1949), 22–46.

CREIGHTON, D. G. "Economic Nationalism and Confederation," Canadian Historical Association, *Report*, 1942, 44–51.

——— "Sir John Macdonald and Canadian Historians," *Canadian Historical Review*, XXIX, 1 (March, 1948), 1–13.

——— "The United States and Canadian Confederation," *Canadian Historical Review*, XXXIX, 3 (Sept., 1958), 209–22.

DAFOE, JOHN W. "The Fenian Invasion of Quebec, 1866," *Canadian Magazine*, X, 4 (Feb., 1898), 339–47.

——— "Early Winnipeg Newspapers," Historical and Scientific Society of Manitoba, *Papers*, Series III, 1947, 14–24.

DAVIS, W. A. "The Fenian Raid on New Brunswick," *Canadian Historical Review*, XXXVI, 4 (Dec., 1955), 316–34.

DOUGHTY, A. G. "The Awakening of Canadian Interest in the Northwest," Canadian Historical Association, *Report*, 1928, 5–11.

FRASER, A. M. "The Issue of Confederation, 1864–1870," in R. A. MACKAY, ed., *Newfoundland: Economic, Diplomatic, and Strategic Studies*, Toronto, 1946, 411–43.

——— "The Nineteenth Century Negotiations for Confederation of Newfoundland with Canada," Canadian Historical Association, *Report*, 1949, 14–21.

GALBRAITH, J. S. "The Hudson's Bay Company under Fire, 1847–1862," *Canadian Historical Review*, XXX, 4 (Dec., 1949), 325–35.

GIBSON, J. A. "Sir Edmund Head's Memorandum," *Canadian Historical Review*, XVI, 4 (Dec., 1935), 411–17.

——— "The Colonial Office View of Canadian Federation, 1856–1868," *Canadian Historical Revew*, XXXV, 4 (Dec., 1954), 279–313.

HARVEY, D. C. "The Maritime Provinces and Confederation," Canadian Historical Association, *Report*, 1927, 39–49.

——— "Confederation in Prince Edward Island," *Canadian Historical Review*, XIV, 2 (June, 1933), 143–60.

———— "Incidents of Repeal Agitation in Nova Scotia," *Canadian Historical Revew*, XV, 1 (March, 1934), 48–57.

HEMMEAN, J. C. "Tariffs and Trade in the British North American Provinces before Confederation," Canadian Political Science Association, *Papers and Proceedings*, 1934, 51–9.

HEISLER, J. P. "The Attitude of the Halifax Press towards Union of the British North American Provinces, 1856–1864," *Dalhousie Review*, XXX, 2 (July, 1950), 188–95.

HOWAY, F. W. "The Attitude of Governor Seymour toward Confederation," Royal Society of Canada, *Transactions*, 3rd series, vol. XXIV, s. 2 (1920), 31–49.

———— "Governor Musgrave and Confederation," Royal Society of Canada, *Transactions*, 3rd series, vol. XV, s. 2 (1921), 15–31.

IRELAND, W. E. "The Annexation Petition of 1869," *British Columbia Historical Quarterly*, IV, 1940, 267–87.

———— "A Further Note on the Annexation Petition of 1869," *British Columbia Historical Quarterly*, 1941, 67–72.

———— "Pre-Confederation Defence Problems of the Pacific Colonies," Canadian Historical Association, *Report*, 1941, 41–54.

———— "British Columbia's American Heritage," Canadian Historical Association, *Report*, 1948, 67–73.

KERR, D. G. G. "Edmund Head, Robert Lowe, and Confederation," *Canadian Historical Review*, XX, 4 (Dec., 1939), 409–20.

———— "The New Brunswick Background of Sir Edmund Head's Views on Confederation," Canadian Historical Association, *Report*, 1949, 7–13.

LANCTOT, G. "Deux Appréciations sommaires de la confédération," Canadian Historical Association, *Report*, 1927, 97–101.

LANDON, F. "Canadian Opinion of Southern Secession, 1860–1861," *Canadian Historical Review*, I, 3 (Sept., 1920), 255–66.

———— "The American Civil War and Canadian Confederation," Royal Society of Canada, *Transactions*, 3rd series, vol. XXI, s. 2 (1927), 55–62.

LARMOUR, R. "With Booker's Column," *Canadian Magazine*, X, 2 (Dec., 1897), 121–7; X, 3 (Jan., 1898), 228–31. Personal reminiscences of June, 1866.

LASH, Z. A. "The Working of Federal Institutions in Canada," in G. M. WRONG, et al., *The Federation of Canada*, Toronto, 1917, 77–108.

LOCKHART, A. D. "The Contribution of Macdonald Conservatism to National Unity, 1854–1878," Canadian Historical Association, *Report*, 1939, 124–32.

LONGLEY, R. S. "Fisheries in Nova Scotia Politics, 1865–1871," Nova Scotia Historical Society, *Collections*, XXV, 75–94.

MacDERMOTT, T. W. L. "The Political Ideas of John A. Macdonald," *Canadian Historical Review*, XIV, 3 (Sept., 1933), 247–64.

McINNIS, E. "Two North American Federations: A Comparison," in R. FLENLEY, ed., *Essays in Canadian History Presented to George Mackinnon Wrong*, Toronto, 1939, 94–118.

MacKIRDY, K. A. "Problems of Adjustment in Nation-Building: Maritime Provinces and Tasmania," *Canadian Journal of Economics and Political Science*, XX, 1 (Feb., 1954), 27–43.

MARTELL, J. S. "Intercolonial Communications, 1840–1867," Canadian Historical Association, *Report*, 1938, 41–61.

MARTIN, CHESTER. "Confederation and the West," Canadian Historical Association, *Report*, 1927, 20–8.

———— "Sir Edmund Head's First Project of Confederation," Canadian Historical Association, *Report*, 1928, 14–26.

———— "British Policy in Canadian Confederation," *Canadian Historical Review*, XIII, 1 (March, 1932), 3–19.

MAYO, H. B. "Newfoundland and Confederation in the Eighteen-Sixties," *Canadian Historical Review*, XXIX, 2 (June, 1948), 125–42.

MEAGHER, H. H. "The Life of the Hon. Jonathan McCully," Nova Scotia Historical Society, *Collections*, XXI, 73–114.

MITCHELL, ELAINE A. "Edward Watkin and the Buying Out of the Hudson's Bay Company," *Canadian Historical Review*, XXXIV, 3 (Sept., 1953), 219–44.

MITCHELL, H. "Canada's Negotiations with Newfoundland, 1887–1895," *Canadian Historical Review*, XL, 4 (Dec., 1959), 277–93.

MORISON, J. L. "Parties and Politics, 1841–1867," in *Canada and Its Provinces*. V. *United Canada*.

PATTERSON, G. "An Unexplained Incident of Confederation in Nova Scotia," *Dalhousie Review*, VII, 4 (Jan., 1928), 442–6.

Observer [E. S. CARTER]. "Linking the Past with the Present," Saint John *Telegraph-Journal*, Aug. 1929–Dec. 1931.

PERRAULT, J.-E. "La Confédération canadienne, est-elle née viable?" *Revue de l'Université d'Ottawa*, 1935, 8–25.

ROBITAILLE, G. "La Confédération canadienne," Canadian Historical Association, *Report*, 1927, 62–6.

ROGERS, N. McL. "The Confederate Council of Trade," *Canadian Historical Review*, VII, 4 (Dec., 1926), 277–86.

———— "The Genesis of Provincial Rights," *Canadian Historical Review*, XIV, 1 (March, 1933), 9–23.

SAGE, W. N. "The Annexationist Movement in British Columbia," Royal Society of Canada, *Transactions*, 3rd series, vol. XXI, 1927, 97–110.

———— "Amor De Cosmos, Journalist and Politician," *British Columbia Historical Quarterly*, VIII, 1944, 189–212.

SAUNDERS, E. M. "The Maritime Provinces and Reciprocity," *Dalhousie Review*, XIV (Oct., 1934), 355–71.

SCOTT, F. R. "Political Nationalism and Confederation," *Canadian Journal of Economics and Political Science*, VIII, 3 (Aug., 1942), 386–415.

SHANNON, JOSEPHINE. "Two Forgotten Patriots," *Dalhousie Review*, XIV, 1 (April, 1934), 85–98. William Garvie and E. M. Macdonald.

SISSONS, C. B. "Canadian Political Ideas in the Sixties and Seventies: Egerton Ryerson," Canadian Historical Association, *Report*, 1942, 94–103.

SKELTON, O. D. "Galt and the 1858 Draft of the Canadian Constitution," Royal Society of Canada, *Transactions*, 3rd series, vol. XI, s. 2, 1917, 99–104.

SMITH, J. F. "American Republican Leadership and the Movement for the Annexation of Canada in the Eighteen-Sixties," Canadian Historical Association, *Report*, 1935, 67–75.

STACEY, C. P. "Fenianism and the Rise of National Feeling in Canada at the Time of Confederation," *Canadian Historical Review*, XII, 3 (Sept., 1931), 238–61.

—— "A Fenian Interlude: The Story of Michael Murphy," *Canadian Historical Review*, XV, 2 (June, 1934), 133–54.

—— "Lord Monck and the Canadian Nation," *Dalhousie Review*, XIV (July, 1934), 179–91.

—— "The Backbone of Canada," Canadian Historical Association, *Report*, 1953, 1–13.

—— "Britain's Withdrawal from North America, 1864–1871," *Canadian Historical Review*, XXXVI, 3 (Sept., 1955), 185–98.

STANLEY, G. F. G. "Act or Pact? Another Look at Confederation," Canadian Historical Association, *Report*, 1956, 1–25.

STAPLES, LILA. "The Honourable Alexander Morris, the Man, his Work," Canadian Historical Association, *Report*, 1928, 91–100.

STEWART, ALICE. "Sir Edmund Head's Memorandum of 1857 on Maritime Union: A Lost Confederation Document," *Canadian Historical Review*, XXVI, 4 (Dec., 1945), 406–19.

—— "The State of Maine and Canadian Confederation," *Canadian Historical Review*, XXXIII, 2 (June, 1952), 148–64.

TACHÉ, LOUIS. "Sir E.-P. Taché et la confédération canadienne," *Revue de l'Université d'Ottawa*, 1935, 231–55.

TROTTER, R. G. "Lord Monck and the Great Coalition of 1864," *Canadian Historical Review*, III, 2 (June, 1922), 181–6.

—— "Some American Influences upon the Canadian Federation Movement," *Canadian Historical Review*, V, 3 (Sept., 1924), 213–27.

UNDERHILL, F. H. "Some Aspects of Upper Canadian Radical Opinion in the Decade before Confederation," Canadian Historical Association, *Report*, 1927, 46–61.

—— "Canada's Relations with the Empire as Seen by the Toronto *Globe*, 1857–1867," *Canadian Historical Review*, X, 2 (June, 1929), 106–28.

VROOM, J. "Fenians on the St. Croix," *Canadian Magazine*, X, 5 (March, 1898), 411–13.

WAITE, P. B. "A Chapter in the History of the Intercolonial Railway, 1864," *Canadian Historical Review*, XXXII, 4 (Dec., 1951), 356–69.

—— "Halifax Newspapers and the Federal Principle, 1864–1865," *Dalhousie Review*, XXXVII, 1 (Spring, 1957), 72–84.

—— "*Le Courrier du Canada* and the Quebec Resolutions, 1864–5," *Canadian Historical Review*, XL, 4 (Dec., 1959), 294–303.

—— "Edward Whelan Reports from the Quebec Conference," *Canadian Historical Review*, XLII, I (March, 1961), 23–45.

WAITES, K. A. "Responsible Government and Confederation," *British Columbia Historical Quarterly*, VI, 1942, 97–106.

WHITELAW, W. M. "American Influence on British Federal Systems," in CONYERS READ, ed., *The Constitution Reconsidered*, New York, 1938, 297–314.

—— "Reconstructing the Quebec Conference," *Canadian Historical Review*, XIX, 2 (June, 1938), 123–37.

———— "Lord Monck and the Canadian Constitution," *Canadian Historical Review*, XXI, 3 (Sept., 1940), 298–9.

WILLISON, J. "Some Political Leaders in the Canadian Federation," in G. M. WRONG, *et al.*, *The Federation of Canada*, Toronto, 1917, 39–76.

WILSON, G. E. "New Brunswick's Entrance into Confederation," *Canadian Historical Review*, IX, 1 (March, 1928), 4–24.

BIBLIOGRAPHICAL AIDS

Canada. Archives. *Catalogue of the Pamphlets in the Public Archives of Canada, 1493–1877*, Ottawa, 1931.

Canadian Library Association. *List of Newspapers on Microfilm*, Ottawa, 1959.

Canadian Press Association. *History of Canadian Journalism*, Toronto, 1908.

GREGORY, W., ed., *Union List of Newspapers*, New York, 1937.

HARVEY, D. C. "The Newspapers of Nova Scotia, 1840–1867," *Canadian Historical Review*, XXVI, 3 (Sept., 1945), 279–99.

HEWITT, A. R. *Union List of Commonwealth Newspapers in London, Oxford and Cambridge, 1843–1870*, London, 1960.

HIGGINS, M. V. *A Bibliography of Canadian Bibliographies*, Montreal, 1930.

LOCKE, G. H., and WALLACE, W. S. *A Joint Catalogue of the Periodicals and Serials in the Libraries of the City of Toronto*, Toronto, 1934.

MILLER, H. O. "The History of the Newspaper Press in London, 1830–1875," Ontario Historical Society, *Papers and Records*, XXXII, 1937, 114–39.

MORGAN, H. J. *Biblioteca Canadensis*, Ottawa, 1867.

Nova Scotia. Archives. *Report for 1933*. Appendix B. "List of the newspapers in the Public Archives of Nova Scotia."

[Queen's University] *Canadiana, 1698–1900*, Kingston, 1932.

Russell and Co. *American Newspaper Directory*, New York, 1869.

STATON, F. M., and TREMAINE, M., eds. *A Bibliography of Canadiana*, Toronto, 1935.

TALMAN, J. J. "The Newspaper Press of Canada West, 1850–1860," Royal Society of Canada, *Transactions*, 3rd series, vol. XXXIII, s. 2 (1939), 149–74.

TETU, H. *Historique des journaux de Québec*, Quebec, 1873.

TOD, D. D., and CORDINGLEY, A. "A Bibliography of Canadian Literary Periodicals, 1789–1900," Royal Society of Canada, *Transactions*, 3rd series, vol. XXVI, s. 2 (1932), 87–96.

TRATT, G. E. N. A Survey and Listing of Nova Scotian Newspapers; With Particular Reference to the Period before 1867. M.A. thesis, Mount Allison University, 1957.

WALLACE, W. S. "The Periodical Literature of Upper Canada," *Canadian Historical Review*, XII, 1 (March, 1931), 4–22.

Index

Quebec Daily Mercury: and John Sandfield Macdonald, 9–10; supports Sandfield Macdonald on 1863 Intercolonial issue, 55; and visit to Maritimes, 1864, 67, 70n; criticizes Brown, 297; on Northwest, 309

Quebec Daily News: on Nova Scotian ambitions, 15; on Quebec Conference, 91–2; on Reformers at Conference, 97; other reference to, 87

Quebec Gazette, against dissolution of Union, 136

Quebec Resolutions: Prince Edward Island land proposals omitted from, 82; additions after Charlottetown Conference, 83; publication of, 105–6, 166; exposition of, 106–8; practical purpose of, 111–12, 203; criticism of, by *Perth Courier*, 130; interpretation of, by Bleus, 142–4, 147; interpretation of, by Rouges, 142; criticism of, by Montreal *True Witness*, 149; introduced in Canadian Parliament, 152; criticism of by Dunkin, 153–4; "monarchical spirit" of, 165; in Newfoundland legislature, 168; unfair to Prince Edward Island, 187; defended by Tupper, 203; changes suggested in, to accommodate Maritimes, 221, 254, 255n, 269; considered by New Brunswick cabinet, 236. *See also* Quebec Conference

Queen Victoria (Canadian government steamer): voyage to Charlottetown of, 73–4, 75; luncheon aboard, for Conference, 77–8; trip from Charlottetown to Halifax, 79–80

Queens County, N.B., 246

Queen's University, 201n

RAILWAYS: their influence in establishing a metropolian press, 7–8, 201; at Toronto, 117–18; and loyalties, 321. *See also* Western extension; railways by name: Canadian Pacific; European and North American; Grand Trunk; Great Western; Intercolonial; Northern

Reciprocity Treaty with the United States: abrogation of, 32; attempts to renew, 215–16, 275; other references to, 210, 253. *See also* Detroit Convention; Confederate Council for Trade

Redpath, Peter, 134

Red River Colony: troops leave, 1861, 26, 309; position of, 308, 328; and Confederation, 310; helplessness of, 311. *See also* Hudson's Bay Company; Northwest; Rupert's Land

Nor'Wester: founding of, 308; attitude to Great Britain of, 308–9; and Confederation, 308, 309–10; other references to, 26n, 30, 307. *See also* Buckingham, William

Reekie, R. J., 92

Reform party: attitude to Great Britain of, 22–3; and "rep. by pop.," 35, 36–7; Convention of 1859, 37–8, 40–1, 307; attitude to Confederation, 1858–9, 39; supports coalition of 1864, 42–5, 126; supports Confederation, 126–30; attitude to Senate, 129; and local constitution for Canada West, 287–8; on the coalition in 1867, 296–8; Convention of 1867, 298–9, 319. *See also* Brown, George; Liberals; Toronto, *Globe*

Regulator, U.S.S., at Eastport, 267

Reilly, Edward (editor of Charlottetown *Herald*), 191

Reilly, J. O., his letter to Macdonald, 289n

Religious divisions: in Canada West, 117, 126; in Canada East, 135; in Newfoundland, 171n; in Prince Edward Island, 179; in Nova Scotia, 195; in New Brunswick, 238n. *See also* under various denominations

Renouf, H., on Newfoundland's isolation from Canada, 162, 170

Reporter. *See* Fredericton; *Galt Reporter*

Representative government in Newfoundland, difficulties of, 13, 164–5

Republican party (of United States), its relations with Fenians, 264

Restigouche River, 56

Revue Canadienne, La: on New World militarism, 29; feels changes essential, 138; on calm of Canadian politics, 1865, 157